BANDA BAHADUR
ASHT RATNAS ETC.

THE GREAT GURUS OF THE SIKHS SERIES

BANDA BAHADUR AND ASHT RATNAS

Editor-in-Chief

O. P. RALHAN

ANMOL PUBLICATIONS PVT. LTD.

NEW DELHI-110002 (INDIA)

ANMOL PUBLICATIONS PVT. LTD.
4374/4B, Ansari Road, Daryaganj
New Delhi-110 002

Banda Bahadur, Asht Ratnas etc.

First Edition 1998

ISBN 81-7488-697-4

PRINTED IN INDIA

Published by J. L. Kumar for Anmol Publications Pvt. Ltd., New Delhi-110 002 and Printed at Mehra Offset Press, Delhi.

Preface

'Great Gurus of the Sikhs' in six volumes is a monumental work by the editor drawing every succinct information on each of the ten Gurus from unapproachable historical and religious sources.

These volumes should not be treated simply in biographical sketches of their lives or travelogue of their lives, but an account of their teachings, philosophies, travelogue, their sufferings and sacrifices for the country, their mythological and theological aspects, socio-economic reforms, their political contention and wars with the autocracy at their times and many more touching incidents of their lives, miracles which they manifested on several occasions—all have been contained in them. These volumes are treasures of religious wealth enshrined in their sacred *Vanis*—viz. Guru Granth Sahib and on political scenario of their times.

The sufferings of the Gurus were immense during Mughal period. Guru Arjun Dev, Guru Teg Bahadur and Guru Gobind Singh sacrificed every thing for the sake of their sincere love for humanity and reforming zeal. Repressive policies and numerous maneuvre could not bend them, instead. The rulers have to bow before them for their unparallelled and unmatched chivalry shown by them in spite of great emotional hurdles.

These volumes are faithful and sincere narration of the political conditions, social conditions, religious fanaticity of the rulers, prevailing at that times and how all those Great Gurus not only fought against heavy odds but simultaneously never allowed to fade away the spiritual lamp lighted by them which even today imparts eternal peace to thousands of people not only of Sikh people but all other religions.

These volumes on Great Gurus of the Sikhs advocate tenaciously a superb, enchanting study for each and every one. Highly recommended for teachers, students, social reformers, historians. A useful and worthy of acquisition for each library. Section of Sikh history in each library remain incomplete without such a marvellous set.

Contents

BANDA BAHADUR

1

Banda Bahadur (1709-1715)

Banda Bahadur's Life Sketch

The story goes that Banda's original name was Lachhman Dev. He was born in Kartik 1727 Bikrami Samvat, October-November 1670, four years after the birth of Guru Gobind Singh. He belonged either to Kashmir or Punjab. He was a Rajput cultivator. By the time he was just turned twenty, his astonishing mind was set on its task. He had a reputation of being a great hunter. One day he killed a doe which immediately delivered itself of two cubs which expired in his presence. The sight shocked him. He renounced worldly life and became a Bairagi Sadhu or a wandering hermit and ultimately settled at Nander on the banks of river Godavari in Maharashtra. He won great fame as a sorceror under the name of Madhodas and commanded thousands of followers.

Guru Gobind Singh went to his hermitage. Madhodas was away. The Guru ordered his disciples to kill a few goats of the Bairagi and cook meat there and then. The matter was reported to the Bairagi. The Guru asked him who he was. Madhodas replied, he was Banda or Guru's slave. The Guru enquired, if he knew whom he was talking to. He said he was none other than Guru Gobind Singh. At that time Banda was 38 years old and the Guru was of 42 years. The Guru encouraged him to give up his present way of living and resume the duties of a real Rajput. In a few days the Guru held a durbar, conferred the title of Banda Bahadur on him and appointed him his military lieutenant to punish the Governor of Sarhind who had killed his two youngest sons, and was mainly responsible for the death of his two elder sons, his mother and thousands of Sikhs and Hindus. He was given a council of advisers of five Sikhs who on their arrival in Punjab were to assure the Sikhs that Banda was Guru's nominee and deputy to organise them in order to lead an expedition against Sarhind.

Banda came to Punjab and was joined by thousands of Sikhs and Hindus. He plundered all the Muslim towns and villages on the way, conquered Sarhind and killed Wazir Khan, its Governor. He appointed Sikh officers in place of Muslims in the Sarhind province lying between the rivers Satluj and Jamuna up to Karnal and Panipat. Then he extended his rule up to river Ravi and occupied the whole of Indian Panjab and Haryana, while the Rajas of Himachal Pradesh became his tributaries. He led expeditions into the Ganga

Doab also. He set up his headquarters at Lohgarh, a small fortalice, situated in the lower Shiwalik hills south of Nahan and north-east of Sadhaura, in Nahan district. After five years' rule he was defeated and killed by the Mughal Emperor, Farrukh Siyar.

Now three questions of importance arise: Where was Banda's original home, whether he was known to Guru Gobind Singh before their meeting at Nander, and if Banda was baptised.

Banda's original home

There are a couple of theories about the original home of Banda Bahadur. Most of the historians hold that his birth place was at Rajauri in Punchh district of Kashmir. Sixty years after Banda, James Browne wrote that he was born in the Jullundur Doab. J.D. Cunningham says, "he was a native of the south of India." The view is that Banda belonged to Sarmur State now District of Nahan in Himachal Pradesh. This conclusion is based on the following grounds:

1. Guru Gobind Singh's field of activities had been the region lying between the rivers Satluj and Jamuna. He stayed at Paonta in Nahan district of Himachal Pradesh form 1685 to 1688. The Guru frequently went on hunting expeditions around Paonta as well as in the hilly areas south of Paonta and Nahan. This part of the country surrounded by Paonta, Nahan, Morni, Kalka, Pinjor, Chandi Mandir, Tilokpur below Morni, Tilokpur below Nahan, Kala Am and Mukhlispur was the famous hunting ground for tigers, leopards, bears, wild boars and deer, particularly in winter. Ahmad Shah Abdali hunted tigers and bears here in February 1765. The Governor-Generals from Calcutta came here to hunt. On March 28, 1838 Lord Auckland killed eight tigers near Kala Am in the dry bed of river Markanda in a few hours.

Banda was also a mighty hunter. During these hunting excursions the Guru seems to have met Banda many a time. Without any previous acquaintance, the Guru would not have undertaken a long journey of nearly two thousands kilometres and appointed Banda his Deputy on a fortnight's experience at Nander to guide the destiny of his beloved Khalsa.

2. Banda's outward appearance as a Bairagi must have considerably changed due to his long hair and ash-smeared body. The Guru must have recognised him, but to make himself quite sure he enquired who he was. Banda recognised the Guru at once, and replied that he was Guru's slave.

3. Guru Gobind Singh spoke a language which was a mixture of Hindi and Panjabi. Such a language must have been spoken by Banda, otherwise the Sikhs would not have followed him so quickly and Hindus would not have joined him so speedily. Both the Sikhs and the Hindus took him as one of themselves for this reason. This language is still spoken in Ambala district and southern parts of Nahan district even today.

4. Banda's exploits in this region clearly prove that he was familiar with every nook and corner of this tract.

5. The establishment of his headquarters at Mukhlispur is another proof of Banda's knowledge of this area. Mukhlis Khan, the Governor of Sarhind, often hunted in these jungles. In the heart of a dense forest he built a rest house for himself on the top of a hill in 1677 and called if after his own name Mukhlispur. It looked like a small fort. That is why Khafi Khan calls it *Qilachi*.

6. Banda's disappearance into the hills and emergence at Kiratpur in one day indicates his familiarity with the submontane tract of Shiwalik hills.

7. After Banda's escape from this fort in December 1710, Raja Bhup Prakash of Nahan was arrested, put in an iron cage and sent to Delhi. Banda passed through the states of Nahan, Nalagarh Bilaspur, Kangra and Chamba. No action was taken against any other state. It seems clear that the Raja of Nahan was punished not that Banda escaped through his territory, but that Banda was his subject, and it was his duty to apprehend him.

8. Banda's abolition of zamindari system also demonstrates his knowledge of this region. The land there belonged to zamindars under the feudal system. This practice was not confined to Nahan state but also extended to parts of Ambala district, lying at the foot of Shiwalik hills. There the landlords were mainly Muslims and tenants were mostly Hindu Jats and Gujars.

9. Banda changed the name of Mukhlispur to that of Lohgarh. From here he issued his own coins. In addition to the names of Nanak and Gobind Singh, they bore the words 'Sachcha Sahib.' In the language of this tract 'Sahib' meant God. When a Hindu met a Muslim, he greeted him with 'Sahib Salaam' (Salute to God), and the reply given was ' Sahib ko Salaam.' The Hindus among themselves greeted each other with 'Ram Ram.' Sachcha Sahib therefore meant True Lord God. In his letters and orders Banda used the words 'Sri Sachcha Sahib,' not for himself, but for God and the Guru. The other Gurus after Nanak in their letters wrote their names as Nanak. Banda could not write Nanak as he was not the Guru. He adopted the term of Sachcha Sahib. The word Sahib was chiefly used there.

10. In the battle of Sarhind Sher Muhammad Khan, Nawab of Malerkotla, had fought hard against Banda. The Nawab was killed while fighting. In order to punish the Nawab's family, Banda attacked Malerkotla. To save the town from pillage Kishan Das Banya, an old acquaintance of the Bairagi, came to see him. Banda embraced him. On his recommendation the town was saved on payment of two lakhs of rupees as fine. The shopkeepers of the plains visited Shiwalik hills for the purpose of trade. They exchanged sugar, oil, salt and cloth for the hilly products such as blankets, ginger, turmeric and honey. In some of these visits Kishan Das might have met Banda Bahadur.

Was Banda baptised by the Guru?

There is no doubt about it that Banda became a disciple of Guru Gobind Singh, but he was not baptised according to his new ceremony of administering *pahul.* It appears that the Guru did so deliberately for certain reasons:

1. Banda was already known as Guru in Maharashtra and he commanded a large following. The Guru did not want to enhance Banda's prestige as a religious leader of the Sikhs.

2. He was over-active and over-energetic (Bara-Tejdhari), both in worldly life as well as in spiritual domain. The Guru was fully familiar with the Masands' role. He had abolished that institution, and was not prepared to create another masand so aggressive and powerful as Banda.

3. By making him a regular Sikh, the Guru feared lest he might claim Guruship in course of time. Without baptism the Khalsa would not accept him as the Guru. This actually happened. Ratan Singh Bhangu and Santokh Singh write that later on Banda declared himself Guru, and the Khalsa rejected his claim. They insisted on his getting himself baptised and taking meat diet.

Bhai Santokh Singh in *Suraj Granth* says: "He was not in accord with the Khalsa. Without the Guru's approval he started his own sect. He did not take baptism of the dagger. He did not adopt the Sikh way of life (keeping five K's). He did not eat meat and drink wine, and did not wear black clothes."

Gian Singh also says that the Guru did not baptise him. Khazan Singh is of the view that "although Banda became his disciple the Guru did not deem it advisable to initiate him with *Pahul.*" He further observes: The Guru "selected and deputed Banda Bahadur, not as successor and leader of the Khalsa, but as an avenging agent without admitting him into the Khalsa order with the usual initiation of Amrit baptism."

Kartar Singh Kalaswalia says that the Guru presented Banda at the time of his departure for Panjab with his own special dagger which he always wore around his neck. At this his Khalsa shouted: "We will never allow a non-Khalsa to have it. We will sacrifice our lives after killing him." Further he says Banda "was neither a baptised Sikh nor a *Sahajdhari.*"

Karam Singh, the well-known Sikh historian, declares that "although Banda had come within the fold of the Sikhs, he had no time to take *Amrit.*"

4. Had Banda been baptised, he would not have changed the Guru's salutation of *Wah Guru ji ka Khalsa, Wah Guru ji ki Fatah* to *Fatah Darshan.*

5. In case of his being a regular Sikh, a schism could not have taken place among his followers into Tatva Khalsa and Bandai Sikhs.

6. There are no contemporary or near contemporary sources to establish the fact that Banda had been baptised. All sources quoted in support of this assertion are one hundred years or more later.

Banda invested with temporal authority

At a durbar held at Nander about the middle of September 1708, the Guru conferred the title of Bahadur on Banda and invested him with full political and military authority as his Deputy to carry on the national struggle in the Panjab and to punish Wazir Khan of Sarhind and his supporters. He was supplied with a standard and a drum as symbols of temporal authority. He was given an advisory council of five devoted Khalsa: Baj singh, a descendant of the family of the third Guru, Amar Das, his brother Ram Singh, Binod Singh, who descended form Guru Angad, his son Kahan Singh and Fatah Singh. Twenty-five sikh soldiers were given to him as his bodyguard. A rescript called *hukamnamah* or a letter of authority in the handwriting of the Guru instructing the Sikhs to join Banda Bahadur in his national war against Mughal tyranny was provided. As an insignia of his temporal authority invested in him, the Guru gave Banda Bahadur his own sword, green bow and five arrows from his quiver. Three hundred Sikh cavaliers in battle array accompanied Banda to a distance of eight kilometres to give him the final send off.

Banda on his journey, 1708-09

The Guru refused to accompany the Emperor beyond Nander. He had been severely wounded by a Pathan set on the Guru by Wazir Khan with the connivance of the court nobles. The despatch of Banda to the Panjab had infuriated Emperor Bahadur Shah. As a result of his intrigue the Guru passed away on October 7, 1708. Banda had not gone for when he heard the sad news. This did not discourage him. On the contrary it doubled his zeal and set the fire of vengeance ablaze in his heart. Besides Banda had seen with his own eyes how Tara Bai, a young widow five years younger than he, had set Aurangzeb's teeth on edge from 1700 to 1707. Sir Jadunath Sarkar writes, "During this period the supreme guiding force in Maharashtra was not any minister but the Dowager queen Tara Bai Mohite. Her administrative genius and strength of character saved the nation in that awful crisis that threatened it in consequence of Rajaram's death." He now feared the safety of his own person and his men on account of Emperor's hostility. He wanted to reach Panjab before the Emperor was free from the revolt of his brother Kam Bakhsh at Hyderabad.

Banda seems to have travelled in disguise and by circuitous routes to avoid detection. Generally he adopted the same route across Maharashtra and Rajasthan as was followed by Guru Gobind Singh. The distance between Nander and Hissar in Haryana by that route was 1,600 kms.

Aurangzeb, V, 200.

Nander to Mandsaur	=	857 kms
Mandsaur to Ajmer	=	291 kms
Ajmer to Phulera	=	74 kms
Phulera to Ringas	=	66 kms
Ringas to Sikar	=	50 kms
Sikar to Churu	=	134 kms
Churu to Sadulpur	=	58 kms
Sadulpur to Hissar	=	70 kms
		1600 kms

At the rate of 16 kms or 10 miles a day on an average, Banda should not have taken more than 100 days during his journey, but he actually took about a year. It means that he might have been frequently in hiding. The Emperor should have instructed his officers to make short work of Banda and his party, as this much of diplomacy he could not have ignored. That is why Banda travelled right across Maharashtra and Rajasthan, both of which were in revolt against the Mughals.

Banda in Haryana, 1709

Narnaul: Banda arrived at Narnaul. There he saw complete destruction of Satnamis with his own eyes. His blood boiled on learning that the entire sect of Satnamis, men, women and children, one and all, had been wiped out of existence. It was here that Banda made up his mind to retaliate upon Muslims. Here he suppressed some dacoits and robbers.

Bhiwani: At Bhiwani Banda looted the government treasury and distributed it among his followers. This liberality attracted a large number of young men to join him.

Hissar: In Hissar district called the Bagar desh where Banda was in October 1709, he was well received by the Hindus and Sikhs as a leader of the nationalist movement and deputy of Guru Gobind Singh. Liberal offerings were made to him in the cause of the country and dharam (religion and virtue) which he distributed among his followers and the poor and the needy. In this region he took to suppressing dacoits and robbers, seized their booty and gave it to the poor people. Young men of narrow means and daredevils began to flock under his banners, and the number of his retinue was swelling.

Tohana: Here Banda issued letters to Malwa Sikhs to join him in his crusade against Wazir Khan of Sarhind.

Never perhaps in the history of Panjab did the circumstances of the time offer so fair a field to the ambition of a leader, conscious of great talents, and called to the command of a warlike people, only too eager to support him in any enterprise he might undertake. The Emperor was away in the Deccan, and many of his notable chiefs and commanders had been killed in the recently fought civil war. The Governors of Delhi, Sarhind, Lahore and Jammu acted independently and had no cooperation among themselves. Banda directed his attention to the east towards Delhi. There were two motives behind this move. He wanted to leave Mata Sahib Devi in Delhi and plunder the Government officials and rich Muslims of the fertile areas of Haryana. From Kharkhauda about 50 kms north-west of Delhi, Mata Sahib Devi was sent to Delhi under proper escort, to join Mata Sundari, who was acting as head of the Khalsa. She might have resented Banda's ignoring her for not having visited her at the capital before starting on his crusade.

Sonepat: At Sonepat, 50 kms north of Delhi, early in November 1709 Banda commanded about 500 followers. He attacked the government treasury, plundered it and distributed it among his retinue. This was his second success against the government and it considerably raised his prestige. By slow marches he advanced towards Sarhind.

Kaithal: Near Kaithal, about 100 kms farther north, Banda seized a government treasury which was on its way from the northern districts to Delhi. He kept nothing out of it for himself and gave it away to his rank and file.

Samana: Samana, 50 kms farther north was the native place of Jalal-ud-din Jallad, the professional executioner, who had beheaded Guru Tegh Bahadur, while his son had beheaded the two younger sons of Guru Gobind Singh. Ali Husain who by false promises had lured Guru Gobind Singh to evacuate Anandpur also belonged to Samana. It was an accursed place in the eyes of the Sikhs. The entire peasantry of the neighbourhood was now up in arms, and Banda's following had risen to several thousands. Banda fell upon the town on November 26, 1709. The inhabitants were massacred in cold blood and the town was thoroughly squeezed. Samana was the district town and had nine parganahs attached to it. It was placed under charge of Fatah Singh. Samana was the first territorial conquest and the first administrative unit of Banda. A large quantity of gold, arms and ammunition fell into his hands, while everybody fighting under him became rich and prosperous. Fatah Singh was given a body of troopers to maintain peace and order.

Other Muslim Towns: Kunjpura, Ghuram and Thaska, inhabited by Muslim Ranghars, notorious for rape and rapine, was destroyed next. Damla was the village of those Pathans who had deserted Guru Gobind Singh in the battle of Bhangani. It was ravaged. Shahabad Markanda, 25 kms south of Ambala, a Muslim town, fell Banda's victim. Mustafabad, 40 kms south-west of Ambala, was laid waste. The Nawab of Kapuri who was lewd and lustful was killed and his fort was razed to the ground.

Sadhaura: Usman Khan, the chief of Sadhaura, 25 kms distant, had persecuted Sayyid Budhu Shah for helping Guru Gobind Singh in the battle of

Bhangani. The Muslim population maltreated the local Hindus. On the approach of Banda the leading Muslims gathered in a big and strongly built mansion. They were all massacred. This building came to be called Qatal Garhi. Banda attacked the town and destroyed it.

The contemporary historian Khafi Khan wrote: "In two or three months' time, four to five thousands pony-riders, and seven to eight thousand warlike footmen joined him. Day by day their number increased, and abundant money and material by pillage fell into their hands. Soon eighteen to nineteen thousand men in arms under him raised aloft the standard of plunder and persecution." Further on he says: "Numerous villages were laid waste, and he appointed his own police officers *(thanedars)* and collectors of revenue *(tahsildar-e-mal)*."

Lohgarh: The ultimate aim of Banda was to punish Wazir Khan and conquer Sarhind. It required time to consolidate his material and territorial gains. He also wanted to study the military resources of Sarhind. He was anxious to see what steps the Government would take against him. He therefore established his headquarters, in the beginning of February 1710, at Mukhlispur situated in lower Shiwalik hills south of Nahan, about 20 kms from Sadhaura. Its fort stood on a kill top. Two kuhls or water channels flowed at its base and supplied water to it. This fort was repaired and put in a state of defence. All the money, gold and costly material acquired in these expeditions were deposited here. He struck coins and issued orders under his own seal. The name of Mukhlispur was changed to Lohgarh, and it became the capital of the first Sikh State. "Although he declared himself as the slave of the Guru, yet the Khalsa looked upon him as the Guru and became his followers."

Banda ruled over the region bounded on the north by the Shiwalik hills, on the west by river Tangri, on the east by river Jamuna, and in the south by a line passing through Samana, Thanesar, Kaithal and Karnal. He abolished the Zamindari system of land tenure prevailing under the Mughals and declared the actual cultivators as the owners of land. Thus he established the peasant proprietorship, and won the approbation and support of the overwhelming majority of the population. Khafi Khan says that Banda "issued orders to imperial officers and agents and big jagirdars to submit and give up their business." So Guru Gobind Singh's dream of political sovereignty was realized within a year of his death.

Banda's name struck terror into the hearts of lawless people, and thefts and brigandage became a thing of the past. "In all the parganahs occupied by the Sikhs," writes Irvine, "the reversal of the previous customs was striking and complete. A low scavenger of leather dresser, the lowest of the low in Indian estimation, had only to leave home and join the Guru, when in a short time he would return to his birthplace as its ruler with his order of appointment in his hand. As soon as he set foot within the boundaries, the well-born and wealthy went out to greet him and escort him home. Arrived there, they stood before him with joined palms awaiting his orders... Not a soul dared to disobey an order, and men who had often risked themselves in battlefields, became so cowed down that they were afraid even to remonstrate. Hindus who had not joined the sect were not exempt from these."

Banda's troops

Banda devoted three months in organizing his civil and military administration. Bahadur Shah was still away from Delhi. The Delhi Government had made no attempt to recover their lost territory from him. Wazir Khan of Sarhind was making his own preparations independently to meet the danger from Banda.

Banda's troops consisted of two classes of people. The old Sikhs who had fought under Guru Gobind Singh joined him purely to punish Wazir Khan. They also wished to see the fulfillment of the Guru's prophecy for Sikh sovereignty in Punjab. They numbered about five thousands. Another class of Sikhs of about the same number comprised young men who wanted to punish and plunder the enemies of their faith. The third group of Hindu Jats, Gujars and Rajputs, about ten thousands in number were intent on plunder alone. Most of them were untrained, raw levies, not fully armed. Banda possessed no elephants, no good horses and no guns. His followers had matchlocks, swords, spears, bows and arrows. According to Khafi Khan the number of Sikhs had risen to thirty or forty thousands.

Wazir Khan's preparations

Wazir Khan had proclaimed a *jihad* or a holy war against Banda. He was joined by the Nawab of Malerkotla, all other Muslim chiefs and jagirdars as well as by Ranghars in large numbers. His men were fully equipped with fine, up-to-date arms. Majority of his soldiers were trained men. Wazir Khan's own troops were "five or six thousand horse and seven or eight thousand musketeers *(barqandaz)* and archers, and with these, some artillery and elephants." In addition there were about eight thousand *ghazis.* The total number of his troops was about twenty thousands.

Banda advanced from Lohgarh and halted at Banur, near Ambala, 14 kms from Rajpura. The Muslims of that town used to seize cows and oxen of Hindus and slaughter them in their presence. Banda sacked it, and then went ahead towards Sarhind.

On hearing the news of Banda's advance, the Sikhs of the Jullundur and Bari Doabs gathered at Kiratpur to join his forces. Their passage was barred near Rupar by Sher Muhammad Khan of Malerkotla. He was defeated. They met Banda between Banur and Kharar on the road leading from Ambala to Rupar.

The battle of Sarhind, May 12, 1710

The battle was fought at Chhappar Chiri, 20 kms from Sarhind on May 12, 1710. On the Mughal side Sher Muhammad Khan, Nawab of Malerkotla, was the leader of the right wing. Wazir Khan was in command of the centre. Suchanand, chief secretary of the Nawab, was put on the left. On the Sikh side, Baj Singh headed the right flank and Binod Singh the left flank, while Banda commanded the centre facing Wazir Khan. Shouts of Sachcha *Padishah, Fatah Darshan, Akal, Akal* and *Ya Ali, Ya Ali,* rent the sky. Suchanand could not withstand the ferocity of Baj Singh. He was soon vanquished and fled away. The artillery fire of the Mughals told heavily on the plunderers in Banda's camp. They were equally divided between the forces of Banda and Binod, and they took to flight. Sher Muhammad was about to overpower Binod Singh's wing when he was suddenly struck by a bullet and was instantly killed. His men immediately dispersed. Wazir Khan was rushing upon Banda who stuck fast to his ground and discharged arrows relentlessly. There a bloody battle was going on. Baj Singh and Binod Singh now joined Banda. Banda and the Sikh leaders now converged around Wazir Khan, who was killed.

Wazir Khan's death is variously described. Khafi Khan says that he was struck by a musket ball. Mir Muhammad Ahsan Ijad says that Baj Singh rushed upon Wazir Khan. The Governor threw his spear at him. Baj Singh caught hold of it. He flung the same spear upon Wazir Khan. It struck the forehead of his horse. Wazir Khan discharged an arrow which hit Baj Singh's arm. He then rushed upon him with sword. At this juncture Fatah Singh came to the rescue of Baj Singh. His sword cut the Khan from shoulder to the waist.

Akhbarat-e-Durbar-e-Mualla dated May 13, 1710 stated that the battle began in the morning and lasted until afternoon. Wazir Khan was wounded by arrows and bullets and fell dead. His son and son-in-law also perished.

Latif writes that he was killed by an arrow which pierced his breast. Kanhiyalal says he was struck by a bullet in breast. Macauliffe holds that his head was cut off by Banda himself in a scuffle.

Pursuit of fugitives

Wazir Khan's head was stuck up on a spear and lifted high up by a Sikh who took his seat in the deceased's howdah. The Sikhs with one voice and in wild excitement raised the sky-rending shouts of *Sat Sri Akal.* The Muslim troops on beholding the Nawab's head took alarm, and trembling fled helter skelter in dismay and despair. The Sikhs fell upon them and there was terrible carnage. Blood flowed freely not only in the battlefield but on a wide tract up to the city of Sarhind, 20 kms distant. Wazir Khan's body was dragged by oxen and was then burnt. Khafi Khan writes that in the course of flight "not a man of the army of Islam escaped with more than his life and clothes he stood in.

Horsemen and footmen fell under the swords of the infidels who pursued them as far as Sarhind."

The city of Sarhind

The Sikhs reached Sarhind by nightfall. The gates of the city were closed. The guns mounted on the walls of the fort commenced bombardment. The Sikhs laid siege to the place. They took rest in the night and gained strength for another trail the following day. Wazir Khan's family and the Muslim nobles fled to Delhi at night.

Severe fighting took place on May 13, 1710. The fort guns caused great havoc among Sikhs, and about 500 of them lost their lives. The Sikhs in knots were hammering at the gates, and the Mughal gunners obviously were playing a losing game. By afternoon they succeeded in breaking open a couple of gates, and Banda's troops entered the town. Inside the town destruction of life and property knew no bounds. Whole families were wiped out of existence. Every follower of Banda seized as much in cash and kind as much he could carry home. The Government treasury and movable property worth two crores fell into the hands of Banda and it was removed to Lohgarh. Several Muslims of note saved their lives by embracing Sikhism. Dindar Khan son of Jalal Khan Rohilla became Dindar Singh. The official newswriter of Sarhind Mir Nasir-ud-din changed his name to Mir Nasir Singh.

The province of Sarhind occupied

The entire province of Sarhind consisting of twenty-eight parganahs and extending from the Satluj to the Jamuna and from the Shiwalik hills to Kunjpura, Karnal and Kaithal, yielding 52 lakhs annually (Bawani Sarhind) came into Banda's possession. Baj Singh was appointed Governor of Sarhind. Ali Singh was made his deputy. Their chief responsibility was to be on guard against the Mughal troops from Lahore and Jammu. Fatah Singh retained charge of Samana. Ram Singh, brother of Baj Singh, became chief of Thanesar. Binod Singh, in addition to his post of the revenue minister, was entrusted with the administration of Karnal and Panipat. His main duty was to guard the road from Delhi. Banda retired to his capital at Lohgarh. His era began from May 12, 1710, the date of his victory in the battle of Sarhind. The zamindari system was abolished in the whole province at one stroke.

Banda advances towards Lahore, June 1710

Having set up the administrative machinery, Banda advanced from Sarhind to Malerkotla to punish the family of Sher Muhammad Khan. The town was saved for a ransom of two lakhs on the re-commendation of Kishan Das Banya, an old acquaintance of Banda. From there he marched to Morinda. He chastized the Brahmins and Ranghars who had made over Guru Gobind Singh's mother and his two youngest sons to Wazir Khan. Then he visited Kiratpur and Anandpur to pay homage at the holy shrines. He took Hoshirpur and

Jullundur and carried fire and sword everywhere. Banda crossed the Beas and fell upon Batala. Shaikh-ul-Ahad, a leading Muslim chief and theologian, was killed. Several other places including Kalanaur were captured. He went on a pilgrimage to Derah Baba Nanak. At Amritsar Banda made large offerings. He invited young men to embrace Sikhism promising remission of land revenue and other rewards. Thereupon the people of Majha joined the Khalsa.

Banda marched to Lahore. Sayyid Islam Khan, the Governor, mounted guns on the walls of the city. He was joined by all the Muslims of the neighbourhood. A fierce action took place at a distance from the city. Thousands were killed on both sides. The Muslims were defeated. They assembled the next day, "but were again defeated with great slaughter." Lahore must have fallen, but Banda was in a hurry to look after his Government.

Thus the city remained safe owing to its strong fortifications. But the entire suburbs for miles around were completely devastated. In this campaign Banda was joined by thousands of low-caste Hindus.

Banda in the Upper Ganga Doab, July 1710

Banda returned to Sarhind, toured over the province to see that the administration was going on well. Then he returned to Lohgrah. In the course of his excursions tales of bigotry of the Muslims of the Upper Ganga Doab were brought to his notice. He lost no time, and crossed the river Jamuna at Rajghat near Buria and entered the district of Saharanpur. He punished and plundered the people of Saharanpur, Behat, Nanautah and Jalalabad. The people submitted after a tough resistance. Thus Banda's rule extended from the river Ravi to the Ganga, and from the neighbourhood of Lahore to the vicinity of Panipat.

The Haidari Flag, September-October 1710

Immediately on his return, the Muslims of Lahore district and its vicinity declared a holy war against the Sikhs. Thousands of Muslims gathered under a huge standard with a green flag, called *Haidari Jhanda*, to crush the Sikh revolt. The Sikhs assembled under their local leaders in self-defence. Three main battles were fought at Qaila Bhagwant Rae, not far from Lahore, Kotla Begam near Chamyari and Bhilowal. The Muslims were defeated and dispersed.

The battle of Rahon, October-November 1710

The Sikhs fell back. They captured Rahon situated on a high mound near the Satluj in the Jullundur Doab. Shams Khan, faujdar of the Jullundur Doab, had his headquarters at Sultanpur Lodi. At the head of 5,000 men he marched against the Sikhs. There were no provisions in the fort of Rahon. They left the fort and came out to oppose Shams Khan. A hard battle was fought in Yaqub

Khan's garden. Shams Khan was joined by his uncle Bayazid Khan, Governor of Jammu. Umar Khan, an Afghan chief of Kasur, also united with them. A tough fight followed. The Sikhs held together for a few days. Finding the situation untenable they entered Rahon in the night. The place was immediately besieged. They stood their ground for some time, eating whatever could be had from the deserted houses. The fort fell in November and the Sikhs were driven away. Shams Khan then advanced upon Sarhind. Baj Singh and Ali Singh were defeated. They fled away to Lohgarh. Shams Khan occupied Sarhind and killed a number of Sikhs.

Bahadur Shah marches against Banda

Emperor Bahadur Shah had defeated and killed his only surviving brother Kam Bakhsh in January 1709. He remained in the Deccan for about a year to establish his own administration. Meanwhile several Rajput princes had revolted in Rajasthan. Bahadur Shah came there in May 1710. At Ajmer he got the news of Sikh rebellion in Panjab. He hurriedly settled terms with the Rajputs and left for Panjab towards the close of June 1710.

Several Hindu chiefs such as Chatarsal Bundela and Udet Singh Bundela followed in his train. The Governors of Allahabad, Lucknow, Moradabad, Delhi and Sayyid Abdullah of Barah Sadat in Muzaffarnagar district were ordered to join him.

In July 1710 the Emperor appointed Zain-ud-din Ahamd Khan Governor of Sarhind. In August 1710 Firoz Khan Mewati was placed in command of the advance-guard. Muhammad Amin Khan, Governor of Moradabad, with his son Qamar-ud-din Khan (both of whom became prime ministers of Delhi later on) joined the Emperor in Haryana. Another force under Sayyid Wahih-ud-din Khan of Barah Sadat was sent to reinforce Firoz Khan Mewati. By a proclamation ingress into and egress form Delhi was strictly forbidden. Kokaltash Khan was given charge of Sonepat.

Early in September 1710 all the Hindus in the camp were clean shaved to avoid any resemblance with the Sikhs. Muslim chiefs and jagirdars joined the imperial forces on their way. Churaman Jat of Bharatpur reported himself on duty in the royal camp near Delhi.

The Emperor was so much worried that he did not enter his capital and marched straight to Sonepat in the last week of October. Here he learnt the news of a couple of engagements with the Sikhs. Firoz Khan Mewati had fought an action with Binod Singh at Amin, 24 kms north of Karnal, and he presented 300 Sikh heads to the Emperor at Sonepat. He was given one lakh of rupees and appointed Governor of Sarhind in superession of his previous orders for the appointment of Zain-ud-din Khan. Firoz Khan Mewati fought two more battles against Binod Singh and Ram Singh at Traori and Thanesar, defeated them and established his own military posts there. Hundreds of Sikh heads with their long flowing hair were hung up on trees all along the road. He then advancde to Shahabad, and captured it.

In November 1710 the Emperor passed through Painpat, Karnal, Thanesar and Shahabad. He encamped at Barara. In on month he covered a distance of 150 kms. In the begining of December 1710 he reached Sadhaura which became the base of his operations. There the Emperor received 300 Sikh heads sent by Shams Khan from Sarhind. Frioz Khan Mewati was ordered to restore Emperor's authority in the rural areas.

Clashes with Imperial forces

Bahadur Shah planned to advance upon Banda's stronghold at Lohgrah. The Imperial forces were terror-stricken *(tars-o-haras)*. "According to the popular voice," writes Irvine, "he was a most powerful magician, greater even than he who made a calf to talk; he could turn a bullet from its course and could work such spells that spear and sword had little or no effect upon his followers. Owing to those idle rumours the Emperor and the nobles and the soliders were much disturbed in mind and were disheartened. The Sikhs, on the other hand, were encouraged by the belief instilled into them by Banda that all who lost their lives in this war would be recreated at once in a higher rank."

A strong Mughal force under Rustamdil Khan advanced from their base at Sadhaura towards Lohgarh to examine the position bo Banda's defences. At a distance of 5 kms they were suddenly attacked by Banda's troops. Khafi Khan writes: "It is impossible for me to describe the fight which followed. The Sikhs in their *faqir* dress struck terror into the royal troops. The number of the dead and dying of the Imperialists was so large that, for a time, it seemed they were losing ground. A nephew of Firoz Khan Mewati was killed and his son wounded." In the battle Banda lost 1,500 Sikhs and two Sardars. Banda cut off convoys and other detachment, and killed two or three faujdars. It rained for four or five days and weather became very cold. Thousands of soldiers fell ill and many horses died. Their stench was unbearable. The soldiers attributed this calamity to the sorcery of Banda.

Another big contingent under command of Emperor's son Prince Rafi-us-Shan, was ordered to reinforce Rustamdil Khan. Kamwar Khan in his *Tazkirat-ul-Salatin* writes: "This humble person was then present with troops of Prince Rafi-us-Shaṇ, and saw with his own eyes that everyone of the cursed Sikhs came out of the entrenchments, challenged the Imperial troops, and after great struggle and trail, fell under the swords of the *Ghazis*." Rustamdil Khan was raised to the *mansab* of 4,000 *Zat* and 3,000 *Sawar* with the title of Ghazi Khan Rustam-e-Jang.

The siege of Lohgarh

Rustamdil Khan made farther advance by 4 kms, and reached the stream Som. From there the fort of Lohgarh was visible. It was perched on the top of a hill. Between the stream Som and Lohgarh lay a dense forest. It produced frightful sounds at night. The imperial camp arrived there on December 9, 1710. The prime minister Munim Khan and his son Mahabat Khan were assigned the duty to guard the royal camp.

The following day on December 10, 1710, the Imperial army, 60,000 strong, pushed forward in battle array so as to surround the fort of Lohgarh on all sides. Wazir Munim Khan, his son Mahabat Khan and Chatarsal Bundela were in charge of the right wing. Udet Singh Bundela and Churaman Jat commanded the left wing. Rustamdil Khan was in the centre. When they reached within range of the Sikh guns, they were heavily shelled. The Mughal troops entered the trenches at the foot of the hill. The Sikhs fought hard, but they were repulsed. The survivors retreated up the hill. Large numbers of Muslims were also killed.

The fort of Lohgarh was small. There was no space for storing large quantities of grain and fodder. Their supplies had run short. "The infidels bought what they could from the grain-dealers with the royal army, and pulled it up with ropes." In this exigency Banda decided to escape. A Sikh Gulab Singh by name, a Khatri and formerly a tobacco-seller, had a great resemblance with Banda Bahadur. He put on Banda's clothes and took up position in his place. At 3 o'clock in the morning on December 11, 1710, a hollow truck of a big tamarind tree lying in the lower parts of the hill was filled with gunpowder. The guns in the fort were also kept ready to fire simultaneously. Just when the gunpowder in the tree trunk wea blown off and the guns in the fort fired, Banda and his men escaped in the great confusion prevailing in the Mughal camp. They safely disappeared into the Sarmur hills.

From Sarmur right across lower parts of the Shiwalik hills, Banda passed through Hindur (Nalagarh), Kahlur (Bilaspur), Kutlehr, Jaswan, Siba and Nurpur, to Chamba.

With the sunrise on December 11, 1710, the imperials delivered a vehement assault on the fort. Gulab Singh and his companions kept in firing from the fort. The Mughal troopers continued climbing up the hill. Gulab Singh and thirty of his companions were captured. A number of women and children of the neighbouring village had taken up shelter in the Sikhfort. They were taken prisoners. The booty in the fort comprised many horses and camels, five elephants, three big guns, seventeen light guns and silver muskets and swords, a canopy with silver poles, gold and silver coins worth eight lakhs of rupees, and from underground gold coins to the value of twenty lakhs of rupees.

There were great rejoicings in the Imperial camp. On December 12, 1710 a great durbar was held, and various honours were conferred on all the commanders. In the evening it was discovered that thy real Banda had escaped and that it was his duplicate who had been captured. According to Khafi Khan "the hawk had flown and an owl had been caught." All were thoroughly disappointed. The Mughal camp wore a mourning appearance. The Emperor summoned Prime Minister Munim Khan and administered to him sharp rebuke. The Wazir took the insult to heart, fell ill, and died two and a half months afterwards, when the Emperor was halting at Badhauli not far from Sadhaura on his way to Lahore.

On December 13, a contingent of Mughal troops was despatched to seize the Barfi Raja of Nahan, Bhup Prakash, whose younger brother had been offered the *gaddi* be Aurangzeb if he would embrace Islam. The Raja was seized. He and Gulab Singh, Banda's substitute, were both put in an iron cage, sent to Delhi and imprisoned in the Red fort. Gulab Singh's thirty companions were beheaded. Muhammad Khan came from Sarhind and presented to the Emperor six cartloads of Sikh heads.

It was the duty of the Raja of Nahan to supply ice in summer to the Imperial capital. In winter ice was stored in pits at the fort of hills. In hot weather it was carried wrapped in thick blankets by porters to Dhamras on the river Yamuna. There it was packed in boxes and floated down the river in rafts to Daryapur near Khizarabad in Ambala district. At this place it was loaded in boats and reached Delhi in three days.

Banda at Kiratpur, December 12, 1710

One day after his escape from Lohgarh Banda arrived at Kiratpur. On December 12, 1710 he addressed a number of letters to various centres of Sikhs inviting them to gather at Anandpur immediately. One of such letters was addressed to the Sangat at Jaunpur in U.P. It is reproduced below:

One God! Victory to the Sect!

This is the order to Sri Sachcha Sahib to the entire Khalsa of Jaunpur. The Guru will protect you. Call upon the Guru's name. Your lives will be fruitful. You are the Khalsa of great Immortal God. On seeing this letter repair to the presence, wearing five arms. Observe the rules of conduct laid down for the Khalsa. Do not use bhang, tobacco, poppy, wine or any other intoxicant....

Commit no theft or adultery. We have brought about the golden age *(Satyuga).* Love one another. This is my wish. He who lives according to the rules of the Khalsa shall be saved be the Guru. Poh 12 Samvat 1."

From Kiratpur Banda went to Anandpur, and passing through the hills reached Chamba. Raja Udai Singh offered Banda a princess "a supremely beautiful girl. She had large eyes, her limbs were graceful and delicate, and she is described by the enthusiastic chronicler as the very image of the goddess of love."

Bahadur Shah died, February 28, 1712

The Emperor marched in pursuit of Banda. Passing through Sadhaura, Sarwarpur, Rasulpur and Badhauli, where his prime minister Munim Khan passed away, he reached Rupur on April 30, 1710. He crossed the Satluj on May 17, 1711, and reached Hoshiarpur on June 9, 1711. The river Beas was crossed on June 23. He arrived at Kahnuwan on July 17 where he enjoyed hunting water fowls. He reached Lahore on August 11, 1711. Some time afterwards the Emperor developed signs of insanity and died on February 28, 1712.

The battle of Raipur-Bahrampur, November 1711

Banda came out of the hills in September 1711. He seized Pathankot and Gurdaspur. At the latter place he built a fort and collected stores of munition, grain and fodder. In November Qutb-ud-din Khan Kheshgi, faujdar of Jammu, advanced to oppose him. Banda was then subjugating the country in the neighbourhood of Batala and Kalanaur. Qutb-ud-din lay encamped 40 kms to the north. His nephew Shams Khan proceeded from Sultanpur to join his uncle. Both the chiefs attacked Banda near Raipur-Bahrampur. In a severe scuffle the Sikhs took to their heels. Shams Khan issued out in their pursuit. Qutb-ud-din tried his best to prevent him, but he did not care. The Sikhs suddenly came to a halt, and engaged the Afghans in a fiercely contested battle. Shams Khan was shot dead, while Qutb-ud-din was seriously wounded. He fell unconscious and died after three days.

Kalanaur and Batala

Banda marched upon Batala. Shaikh Muhammad Daim, the faujdar of Batala opposed the Sikhs. He was defeated and he fled away to Lahore. Kalanaur and Santokhgarh fell immediately afterwards. Two Mughal generals, Muhammad Amin Khan and Rustamdil Khan issued in pursuit of Banda. He at once crossed river Ravi. The Mughal forces pursued Banda. In the battle of Pasrur the Mughals were victorious and Banda fled away towards Jammu.

Muhammad Amin Khan and Rustamdil Khan maintained pursuit of Banda. In other engagements fought at Parol 24 kms north-west of Pathankot and at Kathua 11 kms east of Parol he was again repulsed. Rustamdil Khan committed terrible atrocities on the people of Parol-Kathua. He captured young men and women and brought them to Lahore for sale in the slave market.

Muhammad Amin Khan advanced to Jammu, fought a battle with Banda and sent 500 Sikh heads to Lahore. Banda penetrated into the hills and rested on the bank of river Chenab, 75 kms from Jammu. The place came to be called Derah Baba Banda.

Banda recovers Sarhind and Lohgarh, March 1712

On the death of Bahadur Shah a civil war occurred among his sons at Lahore on March 14-17, 1712. The Mughal governors joined one side or the other. Eventually the eldest son Jahandar Shah came out successful.

Banda took advantage of the situation. He appeared into the plains early in March 1712. Islam Khan, Governor of Lahore, marched to check Banda's advance. In a pitched battle Islam Khan was repulsed and he returned to the capital to participate in the contest for the throne among princes.

Banda advanced upon Sarhind. Bayazid Khan, the Governor, opposed him, but he was not successful. After the battle the Governor retired into his tent. A Sikh entered his tent at night and severed his head. Sarhind again fell into Banda's hands. Having appointed Sikh officers Banda took up his position at Lohgarh.

Lohgarh besieged

Jahandar Shah ordered Amin Khan to seize Banda. He besieged Lohgarh, but failed to capture the Sikh leader. When the Emperor was going to Agra to suppress the revolt of farrukh Siyar, son of his youngerr brother Azim-us-Shan, he called Amin Khan to join him. Jahandar Shah was defeated and killed on February 11, 1713. Tarrukh Siyar became the Emperor.

The new Emperor immediately turned his attention to suppress the Sikh revolt. On February 22, 1713 Farrukh Siyar transferred Abdus Samad Khan Diler Jang from Kashmir to Panjab, while his youthful son Zakariya Khan was appointed faujdar of Jammu. Zabardast Khan was given Kashmir. Zain-ud-din Ahmad Khan was made in charge of Sarhind. Strict orders were issued to all of them to put an end to the Sikhs revolt and capture Banda. Abdus Samad Khan and Zain-ud-din Ahmad Khan encamped at Sadhaura in April 1713 and commenced fighting woth the Sikhs. The Sikhs fought so ferociously that the Mughal army was almost overpowered. According to Khan "They over and over again showed the greatest daring." He again repeats that the Sikhs "showed the greatest boldness and daring, and made nocturnal attacks upon the Imperial forces." He further emphasizes that "the enemy exhibited great courage and daring." Banda held his ground for six months. When he ran short of supplies of grain and fodder he escaped into the hills in the beginning of October 1713. This news was recorded at Delhi on October 9, 1713.

Banda retired to his Derah on the bank of river Chenab. Zakariya Khan, the Governor of Jammu, led an expedition against him. A number of Sikhs lost their lives. Their heads were cut off and sent to Delhi. They were produced before Farrukh Siyar on December 13, 1713. Zakariya Khan was granted a robe of honour with the rank of 3,000 Zat and 1,000 Sawars.

Banda came out in August 1714 near Rupar with 7,000 Sikhs. Zain-ud-din

Ahmad Khan, Faujdar of Sarhind, fought an action with him on August 26, 1714. He sent 200 Sikh heads to Delhi. Banda vanished into the hills.

Schism in Banda's ranks, October 1714

A determined effort was now made by Farrukh Siyar to suppress the Sikh rebellion through diplomacy as well as military action. He was disappointed that the Mughal Empire with all the resources at its command had failed in capturing the Sikh leader. He formed at plan to use Mata Sundri widow of Guru Gobind Singh who was livind in Delhi. She was asked to persuad Banda to stop his lawless activities, accept jagirs for himself and other Sikh leaders, and to get his Sikh soldiers recruited in the imperial army. On receiving Mata Sundari's communication Banda replied that he had no faith in Government's promises. The Emperor imprisoned Mata Sundari and Mata Sahib Devi. The Emperor knew that the Sikhs would make submission in order to save the honour of Guru's widows. Mata Sundri again wrote to Banda to submit. Banda said that the ladies must endure all the hardship because his submission implied annihilation of the Khalsa, and failure of his mission entrutsed to him by the Guru. The Emperor tightened the restrictions imposed upon the ladies. Mata Sundari ordered Banda immediately to submit or face excommunication.

Banda replied that "he was merely a Bairagi Faqir and had neither friend nor foe" and that "he was merely carrying out the orders of Guru Gobind Singh in regard to the campaign of vengeance for the destruction of the tyrant, and the protection of the Khalsa.

Mata Sundari charged Banda with disobedience and non-observance of Guru Gobind Singh'a instructions. She issued orders of excommunication of Banda to all the Sikh leaders serving under Banda on the ground that he had married, that he had substituted *Fatah Darshan* for *Wah Guru Ji ka Khalsa, Wah Guru Ji ki Fatah*, and that he wanted to rule over the Singhas as their Guru.

On the receipt of letters of excommunication many Sikh chiefs immediately decided to separate themselves from Banda. The initiative was taken by Miri Singh, a young man in early twenties. His father Kahak Singh and grandfather Binod Singh, Banda's companions from Nander as his principal advisers appointed by Guru Gobind Singh, broke away from Banda with 5,000 Sikhs. Others who hesitated pressed Banda to take *pahul*, begin to eat meat, drink wine and waer black clothes instead of red clothes, in order to retain their loyalty. Banda declined to do so. They also fell off and joined Binod Singh. This party called itself Tatva Khalsa or the real Khalsa. Those who strck fast to Banda were called Bandai Sikhs. They were almost equally divided, each group containing about 15,000 Sikhs.

The Emperor sent presents of doshalas and arms and other articles to the Tatva Khalsa. A contingent of 5,000 Sikhs under command of Kahan Singh, his son Miri Singh, Fatah Singh or Bhagto, and Sham Singh Naurangwalia was taken into service by the Governor of Lahore. Each horseman was paid Rs. 30 p.m., a footman Rs. 15 p.m. and a Sardar Rs. 5 daily. The Sikhs who preferred to stay at Amritsar were paid Rs. 5,000 monthly. The parganah of Jhabal was granted to meet the expenses of the *langar*, and grain and fodder for horses.

The division in the Sikhs was to be confirmed at the sacred shrine of Amritsar. Hence the Sikhs were allowed to celebrate the Diwali at Amritsar in November 1714 without any fear of molestation. On this occasion the Tatva Khalsa made a formal isolated from Bandais, and offered their allegiance as well as active service against the Bandais to the Governor of Lahore.

Revolt of Husain Khan Kheshgi of Kasur

To stabilize the bifurcation the Tatva Khalsa gave a practical proof. Abdus Samad Khan was then busy in suppressing the rebellion of Husain Khan Kheshgi of Kasur. There was only a small force at Lahore. Banda marched from Amritsar and encamped near village Kahali. The next halt was made at village Ghanayki. He then advanced upon Lahore. The Lahore army came out to oppose him. There advance-guard consisted of the Tatva Khalsa under Miri Singh. At the sight of his comrades arrayed on the enemy side Banda felt disgusted. He lost the ground and retired into the hills.

Husain Khan Kheshgi had revolted against the Panjab Governor. Khafi Khan saays he was incited into rebellion by the Sayyid Brothers who headed the Hindustani party in opposition to the Turani party at the Mughal court. Abdus Samad was an important leader of the Turani party. Husain Khan took possession of several places in the neighbourhood of Kasur. He turned out many Imperial jagirdars and faujdars. Abdus Samad sent an expeditionary force to punish him. The Mughal commander was killed in the battle, and his baggage and treasure were plundered by the victor.

Husain Khan recruited an army of about nine thousand horsemen. Abdus Samad also raised a force of equal number and marched against him. Both the armies fought near Chunian, about 30 kms south of Lahore. It was a long and fiercely contested battle. At lenght an arrow struck Husain Khan. His elephant whose driver had been killed ran about at random. A shower of bullets and arrows fell on it. The howdah caught fire. Husain Khan fell dead. Many of his Afghans were killed. The rest took to flight. The Emperor conferred the title of Saif-ud-daulah (Sword of the State) on Abdus Samad Khan.

Banda captured alive, December 1715

The fall of Sikh power was now sure and certain. *(Is ghar ko ag lag gai ghar ke chiragh se).* Banda still had 14,000 combatants with him. However, the courageous Banda did not lose heart and continued to perform his mission of destruction and devastation.

Emperor Farrukh Siyar sent a strong force of 20,000 troops from Delhi, under Qamar-ud-din Khan. He was joined by 5,000 troops from Sarhind. Orders were issued to Abdus Samad Khan and his son Zakariya Khan to seize Banda alive. All the three Turani leaders were related to one another. The mother of Qamar-ud-din and wife of Abdus Samad Khan were real sisters. Zakariya Khan, son of Abdus Samad Khan, was married to the sister of Qamar-ud-din. Thus the campaign became a family affair of the Turani party.

Banda was at that time carrying on operations to the north of Amritsar. Just then the Mughal army appeared on the scene with the determination of a crusader. Banda retired northward with a view to take shelter in the fort of Gurdaspur. It had been recently extended so as to accommodate sixty thousand horse and foot. Large stores of grain and fooder had also been collected there. The Mughal army converged upon him from three sides. The Delhi force of 20,000 men under Qamar-ud-din Khan advanced from the east, the Lahore troops about 10,000 under Abdus Samad Khan marched from the south, and the Jammu soldiery nearly 5,000 under Zakariya Khan moved from the north. To the west lay river Ravi. There was no bridge over it. All the boats had been withdrawn to opposite bank which was closely guarded by numerous local chiefs and government officials. The pursuit was so tight that Banda could not enter his fort at Gurdaspur. He turned west. Finding that all the ways of escape had been barred he rushed into the *haveli* of Dunichand which had a large open compound with a wall around it at village Gurdas Nangal, 6 kms to the west of Gurdarpur. In it Banda accommodated 1,250 men with a small number of horses. The other Sikhs who could not be lodged therein tried to flee in all directions. They fell an easy prey to the fury of the Mughal army. According to Khafi Khan further observes: "Those who escaped the sword, were sent in collars and chains to the Emperor. Abdus Samad sent nearly two thousand heads stuffed with hay and a thousand persons bound with iron chains in charge of his son, Zakariya Khan, and others to the Emperor."

Banda dug a ditch around the enclosure and filled it with water from the canal flowing nearby. The imperialists also dug trenches all around the enclosure. It took place in the begining of April 1715. This news reached Farrukh Siyar on April 17, 1715.

The siege lasted a little over eight months. The full summer from April to June, the entire rainy season from July to September, and half of winter from October to the beginning of December passed in this condition with frequent sorties and occasional skirmishes.

Banda's enclosure was closely invested on all sides. On the east lay the Delhi troops under Qamar-ud-din Khan. On the north was Zakariya Khan, faujdar of Jammu and Zaid-ud-din Ahmad Khan, Governor of Sarhind. To the south was Abdus Samad Khan of Lahore. The western side of the river

Ravi was guarded by petty chiefs and jagirdars such as faujdars of Gujrat, Eminabad, Patti, Kalanaur and Rajas of Kangar and Jasrota.

Banda was popular in Sarhind province for having abolished the Zamindari. In the Bari Doab the people did not support him. The Sikhs offered the most stubborn resistance. Muhammad Qasim who fought against the Sikhs in this campaign wrote: "The brave and daring deeds of the infernal Sikhs were wonderful. Twice or thrice everyday some forty of fifty of the black-faced Sikhs came out of their enclosure to gather grass for their cattle, and when the combined forces of the Imperialists went to oppose them, they made an end of the Mughals with arrows, muskets and small swords, and disappeared. Such was the terror of the Sikhs and the fear of the sorceries of the Sikh Chief that the commanders of this army prayed that God might so ordain things that Banda should seek his safety in flight from the Garhi."

Eventually all supplies of foodstuff and fodder came to a dead stop. All animals died, and their flesh was eaten. Then their bones and bark of trees were powdered and eaten. Many Sikhs died of hunger and the rest were completely famished and reduced to skeletons.

Seeing that resistance had completely ceased, the Mughal army on December 7, 1715, ventured into the enclosure. About three hundred men almost on the verge of death were beheaded. Their bodies were cut up in search of gold coins which they were believed to have swallowed. Banda with his 740 followers was captured. The following articles were recovered from the enclosure:

Swords	1,000
Shields	278
Small Kirpans	217
Matchlocks	180
Bows and arrow cases	173
Daggers	114
Rupees	600
Gold mohars	23
Gold ornaments	a few

With this beggarly equipment in men, money and material and living in a small house with an open compound, Banda had defied the mighty Mughal Empire for over eight months. No better record than this challenge can be traced anywhere else in world history.

Banda's scoffing procession in Delhi

In chains and fetters Banda was put in an iron cage which was hooked up on the back of a tall elephant. The others with ludicrous paper caps on their heads were fastened on camels, horses and asses, and later on chained on feet, waist and neck were tied in twos and threes and were placed in bullock carts. Bandsmen, buglers and drummers playing loudly went ahead, followed by 300 Sikh heads stuck up on spears. Qamar-ud-din's cavalry was in front of all, while Zakariya Khan's horsemen were in the rear. Last of all followed the nobles, faujdars and rajas at the head of their troops. While passing through towns and cities people thronged in the bazars and streets and on house tops and in balconies in crowds. In the countryside spectators stood on both sides of the road.

The prisoners were first led to Lahore and then to Delhi. At Lahore the mother of Bayazid Khan, the deceased Governor of Sarhind, threw a heavy stone from the balcony of the house on the Sikh procession and killed a Sikh. The number of Sikh heads went on increasing by the execution of innocent Sikhs captured on the way. At Lahore the number of Sikh heads was 700, and in Delhi 2,000. In Muslim towns such as Sarhind, Karnal and Panipat the people treated the prisoners with utmost insolence, "usual with bigots and common among barbarous or half-civilized conquerors." They heaped every indignity upon them. They used filthy abuses, mocked, whistled, ridiculed, laughed to scorn, scoffed, jeered, taunted, grinned, sneered at , hissed, hooted, pointed the finger at, turned up their noses at, snapped their fingers at, and spat at. The Sikhs drowned this mockery by singing in chorus hymns from the holy Granth.

They reached the Shalimar Garden near Delhi on February 25, 1716. Muhammad Amin Khan, father of Qamar-ud-din Khan, came to receive them and the following morning led them to the Red Fort.

On February 29, 1716, the Hindu festival day of Holi, they were taken out in a procession. Banda played ahead of all. Then followed 2,000 Sikh heads stuffed with straw fixed on spears and bamboos, their long hair flowing with the wind. After them came the dead body of a cat mounted on a long pole to show that not even a cat or dog was left alive in Sikh homes. Behind it was Banda in an iron cage on a lofty elephant. A red turban with borders embroidered in gold was placed on his head. On his body was a crimson robe of brocade wrought in flowers of gold. It was a mockery of a bridegroom. A stalwart Mughal soldier in a coat of arms with a shining sword in hand stood behind him. The 740 prisoners were behind Banda's elephant. To vilify them their faces were made black in order to have uniformity with their hair. Black sheep-skin high-coned caps with glass beads sewn on them were placed on their heads. Some were dressed in sheep-skins, the woolly side being outward. Their left hands were tied to their necks with two pieces of wood. They were bound back to back in pairs and two pairs were mounted on the bare back of a camel. In the rear of the cavalcade were Amin Khan (later on Prime Minister), his son Qamar-ud-din Khan (also Prime Minister, and his son-in-law Zakariya Khan later Viceroy of Panjab). They rode at the head of a strong contingent of Mughal troops. The road from Shalimar Garden to the Red Fort 10 kms long was lined on both sides with troops and lakhs of exultant spectators.

The eye-witness Mirza Muhammad Harsi writes: On this day I had gone to see the pageant *(tamasha)* as far as the Mandavi-e-Namak. From there I accompanied the procession to Qila-e-Mubarik. There was hardly anyone in the city who had not come out to see the spectacle of the accursed. There was such a crowd in the bazars and streets as had rarely been seen. The Muslims could not contain themselves with joy. But those unfortunate fellows who had been reduced to this misery were thorougly contented with their fate. Their faces bore not the slightest sign of dejection and humility. In fact most of them on camels were busy in singing . If any one of the spectators remarked: 'Now you will be killed,' they replied: "Kill us. When were we afraid of death? Had we been afraid of it, how could we have fought so many battles with you? It was through sheer starvation and want of food that we fell into your hands, otherwise the truth of our bravery is known to you."

Sayyid Muhammad was another beholder. He wrote: "At that time I asked one of them by signs why they had committed such rudeness *(gustakhi)* and mischief *(shokhi)*. He placed his hand on his forehead indicating that it was predestined. This expression pleased me."

The procession passed along the 10 kms long road, abused, scoffed and laughed at throughout. They were brought back to the Red Fort after demonstration. Kahan Singh son of Binod Singh was the leader of Tatva Khalsa who had gone over to the Mughals and fought against Banda at Lahore. He declined to join the imperial army in the siege of Gurdas Nangal. He was arrested and sent in the retinue of Banda to Delhi. When the regular slaughter of the Sikhs began in front of the Kotwali, Mata Sundari planned to save Kahan Singh's life. The Mughal officers and guards on Sikh prisoners were heavily bribed, and Kahan Singh was substituted by another Sikhs. Baj Singh who was a descendant of Guru Amar Das, also escaped.

714 Sikhs are beheaded at Kotwali

Banda and his twenty-six officials were separated from the rest by Sarbrah Khan Kotwal. The remaining Sikhs were divided into seven groups, each of 100 Sikhs to be beheaded on all the seven days of the week. The execution began on March 5,1716. The Sikhs were led in batches to *Kotwali* and made to stand in rows of ten in front of the police office where now stands the fountain *(Fuwara)*. Before execution an offer was made to spare their lives if they could become Musalman. None volunteered to do so. They uttered *Wah Guru, Wah Guru*, and tried to outbid one another in offering themselves for sacrifice saying, "me, *mukta* (deliverer)! kill me first," was the prayer which constantly rang in the ears of the executioner.

All observers, Indian and Europeans, unite in remarking on the wonderful patience and resolution with which these men met their fate. Their attachment and devotion to their leader was astonishing to behold. They had no fear of death, and they called the executioner *Mukta* or the Deliverer.

Among Banda's followers there was a lad on whose face soft hair was just appearing. Being the only son of a widow, he was the centre of all her hopes and ambitions. According to the old custom he had been recently married as he wore the wedding thread on his wrist. He was so deeply touched at the sight of the Sikhs passing through his village on their way to Delhi, that he left his home and joined Banda's parth. His mother and wife entreated him to return home, but he did not yield. Both the women accompanied him weeping and crying. They reached Delhi and sought help from Ratanchand, Diwan of Prime Minister Sayyid Abdullah. They submitted that his life should be spared. On the recommendation of Ratanchand Sayyid Abdullah issued orders for his release. The mother and wife reached the Kotwali and learnt that he was marked for execution on that very day. He was found standing in a row outside the Kotwali.

The further scene was witnessed by Khafi Khan and Khushhal Chand. Khafi Khan says that when a police official was setting him free, the boy declined to go. He shouted: "My mother is a liar. I am heart and soul a devoted disciple of my leader *(Murshid).* Finish me quickly with my companions." Khushhal Chand writes that the lad declined to recognise his mother and wife saying: "I do not know whose mother she is and from where she has brought this girl. I do not understand what she talks. My companions have gone. I have no time to lose. The delay is painful to me."

The heart-breaking lamentations of the mother and the bride, persuasion of officials, and entreaties of bystanders bore no fruit. He rushed back to his place, put his head before the executioner, and lay dead in the twinkling of an eye.

The heads and bodies lay in separate heaps the whole day. In the evening they were taken out of the city in carts and hung upon trees along the roads.

Some Englishmen as representatives of the British East India Company were then present in the capital. On March 10, 1716, they submitted a brief report on the "Arrest and Massacre of the Sikhs at Delhi" to the Governor of Fort William, Culcutta, in which they said about Banda: "He at present has his life prolonged with most of his mutsuddys in hope to get an account of his treasure in the several parts of his kingdom and of those that assisted him, when afterwards he will be executed, for the rest there are 100 each day beheaded. It is not a little remarkable with what patience they undergo their fate, and to the last it has not been found that one apostatised from new formed Religion."

Banda executed near Qutab Minar

Banda's wife, a princess of Chamba, his 4 year-old son Ajai and child's nurse had been arrested at Chamba and brought to Delhi. They were admitted into the harem of Darbar Khan Nazir. Banda and his 26 officials were tortured for three months and a half to disclose places of their hidden treasure. When all attempts had failed, it was decided to execute Banda on June 9, 1716, and his official the following day.

The same old golden turban and cloak were put on Banda. Fettered and chained all over he was placed in an iron cage which was fastened on the back of an elephant. His companions were put on the bare back of camels. They were preceded by Sarbrah Khan Kotwal at the head of his police force. In the rear was Ibrahim-ud-din, Head of Artillery. The procession passed through the main streets of Delhi. They were taken to the tomb of Khwaja Qutab-ud-din Bakhtiyar Kaki near Qutab Minar in Mehrauli 16 kms distant from Red Fort. They were led around the tomb of the late Emperor Bahadur Shah who had failed in suppressing Banda's rebellion so as to give satisfaction to his soul. The leading nobles had already gathered there.

Banda was taken out of the cage and seated on the ground. As usual he was offered life on his embracing Islam. The proposal was rejected. Through heavily chained his right hand was freed. His son, Àjai, was placed in his lap, and a dagger put in his right hand to kill the child. Banda did not stir. Thereupon the dagger was thrust into the body of the child, and his heart and entrails were thrust into Banda's mouth. He shut his mouth and he remained absolutely unmoved. Muhammad Amin Khan, later on Prime Minister, was standing nearby. He came closer and intensely looked into the eyes of Banda. He was deeply impressed with his nobel features. He remarked: "It is surprising that one, who shows so much acuteness in his features, and so much of nobility in his conduct, should have been guilty of such horrors."

In complete composure and tranquillity Banda replied, "I will tell you. Whenever men become so corrupt and wicked as to relinquish the sence of equity and to abandon themselves to all kinds of excesses, then the providence never fails to raise up a scourage like me to chastise a race so depraved; but when the measure of punishment is full then He raises up men like you to bring him to punishment."

After this Banda's right eye was dug out with a sharp pointed dagger. Then the left eye was removed in a similar manner. With a pause his left foot was chopped off. A little while afterwards both of his arms were lopped off. Then with red-hot pincers his flesh was cut off bit by bit. Later his legs, ears and nose were removed from his body. His brain was blown out with a hammer. Last of all his remaining body was hacked to pieces.

This horrid savagery lasted the whole day. Banda displayed heavenly clam, no tears, no cries, no groaninig, no expression of grief, no jerk in the body, and no sign of pain. Throughout he remained composed and collected, serene and steady, unruffled and unstirred. A curious creature was he, this Banda Bahadur. He had a power of concentrating his mind on something away from his body and his surroundings with such intensity as if he were in a trance.

This abominable scene was staged before the very eyes of Banda's officials who included among themselves Fatah Singh, Ali Singh and Gulab Singh Bakhshi who had remained in the Lohgarh fort after Banda's escape. They were beheaded on June 10, 1716, at the same place.

Banda did not die in vain. This tragic event changed the course of not only Sikh history but also of the history of Panjab. Banda had shown to the Sikhs the difference between those who were in power and those who were out of it. The lesson of power once practically taught could not be forgotten by a militant community. They continuously worked to regain what they had lost and in half a century became undisputed masters to the Land of Five Rivers.

Banda's place in history

Banda was a Rajput. The blood of a Kshatriya flowed in his veins. Thus he inherited the spirit of bravery, heroism, love of independence and self-sacrifice from his race. This spirit was further strengthened by his long residence in Maharashtra where he had seen with his own eyes how Shambhuji, son of Shivaji, his step-brother Rajaram and his widow, Tara Bai, had carried on a life and death struggle against Aurangzed who was personally leading a campaign of annihilation against the Marathas. His dormant spirit of nationalism was awakened and put into its practical application by Guru Gobind Singh. His national enthusiasm was further aroused by the Guru's sufferings and sacrifices and ultimately by his death as a result of the Mughal trickery.

Curiously, Banda had a great resemblance in looks with Guru Gobind Singh. He possessed the same medium heigth and bulk of the body and colour of the face. Under his bushy beard and moustaches and long hair on head, the facial features also looked alike. Further bothspoke the same language which was a mixture of Hindi and Panjabi. Both were fond of covering themselves with arms cap-a-pie. Both were in possession of a commanding voice and manner which resulted in implicit obedience from their followers. Both could arouse the zeal for supreme sacrifice of their devotees.

Banda aimed at national awakening and liberation of the country from the oppressive government of the Mughals. Guru Hargobind and Guru Gobind Singh had transformed the Sikhs from a peaceful people into a class of warriors. They fought against the government in self-defence. They never took any offensive. They did not acquire territory, did not take prisoners, and did not seize enemy's property and wealth. The two Gurus never tried to establish their own rule in their own territory. They belived it belonged to the Government. The government rules were obeyed, and government coins were used.

Banda, on the other hand, always took offensive. He fought battles, took prisoners and killed them, seized the enemy's property and lands, and set up his own government. He issued his own coins, had his own official seal and gave orders which had the force of firmans of the Mughal Emperors. He did not want to weaken the Mughal power, but to destroy its root and branch, and to establish in its place national rule or self-government.

Banda was the first man who laid down the foundation of political sovereignty of the Sikhs. He made Sikhism popular with the people of Panjab, not by force or perrsuasion, but by his bravery and generosity. In about a year, more than one lakh of persons embraced Sikhism and became the Khalsa of Guru Gobind Singh. Those who had not heard the names of the Gurus, were attracted towards Sikhism by Banda's victories. Banda had shown what self-government meant. After his fall the lesson was not lost on the Sikhs. He had brought about a revolution in the minds of the people. A will was created in the masses. Heads could be cut off, but the ideas remained, leading ultimately to success.

Banda was a great reformer. He broke down the barriers of caste, creed and religion. He appointed sweepers and cobblers as big officers before whom high caste Hindus, Brahmins and Kshatriyas stood with folded hands awaiting their orders. He believed in socialism. He distributed all his riches among his folowers. He abolished the zamindari system and established peasant-proprietorship making the actual tillers of the soil its masters. He was opposed to the use of intoxicant drugs. He prohibited drinking of bhang and wine and smoking of tobacco or *charas*.

He knew the real cause of the weakness of Hindus. The spirit of mercy, compassion, sympathy, tenderness, forbearance and their melting mood inculcated in them by religion *(Daya Dharam ka mul hai)*, had been responsible for the slavery of the Hindus by people from the north-west. He showed that the only way to meet the eternal foe was to adopt the policy of paying them in their own coin, a tooth for a tooth and an eye for an eye, and to pay off old scores. The Sikhs learnt this lesson from Banda and admirably succeeded in establishing their own rule in their homeland.

Banda possessed the high ideal of life, sincerity, honesty, indomitable spirit, unbounded enthusiasm, rare daring, single-minded devotion to his cause, dare-devilry of the highest type and nobility of character. It was for this reason that none of this 740 followers renounced his faith to save his life. Even a young lad who had been pardoned by the Prime Minister refused to leave Banda in the face of death.

Banda seems to have destroyed about half a lakh of Muslims. This brutality cannot be approved in any age by any people. But some justification can be offered from the condition of the times. Banda was a contemporary of

Aurangzeb. He had killed all the Satnamis even to a man, woman or child, numbering about 50,000. The same number if not more of the Jats of Bharatpur-Agra-Delhi region were destroyed. Rajputs and Marathas must share between themselves a loss of about 50,000 men each. The total number was in no case less than two lakhs. Forcible conversion and on refusal death was in addition. There was almost wholesale destruction of Hindu temples and other religions institutions in northen India.

Banda had travelled from north to south and back again, and he had seen all this destruction, rape and rapine with his own eyes. The Rajput spirit was throbbing in him. It was lying dormant under an ashes-smeared skin. This spirit was aroused by Guru Gobind Singh, and retaliation was a natural consequence. Latif says that Guru Gobind Singh had selected Banda for "avenging the death of his father and two sons, for which purpose he could not have signed out a batter instrument than this ruthless bloodsucker."

After his conquest of Sarhind Banda considerably mellowed down in his fury against the Muslim population. He placed no restrictions of their *Azan* and *Nimaz.* At Kalanaur in April 1711 he recruited 5,000 Muslims in his army.

To sum up, Banda was a demon in the eyes of Muslims, a great national hero for Hindus, and for the Sikhs their first empire builder. In Indian history he occupies the place of a genius spiritual, political and military, consecrated or perverted as one might think. In world history he should rank not less than Alexander the Great, Halaku, Chingiz Khan, Nadir Shah, Ahmad Shah Abdali or Napoleon Bonaparte.

Nasik, situated on the bank of the river Godavari, is known for its sanctity from the days when Sri Ram Chander came during his long exile and stayed in Panchvati Ashram near the river bank. Madho Das remained in Nasik for a long time, during which he came in contact with the *tantric* yogi, Aughar Nath, who trained him in yogic practices and in performing miracles. He was advised to shift to a lonely place where he could practice *tantric* yoga with success. It was according to these instructions that Madho Das had come to Nanded whose situation on the bank of the river Godavari had appealed to his mind. There, during the course of several years stay, he had perfected his *tantric* art and acquired mastery over satanic spirits. But, in the absence of any genuine guide, he was wasting his *tantric* energy and was only adding to the number of followers.

It was in September, 1708 A.D. that Guru Gobind Singh had reached Nanded. He camped at a short distance from the city. Soon, the local Sikhs and those living in adjoining areas started coming and joining in congregations, both in the morinings and in the evenings. The Guru had, in all, two to two and a half hundred armed Sikhs with him. But during the day, when he rode out for hunting, only ten to fifteen armed Sikhs used to accompany him as his bodyguard. One day, while riding alone the river, he approached a neat, shady place, where the river water was flowing smoothly and peacefully below and near which Madho Das had set up his hermitage. The other *bairagi* sadhus used to sleep on the ground, but inside they kept a picture of their mentor, Madho Das, on a cot, with clean sheets laid thereon. They also kept some articles of worship, e.g. flowers, incense, sandlewood etc. near the picture. The Guru approached the place, alighted from his horse and went straight into the lodge. Keeping aside the articles of worship, he sat on the bed, as if knew the owner of the place as a friend, separated for a long time, whose privacy he could disturb without hesitation. Madho Das had gone out. In his absence, the Guru asked his Sikhs to prepare goat meat which all ate with relish.

The disciples of Madho Das were helpless before the Guru who they thought had defiled the *bairagi's* hermitage. They only frowned at the Sikhs and gnawed their teeth in despair. They searched out Madho Das and told him as to what had happened. Before returning to his abode Madho Das exercised all his invisible *tantric* powers by sending controlled spirits to topple the Guru from his bed but they failed to achieve their object. Finding some slight shakiness in the feet of the bed, the Guru fixed arrows on them to keep them in position. When Madho Das realised that some great soul had come to his *ashram*, he came running and, facing the Guru, said, "You believe in violence, why have you killed my goat?" The Guru replied smilingly, "I came here thinking that it was the abode of a mahatma. It was the duty of your disciples to welcome the guests and entertain them but they did not do so. So we have done the job ourselves." Madho Das was surprised at the reply and asked "Who are you who has shown disrespect towards the *ashram of my guru?*" Guru Gobind Singh enquired as to who his guru was and in what condition he was at that time.

The Guru's query surprised Madho Das all the more. He said, "My guru has passed away but the *ashram* is known after his name. I do not know where my guru is and in what condition he is at present. If you know anything about him, then let me know."

The Guru pointed out towards a ripe *bill* (marmelos) fruit on a tree in the compound of the hermitage and told Madho Das, "Your guru is residing inside that fruit as an ansect. If you like to see it you may do so. That insect is alive and is sucking the juice of the fruit. If you call it you will get a response."

When Madho Das got the fruit plucked and broken, he saw a thick and long insect which made a squeamish sound and fell down, dead. The Guru told Madho Das that his guru had been saved the cycle of births and deaths, just as Guru Nanak had redeemed Duni Chand's father from the life of a loin. Madho Das now realised that he had met his match who had by his superior spiritual powers subdued all his *tantric* propensities which had made him leader of so many followers. Normally, sadhus are very obstinate persons. They cannot tolerate insult of their gurus. But here was Madho Das, who, after seenig and testing the Guru's greatness, came to the conclusion that only selfless surrender before him could save the situation.

On the other side, the Guru had also come to redeem Madho Das from the life of the *tantric* and raise him spiritally. During their brief conversation, Madho Das realised who the Guru was and agreed to become his Sikh. The Guru had, no doubt, with him more than two hundred tried and undaunted Sikhs who were heroes of many a battle. He could have got his wishes carried out through any one of them. He had also come across many sadhus in his life, but, except Mahant Kirpal Das, all other had slipped away in times of difficulty. In Madho Das the Guru had seen a seeker of truth from his past lives but unluckily he too had got stuck up in tantric practices and missed the real goal of life. Having gained control over some spirits he was wasting his accumulated yogic energy in display of miracles. The Guru wanted to enlighten him spiritually and direct his misguided energy in the performance of such deeds which might benefit the society and the country and also immortalise his name in national history.

Having told the Guru that he (Madho Das) was his banda (slave), the Guru spoke to him as follows.

"At present Hinduisam stands eclipsed by the despotic Mughal rule. The sadhus, the saints and the cows are not safe. Centres of pilgrimage are being desecrated, holy scriptures have been burnt and lakhs of Hindus have been converted to Islam. In order to stop such atrocities, my father (Guru Teg Bahadur) had sacrificed his life. The city of Anadpur was despoiled by the Mughals. My four sons and mother (Mata Gujri Ji) and thousands of my Sikhs have also laid down their lives. Having suffered all these losses and resigned myself fully before the Divine Will, I have come to this side of the country. Future depend upon God's wishes."

He continued :

"You have called yourself *banda.* If this is a promise and has been made by you sinerely then, as a Rajput, you have to perform the duties of a Kshtri, just as Sri Ram Chander selected Hanuman and made him his dear devotee. I. too want to make you my Sikh and entrust you with the requisite powers to fight out the battle for justice. You know that, in Gita, Sri Krishna had told Arjun that fighting for a just cause would prove benificial to him inasmuch as that if he died on the battle field he would go to heaven but if he became victorious he would rule in the world. These words had emboldened Arjun and enlightened his mind which enabled him to perform his duty as a Kshatri in the battle. So do I want you to act as a true Rajput and pursue the fight against injustice where I have left it in the Panjab."

When the Guru spoke these words there was a wonderous glory on his face. He cast a benign look at Madho Das and deputing him as the Jathedar (leader) of the Sikhs, he blessed him saying, "I have entrusted the glory of the Panth in your hands; you have been made the leader of the Khalsa. You have called yourself banda. This will raise your name high in the world. The rulers will not be able to withstand your onslaughts. In the stormy battles lakhs of persons will die fighting. Only those will be saved who run away from the battle field."

Madho Das felt inspired on hearing these words. He was already keeping long hair on his head and was a known hunter. The Guru administered to him the baptism of the double-edged sword with his own hands and renamed him Banda Singh. Full of love, the Guru was also ready to transfer his sword-belt, along with the sword, to Banda Singh. But Bhai Daya Singh, Bhai Dharam Singh and other leading Sikhs objected to it and said, with folded hands, "Guru Ji, with this sword you baptised us among the five Beloved Ones. We have also served you devotedly with our bodies, minds and souls and remained with you through thick and thin. This *bairagi*, Madho Das, is a fresh convert. Your sword represents not only temporal power but spiritual power also. Therefore, the five Beloved Ones have a prior claim to that sword. It you want to give anything to Banda Singh, then give him arrows and keep the sword for the Khalsa."

The Guru told them, "Don't be impatient. All Khalsa brothers are my sons. This Banda Singh will perform great deeds. He will pick up the enemies of the Khalsa and destroy them. After him it will be the Khalsa who will rule and live happily". Saying this, the Guru gave five arrows to Banda Singh and told him, "In carrying out the duty assigned to you, you will face many difficulties. But do not feel discouraged. Whenever there is an emergency, think of God and shoot out one arrow." A batch of 25 valiant and devoted Sikhs was deputed to accompany him. Prominent among them were Babas Binod Singh, Kahan Singh, Baj Singh, Bijai Singh and Ram Singh who could also satisfy the Sikhs in the Punjab about the leadership of Banda Singh and also help him in his task. After making preparations for some days and receiving the Guru's blessings, the batch under the leadership of Banda Singh left for the Panjab. His achievements there form a golden page in the history of the country.

AN IMPORTANT QUESTION

It was more than a year when the Guru and Bahadur Shah had left Agra for the Deccan. If the emperor was not fulfilling his promise even within the extended period, why did not the Guru disassociate himself from the emperor and go to the Punjab himself instead of sending Banda Bahadur from Nanded? This is the important question that has been raised by Ghulam Hussain in "Sair-ul-Mutarkhin" and in some other books by Muslim and British writers. In their opinion the Guru had become disappointed and did not like to go back to the Panjab again.

Actually, by now Bahadur Shah was firmly in the saddle. He had established his control over the nobles, the army and the provincial rulers. If the Guru had displeased the emperor by disassociating himself from him at that time, the latter might have revived the orders once issued by Aurangzeb but withdrawn later on after receiving the Guru's Zafar Nama. The Nawabs in the Panjab, who had stopped their enemity with the Sikhs on account of the friendship developed by the emperor with the Guru, would have also changed their attitude. Even the emperor himself would have sensed the danger of revolt in the Punjab if the Guru had left the company of Bahadur Shah abruptly and returned to the north. It was on account of all these considerations that the Guru had decided to send Banda Singh first for arousing the Sikhs and preparing the ground for fighting with the Mughals. The Guru would have followed later on and after obtaining reinforcements from the Rajputs and other Hindu rulers on the way, as promised by them, would have, by their combined effort, destroyed the Mughal rule from the Punjab and made Banda Bahadur as the new ruler, just as Sri Ram Chander, after defeating Ravana, had made Babhikhan the ruler of Sri Lanka. That the Guru had planned his stategy along these lines is supported by the evidence provided by the Guru's Hukam Nama sent from Agra to the Sikhs of Dhaul in which he had indicated that he would be coming to the Punjab after a few days and meet the Khalsa brothers in Kahlur (near Anandpur). Evidently, the Guru's displeasing the emperor and returning to the Punjab from the way was fraught with danger. He had only about 300 armed Sikh soldiers with him at that time. If the emperor had decided to order his army commanders to check those Sikhs and the Guru on their way back to the Punjab, the result would have been disasterous.

While departing from Nanded, the Guru had given some instructions to Banda Singh. "So long as you remain a celibate, your power and glory will be on the ascendancy. Do not, therefore, swerve from the path of celibacy. If you accept this advice, no ruler will dare challenge you. Your glory will increases and you will achieve your objectives. But if you marry, the power of these arrows, which I have given to you, will diminish. Go across the Jamuna and bring the tyrants to their knees by spreading havoc in their midst."

STRESS ON CELIBACY

Accepting the advice given by Guru Gobind Singh, Banda Singh, along with the Sikhs who accompained him from Nanded and those who joined from Rajasthan, travelled fast towards the Punjab and after making short stops on the way, reached Khar Khodhe in Sonepat tehsil, thus avoiding the direct route to Delhi.

The Guru had stressed on Banda Bahadur the need to remain celibate because this was necessary for the achievement of the task entrusted to him. Involvement in family life would have stood as obstruction in his way and made him less effective. The Guru, it may be clearfied, was not against adoption of married. He had himself led married life until the time of creating Khalsa Brotherhood, when he took the vow of celibacy so as to be always prepared for taking up arms against the Mughals. The five Beloved Ones he had selected were also married. But after some time they too remained celibates in the company of the Guru. Banda Singh, as a *bairagi* sadhu, was already a *brahamchari*, without any family attractions or fear of death. It was, therefore, necessary for him to stick to that path in order to keep himself ever ready for warfare.

History records that Maharana Partap was a valiant patriot but he could not tolerate the pangs of hunger from which his small children suffered. Had he remained a celebate that situation would not have arisen.

Hitler, the German dictator of the second world war, whose character had shaped him for the life of a military general, did not think of marrying. That was the reason why he succeeded to a great extent in vanquishing his enemies. But when, due to ambition, he went out to distant places to fight, his success turned into failure and before deciding to commit suicide, he wrote in his will as follows:

"During the days when I had to fight in battles it was my belief that I would not be able to bear the burden of married life. That is why I did not go in for marrige. But now, towards the fag end of my life, I have decided to marry the lady who had been my friend for the past several years. Her only desire is that she should die with me as my wife. My decision will thus help her in fulfilling her desire." This will was written by Hitler, in greater detail, on April 29, 1945 A.D.

The examples of Maharana Partap and Hitler have been cited as they were world-known personalities. The Guru knew fully well that the Rajputs, who had offered their daughters and sisters in marrige to the Mughal rulers, would also try to entice Banda Singh with such offers. This was also another reason for the Guru to emphasise the necessity of Banda Singh remaining a bachelor. Had he kept his vow he would not have suffered so much towards the end, as he actually did.

Even then, Banda Singh deserves high praise for the determination and courage with which he agreed to take up cudgels with the imperial army. He did not lose heart when he heard about the Guru's demise in Nanded. On the contrary, he redoubled his efforts to achieve the Guru's mission. He abandoned the role of a recluse and became a full-fledged Singh after receiving the baptism of the double-edged sword. He avenged the death of two small sons and mother of the Guru by killing the Governor of Sarhind who had prepetrated that crime and by reducing that town to shambles. The Sikhs will ever remain grateful to Banda Singh for his heroic deeds and will be only doing their duty by observing his martyrdom day with due solemnity and adoration.

ANOTHER MISUNDERST ANDING CLEARED

Many non-Sikh historians have described Banda Singh as Banda *Bairagi* or Banda Bahadur, nor have they mentioned anything about his having been baptised by the Guru. The another of "Suraj Parkash" has also not been very specific about it. But the fact remains that Banda Singh was made the leader of the Khalsa by the Guru. That status could not have been given to a non-believer in Sikh tents and discipline, nor could have the Guru decided to bestow his arrows to a person who had not accepted his baptism. As already pointed out, even the bestowal of the sword to Banda Singh was objected to by Bhai Daya Singh and other prominent Sikhs. They would have certainly not agreed to be. led by Banda Singh if he had not been baptised.

EK Onkar Fateh Darshan — The true Lord has ordained that the Guru will protect the Khalsa of Jaunpur. Always remember the Guru, your life will be redeemed. You are the Khalsa of the Timeless Lord. Come immediately on receipt of this order, fully equipped with five arms. Follow the 'rehat' (discipline) of the Khalsa. Do not use bhang, tobacco, opium or liquor, also avoid eating meat, fish and onion. Shun thieving and adultery. We have brought heavenly peace to the world, you should love each other. It is my commandment that whoever observes the 'rehat' (discipline) of the Khalsa will be saved the Guru—Miti Poh 12 Samvat Pahla.

Obviously, carelessness on the part of our historians and research scholars has been responsible for allowing the anti-Sikh elements to depict Banda Singh as a non-Amrit-Dhari *bairagi* in their prejudiced writings. In this connection, it would also be desirable to clerity that in using the term 'Fateh Darshan' on top of the Hukam Nama, Banda Singh had the apparent intention of bringing the concepts of 'Fateh' and 'Darshan' together. Having been a vaishnav *bairagi* he was also against the use of meat, liquor and other intoxicants. This matter is, however, of no significance.

BANDA BAHADUR'S SPIRITUAL STRENGTH

We have already mentioned that Banda Bahadur was not an ordinary man. He had, with all his *tantric* powers, tested the Guru's greatness. The Guru also treated him as if he was an old acquaintance of his past lives and with his blessing transformed him from a *tantric bairagi* to a spiritually enlightened soul. The Guru passed away in Nanded in 1708 A.D. It was in 1710 A.D. i.e. after nearly one and half years that Banda Singh had destoyed Sarhind. Meanwhile, he had succeeded in subduing small towns and with the help of the Sikhs whom the Guru had sent with him, won the hearts of numerous fighting men of the Punjab. The blessings bestowed on him by the Guru had redoubled his strength, both physical and spiritual and made him the accepted leader of Khalsa. Rattan Singh Bhangu has protrayed him thus in "Panth Prakash:"

Thus Banda felt satisfied and his mind became restful. He granted the boon of son or milk (prosperity) to whosover came to seek it. If any one in difficulty came to him, he would pray for him and remove his difficulty. He advised everyone to remember and repeat the name of *Waheguru* and granted whatever he wanted. He became so well-known that both the rich and the poor desired to meet him. If any evil-minded person came from a distant place, he too felt so overwhelmed on seeing him that he touched his feet.

Such was the result of the blessings bestowed on Banda Singh by Guru Gobind Singh. Unlike Guru Har Rai who did not go to Aurangzeb himself but sent his elder son, Ram Rai, to attend the emperor's court (where he unwittingly showed seventy two types of miracles to please the emperor), Guru Gonind Singh taught his Sikhs to fight with the enemies and lay down their lives, if necessary, while fighting. But in the case of Banda Singh, he had, in addition to preparing him for fighting with the Mughals, equipped him with enhanced spiritual powers to help the poor and the needy, wherever necessary. Banda Singh, first of all, camped in Khar Khoda, near Sonepat in the Punjab. From there he conquerred Sonepat, Kaithal, Samana, Ghurham, Shahabad, Mustaffabad, Kapuri, Sadhaura etc. and then forced the Governor of Sarhind to surrender—all within a period of one and a half year after starting from Nanded. History records that, with the Guru's blessings and with co-operation of other leaders of the Khalsa Panth, he also conquered Loh Garh, Raj Ghat, Saharanpur, Behat, Nanauta, Jallalabad, Karnal, Kunjpura, Nahan, Behrampur, Raiput, Kalanaur, Batala, Kasur and several other towns and became the supreme ruler of all conquerred areas. Had he continued to co-operate with and remain under the guidance of the Khalsa Panth, as ordained by the Guru, he might have become the sovereign ruler of the entire country. This is, however, the subject of a separate chapter of history.

In the opinion of some people, it might appear that in sending Banda Singh to the Punjab, the Guru had transferred his responsibility to a stranger in order to secure peace of mind for himself. But this was not so. On the other hand, the Guru sought to make use of the interim period to plan his future strategy, vis-a-vis Bahadur Shah and the Mughal rule as a whole. While at Agra, the emperor had asked for a further time limit of one year to fulfil his promise and the Guru had agreed to it. That period of one year had also elapsed. During their stay in Nanded the Guru must have again reminded the emperor but the latter was dodging and giving evasive replies on one pretext or the other. Perhaps, the emperor was thinking that after giving precious gifts and ornamental decoration like *dhuk-dhuki* to the Guru, he had won over the latter and there could be no further danger from him.

But the Guru knew the emperor's mind. He had already written to the Sikhs of Dhaul (near Anandpur) about his impending visit to the Punjab. The purchase of some land in Nanded, as proved to be his own from signs of past life, was apparently a clever move to show to the emperor that he (the Guru) had decided to settle in the Deccan, away from the Punjab. Thus, by diverting the emperor's attention, the Guru had taken the next step in his strategy by sending Banda Singh and some Sikhs in advance to arouse the people of the Punjab and prepare the ground for continuing the fight with the Mughals. The third step that the Guru had planned to take was that when, after being free from the Deccan, the emperor would march on long expedition against the Marathas, the Guru would also move out of Nanded and join Banda Singh without any fear of interception on the way. All these indications must have been given by the Guru to Banda Singh before sending him to the Punjab as commander of the Khalsa forces. No ruler would ever despatch his commander on any fighting expedition without ensuring full support to him.

To fight against the mighty Mughal empire was no easy task. Already seven members of the Guru's family had laid down their lives as martyrs in non-violent and violent fights against the Mughals. But the despotic empire had yet to be rooted out. The Guru could not have, therefore, left that important task to be performed by Banda Singh alone. In fact, he had chalked out an elaborate plan to arouse the Rajputs as well and with their help, join Banda Singh to launch a final attack on the centre of the Mughal authority. Even in selecting Banda Singh for this mission the Guru had to exercise great precaution. Only a really capable and daring person with strong faith in God and with spiritual attainments could have led the Khalsa forces. Just as out of all the five Pandavas, Sri Krishna's choice fell on Arjun, who had almost given up courage to fight and to arouse whose sense of duty, Sri Krishna had to recite eighteen chapters of the Gita, so could Guru Gobind Singh, throughout his journey to the Deccan, locate only Banda Singh who possessed the requisite qualities.. He too had to be weaned away from his *tantric* practices and made to realise his duty by arousing the physical and spiritual powers, which he had gained but which he was frittering away in meaningless pursuits. It was after making such a careful selection that the Guru had send Banda Singh to the Punjab to work according to the plan chalked out by him.

But destiny willed otherwise. Hardly had fifteen to twenty days passed after the departure of Banda Singh that the Guru was attacked with a dagger by an unsuspected Pathan. At that time, Banda Singh was still on his way to the Punjab. According to Lala Nanak Chand Naaz, it was in March 1709 A.D. that Banda Singh reached near mathura and Bharatpur. During the intervening period he must have been travelling through Rajasthan and meeting the rulers there who had promised military aid to the Guru. He had also to approach the Brar Sikhs and seek their armed help after satisfying them about his leadership and the mission entrusted to him by the Guru. It is recorded in "Muntkhib-ul-Lubab" that, in Kaithal, Banda Bahadur had 4000 mounted and several thousands foot soldiers with him from which it appears that he was able to rise only that much strenght from among the Rajputs and the Brars. The Sikhs from Majha could not have yet joined him. That is why, instead of invading Delhi direct, he had first proceeded towards Sonepat in the Punjab. Had the Rajputs provided large reinforcements, to Banda Singh, as they had promised to the Guru, Delhi could have been surrounded and made to surrender, particularly when Bahadur Shah was still stuck up in the Deccan and his brother, Kam Bakhsh, and the Marathas were both inimically inclined towards him.

Banda Singh, it will be recalled, had given a promise to the Guru that he will not marry and will work under the guidance of the Khalsa leaders. So long as he complied with these conditions, he gained victory after victory. He had already started dreaming of becoming an emperor. On the coins that he issued to commemorate his victories, appeared the following words:

"The blessings of deg (economic prosperity to help the poor, teg (sword power to destroy the wicked), *fateh* (victory over the enemies) and instant succour have been bestowed by Guru Nanak—Guru Gobind Singh."

But the hill chieftains, who were not favourably inclined towards the Guru, prompted Banda Singh to break his vow and marry. That engrossed him inworldly affairs and reduced his physical and spiritual strength. He also formed his own separate Panth and called it Bandai Khalsa. Thus, there was an open estrangement with the Tat Khalsa of Guru Gonind Singh, from whom he could not, therefore, expect any more cooperation. He tried, with his followers, to engage the Mughal armies in several battles, but was ultimately arrested and executed mercilessly in Delhi on June 19, 1716 A.D. It must, however, be said to the credit of Banda Singh that right upto the last moment he did not give up his Sikh faith and died with *Waheguru* on his lips.

It must also be recorded here that some years back, Hindu Sabha leaders, like Bhai Parmanand, had started describing Banda Singh as Banda Bairagi. This was an attempt to depict him as a Hindu recluse and not as a full-fledged baptised Sikh. The question arises that if Banda had the powers, why did he not do what he actually did, as a *bairagi.* In fact, knowing full well as to what was happen in the country as a result of the Mughal invasions, he had escaped from the Punjab and come towards the Deccan in the garb of a *tantric* yogi. It was only after his meeting with Guru Gobind Singh and receiving the baptism of the double-edged sword at his hands that he became enlightened and was able to achieve whatever successes stand to his credit in life. He is now a well-known figure in history and we should all be careful that the real facts about any historical personality are not allowed to be distorted.

BRAR SIKHS DEMAND PAY

The Brar Sikhs who had accompanied the Guru to Nanded had seen that the Guru had purchased some land in that town, with the obvious intention of residing there. They had also seen how some Sikhs had already been sent to the Punjab with Banda Singh. They too desired to go back to their homes and not made to stay in the Deccan, so for away from their families. They, along with some other Sikhs, therefore, pressed the Guru to play them the arrears of their pay and allow them to go home like other Sikhs who had already left. The Guru told them to have patience for some more days but they were adamant.

At that time the Guru was sitting at the place in the town, now known as Gurdwara Sangat Sahib. He gave some indications to Bhai Daya Singh of a place where Guru Nanak's treasure lay buried and asked him to dig it out from there and bring it. This was the place where Gurdwara Mal Tekri is now situated at some distance outside the town. The Sikhs found that a Muslim fakir, named Lakkar Shah, was staying at that place and was sweeping it daily. In his presence they dug out the treasure and brought bag-loads of the same to the place where the Guru was sitting. The Guru distributed the money to the Brars and other Sikhs in shield-loads and whatever was left was ordered to be taken back and reburied at the original place. The fakir, who had also come to see the Guru, was greatly astonished but was told not to try to dig out the reburied treasure as he would not be able to find anything there. Instead, he was asked to continue his service of sweeping the place for which he would get some remuneration every day. According to local tradition, Lakkar Shah used to find one gold coin every day in the sweepings.

The purpose for which Banda Singh and five Sikhs had been sent to the Punjab was kept as a close secret among the Guru and a few leading Sikhs, like Bhai Daya Singh and Bhai Dharam Singh. Even the *bairagi* followers of Banda Singh did not know it. This secrecy was necessary as Bahadur Shah was also camping in Nanded during those days and it was not desirable for the secret to leak out. The mere sending of a *bairagi* recluse and a few Sikhs to the north was of no significance for the emperor.

Bahadur Shah knew in his heart that the Guru was not pleased with him on account of the former's inability to fulfil his promise till then. They were also not meeting each other frequently. Once, after enquiring from Bhai Daya Singh about the Guru's daily routine, the emperor met the Guru when the latter had gone to the river bank for a morning walk. He offered a very costly diamond, which he had acquired after killing Tana Shah of the Deccan, to the Guru as a present and expressed his regrets for not being able to make good his pledge on account of fear of Muslim law which might estrange other provines also from him. He admitted that he had not told the truth when he asked for one year's further time limit. The Guru exchanged the usual salutation and, appreciating the quality of the diamond, took it in his hand and threw it in the river. The emperor was astonished at the Guru's indifference and thought it to be an indication of his displeasure. After some cursory talk, the emperor left without saying anything further about the diamond. The place where this event took place is now known as Gurdwara Hira Ghat.

SHIKAR GHAT

About two and a half miles away from Hira Ghat, the Guru. While out for hunting, pursued a running hare and killed it. When the Sikhs enquired about the reason for taking so much trouble to kill such a small animal, the Guru laughed and explained that the hare had, in one of its past lives, lived in human form as Moola *Kirar.* He had affronted Guru Nanak and had, therefore, been passing through a cycle of births and deaths. It was time for his soul to be redeemed which he had done by ending his life as a hare. This place is now known as Shikar Ghat where a beautiful gurdwara and a tank have been built at a cost of several lakhs of rupees. It is situated at a little higher level from the river and the connecting road and commands a magnificient view of the town and surrounding areas.

OFFER OF A NAGINA

Like all great souls, Guru Gobind Singh had a love for places with running waters, green hilltops, gardens and other beautiful scenes of nature. He had enjoyed his stay in Paonta on the bank of the Jamuna and in Babhor on the bank of the Sutlej. Such a place was available in Nanded near the hermitage of Banda *bairagi* on the bank of the river Godavari. TheGuru was once sitting there and musing over the munificence of God, who had created such bewitching scenes of nature, when a rich devotee brought a *nagina* (precious stone) as a present for the Guru. The latter held the glittering stone in his hand, appreciated its beauty, and threw it in the river. The devotee was astonished and he felt in his heart that the Guru had simply wasted away an article of such a high value. The Guru noticed his bewilderment and told him that if the stone was so valuable he should dive in the river and recover it from there. When the man actually dived, he came across numerous precious stones of the type he had offered to the Guru. He realised his folly and begged to be excused. The place where that precious stone was thrown in the river is now knows as Nagina Ghat.

A pertinent point that can be raised here is that the Guru had seldom refused to accept offerings from his devotees, irrespective of their value. What prompted him to throw away that particular offer made to him? The obvious explanation could be that, having thrown away the emperor's diamond in the river a few days earlier, the Guru did not like to create an impression that he had discriminated against the emperor and there by insulted him. The news about the devotee's previous stone having been thrown in the river was bound to reach the emperor who was camping in the same town. It was through foresight that the Guru accorded the similar treatment to both the offers.

PAYMENT OF A LOAN

Once when the Guru was sitting in the congregation, a few known Pathans came and showed to the Guru a sort of promissory note, which the latter had given to them in Anandpur in lieu of price of the horses purchased from them. The Guru recognised his signatures on the note and told them:

"Your claim is genuine but here in Nanded our financial position is tight. We are having even the daily provisions from the royal store. If you wait for some more time and show this note of mine to any of the Sikh sardars in the Punjab, he will pay to you the actual amount, along with interest thereon". The Pathans replied, "But, Sir, it is not permissible for us to accept interest". The Guru was pleased with the reply and they went away after receiving the Guru's blessings. Later on, during Banda Singh's times or the Misal period, those Pathans were able to recover many times more money by showing the Guru's note to several Sikh sardars.

BATCH OF UDASIS ARRIVES

Some Udasi folowers of Bhai Gurditta (uncle of Guru Gobing Singh) had been sent to places like Hyderabad and Jagan Nath Puri for missionary work. Two of the prominent followers, Gopal Das and Balū Hasna, came to meet their co-religionist, name Govind Sahib, in the Deccan. When they all heard that Guru Gobind Singh was staying in Nanded, they went in a batch to meet him there. There were also other religious centres, like Mata Anjali's temple, near Shikar Ghat, which used to be visited by roaming pilgrims.

The Guru was also pleased to meet them after such a long time and they all stayed in the Guru's camp. When the emperor came to know that a large number of visitors had arrived in the Guru's camp. He ordered the quantity of provisions being supplied from the royal store to be doubled. According to Aurangzeb's orders the entire expenditure on the Guru's entourage to the Deccan was being met from out of the confiscarted property of the Guru. Although Bahadur Shah had become friendly with the Guru, he was not allowing the latter's property to be returned to him fully, lest he might restart preparations to oppose the imperial government.

MATA SAHIB DEVI SENT BACK TO DELHI

The Guru had come to know that Bahadur Shah had decided to go towards Hyderabad. He was also, therefore, looking for a suitable opportunity to return to the Punjab. In anticipation of this move, he decided to send back Mata Sahib Devi to Delhi, under the care of the elderly Bhai Ram Kuar, who was an esteemed descendent of Baba Buddha. Through both Mata Sahib Devi and Bhai Ram Kuar were reluctant to get separated from the Guru, they were prevailed upon to act according to the Guru's wishes in view of the peculiar situation developing around him. Mata Sahib Devi was advised by the Guru to keep company with the Mata Sundri Ji in Delhi and also to spend her time in meditating on God's Name.

It was Bhai Ram Kuar, who, on return to Delhi, recorded all that had happened in the Deccan, through the pen of Bhai Sahib Singh, the script-writer. The "Nanak Prakash" and the "Suraj Prakash", compiled later on by Bhai Santokh Singh, are based on the evidences recorded by Bhai Ram Kaur.

BAHADUR SHAH'S MARCH TOWARDS HYDERABAD

After two to three months of stay in Nanded, Bahadur Shah decided to march towards Hyderabad himself. His commanders had, by then, subdued most of the leading rebel rulers of the Deccan but the Maratha sardars in the south had still not surrendered themselves and accepted the suzerainty of the Mughal emperor. Before leaving he came to see the Guru and requested him to accompany him on that expedition also. With him came his courtiers, ministers, scholars and judicial officers, all wearing costly jewellery, with the object of making an impression on the Guru about their wealth and prosperity.

They were received with the customary salutations and seated in appropriate places. The Guru enquired from the emperor about the developments in the Deccan and the object of his march towards Hyderabad. He knew what was in the mind of the emperor and replied to him on the following lines:

"You may march towards Hyderabad according to your own plan, but I have no desire to go further south from here. I had undertaken to support your cause against your brother, Tara Azam, in order to remove the injustice being done to you. But it is not proper for me to join you in proceeding against the Marathas. You may not, therefore, depend on me for this purpose."

The emperor understood the tone of the Guru's reply but still smilingly said:

"I have to go quickly but will still hope that you would be good enough to follow me at your convenience, may be for sight-seeing and for going out on walks, as before."

HINDUISM, ISLAM AND KHALSA PANTH

At the time of parting, when talk in lighter vein was gonig on, the emperor started a religious discussion by addressing the Guru as follows:

"What type of religion do the Hindus have? It is a hollow faith under which they make idols out of stones, draw portraits on the walls and then worship them. Then they palce food and sweets before them and think they have fed their gods and goddessed. But everything remains lying there, which they later on eat themselves. What can those gods do which are made by the devotees themselves?

"Then they throw water towards the sun. How can that water reach their dead ancestors? They also feed the *brahmins* lavishly with varieties of food and fruits and also burn incense, sesame seeds and ghi in fire. All this is called *havan* which we consider to be a false ritual. But Hindus take it to be true mode of worship. What are your views about it?"

The Guru replied : "It is correct that all these practices are prevalent in Hindu faith. Just as the farmers till their land and feed their cattle in the hope that they will reap the crops and collect the milk, so do the Hindus love and worship the idols and portraits of their gods and goddesses and concentrate their attention on them in order to have their desires fulfilled.

"God has created both theists and atheists in the world. The formar are mostly Hindus and the latter are mostly Muslims. Hindus are theists because they believe in God, and in the concept of the next world; they perform deeds according to their rites and customs and in return, expect to go to heaven. They also believe in transmigration of soul. The Muslims too believe in God and in the existence of heavens and hell. But they are atheists in the sense that they do not have faith in the doctrines of Karma and Transmigration of Soul. Still they do not deny that on the day of judgement they will have to get their accounts settled. In this background, everyone likes his own religion. To you, your religion is good and for us, our religion is good.

"Then the rituals performed by Hindus are like giving water to the roots of a tree. The fruits are gained from the top. They believe that their dead ancestors receive the fruits of their deeds. This may be correct provided the deeds are performed with good intentions and honest earings."

He continued : "Those who have faith in Islam worship tombs and graves of their ancestors who lie buried thereunder and whose mortal frames become one with the dust from which they are made. Just as Muslims expect some rewards from the spirits of their elders, so do the Hindus seek benifits from the spirits of their ancestors and therefore, try to keep them happy."

Guru Gobind Singh further told the emperor :

"Again, the Muslims call themselves God's slaves and say their prayers before Him. He is called Allah, the pure and deceitless. But He is not seen anywhere, for He has no shape or a particular abode. Still they pray with their faces towards the *kaaba*, keep fasts and recite darood (prayer) while offering thick wheat cakes through the priests or Sultan Pir. Is this not all meaningless? If it is not, then rest assured that whatever is done with good intentions, is acceptable, whether it is done by a Muslim or a Hindu."

Continuing, the Guru said :

"Just as the Muslims consider their prophets to be ever alive before whom they bow and pray five times a day, so do the Hindus perform worship before the idols thrice daily. The difference is only of name and language used in invocations. Only those among them are noble who recite the name of Allah or Ram with sincerity and purity of mind. The rest is all show and hypocrisy. Guru Nanak has, therefore, said :

"Remember God's name with purity of heart. All order practices are mere false shows."

"No one is acceptable in the court of the Lord, without good intentions. Only he can approach Him who does not differentiate between *Khuda* and *Ishwar*. All others waste their lives in performing meaningless rituals." Guru Nanak has tought that "unnecessary discussions create only dissensions in the world. Without faith in God, we only fritter away our energies."

"Because I found both the Muslims and the Hindus treading the path of duality, I have started a third faith, called the Khalsa Panth, which will worship only one Timeless God and give up beliefs and rituals which lead to communal strifes. The Khalsa is still like a new-born child. When it grows up, it will gain strength. It will not worship idols, graves and tombs but will adore only one eternal and formless God. This Khalsa is God's own army and has been created with His pleasure and desire."

The Guru further spoke to the emperor as follows :

"Just as for worldly men, it is necessary to have money for expenditure, so do their souls, after death, need some succour. Some souls remain satisfied with the benefits accrued from *bhakti* performed by them during their own lifetime, but for others, the Hindus give charities in the belief that these would reach the souls of their dead ancestors. Similarly, the Turks also pray for their dead relatives and recite special prayers on making offerings at tombs etc. Both have the same significance."

It is evident that the emperor came to the Guru along with his ministerial, religious and judicial officers, and intentionally started religious discussion in their presence in order to impress on them his deep faith in Islamic concepts by making a mockery of Hindu faith and practices. Otherwise, at the time of his departure for Hyderabad, he would have come to meet the Guru alone or in the company of only a few attendants. By adopting such a course, the emperor wanted to create a feeling of dislike for the Hindus in the mind of the Guru and make the latter agree to accompany him on the expedition against Hindus

Marathas. He also tried to show that by converting Hindus to Islam, he was performing a good deed for the infidels. But the Guru's replies put him on the guard and he had nothing to say in defence of what he had said. The whole conversation between the emperor and the Guru must have displeased the *mullahs* who had come with the emperor. Those were the persons who used to decree that the non-believes should be either converted to Islam or put to death. In any case they could not tolerate any leading Hindu or Sikh to remain outside the pale of Islam. It was on account of their fear that Bahadur Shah was unable so far to make good the promise he had given to the Guru that he would do justice.

It was evident that the emperor and the Guru had different religious views. The former looked at religious matters from political angle, whereas the latter had higher matters from political angle, whereas the latter had higher spiritual approach. The two had, therefore, to adopt different paths. This is also the conclusion drawn by Shri Ranbir in his book on Guru Gobind Singh. No wonder, therefore, if on their return to the royal camp, the mullahs might have instigated the emperor against the Guru and obtained his approval of the conspiracy which they had been hatching eversince they found the emperor developing friendly relations with the Guru.

ROYAL CONSPIRACY TO ASSASSINATE THE GURU

It will be recalled that the Zafar Nama written by Guru Gonind Singh from Dina had brought about a feeling of repentence in the mind of the then emperor Aurangzeb. As a result, he had issued instructions to the governors of the provinces to withdraw all orders issued against the Guru. Those instructions must have also been received by the Governor of Sirhind, although he did not know the real reason. But as compliance of royal orders was obligatory, the Governor of Sirhind had stopped taking any open action against the Guru or oppressing the Hindu and Sikh population of the Punjab to any great extent.

After some time the Guru had left the Deccan on the invitation of Aurangzeb but, before he could reach there, Aurangzeb had died. Then the Guru had to help Bahadur Shah against his brother, Tata Azam, in the war of succession. This was done by the Guru on the recommendation of Bhai Nand Lal and on the understanding that Bhadur Shah would fulfil his promise of doing justice in the matter of atrocities committed by the Governor of Sirhind against the members of the Guru's family. It was in response to Bahadur Shah's invitation that the Guru went to Agra and stayed there for some months as the emperor's guest. The emperor had also instructed the Governor of Sirhind to pay rupees three hundred every day to Guru Gobind Singh by way of compensation, but the Guru was at that time in Agra. Even otherwise he would not have accepted such a compensation.

from Agra, the Guru had accompanied the emperor towards the Deccan. The Governor of Sarhind must have, through secret intelligence, kept himself in touch with these developments, because he knew that the growing friendship between the emperor and the Guru would not be in his interest. Agra is only about five days horse journey from Sirhind and special messengers could easily move between these places to bring the day to day news.

Dreading similar reprisals as were meted out to Chandu Lal at the hands of Guru Hargobind, with the connivance of emperor Jehangir, Wazid Khan, the governor of Sarhind, had planned to finish the Guru while he was still in the Deccan. He, therefore, planned to hire a Pathan, who was the son of Painde Khan, whom Guru Hargobind had killed in battle, to do the job. That Pathan originally belonged to Jalandhar but had settled in Sarhind. He was at first not agreeable to go to such a distant place, but his sons, Gul Khan and Attaullah Khan, aged 20-25 years, were made to agree. It is possible that these youngsters might have already been in the employment of Wazir Khan. According to Bhai Kahan Singh, thay were prompted to take revenge from the Guru for the murder of their grandfather, Painde Khan, by Guru Hargobind. They first came to Delhi and with great humility enquired about the whereabouts of the Guru from Mata Sundri Ji. Then they went to Nanded and managed to stay close to the Guru's camp there. They also started working as water-carriers in the royal camp. During their spare time they would come and do wood-cutting or sweeping jobs in the Guru's camp in order to show their fidelity to the Sikhs. They saw an atmosphere of friendship between the Mughals in the emperor's camp and the Sikh followers of the Guru. They could also see that the emperor respected the Guru very much. So they were afraid of divulging their intentions to any one and had to keep it as a secret to themselves. But as they were coming in the Guru's camp frequently they remained on the lookout for a suitable opportunity to carry out their nefarious design.

According to "Suraj Prakash", when Gul Khan first saw Guru Gobind Singh in Nanded, he bowed before him and, on inquiry, said that he was the grandson of Painde Khan whom the Guru's grandfather had killed in battle but whose face he had, out of sympathy, shaded at the time of death with his shield. He told the Guru that his mother had told her that his grandfather, Painde Khan, was to blame. He had been brought up, married and nourished as a wrestler by Guru Hargobind but he proved so ungrateful that he fought with his benefactor and was consequently killed. The Guru liked this truthful version of Gul Khan and gave him five gold coins as a reward. With this, Gul Khan felt encouraged and started doing service in close quarters to the Guru.

Some writers, including Bhai Santokh Singh, have mistakenly stated that he Guru rewarded Gul Khan to prompt him, due to disappointment with life, to take his grandfather's revenge from him (the Guru). This could not have been correct in view of the plans the Guru had made to go to the Punjab in orderr to reinforce the struggle launched by Banda Singh there.

It is also belied by the tone of Zafar Nama (the Epistle of Victory) which the Guru had written to Aurangzeb. Obviously, such writers have not been able to understand the conspiracy engineered, with the connivance and approval of Bahadur Shah, to assassinate the Guru. Only a writer of independent views, like Lala Daulat Ram Arya, could understand the reality and he has stressed it accordingly in his book.

Beacuse the Panthan brothers were now moving about freely in Nanded, without raising any suspicion in the minds of the people, it is most likely that they were present at the time of the emperor's meeting with the Guru, before the former left for Hyderabad. They must have also come to know from the *mullahs* about the demoralising effect of the religious discussion which the emperor had with the Guru on the former's mind. They also must have noticed that the reported friendship between the two was shallow. They, therefore, thought it to be appropriate time to divulge the real objective for which they had been sent to Nanded by the Governor of Sarhind. The *mullahs* thought the presence of the Pathan brothers there to be a blessing in disguise. They would be able, by their intended action, to end the life of one who had expressed views opposed to Muslim law and at the same time save the emperor from the ignominy of being ungrateful to the Guru personally. The whole episode was intended to be depicted as a case of revenge taken by two brave grandsons of a killed Pathan.

Just as a general's orders have to be carried out by the rank and file in the army, so do the gurns and saints find it obligatory to submit to the unalterable divine will of their sole commander i.e. God, otherwise they no longer remain His messengers.

Sri Krishna used his supernatural powers to save Draupadi from becoming naked in the court of Duryodhan, but he did not obstruct the hunter from hitting him with a mortal arrow while he was lying under a tree in the jungle..

Guru Tegh Bahadur, while sitting in meditation in an underground cell in Baba Bakala, had to employ his spiritual powers to save the sinking ship of Makhan Shah Lubaana, but when it came to sacrificing his own life for the sake of protecting Hindu *dharma*, he did nothing to save himself.

Similarly, Guru Gobind Singh, while sitting in Anandpur, saved Bhai Joga Singh, on his way from Peshawar, from falling in sin by standing guard at a prostitute's house. But he did not, with all his plans and powers, shirk from the inevitable end when it came suddenly. It was the pathan's dagger which had to strike at him and it was his sword which had to cut the pathan killer into two. This is how things were ordained under the Divine dispensation.

THE GURU STABBED WITH DAGGER

So long as Mata Sahib Devi stayed in Nanded, she looked after the security arrangements in the Guru's camp. There would always be armed attendants on guard duty outside the tent, where the Guru rested during the day. There is why the mean pathans, who were deputed to assassinate the Guru, could not get an opportunity to carry out their dastardly act till then. But they now knew about her departure for Delhi and also about the unreal sympathy shown by the emperor towards the Guru.

The Guru used to keep his sword and other arms near his bed while resting. Among those arms were two sharp steel daggers which had specially been made and offered to the Guru by a devotee. Gul Khan, who had become a frequent visitor to the Guru's camp, knew where those daggers were kept. It was a cold November night when the Guru lay asleep on his bed on his left side, with his left arm as the headrest. It so happened that the attended, named Lakha Singh on guard duty, dozed off while sitting outside the tent.. On the other side of the tent, Sant Atma Dass, *udasi,* who had come from Burhanpur, was sitting deep in meditation. This situation gave a good chance to Gul Khan to strike. He advised his brother to stand at some distance for help, if needed, and himself sneaked into the tent with naked feet. He picked up one of those two sharp daggers and thrust it on the back of the Guru. This awakened the Guru abruptly and picking up his sword instantaneously, he chopped off the head of the assassin there and then before he could escape. On hearing the noise and on seeing blood oozing out of the Guru's body, Lakha Singh, enraged at Gul Khan's dastardly act, further cut his body into two. The Guru said to Lakha Singh, "I have already disposed him off to hell, there was no need for you to wield your sword".

The other pathan brother tried to run away but he too was done to death by other Sikhs who had by then reached there. Not knowing who the conspirators were behind this dastardly act, they sent their fast horseriders to inform Bahadur Shah, who had, by then, hardly covered on stage of his journey, of what had happened. The emperor was aware of the conspiracy and was awaiting the news. In order to show his sympathy towards the Guru, and in order to ward off any suspicious against him, he sent his British surgeon (Dr. Cole) to attend to the Guru. That surgeon rushed to Nanded, cleaned the Guru's wound and stitched it with great care and sympathy. When the wound healed up and the stitches were removed, the Guru rewarded the surgeon with cash and robe of honour. The Sikhs were rejoined to see the Guru having regained his health.

It is surprising that Shri Ranbir, editor of the 'Milap' has, in his first book written that the Guru was not attacked by any one but was involved in some accident. But in his second book he himself and some other writers, whom he has quoted, have expressed the correct views. There are clear evidences in "Bahadur Shah Nama", "Guru Sobha Granth" by Kavi Sainapat and in "Gohaj

Katha" written by Sant Atam Das *udasi*, in which there is mention of the Guru having been attacked by a pathan with dagger. Lala Daulat Ram Arya has also, in his book, stated that Bahadur Shah, in his heart of heart, was not happy with the presence of Guru Gobind Singh who was pricking in his side like a thorn. He also knew very well the religious and political views of the Guru. He was dodging him continuously for two years and was looking for a suitable occasion to do away with him". Many other writers have also expressed the same view.

ASHT RATNAS

2

Asht Ratnas

BHAI BUDDHA

Baba Buddha whose original name was Bura was born on October 22, 1506 A.D. His father's name was Sugha Randhawa and mother's Gauran. They lived in Kathu Nangal, a village of Amritsar district. After some time they settled down in Dhalla village not far away from river Ravi opposite Kartarpur.

In 1524, when Guru Nanak was returning to Kartarpur on the western bank of the river Ravi, he saw a boy grazing cattle in the fields nearby. The boy rushed to him, made obeisance and offered if he could do him any service. The Guru was much impressed by the demeanour and civility of the boy, who also grew fond of the Guru.

Bura, having found out the name of the village where Guru Nanak lived, decided to pay him a visit. Next morning he took a pot, full of butter-milk with a lump of butter floating in it, and went to the Guru. He presented his gift in all reverence and humility and listened to the Guru's sermons with devotion of a true seeker. Then he beseeched Guru to tell him the way to attain the state of bliss. Nanak tried to put him off thinking that such a problem did not concern a boy of his age. Bura's questions were so deep and relevant, that Guru remarked that Bura was young in age but old in wisdom and was not Bura but Burha or Buddha, an awakened being. Since then Bura came to be called as Bhai Buddha. He became a sincere devotee of the Guru, spent a good deal of his time with him, and lived like a lotus. Bhai Buddha entered into discipleship of the Guru at the age of ten.

Guru Nanak considered him to be one of his chosen apostles and appointed him Master of ceremonies over the coronation of his successor. Bhai Buddha had the unique privilege of crowning the first six Gurus in succession. All the Gurus respected him as their teacher, guardian Angel and godfather. They never commanded him to do anything and they never refused any of his requests. His word was considered law. His utterances were deemed prophetic.

Bhai Buddha always looked after the welfare of the Sikhs and spared no pains to spread the Sikh faith among the people. Whenever a crisis overtook the Sikh community or Sikh church, he was never found lacking in some solution to it.

On Guru Nanak's death in 1539, Guru Angad left Kartarpur and established his seat at Khadur near river Beas. Sri Chand, the elder son of Guru Nanak was not happy at his supperssion in favour of Angad. Guru Angad, to avoid open clash with the son of the Guru Nanak, hid himself in the house of an old woman named Bhiragi at village Sanghar. Bhai Buddha came all the way from Kartarpur to Khadur and prevailed upon the Guru to give up seclusion and resume his duties. At the time of Amar Das's nomination to Guruship similar crisis gripped the Sikhs. Guru Amar Das, because of his deep regard for Guru Angad Dev, did not want to annoy his son, Datu who burned with jealousy at the succession of Guru Amar Das to Gur-Gaddi. He. therefore, hid himself in a hut in the jungle near Basarke village, with instructions that he should not be disturbed. Bhai Buddha persuaded the Guru to attend the Sikhs who were regularly calling at Goindwal and exercised his influence to assuage Shri Datu.

At the assumption of the pontificate by Guru Arjan Dev, Prithi Chand who himself wanted to be the pontiff entered into collusive arrangement with the Masands and projected that he was the real Guru. Bhai Buddha was one of the few disciples who with resoluteness denounced Prithi Chand and foiled him in his cunning attempts to seat himself on Guru-gaddi. It was primarily due to his lead that Prithi Chand did not succeed in bringing about scheism among the Sikhs, although he had tried hard. Guru Arjan Dev held Bhai Buddha in high esteem, so much so that he regarded it a boon to have his blessing. As Guru Arjan Dev had no issue for many years, Prithi aproclaimed that the Guru was not destined to have any offspring, and the Guruship would eventually come to him. The Guru's wife Ganga was cut to the quick at such remarks. She begged the Guru to bless her with a son. He told her to get the blessing of Bhai Buddha. The Baba was then living in the jungle of Basarke village. Mata Ganga waited upon Buddha in a grand procession with rich presents of food, sweets and fruits. Buddha did not like this show and remained cold. She complained to the Guru. He advised her to go there again like a peasent woman with bread, butter-milk and onions only. The lady was blessed. The sixth Guru, Hargobind was her only child.

Bhai Buddha was great mystic and a great teacher. Though records do not speak much as to how he received education; but it is reasonable to surmise that he received his education at Kartarpur at the feet of Guru Nanak. He was well-versed in the sacred hymns of Guru Nanak and other Gurus, and with remarkable case could quote them. When Guru Angad decided to popularise Punjabi alphabet and Punjabi language, he assigned to himself the task of teaching it. He was the veritable tutor of Hargobind. It is not wrong to assume that Guru Hargobind's psyche was much influenced by Bhai Buddha.

It is only reasonable to think that Bhai Buddha must have told his pupil how the Mughals forcibly destroyed the crops of his father and no one could withhold the band of a tyrant. Guru Tegh Bahadur was also taught by Bhai Buddha. "Guru Hargobind personally took him (Tegh Bahadur) to Bhai Buddha, the wisest among teachers and said : 'you were kind enough to be my teacher, O Enlightened one, accept Tegh Bahadur as your pupil'. Tegh Bahadur bowed before the sage who blessed him and accepted him as his student." According to Dr. Fauja Singh, Tegh Bahadur imbibed the mysticism from Bhai Buddha. Bhai Buddha taught him Panjabi and passed on to him the deep spiritual experience which he had gained. Besides this, he along with Bhai Gurdas made arrangement for his education in subjects such as Languages, History, Arithmetic. At a little maturer age, he was taught Metaphysics, Logic, Theology, Six Systems and classics like the Bhagvad Gita, Mahabharata, Ramayana. Elementary Islamic philosophy, Koranic Lore, and Sufi texts were also taught to Hargobind.

Bhai Buddha being an activist, took part in almost all important projects initiated by the Guru. When Guru Ram Das started digging the tank of Amritsar, Bhai Buddha took upon himself the responsibility of supervising the digging operations. It was under his fostering care that the tank was completed. Again during Guru Arjan Dev's time, he was the person who saw to the conduct of the digging operation of Santokhsar. Kaulsar was also excavated under his supervision. The emergence of the city of Amritsar also owed much to his sagacious advice and the devotion with which he prevailed upon the people in the neighbouring area to settle there.

When Guru Arjan decided to compile Adi Granth, Buddha was sent to Mohan to procure the hymns of the previous Gurus. Although Mohan refused to give the sacred treasure and parted with only when Guru Arjan personally went to him, yet the incident is manifestative of the Guru's unshakable trust in him. On the completion of Adi Granth, he was made the first priest of the Hari Mandir. Having placed the bound copy of the Holy Granth on a cot, Baba Buddha carried it on his head bare-foot to Hari Mandir followed by Guru Arjan also bare-foot with a peacock feathers for waving over the sacred scripture. Bhai Gurdas was the third to follow at the head of Sangat. The first recitation was done by Bhai Gurdas. As the head-priest of Hari Mandir, Bhai Buddha, exerted to the maximum to the effect that Adi Granth might be held in proper reverence and he laid down programme to be followed meticulously in Hari Mandir. He was always awake to the exigencies of the circumstances and lost no time to take steps. When Guru Hargobind was imprisoned in the fort and there was apprehension that the Sikhs might not sag in spirit, he lost no time to act. He contacted the people of influence to put pressure on Jahangir to release the Guru. It is said that Buddha ji himself went to Gwalior to bring the news about the Guru.

The greatest contribution of Bhai Buddha was to render much-needed help to the Guru in making explicit the policy of Miri and Piri, which meant that the political as well as spiritual sovereignty vested in the Guru. The concept was first framed by Guru Arjan Dev, although its rudiments could be found in the sacred utterances of the previous Gurus as well. Guru Arjan Dev trained Guru Hargobind in the philosophy of this dual responsibility. The authenticity of this fact is vouchsafed by Bhai Mani Singh in his book "Bhagat Ratnavli." He says;

> "Bhai Sigaru and Bhai Jaita were great warriors and philanthrophists. They were asked to live in the service to Guru Hargobind. Guru Arjan said to them the House of the Guru will take up arms under Hargobind. The dark age prevails. After learning the use of weapons, the Sikhs will wrest political power from the rulers and through the love of Divine Word (Shabad) they will acquire the spiritual wisdom of Divine Teachers. Abide with Hargobind'."

Bhai Buddha true to the advice of Guru Arjan Dev put on two swords on both sides of Guru Hargobind, one as the symbol of Miri (temporal sovereignty) and the other as the symbol of Piri (spiritual sovereignty). This explicit pronouncement caused a furore among the Sikhs. Some of them who were incapable of grasping the import of the Sikh Movement in all its aspects began to entertain doubts regarding the validity, even desirability of the policy. Bhai Buddha not only did his best to remove misgivings of such people but also made them understand the changed perspective which was responsible for the enunciation of such a policy.

The great sage passed away in the winter of the year 1631 A.D. at the age of 125 years in village Ramdaspur about twenty-seven miles from Amritsar. Guru Hargobind who had come to Ramdaspur a few days earlier was deeply moved at the death. Tears rolled down the cheeks of the Guru as the flames went up.

MARDANA

Mardana was the closest associate and the dearest disciple of Guru Nanak. According to Bhai Manohar Dass Meharban, Mardana had been the companion of Guru Nanak since childhood. Both Mardana and Guru Nanak were born at Talwandi Rai Bhoi Ki, Mardana in 1459 and Guru Nanak in 1469. Mardana's original name was Dana. 'Mardana' was the title conferred on him by Guru Nanak. The names of Dana's revered father and mother were Bhai Badrev and Lakho. According to Bhai Kahan Singh, Mardana breathed his last in 1534 at Kurum and Guru Nanak himself performed the last rites. But this date does not stand the test of historical scrutiny. Guru Nanak could not be at Kurum in 1534. Even if Mardana had himself gone to Kurum and expired there, how could, then, Guru Nanak be there at his funeral. In fact he died at Kartarpur and was cremated on the banks of the Ravi in Guru Nanak's presence. Mardana had two sons, Shahzada and Raizada and a daughter.

Mardana's father was the family bard of Mehta Kalu. Badrev and Mardana called every morning at the houses of local residents and obtained alms generally in kind in the form of flour or some eatables. Both would sing to the accompaniment of music or rebec and receiving charity would move next door. Nanak as a child listened to their sweet music and felt elated. According to Professor Satbir Singh, "Nanak and Mardana first came into contact in A.D. 1480. It all happened at Talwandi while, once lying under a tree the sound of someone's playing on the rebec passed his (Guru Nanak's) ears. He arose, approached the man playing on the rebec and asked his name. He answered, Sir, Mirassi (bard) people call me by the name Dana'. Hearing this, Baba appreciated his fine playing on the rebec and his excellent understanding of Ragas. Baba suggested, in case he accompanied him and sang 'ragas' along with Shabad, he would get the better of both the worlds. To this Dana replied, 'We hardly make our both ends meet, by singing Ragas before the rich. In case we follow you, our families would perish for want of food and being starved, we shall miss our prayer (Namaz) even, and thus, we shall stand condemned in both the worlds. How do you plan to liberate me?' Then Guru Nanak said 'O Dana: You are ignorant. God protects and feeds us all. Namaz (Prayer) and Roza (fast) are benedictions bestowed by God. God's abode is the heart of the saints. At the final judgement, none shall come to the rescue.' Guru Nanak further emphasized, "Dana, in case you now turn to be 'Mardana' (brave) and sing Raga along with the word of God (Shabad) you will gain in both the worlds." Dana now turned to Mardana set out with Guru Nanak to enlighten the people living in this world. Mardana played on rebec and Guru Nanak sang Shabads. Quite often Mardana also sang the divine words along with the Guru. Thus the Kirtan came into existence. Kirtan is the divine words (Shabads) sung in accompaniment of the music. Bhai Mardana once asked, 'Baba, is this the word of God that we sing in Kirtan? Is this the word that contains salvation or is it some other?' To this Guru replied, `Kirtan is the word that Guru utters. Contemplation of the word leads to salvation.'

In course of time, Nanak left Talwandi and went to Sultanpur Lodi where he was employed in the service of Daulat Khan Lodi, the Governor of Jullundur Doab. Nanak after some time, sent for him from Talwandi. He came in response to Guru Nanak's call and began to reside at Sultanpur with Guru Nanak.

It became usual with both of them to sing songs in praise of God in a public place. Their melodious voice and soft strains on rebec touched the hearts of listeners and transported them into a state of bliss. This drama was daily enacted in the streets of Sultanpur for seven long years.

After the divine experience at Sultanpur, the Guru became a missionary and he decided to awaken the people to the reality by undertaking long and arduous journeys in all directions. To begin with he proceeded to the eastern part of the country. Thence-from he visited places in the south. After this he went to Ceylon.

All the time, during this travels, Mardana was with Guru Nanak. He suffered the hardships of journey, and pangs of separation from his family and kith but he remained unflinching in his faith in Guru Nanak.

Janam Sakhis are replete with anecdotes portraying wit and wisdom of Mardana. Barring a few questions which are either concocted or connected purposely with the fair name of Mardana in order to ridicule him possibly to emphasise that the Guru had the unique power of transforming brass into gold, all other questions touch the deepest chords of human heart as also the root problems of the worldly persons which hamper them from taking cudgels to better their own lot and of the people at large. Hunger, thirst, family comfort, poverty, insecurity were some of the things which often tormented Mardana as much as every human being but the beauty of Mardana was was that he did not allow himself to be given to them, and with sustained efforts reached the stage of identification between himself and the Guru. Visualising the approaching end of Mardana, Guru Nanak once asked, "Consequent upon your wises, your body after death, may be let into water like Brahmins, or it may be cremated like Khatris, or it may be thrown to winds like one of Parsee or it may be buried like that of a Muslim." Mardana answered, "Well, Baba, you still think of the body. By the grace of your teachings, I have entirely forgotten about it. Now I regard my soul as the sole guardian of my body." Again Guru Nanak exclaimed, "Shall I make you famous by constructing a suitable tomb and render thee, famous in the world?" Mardana replied, "When my soul has been separated from its bodily tomb, why shut it up in the stone tomb?" Baba stepped in forward, embraced Mardana and declared, "Mardana, you have realised the Infinite." At the close of the first itinerary, Mardana reached Talwandi. His wife and children tried to retain him, but he did not agree. Now he was awakened, he again accompanied Nanak in his journey into the west Asian countries.

At the harbour of Surat, Nanak and Mardana sailed in the boat for Saudi Arabia. Having visited Mecca and Madina they reached Baghdad, the capital of the caliph of Islam. As usual, they stayed outside the town near graveyard. Nanak's visit to Baghdad is recorded in the Vars of Bhai Gurdas who writes :-

> Baba gaya Baghdad nun Bahar Jai Kiya Asthana
> Ik Baba akal rup duja rababi Mardana.
>
> [Baba went to Baghdad and put up outside.
> The immortal Baba was accompanied by the rebecplayer Mardana.]

On the roadside, Nanak began to sing hymna in praise of God, and Mardana played a symphonic strain on his musical instrument. Although the people could not understand the language of the hymns, yet the melodious voice with which the hymns were being sung, produced a sooting effect on their minds. as a result, the local pir was converted to Guru Nanak's views and became his disciple.

Nanak settled at Kartarpur, Mardana also came to this place. Mardana was a master-rebec player. He improved the old form of instrument by fixing to strings to a hollow gourd so as to produce deep and melodious strain.

He composed verses also, three of which are included in the Adi Granth in Bihagre ki Var. In the first Sloka Mardana compares human personality of those living in the dark age to the vessel used for the extraction of wine. Lust is the wine that human heart continues to consume. Human wrath makes the cup of temptations, fill it and vanity feeds it. By partaking this wine in the company of unsanctified beings, human heart is degrading itself continuously.

In the second Sloka, Mardana regards it a further plunge into evils for those who partake of this fictitious wine.

In the third Śloka, suggesting a way out from these evils, Mardana thinks, "man can find an escape from the evils provided his body (vessel) partakes the wine of Nector— a wine that inspires the urge for inner realisation and immortality from a cup of devotion in the company of honest and chaste persons."

GURDAS

A brilliant scholar, a great poet, a devoted Sikh, a zealous missionary, a great organiser and a great visionary, Bhai Gurdas was born in 1551 A.D. He was the son of Guru Amar Das's brother, Tej Bhan. His mother's name was Jiwani. He was thus the first cousin of Bibi Bhani who was the daughter of Guru Amar Das, wife of Guru Ram Das and mother of Guru Arjan Dev. His parents belonged to Basarke but later on they migrated to Goindwal, the headquarter of Guru Amar Das. Since his childhood, Gurdas had fascination for Sikh Sangats. According to Hari Ram Gupta, "he possessed a sweet and melodious voice, and enthusiastically participated in singing hymns. He developed great love and affection for the Guru's teachings. He picked up Gurmukhi and learnt by heart Gurbani or the Guru's hymns, prayers and chants. He seldom missed any divine service."

Note much is known as to how and wherefrom he received his education but one thing is certain that he was well-versed in Punjabi, Sanskrit, Braj Bhasha and in the science of Music. He was a keen observer, extremely sensitive, high perceptive, wide awake and broad-minded.

His stance and psych bore the stamp of the Gurus, and there is no wonder that he was ever ready to do anything for the Guru.

He being an erudite scholar was entrusted the duty of writing the Granth at Guru's dictation. Guru Arjan selected a beautiful site two kilometres to the east of the holy tank in the grove of Beri (Zizphus Jujuha) trees on the bank of a tank, called Ramsar. There he sat on a cot inside and Bhai Gurdas outside. For four hours everyday the Guru gave dictation and Bhai Gurdas went on writing without a pause or murmur. The Granth was written in the modified Gurmukhi script. Having included the hymns of Bhaktas in Adi Granth, the Guru asked Bhai ji to insert his own Vars and Kabits also. Bhai ji declined saying that he had not achieved that degree of spirituality as the Bhaktas had got.

In 1605 Emperor Akbar on a visit to Lahore stayed at Batala. Prithi Chand managed to complain to the Emperor to the effect that Guru Arjan Dev in 'Adi Granth' had denounced both Hinduism and Islam. The Emperor called for the Granth. Guru Arjan Dev sent it under the custody of Bhai Gurdas and Bhai Buddha. Akbar asked Bhai Gurdas to read as a certain place. Bhai Gurdas at once complied but the Emperor found nothing offensive to Muslim susceptibilities. Then Akbar asked his clerk, Munshi Sarb Dayal who knew Gurmukhi to read the sacred Granth Sahib from another place. Now it was read as under:

Koi Bole Ram Ram Koi Khoda
(Some call Him Ram Ram, others Khuda)

The Emperor was pleased as the readings echoed his feelings. This being so, he made an offering of 51 gold mohars to the Granth Sahib, and awarded robes of honour to its two bearers with another Khilat for the Guru.

Bhai ji suffered from extreme mental agony when Guru Arjan Dev was executed. He was present in the congress of the important Sikhs held at the instance of the Guru on the eve of his departure to Lahore in response to the summons of Jahangir. He listened to the parting message of the Guru.

After the execution of the fifth Guru and during the years when Guru Hargobind was in prison in Gwalior, the affairs of the Sikh community were left in the hands of trusted followers, among whom were Bhai Buddha and Bhai Gurdas. On the release of Guru Hargobind from the prison of Gwalior Gurudas was sent on a mission to purchase horses from Kabul. Before he could complete the deal, his money was stolen and the crest-fallen Gurdas being unable to face his master fled to Benaras. He was apprehended and brought to Amritsar. The Guru forgave him and he again resumed his duties as the chief organiser of the Sikh community.

Bhai Gurdas supported Guru Hargobind in initiating his new policy whereby he claimed that he symbolized in himself Miri (temporal sovereignty) and Piri (spiritual sovereignty), and to lend substance to his policy, the Guru adopted militant ways. This policy caused unrest in the Sikh community. Bhai Gurdas rose to the defence of his master. He described the Guru, "the destroyer of enemy hordes, the hero of battles, the great warrior, as well as the great benefactor."

Bhai Gurdas will ever be remembered for his compositions, known as vars in which he explained main tenets of Sikhism apart from giving general information regarding men and matters. He wrote 39 vars (ballads in heroic metre in Panjabi), Kabits (couplet) in Brij, are written by a Sindhi poet of Shikarpur of the same name. In the copies of Gurdas's vars which are current to-day, there is the 40th var written by a Sindhi poet of Shikarpur of the same name. The Sindhi Gurdas lived in the time of Banda. These compositions contain several references to persons and events which are of great importance to the historians of today.

There are 85 passages in 39 vars which deserve attention viz. var 1 pauri 17-48, var 11, var 21 pauri 13-31, var 24 pauri 1-25, var 3 pauri 12, var 20 pauri 1 and var 38 pauri 20. It is really surprising that Bhai Gurdas did not say anything about the compilation of Adi Granth and the execution of Guru Arjan Dev. In the list of important disciples of Guru Nanak, he made notable omissions of Rai Bular and various others who were the devote disciples of Guru Nanak. The reference to the execution of the fifth Guru is indirect and vague. Bhai Gurdas says :-

> "The Guru hath taken his abode in the river among the fish,
> As moths that see the flame fall upon it and merge their light with His Light,
> As deer hear the sound of a distant drum and run to it without a care of doom,
> As butterflies seattle on the lotus and die on it during the night,
> The Guru's teachings we forget not and like the monsoon birds are ever calling,
> The Good have peace, the nectar of love and the company of the gentle.
> Thus is my life a sacrifice to Guru Arjan.

Bhai Gurdas's compositions are a key to the understanding of Sikh doctrines, Sikh organisation, Sikh cosmology, Sikh Metaphysics and Sikh Theology. He dwelt on the disciple-preceptor relationship and the spirit that the Gurus were. He heralded to the world, perhaps for the first time, in unambiguous terms that the Sikh religion was not only the need of the hour but enshrined in itself hope for future generations. His compositions provide perspective which enable a reader to grasp the true import of the theme. He presented the Gurus as God incarnates, benefactors, redeemers, prophets, the spirit. He regarded Sangat, a school for spiritualization of individuals, soul culturalization, socialization of the individuals. Moreover, he spelt very methodically the process of regenerating the degenerate man. He also viewed Sikh religion as Universal Brotherhood. Gurdas remained celebrate and died in 1631.

BHAI MANI SINGH

Bhai Mani Singh, one of the galaxy of the eminent Sikhs of the Guru period and the later Mughal period, was born on March 10, 1644 A.D. at Alipur, District Muzaffar Garh to Mai Das and his wife Mudri Bai. Much is not known about his childhood but one thing is almost certain that his sensibilities were shaped by the environment which was essentially Sikh because of the deep faith of his parents and brothers in Sikhism. According to Bhat Vahis Talauda Bhai Mani Singh's grandfather Ballu had died at Amritsar in A.D. 1634 fighting against the Mughal forces on behalf of Guru Hargobind. In A.D. 1654, it was for the first time that he got chance to have the first contact with Sikh movement when he was taken by his father to Guru Har Rai at Kiratpur. Guru Har Rai's piety, his hallowed personality, and his meaningful utterances moved him so much that his heart began to overflow with devotion for the Guru. Henceforth, he began to serve the Guru and his successors in various capacities. At the age of fifteen, he was married to Sato Bai, the daughter of celebrated Lakhi Shah who, later on, cremated the headless body of Guru Tagh Bahadur at great personal risk.

Shortly after marriage, he alone with his elder brothers, Dayala and Jetha came to Kiratpur. The way he conducted himself at Kiratpur was atonce impressive and expressive of his love for the cause. He unhesitatingly and regularly cleansed the utensils in the kitchen, served meals to the people and listened to the instructions of the Guru. This being so, he rose in the estimation of the Guru. The Sikhs also began to adore him.

At the death of Guru Har Rai, Bhai Mani Singh decided to stay on at Kiratpur to serve Guru Har Krishan, the successor to Guru Har Rai. According to the author of Shahid Bilas, he was one of the privileged few who accompanied Guru Har Krishan to Delhi. He served the Guru to the best of his capacity and capability till the Guru passed away (March 30, 1664).

Bhai ji came to Bakala along with Mata Sulakhni, the mother of the late Guru. At that time he was running the 20th year of his age. He was in the prime of his youth, but despite this, he was mature far beyond his age and his advice mattered. When Guru Tegh Bahadur was executed at Delhi in A.D. 1675, Bhai ji was at Anandpur with Guru Gobind Singh. He saw for himself the deputation of sixteen Kashmiri Brahmans supplicating the Guru Tagh Bahadur to save them from the onslaught of Aurangzebian communal Imperialism. He also witnessed the preparation of the Guru to go to Aurangzeb probably to make him understand the fulfility of his stand vis-a-vis the non-Muslims. He also experienced the agony when, in response to the other of the Mughal authorities, the Guru was arrested at Malikpur Rangharan and taken to Sarhind wherefrom, after four months of imprisonment, he was removed to Delhi. Mani Singh put up with all this full with equipoise.

Up to this time, Bhai Mani Singh had known fully the different facets of the Sikh movement, its rationale, its objectives and reactions it had evoked in the minds of the Mughal authorities. Besides this, he had equipped himself to be classed as first rate scholar. He had acquired knowledge of Sikh scriptures by attending regularly the congregations to be addressed by Guru Hari Rai, and Guru Tegh Bahadur. He had the mastery of the languages such as Braj Bhasha, Panjabi and Sanskrit. It is possible, for much of his learning, he owed to the teachers of Guru Gobind Singh with whom he had initimate association. He also learnt military tactics, handling of weapons and management of men during battles. According to Swea Singh, he was also a great warrior.

Guru Gobind Singh loved Bhai Mani Singh and assigned him those tasks. which involved high degree of responsibility. In 1678 A.D. Bhai ji was asked to prepare copies of Adi Granth, the task which was obviously important because firstly its fulfilment was sure to deal a heavy blow to the prestige of Dhir Mal who was in possession of the original copy and was unwilling to loan out Guru Gobind Singh, and secondly if the word of the Guru was precious, the Guru must offer them the opportunity to be in tune with it. Thus at the age of thirty-five, Bhai ji emerged as a great scholar, poised to undertake the important job of preparing copies of Adi Granth.

Bhai Mani Singh accompanied Guru Gobind Singh to Nanhan in A.D. 1687. According to Shahid Bilas the Bhai was one of the important poets of the Guru's court.

Bhai ji had the privilege of accompanying Guru Gobind Singh when he went to Dehra Dun on the seventeenth day after the death of Ram Rai to condole with Punjab Kaur, the wife of Baba Ram Rai. Next year the Guru sent fifty elect Sikhs to attend the function in connection with the death anniversary or Ram Rai. One of the fifty Sikhs was Bhai Mani Singh.

In A.D. 1691, Guru Gobind Singh appointed him as his Dewan, in which capacity he had to attend to variegated duties. Inspite of his pre-occupation with the work of Dewan, he was very regular in giving discourses to convey the. meaning of hymns of the Gurus. It appears that his method of the transmission of the utterances of the Guru was proved to be so effective that, in course of time, a definite school of the Sikh Thought, popularly known as Giani Sampardai (Giani School of Thought) emerged. In 1699 A.D., on the occasion of the creation of the Khalsa, after the five Beloved ones, Mani Singh received baptism from Guru Gobind Singh and became Mani Singh. Bhai ji's five sons were also initiated into the order of the Khalsa by administering Amrit to them.

Amritsar had long been in the hands of the rival Sodhis, Guru Tegh Bahadur had not been allowed to enter the Hari Mandir. When in A.D. 1699, Guru Gobind Singh sent out several batches of the Sikhs to preach the Khalsa way (Sainapat, Sri Gur Sobha 48) Bhai Mani Singh was commissioned to take over the Hari Mandir. He soon made Amritsar the centre for the Khalsa. According to Sewa Singh, he discarded much that was made vogue in Hari Mandir by the rival Sodhis to strengthen their own cause. According to Sodhi Darbari, 'except regarding Prithi Chand, Meharban and Harji as the sixth, seventh and eighth Gurus, no other change in the routine programme of Hari Mandir was made by the Sodhis.'

Mani Singh used to come to Anandpur off and on along with Sangat to be enlightened by the tenth Guru himself. On the even of the first battle of Anandpur (1st September, 1700) Mani Singh who was with the Guru was asked to take part in the ensuing battle. His son Bachittar Singh and Udey Singh also participated in the battle. Vir Singh Bal in his book "Singh Sagar Chapter 11" says that the Guru called Bhai ji, gave him sword, shield and arrows and sent him to the battle-field. In this battle, Bhai ji as also his three sons showed remarkable valour.

When hill chiefs were despaired of capturing Anandpur, they appealed to the Guru's sense of chivalry by requesting him to leave Anandpur to them as gao-bhet, that is, the food for the cow. The Guru left Anandpur and established himself at Nirmoh. But Raja Bhim Chand threw to winds all the promises and assisted by Wazir Chand attacked the Guru. A fierce battle took place. All his sons played their part well. The Guru felt pleased at their performance and honoured them by awarding them a special letter of appreciation (Hukamnama).

At the time of evacuation of Anandpur by Guru Gobind Singh in December 1704, Mani Singh followed the Guru. When on the bank of river Sarsa, the Guru was suddenly attacked at night by Mughal forces, all were scarttered in different sides. The Guru's mother and his two youngest sons went in one direction. The Guru's wives, Mata Sundari and Mata Sahib Devi, followed another route. Mani Singh immediately joined the ladies. He led them across the river the following day when the flood water had subsided. He guided them to Ambala. His aim was to take them to Nạhan, the capital of the friendly Raja in whose territory the Guru has spent three years at Paonta. But since the streams en route were flooded on account of heavy rains, he made straight to Delhi, and posing himself as a Muslim stayed in Matya Mahal, a purely Muslim locality even upto now out of sheer necesity for security.

When he got wind of the Guru's station at Talwandi Saboke, now called Damdama, he along with Guru's wives reached there and contributed his best to the process of the reorganisation of the Khalsa as also to the literary activities conducted at the instance of the Guru himself.

Having spent one year and a half at Damdama the Guru decided to leave for the Deccan to see Aurangzeb. Bhai Mani Singh was one of the few Sikhs who accompanied the Guru.

At Baghaur, the Guru learnt that the Emperor was no more. He changed his programme and turned towards Delhi. He joined the new Emperor, Bahadur Shah, at Agra in July 1707. Mata Sundari was left in Delhi, while Mata Sahib Kaur accompanied him. Bhai Mani Singh remained in attendance upon the Guru.

Guru Gobind Singh passed away at Nander on October 17, 1708. Bhai Mani Singh was present there. He escorted Mata Sahib Kaur to Delhi where she lived with Mata Sundari for the rest of the life.

Shortly afterwards, Bhai ji returned to Amritsar with specific purpose of relieving the Sikhs of the sadness which had gripped them because of the death of their Guru. Bhai ji assuaged them, encouraged them and revitalised them. The method employed to this purpose was to make them realise their own greatness and the greatness of the Gurus by relating to them the stories of the heroic efforts of the Gurus to fight the evil. On the Baisakhi day in 1709, Bhai ji not only ensured a huge gathering by issuing letter far and wide but also he made incumbent on himself that they should be apprised of the latest development.

In April 1709, Bhai Mani Singh had to fight against Chaudhri Deva who was commanding Mulkias and his own force. The cause of the battle was that one Ramu Mal follower of Sodhi Niranjan picked up a quarrel with the Sikhs over a trifle and to prove his superiority he approached Aslam Khan the Nizam of Lahore who ordered Har Sahai, the faujdar of Patti to punish the Sikhs. Har Sahai at once proceeded to implement the order but was killed by Tara Singh Van in an encounter. Ramu Mal's father Chuhar Mal again approached the Nazim. He sent Chaudhri Deva to punish the Sikhs. Bhai Mani Singh and the Sikhs fought so bravely that the enemy had to flee from the field. The victory of Bhai Mani Singh exploded the myth of the invincibility of the Mughal rule. This thing created new confidence among the Sikhs.

When Banda Bahadur, piqued up at the murderous assault on Guru Gobind Singh and goaded by the desire to cosummate the ideals of Sikhism declared open defiance of the Mughal authority, the Government reacted to it and took stringent measures against the Sikhs. Many Sikhs who were putting up with Bhai ji at Hari Mandir left him out of fear of the wrath of the government. Bhai ji, however, remained unshaken and continued to do his duty at Hari Mandir as assiduously as he used to do earlier.

In 1714-15, Bhai ji undertook proselytizing tour of the District Jhang of. Punjab. He sojourned for sometime at village Baga-Wala at the place where now Gurdwara 'Nanaksar' stands and related the story of Guru Hargobind. Shortly after, Bhai ji returned to Amritsar.

The defeat and execution of Banda had adverse effect on the body-social of the Sikhs. The Khalsa were divided between the 'Bandai' who wished to deify Banda and 'Tat Khalsa' who while revering the memory of their leader, disapproved of the attempt to apotheosize him. The differences between the two groups found expression in the matters of trivial detail, but, as is usual with frustrated people, the trivialities assumed unwarranted importance. This led to squabbling and then an open fight to gain control over the Hari Mandir in Amritsar. The position became serious. Bhai Mani Singh was then in charge of Hari Mandir. He decided the case in a simple way. On two pieces of paper he wrote the words 'Tat Khalsa' and 'Bandai Khalsa'. The papers were rolled up into a ball and thrown into the holy tank of Har Ki Pauri. The paper bearing the name Tat Khalsa came up the water first, and the holy places were immediately handed over to 'Tat Khalsa'. The fact that Bhai ji prevailed upon the aforesaid warring groups to agree to the solution as stated above bears eloquent testimony to the deft handling of the delicate issues and speak volumes of his understanding of men and matters.

During these years and after, the unflinching faith which Bhai Mani Singh showed in the Guru's mission served as a source of inspiration and encouragement to others. He reassured the Sikhs that there was no cause for anxiety, because the message of Nanak had a divine sanction behind it and was therefore imperishable. He looked to the future for a new dawn of Sikhs Power, thus dispelling the despondency into which the followers of Guru Gobind Singh had fallen after A.D. 1716.

As has it been in the foregoing passages, Bhai ji was a brave soldier and had taken part in the battles of Bhangani, Nadaun, and Anandpur. From this experience arose his attitude and philosophy of resistance. The attainment of sovereignty and the establishment of just rule was the mission of the Khalsa Panth. Bhai ji vouchsafed that this was laid down by the Guru himself and willed by God. In order to hasten the liquidation of the Mughal rule, the Khalsa must seriously take to 'Danga', a sort of a guerrilla warfare as the most effective method of resistance suited to a numerically inferior people. The objective of the Khalsa was the acquisition of sovereign status. Possessed of this belief, the Khalsa Panth refused to identify itself with the existing state and cheerfully made sacrifices with the hope of establishing their own independent power.

Obviously, Bhai Mani Singh's activities could not be tolerated for long by the existing political establishment whose head was Zakariya Khan. In 1733, the leaders of the Sikhs met at Akal Takht to decide whether or not they should accept the offer of Jagir from the Government. In the course of discussion one significant argument was put forth which was that the Khalsa being sovereign by the grace of their Guru and God could not accept such an offer from a power which they did not recognise. This argument clearly reflected the philosophy of Bhai Mani Singh. In all probability, the matter was reported to Zakariya Khan who must have been angered at this.

The writing on the wall in the case of Bhai ji was clear, but Zakariya took his own time.

The Mughal Government of Lahore had strictly forbidden Sikhs to visit Amritsar and bathe in the holy tank. On all sides of the city, strong contingents were posted to arrest Sikhs approaching their sacred shrines.

In October 1734, just before Diwali, Bhai Mani Singh applied to the Government that the Sikhs might be allowed to attend the Diwali fair for a tribute of Rs. 5000. Permission was granted, but the real object of the Government was to destroy the Sikhs en-bloc. Bhai Mani Singh, ignorant of this, sent messages all over the Punjab inviting the Sikhs to celebrate the Diwali fair. Soon after, Bhai ji sensed the nefarious designs of the Government and informed the Sikhs not to visit Amritsar on the Diwali Day.

No fair was held and no offerings came. Bhai Mani Singh who had planned to play five thousand rupees out of the offerings could not do so, nor had he any other source of income to make payment. The Government demanded the promised fee. Mani Singh blamed the Government for not allowing the Sikhs to assemble on the Diwali day. The Government arrested him in 1734 and took him to Lahore. The Qazi pronounced the judgement and he was cut to pieces limb by limb.

Bhai Mani Singh's martyrdom furthered the cause for which he had been patiently labouring throughout his life. His idea that the Khalsa must possess sovereign power received baptism of martyr's blood and became part of the psyche of the nation.

BHAI JAITA

The Sikh religion up to the time of Guru Gobind Singh had caught the imagination of the Panjab and outside. The down-trodden section of the people which is always the biggest one in the feudal social structure was specially attracted towards it because of its emphasis on ameliorating the condition of the people both on social and economic planes. If statistical data is considered to be a reliable pointer, it can be safely surmised that the people whom the Gurus met or about whom he spoke were mostly the poor, the down-trodden and the so-called low caste people. The Gurus focalised notice of such people led him to the framing of ideology whose focal point was such people. Hence the emergence of such people as the staunchest supporter of the Gurus was a must, and no wonder, Bhai Jaita served the cause of the Guru even at the risk of his life like so many others of his social status.

Who Bhai Jaita was has been a matter of great controversy. Shri Gill has tried to prove that he was a son of Sada Nand, a Brahmin who was employed as an astrologer in the court of Aurangzeb and who belonged to Mathura. Sardar Gill quotes from 'Sisnama' a book written by Giani Chatur Singh. But the view is wrong because Chatur Singh does not quote any source. Moreover there are certain indefensible facts which inhere the description of Bhai Jaita by Giani Chatur Singh. Giani ji says, "that day Sada Nand went to Aurangzeb to give his predictions. Before doing so, he recited a Shabad upon which Aurangzeb lost temper, ordered him to get off. Sada's father, Jas Bhan turned him, out of his house making out to the people that he had turned mad."

The story suffers from serious snags. In the first instace Aurangzeb did not like to consult any Hindu astrologer and secondly no astrologer of the name of Sada is mentioned in any contemporary records. So far as the recitation of Shabad is concerned, it contains nothing which can annoy anybody. Moreover, had he been a Brahman or a Khatri, there was no need on the part of the Guru to call him 'Rangretta Guru ka Beta'. In that case, he would have said "Brahmin or Kshatriya Guru ka beta." In fact, Bhai Jaita belonged to scavenger's class and Rangretta is the name given to it and they are called by this name even today in different parts of the Punjab.

Which place did he belong to is also a matter of controversy among the scholars. Chatur Singh says, "that his parents belonged to Mathura." Professor Kartar Singh regard him as the inhabitant of Ramdaspur near Amritsar. Prof. Kartar Singh mentions that Sada left Ramdaspur in the wake of the death of his beloved wife, Bibi Premo along with his infant son Jaita and went to Bakala at the time when as a result of the efforts of Makhan Shah and others, the fictitious Gurus were fully exposed and constrained to leave Bakala. There he embraced Sikhism and became a devout Sikh of Guru Tegh Bahadur.

Through we have not come across any contemporary or semi-contemporary evidence, yet the tradition of Ramdas being the cradle place of Bhai Jaita is too strong to be brushed aside.

Recently we have come across the following entry in Bhat Vahi Multani Sindhi which records that Bhai Jaita's father's name was Agya Ram who was the resident of Mohalla Dilwali Sikhan Delhi. In view of this, evident conclusion may be drawn that Bhai Jaita belonged to Delhi and his father was not Sada but some other man. But a little probe into matter will bring into relief the reality. In fact Bhai Agya, after the death of his wife began to live a life of resignation, self-absorbed and oblivious of the world around. People often unable to penerate into the real self of the man began to call him 'Sada', the simpletan.

After his visit to Bakala, Sada decided to pass his days while rendering service to the Guru and thereafter he seemed to have always been in attendance upon the Guru. Bhai Jaita also remained in the court of the Guru, of course, with his father. All Sikh records say that when Jaita was taken to Baba Bakala by Agya, he was yet a child. If childhood is assigned 5 years or a little more, it means that he had the privilege of long company of Guru Tegh Bahadur upto the age of seventeen. During these years, he must have imbibed the requisite spirit of espousing the cause of Sikhism. Whether he accompanies the Guru in his tours, nothing can be said with certainty, but there is every possibility that he was with the Guru when he left Kiratpur for tours to the places in the north and west of India. On way back to Kiratpur, it seems that Bhai Agya and his son Jaita decided to settle at Mohalla Diwali, Delhi. Bhai Jaita, as also his father, being dedicated Sikhs, took to preaching the Guru's Gospel and they were quite well-known, having intimate contact with all important Sikhs including Lakhi Shah and his sons.

Bhai Jaita used to come to Anandpur off and on to keep himself abreast of the latest instructions of the Guru and when Guru Tegh Bahadur was arrested and taken to Delhi, Bhai Jaita came to Anandpur to pay his homage to the young Guru Gobind Singh and also to apprise him of the situation and the mind of the Mughal Government. Whether Guru Gobind Singh gave him certain instructions or not, one thing is clear that he must have gone back to Delhi, fully inspired and duly determined to do his best to serve the cause of the Guru.

The fateful day came on November 11, 1675 and executioner's sword severed the head of the Guru. The headless body and the head lay in front of Kotawali in the Chandni Chowk which used to be the most throned place in the city. The plan of the Government was to cut the body into four pieces and to quarter them on all sides of Delhi. Bhai Jaita could not withstand all this. Bhai Nanu a washerman Sikh, also of Dilwali Gate, also felt like Jaita. Both of them met each other. Bhai Agya also took part in the deliberation. According to Banswali Nama and Bhat Vahis, Bhai Nanu picked up the head, went home and asked Bhai Jaita to do the needful. Jaita wrapped the head in a piece of cloth, put the sacred head in a basket and covered it with flowers. He, regardless of the danger of the Mughal pursuers and caring little for physical inconvenience ran towards Anandpur. He was accompanied by his father and Nanu. On the way, he stopped at four places viz Sonepat, Ambala, Nabha (near Chandigarh) and Kiratpur. At Kiratpur Guru Gobind Singh received the hallowed head of his father, took it with all reverence to Anandpur where it was consigned to fire. Guru Gobind Singh was so much moved at the courage and devotion of Bhai Jaita that he took him in tight embrace, kissed him and announced 'Rangretta Guru ka Beta' i.e. to say 'Bhai Jaita is the son of the Guru.'

Since then Bhai Jaita had started living at Anandpur. The Guru was all affection for him, and had full faith in his capability to further Guru's cause. The archaeological evidence is pertment at this point. At Anandpur, there is a building known as Tap Asthan 'place of meditation' of Bhai Jaita, very close to

Guru Gobind Singh's dwelling place. No other Sikh had his house as near as Bhai Jaita's. This thing leads us to conclude that Guru Gobind Singh had special regard for Jaita. Tradition says that Bhai Jaita not only used to meditate and reflect on Guru's word but also gave lessons on Sikhism to the people. 'Tap Asthan' in Sikh context does not mean a place of an ascetic, rather by this is meant the place where Sikh culture is imbibed and steps taken to inculcate it among the people.

Bhai Jaita witnessed variegated activities of Guru Gobind Singh at paonta and possibly it was here that Bhai Jaita became an adept in the art of archery, gunnary, swordsmanship and horsemanship.

In the battle of Bhangani and various other battles which Guru Gobind Singh fought, Jaita played his part well. In the absence of any recorded account, it is not possible for us to give any details of his acts of bravery, yet it is irrefutable that he was one of the greatest generals of the Guru's army.

On March 30, 1699, when Guru Gobind Singh inaugurated the order of the Khalsa he took 'Khande ki Pahul' and was then given a new name, Jiwan Singh.

Guru Gobind Singh evacuated Anandpur on the night of 6-7 Poh Samvat 1762 B.K. (5-6 December, 1705). The moment the enemy got wind of the departure of the Sikhs, they forgot all about their pledges and set out in hot pursuit immediately. Skirmishes commenced from Kiratpur onwards. Realizing the impending damage, Guru Gobind Singh gave a band of 50 men to Bhai Udey Singh and charged him with the responsibility of checking the enemy's advancement. Bhai Udey Singh fought at Shahi Tibbi with the enemy with a handful of men; all of them perished fighting covering themselves with imperishable glory.

When the battle of Shahi Tibbi was in progress, Guru Gobind Singh, along with the rest of Caravan lost no time to reach the bank of Sarsa river. Bhai Jaita was with the Guru, advancing and planning.

About this time, the news arrived that a contingent of enemy troops was fast approaching and was likely to launch an attack in a short time. The river was in high flood at that time, and it was apprehended that in the eventuality of an attack from the enemy, it would become all the more difficult to cross it. Under the circumstances, it was considered imperative by the Guru to set apart a Jatha out of his Sikhs for checking the further advance of the enemy. The choice of the leadership of the Jatha fell on Bhai Jiwan Singh who proved himself worthy of the trust reposed in him by the Master. The Bhai and his brave 100 companions offered a stout and stubborn resistance to the enemy and all of them died martyrs. Sarup Singh Kaushak, the author of 'Guru Kian Sakhian' records as under :—

"A momentous battle was fought on the bank of Sarsa, the arrows of Bhai

Jiwan Singh brought havoc upon the enemies. All the Sikhs fought gallantly with a total disregard of their lives. A large number of the Turks were killed in the battle-field. A hard contest took place between the two parties for half pahar (four and half hours). Then suddenly as a result of a volley of matchlocks Jiwan Singh was shot in his forehead. His departing words were `Wha Guru Ji ki Fateh'. By the sun rise, all the Sikhs had lost their lives."

BHAI NAND LAL

Bhai Nand Lal was one of those blessed Sikhs who had the good fortune of receiving the patronage and guidance of Guru Gobind Singh. He was born in A.D. 1633 at Agra. His father was Diwan Chhajju Ram who, because of his erudite scholarship in Persian and Arabic, was much liked by Dara Shikoh. When Dara was sent to Qandhar to subjugate it, he took Chhajju Ram alongwith him, appointing him to the post of Chief Secretary (Mir Munshi). Sometime after, Dara Shikoh returned to Agra but Chhajju Ram chose to remain at Ghazni working against the post of Mir Munshi of the Governor of Ghazni.

He had great attachment for Nand Lal, perhaps it was because of the fact that he was born in the later years of his life. All possible arrangements were made to ensure good education to the boy. Chhajju Ram himself spared time to give lessons to his son. Shortly, Nand Lal acquired efficiency in Persian and Arabic and could compose verses in Persian at the age of twelve.

Diwan Chhajju Ram was a devote Vaishnavite, although he was not parochial in his religious outlook. Naturally Nand Lal was nourished on the liberal religious views of his father. There was another element that entered into his psyche. During these days, the Sikhs all over northern India and Afghanistan had established their Sangats where they used to pray and discuss spiritual-cum-social views of the Gurus. Bhai Nand Lal came into contact with these Sangats and could not escape the impact of Sikhism which, of course, at the time, was in germinal form.

When Nand Lal grew of age, his father, true to Vaishnavite tradition, asked him to wear around his neck a piece of wood. Nand Lal refused to oblige his father saying that he would wear that rosary whose beads are unbreakable and guarantee real contentment. The father was astonished and failed to convince the boy.

When Bhai ji reached sixteen years of age, his mother died. Three years after, his father also breathed his last. Bhai Nand Lal as per custom, expected the post of his father. He tried for it but the Governor of Ghazni was not willing to oblige him and instead offered him a petty post of a clerk. Bhai ji declined the offer because he did not consider this post in commensurate with his ability and the status of his family. Bhai Nand Lal had no high-placed patron to recommend his case. Dara Shikoh had left Ghazni and Bhai ji did not know that he would visit Ghazni again in A.D. 1653 at the head of third expedition meant to reconquer Qandhar.

Thus finding himself helpless, Nand Lal decided to leave Ghazni. He sold the property which he had inherited and reached Multan alongwith his two brothers and two loyal Pathan servants. He selected Multan for his residence. The choice was a happy one. The city was a great centre of trade and possessed great political importance.

He built a house outside Delhi Gate where quite a few rich Khatris were already living. As the time rolled by, more houses came into being and the place developed into a big Mohalla.

His Pathan servants who were all devotion for Bhai ji used to call him by the epithet 'Aqha' which meant 'Lord'. Soon Bhai ji became very popular—so much so that the Mohalla where he resided began to be called 'Aqapur'. Sir Edward Maclagan says that Mohalla, long before the advent of Nand Lal in the city and borne such name, but we do not agree with him. The reason are not far to seek. In the first instance, for the Mughals the word 'Aqa' was never used and secondly, the suffix 'Pur' is a word of Hindi language.

Shortly after his arrival at Multan, the fame of the scholarship of Nand Lal began to spread. Nawal Wassaf Khan much impressed by Bhai ji's integrity and learning, appointed him to the post of *munshi* in which capacity he worked with distinction and won approbation from all quarters.

After this, he was made the incharge of the fort of Bhakkar. He collected the arrears of revenue from the zamindars of the area and remitted the same to Multan treasury. Soon after, he was made Nazim of Dina, Kehror, Fatehpur and Pargana Mahayyaud-din Pur. He acquitted himself nicely even at this post. The next post which he held was that of Naib Subedar or the Deputy Governor of Multan. About the period of his deputy governorship, no reliable source throws any light and hence it is difficult for us to say anything on this issue.

According to 'Dastur-ul-Insha', the book written by Bhai ji himself, he, as Nazim, made his mark as a military general also. He led a punitive expedition against a notorious dacoit, Sahu who had seven hundred bad characters to support him in his nefarious designs of disturbing peace and committing acts of dacoity. Sahu was arrested and nearly half of his followers were slain.

The dissolution of Sahu's gang not only enchanced the prestige of Bhai ji but also provided atmosphere for the peaceful citizens to progress economically. Besides this, Bhai ji constrained the zamindars to stand surety for the safe passage to the caravans coming into or going from Multan. By this step the volume of foreign trade swelled with the result that the internal trade was also stepped up correspondingly.

According to Dr. Ganda Singh 'Bhai ji' served the state in different capacities for about thirty years. He got the chance of serving Prince Salim and Prince Mohammed Akbar (1678-79).

During the regime of Aurangzeb, Bhai ji was turned out of Government service. The exact reasons for his dismissal are not known, but the probable conjecture is that he had to quit because of his father's good relations with Dara Shikoh, the fact which was unbearable for Aurangzeb.

All the same, subsequent period of his life was fruitful to him in another way. He discovered himself. He came into contact with the Sikh movement and its captain Guru Gobind Singh who wrought a transformation of his psyche. Bhai Nand Lal saw new heights, new horizons, new mountains and new seas. His poetry found new stimuli, symbolised new ideas. The fulcrum of his activities became Guru Gobind Singh, the lord of plume, the lord of Blue steed and the beloved hero of the emaciated humanity.

He went to Anandpur, the seat of Guru Gobind Singh. He saw for himself the Guru, his multi-farious activities, operating with finesse to bring about new awakening among the people and endeavouring to shape new values to fit in the general framework of the society of his ideas. His intellect quickened, his sensibility sharpened, his self responded to his generous gestures and he became beau ideal of a Sikh, embodying the Sikh ethos in its totality.

All out for the Guru's cause, Bhai ji decided to live at the court of the Guru.

After some time, Bhai ji went to Agra where in 1695, he got the post of Mir Munshi of Prince Muazzam who had, just after his release form the prison, assumed the change of subedar of the province of Agra. However, Bhai ji was not destined to work at this post for long.

It is said that once Aurangzeb asked the interpretation of certain excerpt from Al-Quran. Various interpretations were presented to the Emperor, but the version forwarded by Prince Muazzam was considered to be the most appropriate by Aurangzeb. On probe, he came to know that it was Bhai Nand Lal who had interpreted. Aurangzeb felt upset because he did not like a Kafir's mastery over the sacred text. He suggested that such a man of learning should be converted to Islam. In a public Durbar, Nand Lal was awarded a robe of honour and a cash prize of Rs. 500.

When Aurangzeb's secret desire came to Bhai Nand Lal's knowledge, he felt perturbed. There were only two courses left for him. He could either embrace Islam or go elsewhere. The former cause was rejected by him forthwith because he had, to all intents and purposes, entered into Sikh fold. The second course was not practical for him. he atonce packed up, begged leave of the Prince and reached Lahore. Here he met his pupil, Ghiasud-din, the. Drogha of Agra who had come on leave to this place. Both of them reached Anandpur. Ghiasuddin returned to Lahore after some time, but Bhai Nand Lal continued to stay Anandpur upto 1705.

During this period Bhai Nand Lal drank deep in the fountain of Sikh spiritual thought as enshrined in Adi Granth. He listened to the sacred utterances of the Guru. He keenly observed the Sikh way of life and understood the ultimate goal of the Sikh movement. The inauguration of the order of the Khalsa was also noted by him.

All those things and the splendid personality of Guru Gobind Singh constituted environment wherein Nand Lal's poetic genius quickened and flowered. Bhai ji produced books of Persian poetry. The first book of poetry which he presented to the Guru bore the title 'Bandgi Nama' which was changed to 'Zindgi Nama' by Guru Gobind Singh. The Guru wrote the following verse at the end of the book :

Ab-e-hai-van pur shud, chun jam-e-o
Zindgi Namah shud, Bandgi Namah-e-o

(When his goblet was filled with the water of life,
His Bandgi Namah bacame Zindgi Namah).

The Guru offered him the post of Diwan, but Nand Lal very politely declined the offer, saying that he was fully satisfied with his service in Guru's kitchen.

At Anandpur there were several free community messes for the poor and the needy. One day all the nobles began to praise their own free kitchens. Guru Gobind Singh in disguise of a rustic called at everyone of them and he found only Nand Lal's Langar (kitchen) working properly.

One day during Nand Lal's sojourn at Anandpur, Guru Gobind Singh came to know that his wife and children were living at Multan in his father-in-law's house. The Guru offered to issue Hukamnama (fiat) in the name of the Sangats of Multan and the area around to send their *daswandh* (one tenth of their income) to his family members. Bhai ji thanked the Guru for all this and requested that no order in this respect should be issued, only they should be blessed to earn their livelihood through honest means.

In 1705, when the Guru had to evacuate Anandpur, Bhai ji was with the Guru. But when the Mughal forces in combination with the hill forces attacked the Guru on the bank of the river Sarsa, Bhai ji, as also many other Sikhs, got separated from Guru Gobind Singh.

How did he pass the year of 1706, no one knows but this much is certain that in A.D. 1707 after the death of Aurangzeb Bhai ji went to Prince Muazzam who upto this time had occupied the Mughal throne at Agra under the name of Bahadur Shah.

Even after occupying the throne, Bahadur Shah was not feeling comfortable because Prince Azam was threatening and was advancing at the head of a force from the Deccan to the North India. At this critical juncture Bhai Nand Lal approached Guru Gobind Singh for active assistance for Bahadur Shah. Guru Gobind Singh acceded to the request and ordered his three hundred armed Sikhs to fight for Bahadur Shah whose right to throne seemed legitimate to him. Some scholars are puzzled at this gesture of the Guru, for they cannot find any rationale for Guru's sympathetic attitude towards Bahadur Shah whose father was responsible for the death of Guru Tegh Bahadur and varied difficulties of the Guru. But if they keep in view the mission of the Guru and then try to appreciate the policy of the Guru *vis-a-vis* Bahadur Shah, they would suffer from no contradiction whatsoever. The Guru's mission was to uphold righteousness and to see that the crookedness should not flourish. Since Bahadur Shah was not illiberal in his religious policy and was right in his stand, the Guru offered his help.

Bahadur Shah won victory at Jajau on June 8, 1707. He, in token of the appreciation of the Guru's help, offered him a robe of honour and various other valuable presents.

Shortly after, Bahadur Shah had to attend to the revolt of the Kachhwaha Rajputs of Rajputana. When he had just started operation against the Rajputs, he got the news of the open revolt of his brother Kambakhsh. He atonce marched to square up with him. Guru Gobind Singh, who was negotiating with him on different issues concerning his people and the excesses committed by the Subedar Wazir Khan of Sirhind accompanied Bahadur Shah to the Deccan.

All the time, Bhai Nand Lal was with Bahadur Shah. According to Dhadi Nab Mal writes:

"Nand Lal was one of the councillors of the Emperor. He had the privilege of being a very close associate of the very fortunate Emperor."

Bhai ji must have tried his best to get justice for the Guru and his cause. Emperor's intransigence towards the demands of the Guru must have caused disappointment to him. However, he continued to serve the Emperor upto the latter's death at Lahoare. In 1710 when the Emperor was given the news of Banda's anti-Mughal campaigns in the Punjab, he lost no time in marching towards Punjab. Bhai ji was in the Emperor's camp and reached Lahore along with the Emperor. Bahadur Ṣhah expired in 1712 and Bhai ji forthwith left for Multan.

After this, Bhai ji lived only for a year, but this period of his life was marked for his fruitful activities. He established a school in which he himself imparted higher education in Persian, and Arabic. According to Bhai Parma Nand this school continued to serve the people even after the death of Bhai Sahib and when in 1849 Multan came under the occupation of the British, the school was being run by the people of Bhai Ji's family. Bhai ji expired in A.D. 1713.

Bhai ji wrote ten volumes. As is clear from the diction and thought of these books, it is not difficult to surmise that Bhai ji wrote under the deep impact of Guru Gobind Singh and his philosophy. He composed verses under the pen-name of 'Goya' or 'Lal'.

Zindgi Nama

As it has been said earlier, this was the first creation of Bhai ji. The subject of this book is 'Love for God' and devotion for the Guru. For thoughts and perspective, Bhai ji copiously refers to the hymns of the Guru.

Ghazaliat

This volume is a good attempt to present the inner meanings of Guru's compositions. From the point of view of style, thought, and diction, this composition is superb.

Tosifo-Sana and Khatima

Except Khatima, which is in poetry, the whole composition is in Persian prose. Its style is marked for its verbosity and difficult diction. It contains no historical information, nor does it dwell on any theme worth consideration.

Ganj Nama

This composition is in prose as well as in poetry. In it one comes across the devotion for the Guru with which the author seems to have saturated.

Jot Bigas

This composition is in Persian and explains at full length the doctrine of Unity in the plurality of the Guru. The first Guru had categorically rejected the doctrine of incarnation i.e. the appearance of God on earth in human shape but had studiously advocated by practical illustration the doctrine of blending his spirit with the next and so on. It is in this volume that we find Bhai Nand Lal using epithets such as Badshah Darvesh-king saint, Puran Manukh-perfect man, etc., for Guru Gobind Singh. This book is a great aid to the scholars engaged in the study of the personality of Guru Gobind Singh.

Jot Bigas (Punjabi)

This book is not the copy of the former book; although the subject matter is almost the same.

Rahat Nama and Tankhanama

According to Sardar Attar Singh of Bhadaur, both these compositions are the creations of Bhai ji, although Bhai Kahan Singh does not agree. Rahat Nama gives an account of the code of discipline to be followed by the Sikhs. This book was written on December 4-5, 1695 and hence referred to the code which was required to be observed before the creation of the Khalsa. Tankhanama was written after the creation of the Khalsa and it refers to some of oughts and don'ts which the Khalsa should observe in their day-to-day life.

Dastur-Ul-Insha (Persian Prose)

The book provides information regarding social, economic and political condition contemporaneous of Guru Gobind Singh.

Arzuk-Alfaz (Persian Poetry)

It provides abundant information regarding the spiritual currents which Sikhism had caused. In it, Bhai ji is profuse in his praise for God and Gurus. The Persian and Arabic words which Bhai ji had used are clearly manifestative of Bhai ji's over-flowing devotion for the Guru and his deep scholarship.

MAI BHAG KAUR

Guru Arjan Dev was a vigorous preacher, besides being a great organiser and a creative genius. It was because of his proselytizing campaigns that most of the Majha people having shed off their old beliefs and embraced Sikhism. One of them was Langah, the son of Ahul Khair who was a staunch devotee of Sakhi Sarvar. As chance would have it, his friends happened to be the Sikhs under whose influence he visited Amritsar and saw Guru Arjan Dev for himself. The illumined personality of the Guru wrought transformation of his mind and he entered into the fold of Sikhism. By degrees, through his devotion and selfless service, he rose in the estimation of the Guru who began to repose full trust in him and involved him in the tasks of far-reaching importance for the nascent Sikh community. His brother Pero Shah and his nephew Malo Shah also grew to be devout Sikhs. Malo Shah was much loved by Guru Hargobind.

Mai Bhag Kaur was Malo Shah's daughter. Obviously she was brought up in the atmosphere which was suffused with Sikh culture. Admittedly, Bhag Kaur was imbued with Sikh ideas and her psyche shaped accordingly. She got the chance to have the sacred glimpse of Guru Tegh Bhadur when she was taken to Anandpur by her parents. Again she was lucky enough to be present along with other members of her family on the occasion of the installation ceremony of Guru Gobind Singh on March 30, 1699 when the Khalsa was created at Anandpur, her family members were among the first row of the people who received baptism of double-edged sword.

Immediately after the inauguration of the order of the Khalsa, people on a large scale were administered Khande-ki-Pahul. Bhag Kaur also was baptised.

In A.D. 1701, battle ensued between the Guru on one side and the hill chiefs and the Mughal Government on the other side. The war was prolonged upto 1705.

When the news of the excesses of the Hill Chiefs and the Mughal subedar of Sarhind reached the Sikhs of the Amritsar district they became red with moral rage. The grandsons of Duni Chand, Sardar Anup Singh and Sardar Sarup Singh got ready to participate in the war on behalf of the Guru. Mai Bhag Kaur also expressed her desire to take part in the war. Her brothers and parents did not allow her to have her way. Although they themselves rushed to Anandpur to render muchneeded asssistance to the Guru. Many more people did the same. Though the enemy had taken precautions to disallow the Sikhs to reach Anandpur, yet they would go, sometime in disguise and sometime at great personal risk. Bhag Kaur observed all this.

In 1705, the final battle of Anandpur took place. The Sikhs fought gallantly. The siege lasted for more than seven months. The strategy of the enemy during the siege was to force the Sikhs to surrender by fully closing their access to food and water. The effects of the strategy began to be felt as the days passed.

"None could either go or come. Then how were supplies to reach where needed? Many days did pass accordingly. And the price of food did soar to a rupee per seer.

Four Sikhs would venture for water : two would battle, two would fetch the pitchers."

(Gur Sobha)

The situation deteriorated to this extent that the Sikhs did not have anything to live upon. When the enemy learnt of the distress of the Sikhs, they planned a different strategy to take advantage of the situation. They sent a message to the Guru suggesting that if he decided to abandon Anandpur, he would be allowed a safe passage. Their pledge of a safe passage was unreliabel, since they planned to draw out the Sikhs from within the shelter of the township and attack them. The Guru sensed their secret motive when he received the message and therefore did not accept the suggestion. At this some the Sikhs persisted that the offer of the enemy should be accepted. When the Guru did not listen to them, they disclaimed the Guru and left for their homes.

The Guru ultimately, had to evacuate Anandpur on 5-6 December 1705. The moment the enemy got an inkling of the departure of the Sikhs, they forgot all about their pledges and set out in hot pursuit immediately. The Guru suffered a lot but wended his way to Chamkaur where he gave a battle to the enemy. In this battle the Guru had only forty odd soldiers while the enemy commanded a force running into lacs (according to Zafar Nama). All the

Guru's soldiers except three suffered martyrdom. Most prominent among the Sikh martyrs were Sahibzadas Ajit Singh and Jujhar Singh and three Piyaras (Beloved ones).

After this, the Guru had to move from place to place in search of security. and respite for regrouping the Khalsa. While at Dina, the Guru received definite information about the determination of the Sarhind authorities to send a body of troops against him. This news also reached the Majha area of the Punjab. The self-respecting Khalsa was cut to the quick. Bhag Kaur told his husband that time had come to prove their salt for the cause of the Guru. Her husband assured her of his steadfastness and readiness to make any sacrifice in this connection.

Bhag Kaur, greatly heartened at her husband's gesture, drew her sword out of the scabbard, alighted a horse and called upon all those who had love for the Guru's cause to come forward and march to the Malwa region of the Punjab to forestall the nefarious designs of Wazir Khan. Her exhortations were specially directed at those forty persons who had come back to their homes by signing a disclaimer.

Bhai Kaur's call had a magic effect. She like Joan of Arc of the French History led a band of soldiers to the Khidrana ki Dhab where the Guru had proposed to give a fight the Mughal forces. On the way, she was joined by a large number of Sikhs. Some wise men from Lahore who had thought they had some influence at the Mughal Durbar also joined them.

The party met the Master between Ramiana and Khidrana. The deserters. begged pardon and recommended the newcomers to his grace. The wise men advised him to give up fighting and make peace with the Emperor. They offered to act as negotiators. The Guru spurned their advice saying that it was not possible for him to make peace with tyrants. The wise men from Lahore acquiesced in quititude, and returned to their homes. the Guru continued his advance to his destination.

The rest of the party headed by Bhag Kaur and Mahan Singh of village Sur Singh Wala followed Guru Gobind Singh.

On reaching Khidrana, they found the tank dry. The master had for that reason moved on from the place. Bhai Mahan Singh proposed to engage the enemy there and to allow time to the Guru to reach a place of safety. Big white sheets of khaddar (coarse cloth) were spread on the shrubs so that the enemy might think the Sikhs were encamping there in a large number. Soon the Muhammandan army came up.

The Sikhs under Mai Bhag Kaur and Bhai Mahan Singh bore the brunt of the enemy's attack. All the Sikh soldiers fought with their usual courage and power. Mai Bhag Kaur was seen fighting in the foremost rank. The Mughal soldiers did their best to overpower the Sikhs and advance towards the Guru who from a place of eminence was aiming arrows on the prominent persons of the enemy forces, but they did not succeed. Mai Bhago's movements were not only heartening to the soldiers but also manifestative of the resurgence of the Sikh ladies which had taken place under the dynamic leadership of the Guru.

The Sikhs, having exhausted their ammunition and queer of arrows, were obliged to have recourse of their spears and the swords. Small bands advanced, engaged the enemies in hand to hand fights, killed several times their number, until many of them were killed or seriously injured. They themselves were incapacitated to carry on the fight. They did not win victory, nor were they fighting for it, their aim being the vindication of their faith in the Guru's cause and win over the pleasure of the Guru. All the same, they did succeed in constraining the Mughal forces to retrace their steps to their headquarter.

After they had gone, the Guru visited the scene of battle, and with a fatherly affection went about lifting the heads of the martyrs in his lap wiping their faces, and blessing them one by one. When it was the turn of Bhai Mahan Singh to be thus caressed and blessed, the Master found that there was still some life in him. After a while, Bhai Mahan Singh opened his eyes, and found himself in the lap of the Master. He was filled with surpreme joy. The Guru asked him if he had any desire to be fulfilled, Bhai Mahan Singh said, "No, father. I have seen thee. What else or more could I desire? But if thou has taken compassion on us here, then tear off our disclaimer. "The Guru atonce acceded to his request and remarked, "You have saved the root of Sikhism in the Majha. You and your companions, all forty of you are Muktas or the saved-ones, delivered from the round of births and deaths for ever." Then the Guru went to the place where Bhag Kaur was lying senseless. She had not been severely wounded but had fallen down out of utter exhaustion. A little aid revived her. She told the master what had occurred after he had left the party. He, in turn, told her of the last saving deed of Bhai Mahan Singh.

The Guru was greatly pleased with Mai Bhag Kaur for what she had done. He got her removed from the battlefield and got her wounds treated and healed.

After her recovery, Bhag Kaur chose to stay with the Guru. She led the Sikh way of life in its totality.

She was considered to be the *Braham Giani.* Bhai Santokh Singh in Suraj Parkash says that she having reached the stage of Braham Giani did not care for dress and used to remain nude. This view of Bhai Santokh Singh is a fallacy, cut and dried. Braham Giani, according to Guru Granth Sahib, is a person who remains pure in the midst of impurities and serves the people without any desire of reward for that. He is above petty considerations of caste, creed, clime and country. He in no case, pays scant regard for the decencies of life. As a matter of fact, Bhag Kaur combined in herself virtues both of a saint and a warrior. She was strong in character, firm in faith and unflinching in her determination. In view of these qualities, the Guru allowed her inclusion in the bodyguard of ten Sikhs, meant to guard the bed room. She used to be dressed in male attire. She remained with the Guru at Talwandi Saboki. She was one of these privileged Sikhs who accompanied the Guru in his journey to Khultanpur, where Aurangzeb was sojourning. She was there in the camp of the Guru when he marched along with Bahadur Shah first to Rajasthan and then to the Deccan. She observed for herself the parleys that took place between the Guru and Bahadur Shah and noticed with interest how Banda was converted to Sikhism.

After the death of Guru Gobind Singh at Nander, Bhag Kaur went to Bidar and continued to stay there till the last breath of her life. As long as she lived, she served the cause of the Guru. Her example was that of a person embodying in herself all the virtues of a good Sikh as also of the ideal Sikh woman alive to her duties as much as to her rights, believing in perfect equality among sexes and discarding the oft-held view that woman was primarily an appanage of a man. Her performance, both in the battlefield and the sphere of proselytization spoke high of the regenerating process that Sikhism, since its inception, had set in motion. Her achievements were enduring, her character and conduct were flawless, her leadership was unquestioned, her faith was unflinching and her demeanour was striking. No wonder, she has been a perennial source of inspiration to the ladies to keep their head high and dignity aloft.

ZORAWAR SINGH AND FATEH SINGH

3

Zorawar Singh and Fateh Singh

It is praiseworthy to lay down one's life as a victim of the courage of one's conviction and faith but it is certainly contemptible to die for one's selfish ambition or self-aggrendizement. It is not merely one's death that makes one great or immortal but it is the cause for which one dies that makes one great.

Zorawar Singh and Fateh Singh, the younger sons of Guru Gobind Singh, the Tenth Apostle of the Sikhs shall ever shine in human history for the ages to come. Their dauntless courage, divine strength and selfless sacrifice shall inspire millions of people and the children. It was a befitting occasion to remember such great sacrifices in 1979 A.D., the year during which the International year of The Child was being celebrated all over the world. No event could be properly understood without understanding its background. Therefore, we have got to know first of all the historical perspective of these two Martyr-Brothers.

Zorawar Singh and Fateh Singh had a very glorious history of the sacrifices of their fore-fathers for the sake of the freedom and secuity of the down-trodden, the oppressed, the enslaved, the exploited, the ill-treated, the injured and the ignored, by the high-handed religio-political zealots and foreign Muslim invaders, raiders and rules of India. Their ancestors also fought against the Brahmnical Hindu bane of caste system and untouchability. Their great-great-grand-father, Guru Arjan Dev, the Fifty Guru of the Sikhs was tortured to death in 1606 A.D., seated on a red-hot iron sheets or "loh", but he smilingly gave his life at the altar of his faith and freedom and thus sowed the first seed of martyrdom in the Sikh History. Then their great grand-father Guru Hargobind, the Sixth Guru of the Sikhs, wore two swords one of 'MEERI' or temporal power and the other of 'PEERI' or spiritual power and wrought wonders in both the fields to uplift the under-dog and defeated the troops of the Muslim Kings in several battles. Their grand-father, Guru Tegh Bahadur, the Ninth Guru of the Sikhs, fearlessly faced the tyranny of fanatic Aurangzeb and embraced martyrdom in 1675, refusing to accept Islam, challenging duress or any temptation, tortue and even the royal rewards as he wanted to practically infuse the spirit of freedom in the hearts of non-Muslims that religion or faith is a matter of one's own choice and volition. No amount of force can religionise or spiritualise anybody. Hence he gave his life to uphold individual freedom and liberty to profess any way of life or culture.

He left behind his nine years old, the only son Gobind Rai, to carry on the torch of freedom. Gobind Rai, afterwards became Guru Gobind Singh, and justified the expectations of his martyr-father, the example of which is hard to find in the history of the world. Not to speak of only the Indian admirers of Guru Gobind Singh but also the foreign historians have abundantly acknowledged and praised his wisdom, vision, divine dare, bravery, humanity, nobility, agility, magnetic personality, strength and stamina. He was a peerless poet, doyen of philosophy very great scholar, orator and invincible soldiers and commander in the battle-field. He organised and inspired the Khalsa in the unique way for which he renowned writer have described him like a Grecian Law Giver. He rejected the Brahmnical caste system and baptised the Khalsa out of the people of all castes, high and low, rich and poor, cobbler and Brahman, Shudra and untouchable alike, producing a matchlessly strong human alloy from the dregs of the Hindu society.

He seriously and devotedly assimilated the teachings of his martyr father, Guru Tegh Bahadur who said, " O NANAK LISTEN, ONLY HE IS TO BE DESCRIBED AS A GYANI OR ENLIGHTENED PERSON WHO NEITHER FRIGHTENS ANYBODY NOR IS AFRAID OF ANYBODY". The saint-soldier or Sant-Sipahi Guru Gobind Singh provided all the intellectual and physical environments and opportunities by the virtue of which his followers became the true saint-soldiers to protect the freedom of their culture and country. If on the one hand he had collected and patronised 52 scholars and poets, to pursue and spread their scholarly achievements, on the other hand the tyrant Aurangzeb, his troops, his touts and his Governors or Subas, were passing sleepless nights and dreadful days because of their fear from Guru Gobind Singh and his brave Khalsa soldiers.

Guru Gobind Singh had four sons. The two elders: Ajit Singh and Jujhar Singh and the two, youngers : Zorawar Singh and Fateh Singh in the order of their respective ages. Besides, their mother, the four brother had the consoling, caring, enlightening, encouraging and inspiring love of their grand-mother Mata Gujri, to follow the footprits of their great-father, grand-father and father. So, they developed their devotion to their faith and patriotism towards their motherland, in their very childhood.

Human nature is very strange. From the view point of fortitude, a hero of the present movement may become a traitor of the next moment. After all, what is heroism ? I think this is the victorious passing through a certain moment of misery and suffering, we may say, endurance when one is at the most critical point to bend or bow so that one may not break. Anyhow, as it has happened in the history of many nations and organisations, such a day came in the lives of some Sikhs, besieged by the myriads of the Army of Aurangzed, in the fort of Anandgarh, at Anandpur Sahib. The provisions had run short. The feed of the horses had been exhausted. Nothing could be taken into or out of the besieged fort. No communication was possible. The Guru and his brave Sikhs would never surrender to the enemy under any amount of hardship. So, the starving Sikhs kept coming out of the fort in the groups of five to fight with the enemies who were better armed, fully and richly fed and far more superior in numbers. The Sikhs fought like hungry lions and embraced death as true heroes whose inspiring deeds always decorate the history of nations. The enemies were perusading the Guru and the Sikhs to vacate the fort and go anywhere they could for a protective resort, on the solemn oath of not attacking the vacating Sikhs. Some Sikhs in the fort wanted to vacate the fort but Guru Gobind Singh never agreed to the proposal as he knew the cunning and lie of Aurangzeb, his Muslim army and his allies, the Hindu Rajput Rajas of Shivalik Hills. The Guru knew that out in the open the Moghul Army and its commanders as instructed by Aurangzeb, would betray their oath taken on the Holy Koran and on the Cow as taken by the Hindu allies. So, they would attack the Sikhs without any compuncation or moral consideration. Forty Sikhs, under the leadership of Bhai Mahan Singh determined to leave the fort. They gave a written "Bedava" or disclaimer to the Guru saying, "Neither you are our Guru nor we are your Sikhs and hereby we leave the fort". This was the hardest hit that could be given to him and that also at that critical juncture. At any cost, he never wanted the unwilling allies to be with him. He quietly but meticulously preserved that piese of paper, right in his pocket and let them go. Hence I cannot help realinsing the clairvoyance of the Guru as after some time all those 40 deserters joined with him in the battle of Muktsar, embraced martyrdom led by their same leader, Bhai Mahan Singh who while bleeding and breathing his last begged for tearing away the disclaimer to pardon them. What a wonder of history. Although the Guru had lost his home and all his kith and kin including his sons, mother and wife, yet that piece of paper was intact in his pocket, carefully preserved like his own soul. He wiped the bleeding face of Bhai Mahan Singh, patted him on his shoulders and kissed his forehead, tearing out the disclaimer into pieces. The dying martyr gave a last smile of divine joy and died in an ecstatic peace as a leader of not the deserters but those of the 40 "Muktas" or the emancipated ones.

The misery within Anandgarh Fort increased by leaps and bounds. Most of the inmates wanted to leave the fort. Inspite of knowing the treachery of the enemies, the democratic Guru bowed to the will of his Comrades. It was the dark night of the 20th and 21st of December, 1704 A.D. It was Wednesday. The Guru and his 1,500 other soldiers including his old mother, two wives and four sons, all left the fort.

The teacherous foes behaved as the Guru had expected from them. They attacked the starved Sikhs who were like a pinch of salt in a large heap of flour : just 1,500 out of which only 500 were riding the horses. The drawn appeared when the Sikhs reached Kiratpur Sahib, advancing towards Rapar to cross the

Sirsa river on the way. The defensive marching fight of the Sikhs with the Moghul army, became severer and severer till they reached Sirsa at the night-fall of the 21st of December, 1704. Most of the Sikhs had already been killed, wounded and plundered in their bloody journey from Anandpur Sahib to the bank of Sirsa. Then the enemies found a golden opportunity to attack the Sikhs who were crossing the hissing waves of the angry Sirsa, frantically in flood.

Although the Sikhs and the Guru gave an heroic and examplary fight to the chasing enemy, yet many Sikhs were killed or washed away by the currents of water. Thinking intrinsically, the greatest loss was the washing away of the manuscripts prepared by the hardwork of 52 poets and scholars who pored over books for many years. They were lovingly patronised by Guru Gobind Singh. The men may come and men may go but the manuscripts devoured by the waves of Sirsa could never by regained. How can this loss ever by made good? Only imagination can answer this question.

Only 163 Sikhs could cross the Sirsa, alive. Guru's wives got separated in the tumult of the fight, darkness and the ravage of Sirsa. So, were also separated his two younger sons, Zorawar Singh and Fateh Singh alongwith their grand-mother, Mata Gujri and similarly Guru Gobind Singh, alongwith his two elder sons, Ajit Singh and Jujhar Singh were separated alongwith 150 Sikhs. All the three separated groups ran for their lives, before the chase of the enemies, in any direction their eyes could see safety and their feet could carry them. After many days, Guru's wives reached Delhi, led and escorted by Bhai Daya Singh, the first of the five baptised by Guru Gobind Singh as the Khalsa. The Guru crossed Ropar still fighting with the enemies, who were in hot pursuit to kill or capture him alive. He lost his many companions alongwith horses. The 22nd of December, Thursday, passed in skirmishes.

Again the pitch-black night came. Out of 150 comrades of the Guru, after crossing Sirsa, only 40 were left alive. They entered the mud-fortress in the village of Chamkaur. The enemies besieged it, in cordons round cordons. Guru Gobind Singh's two elder sons Ajit Singh and Jujhar Singh brevely fought to death, killing many enemies and eventually were killed before the very eyes of their father and Guru. All the 40 Sikhs also fought one by one and embraced death as martyrs who sent the Guru out of the fortress under the blanket of the black night. The Guru tried his best to fight to his death also, but the last five comrades commanded him to leave the fortress. He had to obey their Gurmata or Guru-willed-resolution as in the Sikh faith the unity of five or more true devotees compose "Sangat" or holy congregation which is higher than even the Guru. Such is the theo-philosophical and democratic Sikh faith or religion. So, the Guru left the fortress with a pledge to the five behesters to carry on his campaign of putting an end to the Moghul fanatic tyranny to uproot it from the soil of India.

What did happen to Zorawar Singh, Fateh Singh and their old grandmother, Mata Gujri? They were taken by their Brahman cook named Gangoo to his native village of Saheri near Morinda or Baganwala with a pledge to give them a secure shelter to prove his loyalty of a faithful servant. The old mother Gujri and children had a halterful of valuables, including jewels and golden coins, carried by a mule. As a touchstone tests gold, gold tests man. The old lady and children who had undergone untold hardships, fight, fatigue and ferocity of fate, fell into sound sleep. The lustre of gold and lust for gold, unfeeling and remorseless is the last corruption of a degenerate man. Gold turned the head of the hyprocrite Brahmin. He stole the halterful of valuables and shouted aloud, "thief, thief, thief". Mata Gujri was awakened and alarmed with a noise. The children got up. But alas! Their halter of valuables was missing. The old hard-hit lady cool-headedly discussed the matter with Gangoo and calmly tried to make him realise the sin of his batrayal. She implored even to share the wealth with her but keep the secret of giving them shelter so that the enemies in pursuit might not catch them. Of all the vices to which human nature is subject, treachery is the most infamous and detestable, being composed of fraud, cowardice and revenge. So, the coward Gangoo, determined to take revenge of the allegation of being a thief.

The heartless Brahmin informed Wazir Khan, the then Muslim Suba of Governor of Sirhind, of the stay of Mata Gujri and her two young and innocent grand-sons. He curried favour with the Governor describing his hospitality as a snare to help the Muslim rulers to arrest Guru Gobind Singh's mother and his two younger sons. He tried to prove himself to be the loyal informer of the Government. The reverenced Mother Gujri and her grand-sons were got arrested by the Governor. They were taken to Sarhind where they were confined to a domed room called "Thanda Burj" or "Chilly Tomb". All the three parts of the separated family did not know anything about one another's plight. It was killing cold in the month of December. No clothes or beds were provided to the innocent prisoners to callously torture them.

It was the 25th of December, the Christmas Day of 1704 A.D. The X-mas was being celebrated all over the Christian world and the children were being presented with beautiful gifts and sweets but Zorawar Singh and Fateh Singh were handcuffed and taken to the court of Sarhind where all were simply struck with their beauty, deportment and dignity. All were moved with final love for the innocent children. Wazir Khan, the Governor himself was present and the Mullahs, Muftis and Qazis were frightening them to embrace Islam or to espouse death in the cruellest way. Mata Gujri had sent them to the Court tying beautiful turbans on their heads, patting on their backs, remember God, truth, your father's present struggle and your forefathers who sacrificed their lives for their faith and freedom. Maintain their high spiritual and partioic perstige. God shall welcome you in heaven". Both brothers touched the feet of their grandmother, smiled, gazed into her eyes and re-assured her, "Respected

Grand Ma, we will happily sacrifice our lives but will never betray our faith".

They entered the Court with a loud Sikh war slogan "Bolay So Nihall, Sat-Siri Akall" (Whosover utters the Name of the Eternal God shall be blessed). Then they emphatically and fearlessly uttered, "Wahe Guru Ji Ka Khalsa, Wahe Guru Ji Ki Fateh" (The Khalsa belongs to the Lord and so his victory also belongs to Him). All the pressures, persuasions, threats and temptations could not cut any ice with them, come what may, and they would not renounce their faith to accept Islam in order to save their lives. All the audience were astonished at their fearlessness when none was there to plead their case or help them in any way. Anyhow, "they were given another day to reappear in the Court and were taken back to their grand-mother. This was another way to weaken their determination. They passed another night exposed to freezing cold, but with a sweet resignation to the will of the Lord. Next day, again the same drama was repeated by the Muslim authorities giving the worst threats but they were spurned away by the children still more chivalrously. The night of 26th of December passed in the same plight of the confinement.

The 27th of December, 1704 appeared with the red dawn full of blood of those two brothers. It was the final chance to pardon them for life, if they could accept Islam. Mother Gujri died of cold in that domed and domed room. Zorawar Singh (literally, the Powerful Lion) and Fateh Singh (literally, the Victorious Lion), finally told the Governor not to protract his decision and do whatever he wanted to do, at the earliest. The beauty, divinely blessed behaviour of the children for their faith and their diginity had fascinated all the people who had seen them, including Wazir Khan who wanted them to accept Islam.

No argumentation of the Mullas and Muftis could influence the Shaibzadas, the sons of the respected Guru, to budge even an inch from their original andunshakable stand. At last, Wazir Khan himself addressed the children, saying "Look, you are innocent children, beautiful and impressive. I do not want to kill you and if I set you free, out of mercy for you, what would you do when you have lost your parents, brothers, home and supporting Sikhs." History relates that both of them shouted with burning ire, "We will organise the disbanded Sikhs and give an examplary fight to a tyrant ruler like you." He could not expect such an answer from them and so was cut to the quick. He again questioned them, "All right, if you are defeated having so meagre the military resources in the face of the imperial Mughal power, then what will you do?' They again roared with one voice like the wounded lions, Wicked Wazir Khan, we do not care for victory or defeat which are in the hands of God. We will incessantly fight against your tyranny till our last breath."

All were stunned to hear these words which fell on Wazir Khan and other Muslim zealots like the molten lava of a volcano. He was enraged like a burning cinder and instantly ordered to execute them, making them stand within the bricks of a new wall to be built around them. Out of all the audience, only Sher Mohammad Khan, the ancestor of the present Nawab of Malerkotla, condemned the heinous order of Wazir Khan and he walked out of the Court as a protest, although many more felt so much compassion for the children. Yet due to the fear of the Royal power and the "Fatwa" (punishment) passed by the Mullahas, all tongues remained sealed.

Zorawar Singh and Fateh Singh were made to stand within the bricks of a wall being built forthe fatar purpose. It was raied by the mason brick-by-brick and with every layer of lthe bricks, the children were asked to yield to the behest of the Governor, but everytime they snubbed the tyrant with their courage of conviction. They neither trembled, nor cringed, nor cried, nor wailed, nor wept. As the wall became higher and higher, their eyes sparkled, emitting divine light and a beam of smile spread on their faces. At last they raised the Sikh war slogan with a sky-rending voice when the executioner cut off their heads.

Thus they became immortal martyrs and every drop of their blood inspired and created thousands of more martyrs who uprooted the fanatic and calloous Moghul empire from the soil of India. Certainly, Zorawar Singh and Fateh Singh upheld and confirmed the greatness of their forefather, Aurangzeb and Wazir Khan could not finish them as they eternally live in the hearts of millions of people to inspire their children, generation after generation!!!

SEWA PANTH AND NIRMAL PANTH

4

Sewa Panth and Nirmal Panth

SEWA PANTH

The Sikh Gurus were humanist par excellence. They had put man in centre and endeavoured hard to bring him solace and salvation. They not only tried to uplift man on religious plane but also endeavoured to improve the lot of man on religious political plane. Guru Gobind Singh addressed himself to man 'qua man' without the narrow distinctions and antagonisms of east and west, Hindu and Muslim, Masjid and Mandir. The west was not so prominent a factor of influence in India during the 17th century, yet the writings and teachings of the Guru resounded with international humanitarian overtones. That there is no difference between man and man is clearly portrayed by the tenth Guru in the following words :—

> One man by shaving his head to become a holy monk
> Another sets up as a yogi or some other kind of ascetic
> some call themselves Hindus: other call themselves Musalmans
> Among these are the Shiahs, they are sunnis also
> And yet man is of one race in all the world.
> God as creator and God as good
> God in His Bounty and God in His Mercy
> Is all one God. Even in our errors we should not separate God from God
> Worship the one God, for all men the one Divine Teacher
> All men have the same form
> All men have the same soul.

The discrimination between man and man is altogether excluded and the central theme of all activities should be welfare and upliftment of the man.

This theme of the Gurus, on operational place, found expressions in the Gurus' wars, their literary compositions and their actions. It also found its expression in the activities of the order of the Seva Panthis—followers of Path of Service whose sole aim is to see to the welfare of human beings without cherishing any desire for fruit or reward in the mundane sense. They were in fact motivated by purely altruistic impulses.

The founder of this order was Bhai Ghaniya, who belonged to Sodra, a village in Gujranwala district and was Dhamman Kashatri. Since his childhood, he had religious propensies and showed signs of transcending narrow-mindedness and egocentricity. When he was ten years old, he happened to go to Anandpur along with his father, and was much impressed by the towering. personality of the ninth Guru. He again went to Anandpur at the age of sixteen. This time he felt so much attached with the Guru's mission that he decided to pass his life in serving the Guru, and for the Guru's cause. He was handsome, well-built and intelligent. His parents wanted him to marry but he chose to work for the Guru's cause which, in fact, was no other than the people's cause. In spite of the best efforts of his parents, he refused to marry not because he did not believe in this institution, but because he did not want to give divided attention to his mission.

All records show that Bhai ji engrossed himself in rendering service to the Guru, individuals and the people in general. He felt pleasure in rinsing utensils, cleansing campus of Guru ka Langar (Guru's kitchen), bringing water for the kitchen as well as for the thirsty travellers. He slept very little, hardly four hours at night. All the time his attention was fixed on the Great God and his creations. He would spare not even a second without doing something for the people. Bhai ji enjoyed the sweet utterances of the ninth Guru, was elevated by his hallowed darshan and was transported to eternal Bliss by his instructions. He was lucky enough to accompany Guru Tegh Bahadur in his eastern tours. He drank deep at the fountain of Gurbani. He very unassumingly but steadily served the people irrespective of their beliefs and group affiliations.

His dress used to be made of home-spun coarse cloth, expressive of his simplicity and honest living. He was extremely humble and, as a matter of fact, humility was his root tendency. Sometimes when Guru Tegh Bahadur out of amusement told him that people had lodged complaints against him, he would at once say—

"We are stained by the sins which are numerous; only God can purify us."

Guru Tegh Bahadur was executed under orders of Aurangzeb on the 11th November, 1676. Bhai Ghaniya suffered a mental shock at the gruesome execution and could recover only after some time.

As time rolled by, Bhai ji's zeal for sewa (service) redoubled. Day in and day out,he was busy with assuaging the afflicted, dressing the wounds, providing water to the thirsty and comforting the comfortless. Service had become the reeling passion of his life. Bhai ji participated in his own humble way in all the activities of Guru Gobind Singh. He watched for himself the hostility of Hill Chiefs and its implications, and the attitude of the Mughal Government vis-a-vis the Sikhs and their Guru Gobind Singh.

In A.D. 1704 the battle of Anandpur ensued. The enemy forces consisted of the armies of Hill States, of Sirhind and of irregulars such as Ranghars and Gujjars. The Guru had also collected nearly ten thousand men. Although this number was insignificant as compared to the strength of the enemy, yet on the Guru's side there was will of the people to fight and die for their Master.

The actual warfare started on May 20, 1704. The Sikhs fought valiently with the result that the enemy's hope for having easy victory was dashed to the ground.

One day complaints were made to the Guru that a Sikh, Ghaniya by name, had been serving water and rendering first aid not only to the Sikhs but to the wounded enemy. The Guru called Ghaniya and enquired if it was true. The humble Ghaniya replied that he had been serving those who fell in the battlefield. "My eyes could not distinguish between Sikhs and Mughals, as I saw Guru's face in everyone." The Guru appreciated him and remarked that he had really understood his mission. As a mark of approval of his action, the Guru gave him a box of ointment with the mark that he should not serve water alone to the wounded in the battle-field but also ointment to the wounded to ensure their speedy recovery. According to Bhai Kahan Singh the Guru, as a token of his pleasure for his humanistic work, gave him a bed and a handkerchief.

The gifts from the Guru inspired him all the more and he collected round himself a band of the Sikhs, ever prepared to put in service for the people. Guru Gobind Singh evacuated Anandpur on the night of 5-6 December, 1705. The enemy forgot all about their pledges and set out in hot pursuit immediately. Realising the impending danger, Guru Gobind Singh gave a band of 50 men to Bhai Udai Singh and charged him with the responsibility of checking the enemy's advancement. Bhai Udai Singh fought a bloody battle at Shahi Tibbi with the enemy with a handful of his men; all of them perished fighting covering themselves with imperishable glory.

When the battle of Shahi Tibbi was being fought, Guru Gobind Singh along with his men had reached the bank of the Sarsa River. It was now almost the day-break. About this time, the enemy forces mustered themselves to attack the Guru. The Guru ordered Jiwan Singh, a Ranghretta Sikh, to encounter the pursuers and himself with the rest of the people plunged into the flooded Sarsa River. There was confusion all around. Many persons were swept to death by the fast moving water and many more were scattered. Bhai Ghaniya also lost track of the Guru. He moved about in the Malwa region of the Panjab till he reached some place near Jagraon. A Bairagi Sadhu who met him there told him the whereabouts of his Guru. Bhai ji felt overjoyed and lost no time in reaching Talwandi Saboki where the Guru gave him an affectionate pat and told him to devote exclusively to the dissemination of Sikh tenets. Bhai ji stayed for some time with the Guru, but when the Guru moved to the Deccan, he, along with his associatges, undertook tours in different parts of the Panjab, acquainting the people with the Guru's faith and putting in service for the benefit of the people. He could persuade the people to put in joint effort to alleviate their difficulties. He could inspire them to sink wells or to dig tanks to overcome the need of water. He, on his part, would march with vessels full of water laden on both sides of the hump of a string of camels so that he might provide relief too the areas suffering from the shortage of water. He would also provide spiritual balm to the tension-ridden minds of the people.

He established various temples, then known as Dharamshalas where he made arrangements for the propagation of Guru's views and philosophy. Having done a lot of work in Majha and Malwa, he left for the south western Punjab and spread the Guru's Gospel in the villages of Jhang Manghiana and Dera Ismail. He wanted to advance to the province of Sind as well, but he dropped this idea, probably he thought it more useful to convert Sewa Ram who was born at Hyderabad (India) and whose mother had died and father had left home in search of peace and had undertaken tour of different sacred places to find the way to bliss. When he came across Bhai Ghaniya, he felt peculiar placidity and requested Bhai ji to initiate him into his into his order and give him instructions. Bhai ji then acquainted him with the teachings of the Gurus and the regard with which the tenet of service is Sikhism. He said, "To provide comforts to all human beings irrespective of their forms and affiliations and to have faith in the teachings of the gurus in our only advice.'

After this, Bhai ji and Sewa Ram entered the province of Sind. They sojourned at Nurpur. Finding there is a scarcity of water, a programme of sinking well was launched. Sewa Ram took leading part in this work. Bhai ji, infact, used to eliminate egocentricity by putting in service for the people. Service was also rendered in the construction of the Dharamshala of Nurpur. A Dharamshala was also established at Lao Nagar which is situated near Jhang Manghiana. At this place, Ghaniya won over another disciple Addan Shah who had learnt Panjabi from an Uddasi Sait, Gurdas and who possessed religious bent of mind, saturated with love for everyone. In this way, many persons became Bhai ji's followers, and a separate order emerged known in history, as Sewa Panth, the Path of Service. Bhai Ghaniya died but his order carried on his work un-interruptedly. Wherever the members of this order went they preached human sympathy, selflessness, universal brotherhood and since they always evoked respect for themselves, they by implication ender Sikhism among the people. In the later Mughal period if the general Musalmans did not dislike the Sikhs, and Sikhism was regarded as a balm for the afflicted humanity, much of the credit goes to them.

After Ghaniya's death the work was carried on under the over-all guidance of Sewa Ram. Sewa Ram's headquarter was at Nurpur (Sind) wherefrom he used to fan out in different directions to serve the people to make them realise the importance of truthful living.

After Bhai Sewa Ram, his disciple Bhai Santokh Singh took charge of the headquarter. Bhai Santokh Singh belonged to the village, Khari. He, during his life time, had been instructed by Sewa Ram who said, "Recognise the light within every body, serve all and raise yourself above worldly attachments."

Bhai Santokh Singh was succeeded by Bhai Budhan Ram and Sahib Ram. Sewa Panthis from Nurpur headquarter had been rendering yeoman's service to the people.

Bhai Ghaniya's another disciple, Addan Shah also made a mark in rendering service to the people. He belonged to village Lao and often lived there. He stayed at Phagwara and Kartarpur also. He did a lot of travelling, to sacred places. He had his admirers among big zamindars and masses alike. His charismatic personality won over quite a large number of disciples. He used to spin coarse yarn, prepare ink for his livelihood. He advised his disciples also to earn livelihood through honest earning, without becoming rich. In 1757 this great man expired at Jammu. This was the time when Panjab was suffering from political termoil caused by Ahmed Shah Abdali's invasion.

After 1757, Sewa Panthis made a lot of progress as regards general popularity and organisation. Many Dharamshalas were raised in different parts of the country. Bhai Aya Ram, Bhai Ranga ji, Bhai Daya Ram, Bhai Dayal, Bhai Soma, Bhai Paras Ram were the most important among many Sewa Panthis of the later Mughal period. Paras Ram being a *Pingal* could not walk easily, but still the zest for service which he showed was unsurpassed. The Dharamshala from where he operated still stands in the Jangi Shivala Bazaar, Amritsar. He and his disciples did not allow the earthen lamp to extinguish in Hari Mandir during the times of Zakariya Khan when the Government was bent upon destroying the Sikhs root and branch.

Many other Sewa Panthis served Sikhism and people. Bhai Jawahar Singh of Mitha Tiwana was another luminary of the galaxy of the line who served the people from 1900 to 1950. Now his disciple Sant Nischal Singh ji has been serving the people of Haryana from his headquarter at Jagadhari.

The Sewa Panthi order was just like the Servants of the People's Society of the Red Cross Society whose objective is to bring about consciousness among people to love one-another, to help one-another and to respect one-another. The members of this order were committed to the aforesaid objectives and regarded service (Sewa) as the true path to salvation, for doing service unto others was possible only when one had transcended narrowself.

For their own sustenance, they did not like depending upon alms or collecting their requirements through begging. Unlike many orders of saints in India, they never roamed about begging the eatables or other requisite things.

Bhai Aya Ram advised Bhai Dharm Das, "Never get offerings, Live upon the earning of your labour. Make ropes or strings out of hemp yarn, sell them and live by the earnings you get. Bhai Bhall Ram said to his disciples, "You should not keep more than five rupees with you. More wealth distracts one from social service." Addan Shah's advice was that his disciples should work honestly and diligently. He said, "the ropes must be made nicely; the work to be done should be done properly."

One can adopt any profession according to one's capacity and capability. If one did not know making ropes, one could cut grass and sell in the market. According to Dr. Balbir Singh, "Each Sewa Panthi must do some labour. If one cannot do hard labour, one can adopt such jobs which involve less labour; one could prepare ink or pens made of reed. Addan Shah himself wrote books."

Sewa Panthis were prohibited to get loans because they wanted to keep themselves at a safe distance from the implications which were bound to flow from money transactions. They believed in distributing their everything among the people. Bhai Ram Kishen never felt any hesitation while giving even his clothes and shoes to the needy.

Sewa Panthis did not believe in married life. They looked down upon woman and considered her 'a temptress'. When Bhai Bhall went to Nurpur to see Bhai Aya Ram, he got made a veil to be hung between him and the people around so that ladies should not come to him. It is recorded that henceforward. ladies saluted him from outside only.

Sewa Panthis is an order of just monastic order of the Christians in the medieval age. But whereas the Christian monastic order turned to be the hot-bed of intrigues and centre of corruption, Sewa Panthis could keep themselves above these things. The reasons probably were their emphasis on living through honest earnings and keeping needs to the bare minimum.

The source of inspiration of Sewa Panthis is ten Gurus and Guru Granth Sahib. They upto Addan Shah, did not have any particular dress but after Addan Shah they began to wear simple cloth-made caps on their heads and an unstitched sheet of cloth round to cover the lower part of their bodies. Short shirts were used to cover the upper parts of their bodies. They were not particular keeping long hair (Keshas) although Bhai Ghaniya had grown them. Sewa Ram and Addan Shah had never shaved. They were fond of white clothes.

The term 'Nirmal Panth' is as old as Sikhism itself. What is the etymology of term? The reply to this question is given by Kanwar Mrigindra Singh. He says, "The religious order started by Guru Nanak was without any particular form and just comprised the teachings of Guru Nanak and righteous living taught by him to his pupils. But in the course of time, other schools found it necessary to refer to it by some name, for the name 'Sikh' was then ambiguous being used by the Budhhists, Yogis of Gorakh and the followers of all Hindu schools. Therefore, Guru Nanak's school with its emphasis on purity was referred to as the pure path (Nirmal Panth) by others and later even by Guru Nanak's Sikhs in reference to themselves for their distinction." Bhai Gurdas refers to Guru Nanak's school Nirmal Path (Pure Path). Similarly Bhatts use this term in reference to Guru Amar Das and Guru Arjan Dev.

Upto Guru Gobind Singh's time no distinction was made between Nirmal Panth and other names 'Nanak Panth', 'Gurmukh Panth' and 'Guru Sikh Panth'.

But with Guru Gobind Singh, the annotation did not remain as wide as it was before; it began to be used in reference to a particular school commited to definite goals and programmes.

As it is well- known Guru Gobind Singh matured and concretised most of his plans at Panota—one of those plans was the propagation of Sikhism through the medium of literature throughtout India. It was with this object that Guru Gobind Singh wanted to establish a special order of his Sikhs particularly to make comparative study of religions and also interpret classical Indian tradition in terms of the basic philosophy of Sikhism.

The project thus conceived had incidental advantages as well. Since times immemorial learning and teaching had been the exclusive privilege of Brahmins, Sanyasis or Vairagis (ascetics); but the project of the Guru was sure to give a strong blow to the idea of class learning and of missionaries belonging to a particular caste.

Since most of the classical Indian religious literature was available in Sanskrit, the Guru found it imperative to make arrangement for the teaching of Sanskrit to his followers. Accordingly, Guru Gobind Singh asked his court poet Pandit Raghu Nath to do the needful. The Pandit politely and very diplomatically replied that he was prohibited by convention to teach the language of the Gods (Deva Bhasha) and the holy scriptures to non-dvijas, i.e. Shudras and women. Guru Gobind Singh admonished him for his ego and pride for his most unreasonable stand. The same day, Guru Gobind Singh also invited the udasis to assist him in seeing his plans through.

They also did not respond and were not ready to effect any change in their traditional outlook and approach.

Ultimately, the Guru selected a dozen of Sikhs from all classes, castes and sent them to Benaras. Their names were (1) Pnadit Karma Singh, (2) Pandit Rama Singh, (3) Pandit Ganda (Singh), (4) Pandit Vir (Singh), (5) Pandit Sobha Singh, (6) Dharam Singh, (7) Daya Singh, (8) Kesar Singh, (9) Mukham Singh, (10) Gian Singh, (11) Gaja Singh, (12) Chanda Singh, (13) Saina Singh. All these chosen Sikhs studied under the guidence of Pandit Sadda Nand for six years. In the seventh year, they came back to the Guru who now had shifted to Anandpur.

Guru Gobind Singh was much pleased to find that they had become really good scholars and allotted them different duties. Pandit Karma Singh was asked to give sermons on Guru Granth Sahib in the Guru's court in the morning.

He did his job meticulously and nicely. The Guru having been deeply impressed by his exposition directed Bhai Mani Singh to become his student and learn six *darsanas.* Within a short time quite a few hundred scholars belonging to all castes were ready for missionary work.

As the number of Nirmalas increased, they were divided into two distinct branches: (i) Nirmal saints who wore the ascetic pink (Bhagva) robe given by the Guru and did not marry though they did not prohibit it, and in fact asked people to live a pious married life; (ii) the Nirmalas who adored white clothes. The latter were further split into two categories: the unmarried among them were referred to 'saint' but the married were referred to as Giani (knowledged).

Nirmalas exerted a lot to disseminate Sikhism and to bring about general awakening among people. In the life time of Guru Gobind Singh, by his orders, Bhai Punjab Singh Nirmala came to Punjab, settled down at Khadur. He so identified himself with the cause of the people that they adored him and thought it a good luck to enter into Sikh fold. His grand pupil Racha Singh Nirmala was responsible for conversion, on a large scale, in the predominant Muslim areas of Kashmir and Pothohar (West Punjab).

After the death of Guru Gobind Singh, the Nirmalas spared no paints to spread the message of the Guru. They acted not only as torch bearer of Sikhism but also as consience keepers and political advisers of the Sikhs. When differences arose between Vinodh Singh Trehan (in the seventh generation of Guru Angad Dev), Dharam Singh Nirmala advised him to leave Banda Singh Bahadur in larger interest of the Sikhs. It was again Baba Dharam Singh who brought Vinodh Singh in touch with Baba Dip Singh and Baba Ala Singh the founder of Patiala State). Baba Ala Singh took Khande-ki-Pahul in which Baba Dharam Singh, Baba Vinod Singh and Baba Dip Singh acted as Piyaras. Baba Ala Singh so much appreciated the sagacity of Baba Dharam Singh that he gave the land where theceremony was held to Baba Gurmukh Singh Nirmala, a pupil of Baba Dharam Singh Nirmala. One of the Punj Piyaras, Bhai Durgah Singh Nirmala settled down at Kankhal (two miles from Haridwar, U.P.). He was a great marks-man. He fought for Rai Ahmed of Najibabad against the Rohilas. Since Rai Ahmed of Najibabad was victorious, he offered a grant of land to Bhai Durgah Singh Nirmala on account of his service. Sant Nikka Singh was given a gift of thirty villages by Bibi Pradhan, the daughter of Bhai Ala Singh. Santji refused to accept such a big grant for his maintenance and only kept one village, named Khudi near Barnala. Many other such gifts were given to the Nirmalas by the Khalsa for their much-needed services to them.

Sardar Bhyan Singh of Shahbad willed his estate to Sant Karm Singh Nairmala (Chote). Sardar Ganda Singh of Bhangi Misl offered thirteen villages to Sant Jai Singh Nirmala who instead of keeping it for himself passed it on to Udasi Dera of Santokh Das. Similarly Sardar Sadda Singh of Bahirwala gave a patta of seven villages to Sant Bhagat Singh Nirmala in the year A.D. 1766. The offer was declined by the Sant but the Patta is still available at Bunga of Mana Singh Wala, Amritsar. Sardar Jai Singh's daughter-in-law donated two villages in favour of the Nirmala Dera at Kankhal.

In the year 1796, Maharaja Ranjit Singh offered a written sanad to Sant Nihal Singh Nirmala. The Sant passed on the property to Udasi Akhara of Santokh Das.

In the years when there was comparative peace in the Punjab after the failure of Ahmed Shah Abdali in his invasion. Nirmalas stepped up their activities of proselytization. It was during this period that they started visiting different places of the time of the Hindu festivals to conduct their missionary work. This thing as well as the exclusive patronage of the Sikh Chiefs to the Nirmalas caused a lot of heart-burning among the Hindu sects of *Sannyasis* and *Vairagies* who had always thought that the giffts would be given only to them by the chiefs.

The heart-burning led, not unoften, to serious quarrels. At the Kumbh Mela of 1807 at Haridwar there was a polemical discussion between the Nirmalas on one side and the *Sannyasis* and *Bairagis* on the other. The Nirmalas made such a great philosophical impact on the people by showing the distinction between Guru Nanak's spirit-temporal philosophy and other schools of socio-religious philosophy that both Sannyasis and Vairagis accepted that a Nirmala whatever be his caste or creed, could enter any Hindu temple in India.

In the year 1819 at the Kumbha Mela at Kurukshetra the Vairagis physically led an attack on Nirmala gatherings and cut up Guru Granth Sahib with the sword.

This event caused a lot of stir among the Sikhs. The Udasis and Nirmalas put up a request to the various Sikh chiefs for help. Maharaja Karan Singh of Patiala, Sardar Karma Singh Nirmala of Shahbad with Nanu Singh of Shahbad, Sardar Rai Singh of Buria, Sardar Dasaundha Singh of Sadhora, Sardar Bhagat Singh of Malaud, Raja Jogh Singh of Kalsia, Sarda Rup Singh of Rupar and many other Sardars with their forces marched to Haridwar with the Maharaja of Patiala at head. The Sannyasis were easily put to fioght. The Vairagis were also taught a lesson, their camp near Dahsha Prajapati's temples, was ransacked and their monastries were razed to the ground. The Sannyasis were forced to abandon the malpractice of raising a rupee per person whose head was to be shaven there.

After this happening, the Nirmalas began to attend all the four Kumbha Melas at Haridwar, Nasik, Ujjain and Traveni. Most of the Gurdwaras at such places owed their existence to them. The 'Gurdwara Pakki Sangat of Traveni' built to perpetuate the memory of Guru Tegh Bahadur is with the Nirmalas even to-day.

It was through the sustained and consistent efforts of Nirmalas that many persons of the province of Sind (Now in Pakistan) came into the Sikh fold. In the recent past Sant Attar Singh did commendable work of proselytisation in Malwa. At present, Sant Harchand Singh Longowal, the most respect Sikh of the present times is doing invaluable work of rejuvenate the Sikh masses.

Nirmalas have done commendable work in the field of comparative study of classical philosophy and have written books of great value in this connection in Sanskrit, Berija, Hindi, Panjabi both in Gurmukhi script and Devnagri script. Sant Nikka Singh traslated Yoga Vasishtha into Braj and wrote it in Punjabi script. Sant Nihal Singh Nirmala wrote a Sanskrit commentary on the 'Japu' of Guru Granth Sahib. Tara Singh Narotam also produced a few good books such as Gurdwara Darshan etc. The Urdu Language was also enriched by them, as they produced a lot of literature in it for their missionary work.

In 1861 they set up their central organisation to co-ordinate their activities.

It was in this year that yellow flag of Guru Gobind Singh with 'Khanda' super-imposed was flown on the building known as 'Dhrma Dvaja' where the meeting was held to establish the aforesaid organisation.

The Nirmalas are the Khalsa, having full faith in Guru Granth Sahib, Khande-ki-Pahul, five 'akarsa' i.e. to say sword, unshora hair, a pair of shorts (Kachha), comb, iron bracelet. The names of all Nirmalas end with 'Singh'. They do not follow udasis who keep knotted hair (Jatas) and whose names end with 'Das'.

Though they adopt outer symbols, yet they are clear that these without inner purity and discipline have got no meaning. These days, their headquarter is at Kankhal.

SUKHMANI

5

Sukhmani

The Sukhmani is one of the books in the collection known as the *Granth Sahib.* It is a wonderful scripture, the *Sikh Granth.* The Rishis composed the *Upanishads* in quiet communion with Nature. And the Sikh Guru Arjun sat in a tent pitched in a beautiful spot of Nature to compile hymns. He brought together in one book the hymns of Hindu saints and Muslim Fakirs. *Granth* is a scripture of synthesis. There were many Hindus and Muslims who persecuted the Guru for having compiled this scripture of synthesis. Who was he, they argued, to speak of Allah in the same breath with Rama? There were *Kazis* and *Pandits* who complained that the *Granth* had hymns in which Muslim saints and Hindu Gods were spoken of with contempt. The complaints reached the ears of Akbar. That Muslim king was himself in search of some message of synthesis; and on listening to hymns from the *Granth* he said:— "It is a volume worthy of reverence." This scripture was completed in 1604. After three centuries it still has a message for us, a message for the world. Out of World-Soul it rolled. Sukhmani is but one section of this world-scripture.

There are hymns in the *Granth* composed and sung by other Gurus and *bhaktas* and simply brought together by Guru Arjun; but the Sukhmani is a song composed by the Guru himself. Sukhmani is an outpouring of the Guru's soul. The Guru can be viewed in four aspects as an organiser, a poet, a seer of a synthesis, a martyr of faith, as a collosal figure. He lived in the sixteenth century. We of the twentieth may boast of 'science' and 'civilization'. We feel as pigmies in his presence; He organised the Sikhs into a community. He completed the tanks of Amritsar. He extended the city of Ramdaspur. He planned the Harmandir. He founded Taran Taran. He purchased land to build another city and named it Kartarpur. And this organiser was a poet-seer. To him came a perception of the truth that there is one Religion in religions, as in the various forces of nature there is really but one Force, that which in Hindu books has been rightly named *Shakti* Guru Arjun saw the higher harmony of Hindu *bhakti* and Muslim mysticism. And he had the courage, rare in those days, to bring together in the *Granth Sahib,* the sayings of Hindu saints and Muslim *fakirs.* He suffered for it. He was tortured to death by the Government of his day. But he would not, for a moment, falter in his vision. He would not, he said to his king, change even an iota in the *Granth Sahib.* It could not be, "if he would change it, a scripture of synthesis, of human brotherhood," a scripture of that one Spirit "whom the sages call by many names." He preferred death to disloyalty to the faith of his soul. And he had the courage to say to his sovereign: "If in following the truth, this perishable body depart, I shall rejoice deeming it great good fortune."

In this saint dwelt a poet's soul. His hymns are a poet's offerings to the Spirit of Nature,—the Spirit of Humanity.

Make Truth thy prayer
Make Faith thy prayer-carpet
Thy body is the temple,
Thy conscience is the priest,
And the very pure God thy creed
Every heart is His casket,
Every thing is an extension of God:

The Guru's hymns are strewn with such passages at once tender in poetic beauty and philosophic in suggestiveness. "Sukhmani", dwelleth in the heart of the saints. And in the heart of Guru Arjan dwelt the Sukhmani. In his heart was the peace which comes of communion with the ideal. Sukhmani means "The peace (or joy) of the heart." Sukhmani as "Peace-Chant in the Guru's heart was only deepened by the agony of the last few days of his earth-life. Not many in the world's history have suffered in the spirit which sustained the Guru in those days when a cruel Government inflicted on his body indescrible tortures. It is the spirit which to him was of the essence of the Granth and which he expressed in three beautiful words:— Truth, patience and meditation. The Guru was loyal to truth; the Guru was patient in suffering; the Guru met the cruel torture of his body with the weapon of mediation. Blood corpuscles, we are told, swim about in a fluid which contains iron. Our blood has iron. Our blood needs iron. Without iron in the blood there would not be the flame of his life. This is true also meta-physical. The iron entered into the soul of Guru Arjan; and the flame of his life did not flicker. It seems to be will of God that spiritual iron should enter the soul of India for the fulfillment of India's destiny.

Some of the characteristics of the Sukhmani may be illustrated. It lacks dogmatism or speculative theology. Sukhmani is pre-eminently pratcial in its outlook upon the problems of life. When was the world created? How many spirits can dance on the point of a needle? Questions such as these engaged the attention of many theòlogians in Christian Europe during the pre-scientific era. Questions such as these are ignored by the Guru as having no reference to the life of religion. Such questions, are prejudicial to the development of spiritual life in the measure in which they disturb concentration on the vital values of religion. Sukhmani is a gospel of life with its note of devotion to the Ideal. yet a third characteristic of the book is its atmosphere of companionship with the Guru. Every hymn ends on the note: "Nanak says". Guru Arjan merges himself in the first Guru. The Sukmani is, in a deep spiritual sense, the voice of Guru

Nanak himself. There is a beautiful picture, painted by a devout Sikh. It represents Guru Nanak as sitting under the shade of a stately tree. On one side of the Master is Mardana, on the other side is Bala; and the Master is meditating on the mystery of the ages. Under such a tree was the Sukhmani sung by Guru Arjan and written under his dictation by a disciple for the *Granth*. And as I have recited the verses of the Sukhmni I have sometimes felt as though the infinite living Ideal was calling the soul to come and sit, as sat those dear disciples of the Gurus, under the shade of the Tree called in Hindu books the Trees of Life.

The message of the Sukhmani, is preeminently practical. It signs of peace. It also sings of the path to peace. The path is not one of ascentic abstraction from the world. It is a positive path. Through life must we attain to peace. In a beautiful text in the Sukhmani we are told that we are come to this world to get "merchandise". Vakhar is the word used. It means "goods", "merchandise". It suggests the meaning of life. Life, is a pilgrimage. Life, too, is regarded as a voyavge, the world, the *smsar*, being represented as a great sea. Life is a pilgrimage. Life is a voyage. But there is yet another, to my mind a more positive conception. We are in this world to get 'merchandise'. Not to gey away from the world, not to spurn it with the ascetic's scorn, but to have commerce, to carry on certain transactions with the infinite Ideal that calls us to Itself within the veils of time and space. We are in the world as merchants. Our business is to be rich. We are here to enrich ourselves. Life is enrichment. From the World-Heart we came to this earth-plane to gather experiences, to enrich ourselves. We are here to get *vakhar*.

This *aikhar* comes with discipline. The soul is enriched when she fulfils the obligations of life. One recalls the great teaching of Sri Krishana: "Do thy duty". To the Gurus, as to the *Rishis* of the Upanishads, the world had a meaning. Over and over again we read in the Sikh scriputres: "His name is Verity" Again : "He watcheth his own field, at once concealed and mainfest." Yes, He watchety His children in the field and wishes, none to leave his allotted space. In another text we read: "He who created the earth made men's coming and going" in order that men might have the discipline of life, and, cut and polished by pain, may shine in the temple of His servants. It is a three-fold lesson we learn in life's school of discipline. There is, first, the lesson of self-control. A boy is sent to the school. He must learn self-control if he would gather knowledge. Concentration is a form of self-control. The student grows to be man. He must think of his wife. Gradually the lesson is learnt that the marriage is not meant to be a romance, but a *Sadhan*; selfish impulses are aroused only to be subdued. The great lesson is learn that to live is to serve. The husband becomes the father of a family. A child falls ill. The father and mother must keep awake night to nurse the child. They must suffer for the sake of their darling. The child grown into manhood must forego many things for the sake of his aged parents. The great lesson is thus learnt that life's gifts are to be shared with others; are to be poured as a sacrifice on the altar of the Ideal.

Sadhan :— This is the first method of man's education and enrichment. Another method, too, is indicated in the Sukhmani. It is the method of *Sadh-Sang*, the method of fellowship with the *Sadhu*. Who are the *Sadhus*? The question is answered in a number of beautiful verses in the Sukhmani. *Sadhus* are servants of the Ideal. They are the wakened ones. We often sleep in forgetfulness. They are awake to the Ideal. "The beloved of my Lord are awake", says the Guru; "The sadhu lives in the world, but uncontaminated, as the lotus is untouched by the water." His nature, we read, is like that of fire which purifies everything. He is humble, "the dust of all men's feet." "He dwells in peace and is full of tender love." "Nectar rains from his glance." O God!", says the Guru "be gracious to me that my heart may become the dust of the *Sadhus'* feet." In another passage we read: "Reflect in association with the *Sadhus*." There are young men to-day who argue that thought and religion are in conflict. To them the Guru says: "Think, by all means; reflect : but in association with the good." Religion is not irrational; and in the Sukhmani there are passages of rare beauty bearing upon the value of knowledge in religious life. religion without reflective consciousness threatens to become superstition. Reflect; but, says the Guru, not in isolation. Reflect in fellowship with some of the great souls, the *Sadhu* who are in tune with verity. you need vibrations of the good to help you in your quest of Truth. The stimulus of environment helps much in developing thought. And if you are in contact with the environment of a *Sadhu-soul* you will be helped in your thinking. The higher consciousness, often staying below the threshold of waking consciousness, will be stimulated, and you will think better. In the society of the *Sadhus*, as we read in the Sukhmani, "the light of wisdom shines in a man's heart."

There is a third method of education also referred to in the Sukhmani. I may name it the method of inwardness. The Sukhmani signs, again and again, of meditation. The ideal is not afar, but within. In the shrine of the heart is the play of Its story. If we see It not, it is because we sleep on while the Beloved is awake. And even when some awakening comes, we do but wander like Arthur's knights, wander here and there in quest of the Ineffable Presence that is already in the House within. We go searching for Him abroad when He has entered unbidden the temple-niche of the heart and Himself lit the unused lamp to teach us how to worship Him.

Concerning this method of meditation, two things are emphasised in the Sukhmani. The first is : Meditaion on the Name of God.

> Ever ever repeat the Name,
> To utter the Name
> Standing sitting of sleeping
> Is ever the duty of Man
> Gods's Name is the sum-total of all faith.
> Nanak hath meditation on Thy Name

The true Name hath saved him
Men recite the Vadas and sastras to sevure muke
but superior to rites and ceremonies
Is the utterance of the Name
The most wicked sinners have been saved
By the Name

To utter the Name is to evoke an Idea and secure a link in the chain of harmony. But the name must be uttered with love. Meditation on the Name cannot draw us nearer the great Centre of Life if the heart lacks love. Meditation without love is empty. In a deeper sense, indeed, meditation without love a spiritual impossibility. Who there who will receive the "Treasure of His Name" in his Heart and not be stirred to the depths with love? Who will behold the lotus-feet of the Lord not fall down in reverent love?

In most moving stains do the Sikh hymns sing of love for the living Ideal:

With clasped hands Nanak hath entered Thy sanctuary
O beloved Lord! Grant him salvation.
A fish out of water dies being separated from water;
How can I live without the Beloved?
The deer faces the arrow;
Alas: it sacrifices its life
While absorbed in the joy of listening to the hunter's call
Mine eye-lids close not;
I am absorbed in the love of the Dear one
My mind anxiously loodeth for Him night and day
O Night! grow long as I love the Dear One
O Sleep! grow short that I may ever touch His feet
My soul and body feel love for the Beloved:
How shall my heart be satisfied without beholding Him?
I cannot abide for a moment without the lord.
I cry for Him as the *chatak* cries for water.
I wander searching for the fascinating One,
Mine eyes are dyed in the colour of the Beloved;
They rest not even for a moment.
Separate from my Spouse
One moment appears to me as a day;
Wandering and wandering
I weep and wring my hands.

Such love had the Gurus. Such love is sung in hymn after hymn of the *Sukhmani*. Years have passed away since my heart was knit to his great book. As a lisping child I listened to its simple verse.

DAL KHALSA

[illegible] the history of the Sikhs. Because it united them once again in a compact bo[illegible] after a period of 33 years. It served the most useful purpose of giving the Sikhs [illegible] [illegible] unity and power in keeping them bound together by the common tie [illegible] faith [illegible] of the severest persecution and in moulding them into a discipline[illegible] body. They had realised that obedience to their leaders was a religious duty as [illegible] commandment of the Guru imposed upon them by the *panth*, in which body th[illegible] Guru had merged his personality, and every sacrifice made for the *panth* was th[illegible] real service of the Guru. This singleness of purpose and harmony made them th[illegible] strongest military body of the day and prepared the way for the establishment [illegible]

[illegible] Singh [illegible] Dal [illegible] applies the term Dal Khalsa [illegible] [illegible] at a certain place and time. Sohan Lal says that the conquering armies o[illegible] the Sikhs formed Dal Khalsa Ji. Ratan Singh Bhangu calls it The Dal of the Singhs[illegible] Cunningham says it was the 'army of theocracy of Singhs'. Gian Singh names [illegible] *Khalsa Da Dal* or Khalsa Dal. Khalifa Muhammad Hasan writes:

The [illegible] army of [illegible] [illegible] the country f[illegible] the sake of plunder [illegible] the [illegible] army of the rebel[illegible] [illegible]

This is [illegible] to note that the first organisation of the Khalsa under Gu[illegible] Gobind Singh, numbering about five thousand had broken up at the siege o[illegible] Anandpur in 1704 after five years. The second organisation of the Khalsa unde[illegible] [illegible] [illegible] [illegible] [illegible] end of the century, when Ranjit Singh established monarchy on its ruins.

[illegible]

[illegible] describing the battle of Bhangani fought in 1688 [illegible] fought between Guru Gobind Singh and the neighbouring hill rajas.

[illegible]

6

Dal Khalsa, 1745-1748

THE SIKH AGGRESSIONS

Under the impulse of a few successes which the Sikhs scored in their new role, they determined to punish their enemies. They now raided the villages of Naushahra and Majitha and others, and killed Sahib Rai, Rama Randhawa, Karma Chhina, Harbhagat Niranjaniya, Qazi Fazil Ahmad Khan, Khokhar Shaamshir Khan and many other *chaudharis* and *muqaddams,* who had rendered active help to the Government against them. The towns of Batala, Jullundur, Talwan, Bijwara, Dhag, Manjki and Phagwara were also laid waste.

There early successes led the Sikhs to undertake bolder adventure. A band of their daring youths disguised themselves as Mughal soldiers entered the town of Lahore by the Mochi Gate, one evening, in the month of January. This being the coldest month in the year, the people of the city had retired to their houses early. The streets were almost deserted and the dim lights inside the shops and houses failed to disclose the identity of the intruders. The plunderers blocked all exits, put the shopkeepers to the sword, and loading their horses with booty immediately disappeared. Before they left the town, some of the party managed to slay the *qazis* and the *muftis* living in that quarter, as they had been instrumental in the punishments awarded to the Sikh captives.

JASPAT RAI SLAIN BY THE SIKHS, C. MARCH, 1746

After plundering Lahore the Sikhs joined the rest of their body lying concrealed in the jungle on the banks of the Ravi. It was a dreary and arduous task for the pursuing Mughal troops with their loose trousers to pass through the thorny bushes over a marshy soil where the legs of the horses sank in the mud.

Yahiya Khan, the Lahore Governor, on learning what had taken place in the Mochi gate bazar of his capital, ordered Diwan Lakhpat Rai to the take immediate action against the Sikhs. The Diwan sent a strong detachement of cavalry who succeeded in expelling the Sikhs from their swampy haunts and they fled towards Eminabad. Jaspat Rai, brother of Lakhpat Rai, who was *faujdar* of Eminabad, lay encamped at village Khokharan, 25 kms distant. The residents of Gondlanwala approached him complaining that 2,000 Sikh horsemen had suddenly fallen upon the village, and after driving away the flocks of sheep and goats of the village were slaughtering and eating them at Rori Baba Nakan. The Diwan sent them word to return the goats to their owners and to depart immediately. The Sikhs gave him a reply that they had gone without food for the last two or three days and they expected to leave the place the next morning. The *faujdar* again sent them strict orders to disperse at once. But the Sikhs would not move. Then Jaspat mounted on an elephant launched an attact on the Sikhs with whatever troops he had with him. The Sikhs offered a stubborn resistance. During the course of the action, aa Rangretta Sikh named Nibahu Singh, caught hold of the tail of Jaspat's elephat, leapt up like lightning and cut off the head of the *faujdar*. This was the signal for a general stampede of the troops.

LAKHPAT RAI'S MASSACRE OF THE SIKHS OR CHOOTA GHALLUGHARA, C. APRIL—JUNE, 1746

On receiving the news of his brother's tragic end, Diwan Lakhpat Rai swore vengeance on the Sikhs. He is reported to have taken a vow to destroy the Khalsa root and branch. With the approval of Yahiya Khan he arrested all the Sikhs of Labore and slaughenred them at Shahid Ganj. The noted persons of Lahore such as Kaura Mal, Kunjah Mal, Dila Ram, Hari Ram, Kashmiri Mal, Surat Singh, Har Singh, Bhai Des Raj and Chaudhari Jawahir Mal formed a deputation and waited upon Lakhpat Rai to dissuade him form shedding blood of innocent persons, particularly so on the sacred day of *Amawash* (9 April). Lakhpat Rai did not listen to them, burnt the holy book of the Sikhs and demolished their places of worship.

The general body of the Sikhs had taken shelter in the swamps of the upper course of the Ravi, Yahiyaa Khan and Lakhpat Rai personally marched in their pursuit. The Sikhs, keeping themselves concealed in the jungle, moved up the right back of the Ravi into the north-eastern corner of the province. Several skirmishes took place in which the Sikhs were worsted because they were helpless aagainst light artillery. At last they advanced in the direction of Kahnwan on the right bank of the old Beas, 15 kms south of Gurdaspur where there was a thick forest abounding in wild animals.

The Sikhs maintained a guerilla warface by concealing themselves in the day and harassing the enemy in the night. But their strength had begun to dwindle. They were runningg short of provisions aand ammunition. The wild game had grown scarce. Many were dying of starvation and wounds. A number of parents by securing pardon from Lakhpat Rai persuaded their sons to cut off their hair, to relinquish all other symbols of Sikhism and to revert to Hinduism. Others who had joined the Khalsa ranks for the sake of plunder came back, and resumed their peaceful avocations. But those who were true to the new religion remained steadfast.

Being extremely hard-pressed, the Sikhs one night decided to give their enemies the slip under cover of darkness. A few of them who were ready to lay down their lives for their brethren raised loud shouts of "*Wah Guru ji ka Khalsa, Wah Guru jiki Fatah*", and fearlessly dashed into the ranks of their foes. This attracted the whole force of Lakhpat Rai to that particular spot and the other Sikhs succeeded in escaping towards Parol Kathua.

Lakhpat Rai, however, was soon upon them with definite instructions to all the chiefs, *chaudharis* and *lambardars* to co-operated with him. The hill people were to obstruct their progress in the north and to drive them away towards the plains, while the residents of the country along the foot of the hill were to cut off all ways of escape.

The hot pursuit on all sides compelled them to retreat and halt on the spurs of the Basohli hills (between Pathankot and Dalhousie on the Ravi) where the river swept through a deep bed between high banks. Here the Sikhs were brought to bay with the enemy behind them, precipitous mountains in front, a hostile population all around and a swift river flowing to their left.

Some Sikhs wanted to escape by crossing the river, but they were prevented from doing so by the strong current which foamed below between sloping rocky banks of the river. Two of the young Dallewalia Sikhs jumped into the river to see if it could be crossed, but none of them was seen again. The Sikhs tried to ascend the hill which was in some parts perpendicular, and in others irregular in slope, but they made little progress over this steep and slippery ground. Some of them succeeded in reaching the top but the bullets and stones of the hill men made short work of them. The Sikhs, therefore, gave up all these attempts and hid themselves in all possible places which they could find. One dark night they swam accross river Ravi and entered and Bari Doab.

Khushwaqt Rai gives a graphic account of their sufferings. He writes that the enemy entering into every cave and crevice fightened them out and drove them into the plains towrads Batala. All exits being blocked, Lakhpat Rai and Yahiya Khaan fell on them and put four hundred Sikhs to the sword on the spot; while about the same number of them were taken captives. Many Sikhs fell into the river Ravi, while a number of them jumped into a well to save thier lives. Some of them cut off their hair in the twinkling of an eye and escaped in this changed appearance. Among the captives all those who shaved their heads and beards were allowed to depart; while the hair of others was pulled off with their skin, and they were put to death with a thousand tortures. Scouts and military contingents roamed about in search of them, killing every Sikh they came across Lakhpat Rai set five rupees as the price for every Sikh head. The Sikh ranks consequently thinned every day by desertion and death.

The Sikhs who had escaped this massacre ran towards the Beas which flowed at a distance of about 30 kms, fighting their way valiantly against their pursuers. They again suffered teribly in the passage of the Beas, a vivid picture of which is presented by Ratan Singh. He says that Lakhpat Rai overtook them when they reached the Beas. It was mid-day in the month of June. The river was flooded (from the melting of snow on the mountains). The enemy was in hot pursuit. No boats were available. The Sikhs prayed to the Guru and jumped into the river at Goindwal. When they reached the opposite bank, they came upon a deep bed of sand 3 kms long. They wree already dying of huner and fatigue and the pain of their wounds, and now the burning sand added to their torture. They tore out their turbans, tied the pieces of their feet and thus managed to cross it. In the Jullundur Doab they halted near a village. They had hardly begun to cook their food when Adina Beg Khan suddenly fell upon them. They also received the news of Lakhpat Rai's having crossed the Beas. So they gave up cooking, started fighting and piercing through Adina'a troops reached the Satluj. Having crossed it at Tihara and applying cold water compressed on the way, they arrived in Malwa with great difficulty, while Lakhpat Rai returned to Lahore. The Malwa Sikhs sympathised with theirbrethren of the Majha and offered them their homes and nursed their wounds with care and devotion. The leaders with their surviving associates halted at different places. Sukha Singh stayed at Jaito, Jassa Singh at Kot Kapura, Kapur Singh at Dhing Wanjhuke, Hari Singh at Dyalpur, Charat Singh at Pakka Pathrala, while Dip Singh with is devoted band retired to the Lakhi Jungle and many other Sikhs stayed at Tihara and in the neighbourhood of Daroli.

In this campaign seven to eight thousand Sikhs were killed and captured. The captives were brought to Lahore, dressed in paper caps and mounted to camels, and were beheaded at Shahid Ganj, Lakhpat Rai also issued a proclamation at the saame time threatening to rip open the belly of any one taking the name of the Guru. He prohibited calling sugar-cane molases '*Gur*' because it sounded as '*Guru*' and ordered the people of name it '*Rori*' which is steill current in the Panjab.

Such strong measures checked the progress of Sikhism for the time being. The enthusiasm of the votaries of the Guru decreased considerably, and a large number of them who had joined their ranks more for the sake of plunder and love of dare-devilry than for their devotion to the Khalsa faith now began to desert the Khalsa Panth. Lakhpat had the satisfaction of wreaking a thorought vengeance for his brother's death.

CIVIL WAR BETWEEN ZAKARIYA KHAN'S SONS, 21ST NOVEMBER, 1746—21ST MARCH, 1747

The sufferings of the Khalsa were not, however, destined to continue very long, while retribution for Lakhpat Rai and an opportunity for the Sikhs were soon at hand. After about five months, Yahiya's younger brother Shahnawaz Khan rose in insurrection against him. He came to Lahore on the 21st November, 1746, encamped near the Shalimar Garden and through Diwan Surat Singh called upon Yahiya Khan to make a complete division of his father's property. Adina Beg Khan, Kaura Mal and Hashmatullah Khan also joined him.

Yahiya Khan was not willing to pay him anything, while at the same time he avoided fighting. The discussion was prolonged and no decision was arrived at. The soldiers of both the brothers often came to blows. At last Yahiya Khan, with all his old and new chiefs such as Mumin Khan, Lakhpat Rai, Mir Ne'mat Khan and Mir Amin Beg, etc., came out of Lahore and a sharp engagement took place. Yahiya Khan then ended the dispute by paying Shahnawaz Khan Rs. 600,000 from his father's treasure. The latter, thereupon, retired towards Batala where he seized many districts belonging to Yahiya Khan and brought a number of neighbouring chiefs under his subjugation.

This annoyed the Lahore Viceroy and he prepared for another fight. Shahnawaz, on hearing of it, came to Lahore and encamped near the tomb of Hazrat Ishan. The battle begaan on the 17th March, 1747. Adina Beg led the attach and succeeded in forcing Mumin Khan out his trenches. Next day Shahnawaz delivered the assault in person. Mir Mimin was defeated and captured. Yahiya's soldiers whose salaries had been in arrears for the past four or five months since the commencement of hostilities, flocked into the city and clamoured for the payment of their dues. They were easily seduced by Shahnawaz Khan. He entered Lahore quite unopposed on the 21st March, seized the property of Yahiya and took him captive.

Shahnawaz Khan established himself securely in the office of the Panjab Viceroy "by removing from their posts all the old captains who had grown grey-haired in the service of his father and grand-father, and confiscated their houses and property." He nominated Kaura Mal as his Diwan in the place of Lakhpat Rai and confirmed the vigorous Governor Adina Beg Khan in the civil and militiary charge of the Jullundur Doab.

RECOVERY OF STRENGTH BY THE SIKHS, NOVEMBER, 1746—MARCH, 1747

The civil was between the sons of Zakariya Khan which commenced in the month of November, 1746 resulted in the dislocation of the governmental machinery. This period not only gave the Sikhs much needed respite to recover their strength, but also proved favourable for their further rise. The training of the Khalsa in the shcool of adversity had produced that keen insight in them which is a rare gift of nature for enabling one of take the best advantage of one's opportunities. The short interval of five months (July-November) while they were in Malwa had healed their wounds and calmed the horrors of the late war. At the outbreak of the civil war they left their retreats and started paying visits to Amritsar. This was considered to serve a double purpose. The bathing in the sacred tank and prayers in holy shrine of Harimandir would elevate their depressed spirits, enhance their enthusiasm and secure the blessings of the Guru. In the second place, it was to serve them as a rendezvous. Most of their co-religionists had scattered far and wide under the tyrannous rule of Yahiya Khan and it was essential to rally all the forces of *Panth* before entering upon a fresh career.

The Muslim officials of the district were made aware of this move of the Sikhs. The Mughal *faujdar* of Amritsar erected four towers at the four corners of the tank with a view of keeping a sharp lookout on the Sikhs coming there to bathe. Armed police was posted there day and night with orders to shoot every Sikh, approaching the tank. Sukha Singh, a prominent Sikh volunteered himself to take the lead and resolved to bathe there in broad daylight. He dressed himself in Turkish uniform, came to the tank at mid-day, had a dip and went away showing his identity by taking off his turban. His example was followed by other Sikhs and soon the Khalsa of daring spirit began to pour into their holy city in groups of tens and twenties. This news quickly spread all over the country and the other Sikhs who had exchanged their swords for the ploughshare soon began to flock to the Khalsa ranks for the sake of acquiring rich booty. Their venture met with great success, because the district officer of Amritsar had to withdraw to Lahore in view of his scantly resources to cope with the serious situation, and perhaps the presence of his troops was required to fight on the side of Yahiya Khan.

The different bands of the Sikhs then sallied out of Amritsar and fell upon the Bari and Rechna Doabs like birds of prey. They it loose their vengeance to have its full play on the Government officials especially those who had persecuted them. They soon succeeeded in aquiring an immense booty thus replenishing their exhausted stores and fully equipping themselves with arms, ammunition, horses and other necessaries.

THE SIKHS BUILD THE FORT OF RAM RAUNI AT AMRITSAR, C. 30TH MARCH, 1747

In the struggle between Zakariya Khan's sons Shahnawaz Khan had defeated his elder brother Yahiya Khan together with Diwan Lakhpat Rai and Mir Mumin Khan, all of whom had been imprisoned by him. Shahnawaz, as has already been remarked, had appointed Kaura Mal his Diwan and confirmed Adina Beg Kha in the *faujdari* of the Jullundur Doab. Kaura Mal was a Khulasa Sikh (believer in Guru Nanak's religion without having adopted the tenets of Guru Gobind Singh), while Adina Beg Khan had inclinations towards the Sikhs from polity. Out of regard for their patron who occupied the highest authority next to the Viceroy in the Panjab, the Sikhs decided to bring their plundering activities to a stand-still, more so because they really needed a breathing time and leisure to recoup. The Government of Shahnawaz Khan was also not yet stable and his two advisers Kaura Mal and Adina Beg saw advantage in advising then new Governor to let the Siksh alone. Naturally when the Sikhs had no interference from the Government and when they wished the recoup, they were quiet.

In view of the approaching Baisakhi festival which was to fall on the 30th March all the Sikhs assembled at Amritsar, their religious capital, where they celebrated the occasion with great pomp and show after a long, stormy period of about twelve years. On this day a general assembly of the Khalsa was convented in which a *Gurmata* was passed to the effect that a fort should be erected at Amritsar. This wise step was taken because some work had to be provided for the Sikhs who did not want to go their homes and who could not reconcile themselves to a life of inactivity after having been diligently employed for a long time. Moreover, they were not sure how long they were destined to enjoy peace with the Government in those troublour times.

In spite of the two disadvantages, that Amritsar was situated in the immediate neighbourhood of the provincial capital (50 kms north of Lahore), and that it stood on the Grand Trunk Road, thus falling on the way of forces marching between Lahore and Delhi, it was selected as the future site of their military capital as well. There were several factors in favour of such a choice. It was considered by the Sikhs as 'the Guru's Kashi' and it was believed that any Sikh who died there would go straigth to heaven. It stood in the centre of the Majha, their real home, surrounded on all sides by a thick forst of *Palas* trees, and thus they could count on a friendly population and a safe retreat in times of emergency. Besides they could closely watch the policy of the Lahore court and the movements of its forces.

The Sikhs started the work of construction after the festival was over. Its foundation was laid near another holy tank named Ramsar, about 3 kms distant from Hari Mandir. A two metres wide foundation was dug. The Sikhs themselves were the masons, carpenters and labourers. All the four walls of the fort were started at the same time and special provision was made for the gates and towers. A deep and wide ditch was excavated around the fort. It was named 'Rauni' and the fort was called 'Ram Rauni' (God's shelter). It was a small, mud-built fort with an accommodation for 500 men. The reason for such a small undertaking seems to be the idea of not rousing the jealousy of the Government officials. It was a fort for them; but it looked like the house of a zamindar securely built and properly protected, the more so because it had extensive fields on all sides in which wheat, gram and mustard were cultivated in winter and fodder in summer. After the completion of the fort, the Sikhs began to beautify the temple and the tank. Hari Singh Bhangi was also allowed to establish his *Katra* or residential quarters in teh vicinity of the tank of nectar.

Shahnawaz Khan's government

Having placed his brother in confinement, Shahnawaz Khan usurped the government of the province in March, 1747. The new Governnor is described by all contemporary writers as a man of intemperate habits and bloodthirsty character. The author of *Tarikh-e-Muhammad Shahi* depicts him even more cruel than Nadir Shah. His administration was marked by excessive tyranny and oppression. He would often inflict very severe and inhuman punishments for tirvial faults. The amputation of limbs and putting out of eyes was not uncommon.

We are given to understand by several writers that the Nawab's cruel administration drove a good many peasants from peaceful pursuits to lawless habits.

The usurpation of the Panjab Government could not be brooked by the Delhi court, but no drastic action was taken against Shahnawaz Khan because Wazir Qamar-ud-din Khan first wanted to secure the release of his son-in-law Yahiya Khan who, in case of the despatch of a force from Delhi might be put to death. The Wazir wrote several conciliatory letters to Shahnawaz Khan demanding the liberation of Yahiya Khan, but he always replied that Yahiya's freedom from captivity depended on his own confirmation in the Viceroyalty of the Panjab under a royal rescript. Shahnawaz Khan's hopes of reconciliation with his maternal uncle, the Delhi Wazir were dashed to the ground with the escape of Yahiya Khan by the end of July. He made one more effort by sending his ambassador to the Emperor with the request that his misdeed should be forgiven and that he should be appointed deputy-Viceroy under the Wazir. They envoy reached Delhi on the 3rd September, 1747, but nothing came out this mission. Shahnawaz Khan now felt sure that the retribution of the Emperor and his Wazir must fall upon him. Consequently he turned his mind in all directions to secure support. At this juncture the political horizon of India was suddenly overcast with clouds, and once more was the kaliedoscope to re-arrange its disc and glasses.

Confusion caused by the first Durrani campaign, December, 1747—March, 1748

Nadir Shah was murdered on the 9th June, 1747 and his ablest general Ahmad Shah Abdali, also known by the title of the Durrani, rose to power and founded an independent dynasty in Afghanistan. Having driven away Nasir Khan, the son of the old Mughal Governor of Kabul, retained in his office by Nadir Shah, he pursured the retreating Governor as fas as Peshaawar, and wih this place as a suitable base, 'the man-power of Afghanistan' behind him and no hindrance in front, the loot of India, the Eldorado of the western people, become his ruling passion.

Shahnawaz Khan, as we have stated above, was in search of a strong ally in order to secure his position in Lahore. He hailed the presence of Ahmad Shah Durrani in Peshawar and appealed to him for help against the Emperor of Delhi in fear of the consequences of his act. Ahmad Shah, encouraged by the unexpected success of his first efforts, at once accepted his invitation in view of the utter weakness of the Delhi Empire which he had hemself seen when in attendance upon Nadir Shah. He left Peshawar by the middle of December, 1747, and arrived at Shahdara, 6 kms west of Lahore, on the 8th January, 1748. Meanwhile a chnage had taken place in the attitude of Shahnawaz Khan. The Delhi Wazir availing himself of his relationship wrote to his nephew conciliatory and flattering letters and appealed to his sense of honour and patriotism. This touched the young Governor's heart, and he prepared to oppose the invader whom a little while before he had invited.

Ahmad Shah tried his best to bring Shahnawaz Khan back to his allegiance, but failed. He crossed the Ravi on the 10th January and took up his position at the Shalimar Garden. An engagement between the Afghans and the Mughals took place on the 11th January in which Shahnawaz Khan was defeated and he fled to Delhi in the course of the same night.

The Abdali plundered the outer portions of the capital particularly Mohalla Mughalpura, the richest part of the town, but spared the city for a ransom of 30 lakhs. The whole baggage of Shahnawaz Khan, consisting of camp equipage, artillery, elephants, camels and horses, fell into the conqueror's hands and considerably augmented his military resourses. The Abdali stayed in Lahore for over a month to make necessary arrangements for his march on Delhi, and leaving Jumla Khan of Kasur as his Governor in Lahore he left it on the 19th February.

The flight of Shahnawaz Khan to Delhi had stirred the indolent Emperor, his Wazir and the court into activity. A huge army of 2 lakhs under Wazir Qamar-ud-din Khan was despatched to check the progress of the Afghans. The imperialists arrived near Sirhind on the 25th February, and to their utter amazement found that Ali Muhammad, the governor of the place, had deserted his post to avoid fighting with his Afghan brother and fled to Aonla in the Bareilly district. They decided to make Sarhind the base of their operations and before proceeding further they left their heavy baggage, surplus stores of arms and ammunition and their women including the Wazir's harem in the small fort of Sarhind with a garrison of 1,000 horse and foot.

The imperialists committed a fatal blunder in deciding to cross the Satluj, not by the direct route at Ludhiana, but at Machhiwara, 30 kms north-east. A still greater folly was displayed in not maintaining their communications with Sarhind, in not posting a guard at the Ludhiana ford and in not collecting intelligence about the enemy's movements. The enemy on the other hand was extremely agile and vigorous and maintained absolute secrecy about their movements and whereabouts. The Abdali reached the Satluj opposite Ludhiana on the 1st March, 1748, forded the river unopposed, covered the distance of 65 kms in the night, and at dawn on the 2nd March took to fort of Sarhind. He put the garrison to the sword, seized all the stores of war materials and reduced the women to slavery.

Great was the loss of the imperialists and still greater their dismay when they heard about the capture of Sarhind. They returned from Machhiwara to Manupur (15 kms north-west of Sarhind) where they sighted the roving bands of the Afghans and took up an entrenched position. The Abdali kept Sarhind as his base and entrenched his camp 8 kms north-west of Sarhind. Frequent skirmishes took place in the beginning. Alha Singh of Patiala gave great help to the government of Delhi by cutting off Abdali's supplies. His foraging parties were attacked, men were killed, and camels and horses were captured. On the morning of the 11th March whent he Wazir was about to lead the imperial army for a general attack, he was mortally wounded by a cannon short. Calling his son Muin-ul-Mulk he said, "My son! I am done for; it is all over with me. But the Emperor's work is not yet finished. Before this news spreads, quickly take horse and deliver the assault. After that you may look after me."

The Wazir then expired. Muin repressed his filial feelings, rode on his father's elephant with his banners and led the attact. In the centre was Prince Ahmad Shah with Muin in front, on the right wing was Safdar Jang, and Ishwari Singh on the left. The Durrani resorted to stange tactics. 1,000 horse suddenly appeared before each wing, delivered a sharp volley and gradually fell back retiring to the rear, making room for fresh contingents to advance. In this way fresh and vigorous men came to the front every time. Under these new tactics the left wing gave waay and the Rajputs wer indiscriminately massacred. The thickest contest raged in the centre. Muin's skin was grazed, his brother was shot in the foot, Adin Beg was twice wounded and many officers of note were slain. The right wing herocially fought and drove away the Afghans. Safdar Jang then came to the rescue of Muin. Just at this time the Durrani store of rockets and gunpowder caught fire and killed 1,000 Afghans on the spot. The Durranis thus caught between the jaws of a nutcracker fled from the field, and the Panjab was recovered for the Mughal Empire.

The imperialists did not take advantage of this victory by immediately following up the enemy. It was only five days after the battle (16th March) that the Indians ventured to march out of their camp. Ahmad Shah Abdali had already left for home and so the imperialists enjoyed a holiday on the banks of the Satluj till the 12th April, when Prince Ahmad Shah left for Delhi and Muin-ul-Mulk for Lahore to take over charge of his new post as Governor of the Panjab.

Peaceful progress of the Sikhs

In the last chapter we left the Sikhs as having settled either in their homes or at Amritsar where they had commenced building the Ram Rauni fort. The Sikhs who had dispersed to their villages did the most useful work in peacefully propagating the tenets of Guru Gobind Singh. The simple peasants and other villagers had also seen with their own eyes how the Sikhs were augmenting their power even when they seemed to be beaten doen to the dust. Whenever the Sikhs came back to their homes they became the centre of all affairs. The stories of their sufferings and heroic deeds were on everybody's lips. They wer surrounded by the village youths who listened to their aventurous deeds with zeal and rapt attention. They joined them in playing games, in wrestling matches and in hunting expeditinos. The poor men and women thronged at their doors begging alms. The suffering persons sought redress at their hands, because the Sikhs had established it as the foremost principle of their religion to help the poor and the needy and to redress the grievances of the oppressed. Besides, this was the gang age. An individual might do very little of his own, but as a member of a gang would do and dare a great deal. This factor had an important influence upon the development of personality which grew under the shelter and comradeship of the group. These were the causes which wer paving the way for the Sikh religion to make it a mass movement among hte peasntry of the centrel Panjab. When the Sikhs returned from their homes either to Amritsar or some other rendezvous they were followed by a number of village young men to be baptized to Sikhism and recruited to the Khalsa ranks. This is borne out by the fact that the band of a Sikh leader consisted mostly of the young men of his own village or neighbouring village, and the villages of his relations and friends.

Thus, this period of seven months (May-November) was most usefully spent. The Sikhs of Amritsar leisurely finished the Ram Rauni fort, adorned and magnified their temple and tank, and constructed *katras* (residential quarters) in its immediate neighbourhood.

Early in November strong rumours of the impending Durrani invasion spread all over the country. The Sikhs rose up in arms once more. They sent their women and children to the hills of Jammu, Chamba, Kangra and Hoshiarpur as the other inhabitants wer doing, and then gathered at Amritsar pretending to protect their holy places from desecration. On the commencement of hostilities between Ahmad Shah Durrani and his namesake the Delhi Prince, the Majha Sikhs decided not to co-operate either with the Mughals or with the Afghans because their struggle lay against both. The Sikhs seem to have retires to the northern parts of the Bari Doab where their depredations remained for the time unchecked. Thus they busied themselves in settling old scores with their enemies and in acquiring immense booty, and "made themselves masters of a considerable part of the Doab of Ravi and Jullundur, and extended their incursions to the neighbouring countries."

SIKHS FALL UPON THE RETREATING AFGHANS, C. 18TH-26TH MARCH, 1748

Ahmad Shah Abdali was defeated by the Imperialists on the 11th March. He crossed the Satluj at Ludhiana on the 17th March and retired towards Lahore in a hurry in order to avoid any pursuit. He took his goods and property from Lahore in all possible haste and by rapid marches travelled to Afghanistan.

The Sikhs had known all about it and resolved not to let the vanquished general pass through the Panjab unmolested. They fell upon his rear-guard at many places till he reached the Chenab acquiring good booty in the shape of baggage, arms, camels and horses.

THE DAL KHALSA ESTABLISHED, 29TH MARCH, 1748

In 1745 the Sikhs had formed themselves into small bands, in which they welcomed all the fresh recruits and supplied them with arms and horses. The leaders, being guided by their personal ambition, had been so far content with small scale operations. They had no occasion to unite their forces, except in the small Ghallughara, where also they had not fought under the command of one supreme leader.

Even in the absence of the unity of command, the enthusiasm and endurance of the Sikh soldiers were great. With the training of half a century they had become born warrious who despised death, believed in war as the honourable profession for man and regarded hand to hand fight much in the same way as an Englishman regards football or racing. The Sikhs were sober and strong, and their scorn of danger was only equalled by their unlimited pride in themselves and their inborn hatred of the Musalmans. Gureilla warfare, ambushes, sniping and decoys were their favourite tactics and they preferred death to surrender or captivity.

Their small scale organization had shown its obvious advantages. They had learnt to exercise foresight, to submit to command and to conceive of large purposes. The leader who had to felt the joy of command was rewarded by the implicit obedience, unflinching faith, constant attention of his followers, and by a larger share of the spoil. The men whom he had led to victory were devotedly attached to him. They had one common grievance against the oppressors of their faith, and one comman bond of union, their faith. The leader, enriched by the booty, was in a position to strengthen more securely the tie between him and his followers, by occasional gifts and presents, and a further continued succession of fortunate expeditions and conquests resulted in binding them permanently.

In the progressive state of the Khalsa another development was bound to take place in course of time. It was uniting the whole body of the fighting Sikhs in the form of a standing national army. Its idea had been supplied to them in a concrete form by Guru Gobind Singh and Banda Bahadur. Experience in contending with their enemies had taught them the need of some measure of union. The odds were so heavily against them that uniting and acting in one body and on one principle was with them a law of necessity. Being surrounded with danger their only hope of success lay in unity, as this was the sole means of their preservation.

It was due to these causes that some of the far-seeing talented Sikh leaders realized the need of widening the circle of the attachement existing between the soldeirs and the sardars in each group, and this could be effected only by uniting them under one supreme command, thus binding each individual not only with his colleagues and the chief but also with the whole *Panth*. It was also felf that the independent position of as many as 65 chiefs, whose number was rapidly increasing would not lead to any solidarity in making them a power without taking such a step. On the other hand there was the danger that the feelings of jealousy and selfishenss might arise among them if they were allowed to follow their own line of action.

Luckily for the Sikhs, a very capably leader who commanded high respect from all the Sikhs and who possessed remarkable powers of organisation had appeared among them. This was Jassa Singh Ahluwalia, who had received his training under the famous leader Nawab Kapur Singh. The Nawab was the most venerable Sikh leader. Owing to the constant help and guidance of the Nawab and his own sterling virtues, Jassa Singh Ahluwalia had come to occupy a very prominent position among the Sikh leaders. The Nawab was growing old and he wanted to give the leadership of the warlike Khalsa to somebody else. He had his eye on the promising Jassa Singh and he was on the look-out for an opportunity to do so.

This opportunity came handly on the retirement of Ahmad Shan Abdali from the province. On the sacred day of Baisakhi, 29th March, 1748, the Sikhs assembled at Amritsar. It was on this occasion that Nawab Kapur Singh impressed upon the assemblage the need for solidarity of the *Panth*, and placed Jassa Singh in the supreme command of all the Sikh forces. The entire fighting body of the Sikhs was given the name of 'Dal Khalsa'. There were eleven leaders of most prominent ability among the various Sikh chiefs. Hence the 65 groups were leagued together in eleven main divisions, each with a distinguishing title and banner, but varying in strength:

1. The *Ahluwalia Misl* under the leadership of Jassa Singh Ahluwalia, who, in addition to it, held the chief command of the 'Dal Khalsa' at the time of any expedition or battle.
2. The *Bhangi Misl* under Hari Singh Bhangi.
3. The *Dallewalia Misl* under Gulab Singh of village Dallewal near Derah Baba Nanak on the Ravi.
4. The *Faizullahpuria or Singhpuria Misl* under the renowned Nawab Kapur Singh of Village Faizullahpur.
5. The *Kanhiya Misl* under Jai Singh Kanhiya of villaage Kanha in Lahore District.
6. The *Karorasinghia Misl* under Karora Singh of Panjgarh.
7. The *Nakai Misl* under Hira Singh Nakai of village Baharwal in Chunian Tahsil of Lahore District.
8. The *Nishanwal Misl* under Dasaundha Singh, the standardbrearer of the Dal Khalsa.
9. Unit of Nand Singh Sanghaniya, afterwards known as the *Ramgarhia Misl.*
10. Dip Singh's band which came to be called afterwards the *Shahidi Misl* on account of its leader's martyrdom while fighting against the Afghans, as we shall see later on.
11. The *Sukarchakia Misl* under Nodh Singh of village Sukarchak in Gujranwala District.

CONSTITUTION OF THE DAL KHALSA

It seems idle to give the name of a constitution to the crude system of an overshelming state of alliance and dependence established by the Sikhs on this occasion. We should not expect any elaborate plan worked out by the simple illiterate tillers of the soil, as we are accustomed to find it in the enactments of legislative bodies or in the regulations of religious preceptors. The existence of such a scheme, as was adopted by the Sikhs on this occasion, may be better traced in the dictates of common human nature. They system was not devised or purposely adopted and therefore it was rather temporary and incomplete. Every Sikh who believed in the tenents of Guru Gobind Singh, was considered a member of the Dal Khalsa without any need being felt to secure his willingness. It was thought compulsory for each individual to enroll himself in the Khalsa army in order to wage war against the enemies of his faith and his persecutors and therefore each Sikh who was true to his faith, was supposed to have become a member of Dal Khalsa. But nobody was admitted a member of any misl which consitiued the Dal Khalsa, unless he was an active horseman and proficient in the use of arms. Every individual, even of the meanest birth, had the right of choosing the leader he would like to serve.

The joint forces of all the misls took the field either upon any predatory enterprise or to offer a bold front to the enemy. On these occasions the army assumed the denomination of the Dal Khalsa. The chiefs had agreed by common consent that at such times someone from among themselves should be appointed from time to time to be the head of the Dal to guide them in all matters requiring united action, while the other ten chiefs were to constitute an advisory body or council of war.

Their unity was further maintained by the gatherings of the whole body of the Sikhs called the 'Sarbat Khalsa' twice a year at Amritsar on the occasions of the Baisakhi and Diwali festivals, which generally fall in April and October respectively. At these times the Sikh chief held a special council under the presidentship of the chief leader and passed resolutions (*Gurmatas*) on matters of more than ordinary interest to the *panth.* The Akalis, or men wholly and solely devoted to war and worship, formed the central league of the Sikh religion. They had the sole direction of all religious affairs at Amritsar. All the cases of irregularity were referred to them and thus they played the part of the defenders of the faith. They were stern zealots who maintained the purity of the Sikh doctrines, watched over the general conduct of the Sikhs by exercising a fierce scrutiny as censors and took a prominent part in conducting the National Councils. They initiated converts, imposed fines upon those who broke the laws of the community, and in the event of disobedience prevented them from performing worship or going throught any religious ceremony at the Hari Mandir, Amritsar.

Thus a kind of federal union was established and the leader of the Dal Khalsa was looked upon as the head of the Church and State. Whenever there was no emergency, each misl acted independently, or in concert, as necessity or inclination suggested. Each sardar of a misl was to lead his followers in warlike activities and act as an arbiter in times of peace. The sardar did not exercise absolute authority over his comrades. They paid him due regard and treated him with respect; but they were under no obligation to obey him beyond what was required in the interests of the whole *panth*, or of their misl or their own mutual advantage. The chiefs, therefore, were forced on all occasions, to be very careful in looking to the wants and whised of their followers, and in treating them with attention and conciliation. It was only in this way that they could retain them intheir service; otherwise a little indifference on their part was sufficient to cause their desertion and going over to another chief, who was every ready to accord them a warm welcome. This was the reason that even the humblest Sikh in the Dal Khalsa was happy because he was free from all kinds of tyranny and violence from his chiefs and therefore even the lowest Sikh horseman usually assumed an independent attitude of mind.

Thus this system of voluntary service secured not only good treatment from the chiefs but also a share in the booty or land. All the booty taken was divided proportionately among the chiefs, according to the number of their followers, and they in turn sub-divided it among their men. This was the remuneration for their services in the absence of any fixed salary.

Distant relations and friends of the Sardar of the misl formed a link between the highest and the lowest Sikhs. There existed no wide distinction between them. All possessed the same descent to boast of and the same exclusive profession of arms. Moreover, there was the strong bond of brotherhood according to the commands of the last Guru and as found in the bond of *pahul*. They also fought in the same cause and suffered from the same grievances. Thus they developed a similar type of mind and character.

The Sikh chiefs who were at the head of the various misls forming the Dal Khalsa were really great soldiers and men of insight. They possessed a mind that planned broadly, grasped tenaciously and saw clearly. Every one of them was going to be the master-builder in consolidating the Sikh power. He needed tools on which he could absolutely rely. These were supplied to him by the soldiers under him. They all had ambition and therefore they obeyed him, followed him and helped him, and thus the sardar as well as the soldier, united in one common object, passed on the from glory to glory.

The principal point to be borne in mind is that the military system of the Sikhs was not established by the king or the chief. The Sikh sardars did not create and endow their following, but were created and endowed by them. They were, in fact, elected by their soldiers. It was only in later days that by aid of regular troops and military combination they acquired a larger hereditary power.

The foundation of the Dal Khalsa was a step of the greatest significance in the history of the Sikhs, because it united them once again in a compact body after a period of 33 years. It served the most useful purpose of giving the Sikhs an ideal of unity and power, in keeping them bound together by the common tie of faith in the teeth of the severest persecution, and in making them a disciplined body. They had realized that obedience to their leader was a religious duty, as a commandment of the Guru, imposed upon them by the *panth*, in whose body the Guru had merged his personality; and every sacrifice made for the *panth* was the real service of the Guru. This singleness of purpose and harmony made them the strongest military body of the day and prepared the way for their establishment as a political power

The Dal Khalsa is called differently by various names and given diverse definitions. James Browne calls it 'Confederacy Khalsa Gee' or the 'Dull Khalsa Gee.' Sir John Malcolm applies the term Dal Khalsa to the combined forces of Sikh sardars at a certain place and time. Sohan Lal says that the conquering armies of the Sikhs formed Dal Khalsa Jio. Ratan Singh Bhangu calls it 'The Dal of the Singhs.' Cunningham says it was the 'army of theocracy of Singhs.' Gian Singh names it *Khalsa Da Dal* or Khalsa Dal. Khalifa Muhammad Hasan writes :

'The Dal was an army of Sikh freebooters who moved about in the country for the sake of plunder.' N.K. Sinha defines it as 'the grand army' of the Khalsa confederacy.

This is ramarkable to note that the first organisation of the Khalsa under Guru Gobind Singh, numbering, about five thousand had broken up at the siege of Anandpur in 1704 after five years. The second organisation of the Khalsa under Banda Bahadur, about fourteen thousand, was destroyed at Gurdas Nangal in 1715 after six years. The third organisation in 1748 was destined to endure upto to end of the century when Ranjit Singh establised monarchy on its ruins.

Meaning and origin of Misl

Misl is an Arabic word meaning alike, equal or similar. It is closely connected with Persian word Misal, implying example, simile, likeness, similitude or picture. In Sikh history the word was first used by Guru Gobind Singh. He applied the word to a body of troops fighting under a leader of their own choice. Sainapat, an eminent scholar in the service of the Guru, uses the word Misl, while describing the battle of Bhangani, fought in 1688 in District Nahan of Himachal Pradesh between Guru Gobind Singh and the neighbouring hill rajas.

Sainapat was present in the battlefield. He says that at the call of Ranjit Nagara or war-drum, the horsemen of Guru Gobind Singh immediately gathered under their banners. The chiefs rushed into the batttlefield and set up their morchas or trenches at different places at the head of their misls. The word here implies a group or a unit of horsemen.

Sainapat again uses this term when Guru Gobind Singh was staying at Nander on the Godavari in Maharashtra. About middle of September 1708 the Guru held a great durbar. There he conferred the title of Bahadur on Banda and he was invested with political and military authority. He was deputed to Panjab to punish Wazir Khan, Governor of Sarhind and establish Sikh sovereignty there. Sainapat says this durbar was attended by the Sikhs in misls.

Sayyid Imam-ud-din Husaini, writing in 1798, says that a Sikh Misl was a *derah* or an encampment. (Yani' misl kudam sardar ast). Sir David Ochterlony in 1809 described a Sikh misl as a 'tribe or race.' Ratan Singh Bhangu who compiled his work, *Prachin Panth Prakash*, in the early thirties of the nineteenth century, interprets the term at several places in the sense of a thana meaning a military or a police post. The head of a thana is called thanewal by him.

Wilson considered it a voluntary association of the Sikhs. Henry T. Prinsep observes that the misls "were confederacies of equals, under chiefs of their own selection." W. L. M'Gregor calls a misls 'a friendly nation.' H.M.L. Lawrence described the misls as 'brotherhoods'. Major Henry Court states that a misl signified dependency to a chief or a petty ruler who was under the authority of a Raja. To J.D. Cunningham the term meant 'armed men and warlike people.' Payne says: "As membership in such a *Jatha* or group conferred political, religious and social equality on all its members, they began to be designated as Misls." Sir James Douie defined it as 'a political and military organisation.'

Syad Muhammad Latif explains it as follows: "The various clans under their respective chiefs were leagued together, and formed a confederacy, which they denominated misl or 'similitude,' thereby implying that the chief and the followers of one clan were equal to those of another." George Batley Scott writes: 'The several states or confedracies were known as misls, a Persion word meaning alike (applied also to a court file of papers).'

Sita Ram Kohli states: 'A Derah was composed of several subordinate groups called Misals. This term seems to have come into use some time in the latter half of the eighteenth century, and denoted the small groups or bands of horsemen into which the more daring Sikhs had organised themselves during their period of exile.' He adds: 'A Misal, therefore, like the company in a regiment, was a subordinate unit of a Derah.'

Teja Singh declares the Sikh misls as 'power of equal rank.' N.K. Sinha writes: 'The Sikhs formed themselves into misls or confederacies.' Muhammad Baqir of Lahore University stated that a misl was 'a sect of the Sikhs.'

The latest Sikh historian and journalist, Khushwant Singh, considers misls as 'militias.'

LIFE AND MANNERS OF THE SIKHS

7

Life and Manners of the Sikhs

The Jats

The military strength of the Sikhs rested mainly on the Jats of the Majha or Central Bari Doab. The Jats may be identical with Jutes or Getae, but they were neither Scythians nor Huns as alleged by some writers. The name is derived from the Sanskrit word Jesht meaning superior or noble. This word is still applied to the elder brother of the husband, showing his position of superiority and honour. In every respect, they are intensely Aryan, in their features, in their figures, in their language, and particularly in their institution. They belonged to the Vaishya class of the Aryans and were the producers of wealth. The senior class of Vaishyas produced money by trade and through the learned professions. The Jats created money out of soil. They formed the principal agricultural class.

Physique

Accustomed from infancy to the most laborious outdoor life and hardest fare, they grew tall, muscular and healthy. They possessed a light frame which was very often exceedingly wiry and capable of great endurance that really appeared astonishing. The genuins Khalsa knew no occupation but war and agriculture, and hence hardened by bold exploits and inured to climate they acquired a physique far superior to that of the general run of Indians. Their thorough-bred looks, martial bearing and dignified appearance could elicit praise even from their bitterest foes. A Muslim historian, though passing the foulest remarks about the Sikhs, which we refrain from reproducing here says, "It may not be unknow that after the Durranis no other troops can be compared to the Sikhs. This sect abounds in giant-sized and lion-limbed youths whose stroke of the leg would certainly cause instantaneous death to a *Vilayti Qipchaq* horse. Their matchlock strikes a man at a distance of nine hundred paces and each of them covers six hundred Kms on horseback. Clearly enough, had it not been so how would they have succeeded in opposing the Vilayti troops? After all, the Durrani army also admitted the sharpness of the sword of the Sikhs." George Thomas , another contemporary testified to this fact in the following words: " When mounted on horseback, their black flowing locks, and half-naked bodies, which are formed in the stoutest and most athletic mould, the glittering of their arms, and the size and the speed of their horses, render their apperance imposing and formidable, and superior to meet most of the cavalry in Hindostan."

So far as their personal appearance is concerned we can imagine their calm, courteous and striking faces and piercing and animated eyes hidden between the mass of moustache and head. Their faces had regular, strongly-marked and handsome features, full of energy in the expression. Their skin was light brown and very often smooth, and fresh-looking. They had, as a rule, beautiful teeth, white, strong and regular, which they cleaned with the usual tooth-stick. The hair, of course, was black and the beards and moustaches were greatly cared for. Their averege weight as supposed by an intelligent man of their class, was a little less than a quintal, and height from 180 to cms 200.

Disposition

The Sikhs, though not an intellectual race, possessed considerable shrewdness united with unusual independence of character. They were sober and well-disposed with a high spirit and frank, simple and unsophisticated manners. They were well-behaved, brave, self-respecting and honourabl. In their dealing with one another they were good- humoured, cheerful and open, perhaps too confiding. They betrayed no sign of timidity or cringing in their manners. They seemed a jovial, light-hearted people, fond of sport, sociable and upright in their domestic life. They were, by no means, devoid of humour. They indulged in a good deal of somewhat coarse raillery. A Sikh loved a joke when the point was broad enough for him to see and he enjoyed very much an appositely quoted proverb. No inferiority or superiority complex existed among them.

Character

There was no quality possessed by the Sikhs more remarkable than the elasticity of character, the power to adapt themselves to all circumstances, an expansive and contractive principle susceptible of being adjusted to the requirements of the moment. They possessed great vigour of body and mind to withstand the changes of climate. The burning sun, heavy rains, freezing winter and rough weather exercised no deterring influence on them. The utmost presecution by the enemies of their faith, the demolition of their homesteads and sacred buildings and the enslaving of their women and children did not damp their spirits. As a consolation to them amidst their never creasing anxiety, restless movement, everchanging scene and unconsicousness as to what the next day might bring forth, they had in them all a sufficient antidote against the fancies which were bound to arise in solitude and in separation from their dear ones. Thus it was due to these faculties that the Sikhs under the pressure of the severest type of calamities displayed a courage and manifested a perseverance of the most obstinate kind.

The other conspicuous trait of their character was the true blood of loyality and devotion to their *Panth* surging in their veins. They never allowed their private feelings, desires, loves, sorrows, likes and dislikes to come between them and good of the *Panth*. A true Sikh let his body be cut to pieces when fighting for his faith; nay, he considered dying in bittle a means of salvation. Some may say that a soldier sells his head for the petty dole he receives every month; but a Sikh did not do so. He was a different man from a conscripted soldier. He served his country of his own free-will. He was, therefore, full of enthusiasm; proud of his wounds, and glorious in his death. He was comforted even in the most cruel sufferings by his exalation, the love of his country and religion, in the vows he made, and in prayers which he addressed to *Wah Guru* for the triumph of his cause. He devoted his head, heart, body and everything dear to him to preserving the influence of his *Panth*. Death, in all its forms, streaily looked him in the face moreoften than we can imagine, but a Sikh maintained a calm, cheerful and dignified demeanour, muttering slowly, "*Nanak! Das sada qurbani.*" (Thy servant, O Nanak! stands ready for sacrifice). This was the noble expression of his spirit.

On the other hand, their success did not make them lose their head. They remained humble, simple and quiet as they were before and proved themselves true and faithful followers of the Guru in magnanimously playing the part of a hero [Sardar] in times of misfortune and warfare and that of a good fellow [Bhaji] in *halcyon days* of peace and prosperity. They seldom resorted to cold-blooded murder even of their enemies and respected the chastity of women as their faith and honour. Thus we can safely say thta prosperity did not spoil them and adversity could not crush them.

As for the bravery and warlike spirit of the Sikhs, they were full of daring, impetuous valour, unflinching courage, patient endurance of fatigue, high aspirations and manliness of sentiment. No superiority of his enemies in number, no stroke, no shot, no shell could make his heart quial since his *Amrit*, taken at the time of baptism, bound him to fight single-handed against millions. They could ply their swords, pliant as aa cane and sharp as a razor, with the perfect ease and dexteritiy, while in the discharge of matchlocks they were invariably dead shots. In a contest with their enemies, they would rush at them like tigers, moving their swords like forked lightning and even the dreaded Durranis found their match in them.

As a testimony to what we have said above, we hand over the pen to Qazi Nur Muhammad, the bigoted author of the *Jang Namah*, who came in the train of Ahmad Shah Abdali in 1764 to fight against the Sikhs. This Qazi, though he uses most offensive expressions for the Sikhs, their religion and their Gurus, as we have had occasion to quote above, feels rather compelled to present a faithful picture of his formidable enemies. He says:, "Do not call the Sikhs 'dogs', because they are lions and are brave like lions in a battle-field. How can a hero of the battle who fights like a lion be a dog? If you cherish a desire of learning the art of war, come before them in the field. They will show you such (wonderful) feats of war. O, swordsman! If you want to learn the modes of fighting, learn from them how to face the foe like a hero and how to come out unscathed from the battle. You may know that their title is Singh (lion) and it is injustice to call them dogs. O youth! If you are ignorant to the Hindi language (I can tell you that), the meaning of Singh is lion. In fact they are lions at the time of battle and when in festivities they surpasss Hatim (in generosity). When they take hold of the Indian sword in hand they gallop from Hind (Ganga Doad, invaded in February, 1764) upto the country of Sind. Nobody, however strong and wealthy, dared to oppose them. When they fight with a spear, they bring defeat to they army of the enemy. When they hold the spear-head upward they break to pieces even the Caucausus Mountain. When they bend a bow they set in it the foe-killing arrow. When they pull it up to the ear, the body of the enemy trembles like a cane. If their hatchet strikes a coat of mail, then this coat of mail itself on the body of the enemy becomes a shroud. The body of each of them looks like a hillock and in grandeur it excels fifty men. Bahram Gor (an Iranian hero) killed wild asses and could frighten tigers. If Bahram Gor comes before them, he also would admit their superiority.

"In addition to these arms when they take up a musket in hand at the time of battle, they come to the field fiercely sprining and roaring like lions and (immediately) split many a breast and make the blood of many others roll in dust. You may say that this musket was invented in ancient times by these dogs and not by Luqman Hakim (Aesop). Though guns are possessed in large numbers by others, yet nobody knows them better. These bad-tempered (people) discharge hundreds of bullets on the enemy on the right and left and in front and on the back. If you disbelieved in what I say, enquire from the brave warriors who will tell you more than what I have said and would have nothing but praise for their (art of) war. The witnesses of my statement are those thirty thousand heroes who fought with them.

"O hero! if their troops take to flight, do not consider it a defeat. It is a trick of their mode of war. May God forbid the repetition of such a fraud! They resort to this deception in order to make a angry enemy grow bod and run in their pursuit. When they find them separaated from their main body and away from help and reinforcement, they at once turn back and give them the hardest possible time. Did you not see that in the battle they took to flight by way of cunning from before the Khan, then turned back from a distance and surrounded the Khan in a circle ? The world-famous wrestler (the Khan) alighted from his horse, fought against them valiantly and in the end the hero escaped from their midst.

"O valiant fighter! do justice to their (art of) war. One of their armies invaded Multan and gave the city over to plunder. The 'dogs' carried off a lot of booty, and my heart does not permit me (to narrate) what the 'dogs' did there. Nobody remembers (such a catastrophe) from the times of the good-natured Adam. None else had ever subjected Multan to such a plunder and pillage. But as God had ordained such a revolution, each of us submitted to His will.

"Besides their flighting, listen to one thing more in which they excel all other warriors. They never kill a coward and do not obstruct one who flees from the field. They do not rob a woman of her gold and ornaments, may she be a queen or a slave-girl. Adultery also does not exist among the 'dogs'. `None of them is a thief.' A woman whether young or old is called by them a *'Burhiya'*—one who has retired from the world. The meaning of 'burhiya' in Hindi language is an aged woman. The `dogs' never resort to stealing and no thief exists among them and they do not keep company with the adulterer and the thief."

If we have to point out any defect in the character of the Sikh of this period, we might blame him for his raids and plundering expeditions. This can be done on strictly moral grounds. But in coming to this conclusion we lose sight of two important factors. Firstly, we make the mistake of judging him by the present day standard or according to an ideal code of ethics. During the period under review even Government officials attached no importance to property rights. Najabat Khan of Kunjpura, Isa Khan Munj and many others openly resorted to plundering and waylaying travellers. The ministers of the Delhi Empire took no notice of their misdeeds because they also received a share in the booty. Secondly, we forget that the Sikhs were a persecuted people to whom all means of livelihood were denied. Thus they were compelled to such a course by bare necessity.

Moreover organised brigandage was only aa transitional stage to national herosim. It was as a freebooter that Nadir Shah became the greatest national hero of Iran and secured her liberation from the Afghan yoke. Ahmand Shah Abdali followed in his footsteps and made Afghanistan, his homeland, free and independent. The Sikh, though a plunderer and freebooter in the ordinary sense of the word, was impelled by a higher moral force which brought out all his virtues.

Recruitment to the Sikh army

Generally Sikhs were recruited as soldiers in the Sikh army and no consideration was paid to their original caste or creed. Enlistement was voluntry. The fresh recuites could join the contingent of any cheif and had perfect liberty to transfer their services to a more popular leader. Hence it was always incumbent upon the chief to maintain his popularity and to keep his followers in good humour. No records of the soldiers' names, service, payment etc., were kept. This fact accounts for our failure to have an exact number of the strength of the Sikh army. Regarding this matter we are left entirely to guess work and the rough estimate of the contemporararay writers.

Drill and discipline

The Sikh soldiers were given no training in drill, marching, manner of attack or the ways of defence, etc. either individually or in groups. As a matter of fact the Sikhs of those days never dreamed of such things. In spite of this drawback, the Sikhs never proved themselves bad soldiers or wanting in war tactics. This deficiency of the military science was made up by their religious zeal, single-minded devotion to the *Panth*, strong passion of revenge and intense feeling of self-respect. There was no organisation of the Sikh soldiers into regular regiments of uniform size. The contingents of individual chiefs, who were numerous, and whether their number was big or small, formed the units of the Dal Khalsa. When the expedition was organized on a large scale, the whole Dal Khalsa united under the command of one supreme chief, usually Jassa Singh Ahluwalia, and all the heads of the various contingents obeyed him though much was left to their discretion. In cases of disobedience of orders a council of war consisting of five prominent leaders punished them, and these punishments were borne without any grumbling because it was considered that they were decreed by the Guru through his chosen five. The Sikhs, therefore, humorously gave such punishment the name of receiving one's salary. It may be noted that the cases of disobedience were very rare.

Modes of payment

The modes of payment to the Sikh soldiers were various. They were paid no monthly salary or weekly wages. They were permitted to retain a portion of the booty acquired in a raid. To some money was also paid in small sums while others were allotted lands; but the most common method, then in vogue, was to pay them in kind at the time of each harvest. A fixed quantity of grain, cotton, sugar and fodder, and other things, the produce of the country, was allowed to each individual.

Equipment

The accoutrements of a Sikh soldier while on a march consisted of offensive and defensive weapons, priming horns, ammunition pouches, two blankets, a grain bag and heel ropes, while their cooking utensils were carried on panies. Swords, spears, scimitar, sabre, two-edged daggers, lances, muskets, guns, cultasses, pikes, bows and arrows were generally employed. In the handling of these arms, especially the matchlock and the sabre, they were uncommonly expert. Shield of hide and sometimes a coat of arms were the main weapons of defence. The chiefs were only distinguishable from their followers by finer horses and arms. In their excursions or in the camps they carried no tents. The chiefs were sheltered by only a small square canopy of coarse cotton cloth, supported on four lances, planted in the ground, while the soldiers rested on the bare ground under a blanket spread over two lances in case of rain and sun and placing beneath this rude shelter a saddle and a blanket to serve the office of a matterss and pillow; otherwise they wrapped themselves in cotton sheets in summer and in blankets in winter. On a march they put the blankets beneath the saddle, so that with this scantly accountrements they could encamp or decamp in a few minutes at their will.

Method of warfare

The method of warefare of the Sikhs was rather crude. They generally adopted guerilla tractices of warfare, though about 1765 they seem to have taken to settled fighting in ranks. Their method of attack, as is described by contemporary writers, was this. A party of Sikh horsemen numbering from forty upward would advance towards the ranks of the enemy galloping at a quick pace and would suddely draw up their horses who were so expertly trained to this sort of performance that on receiving a stroke of the hand they would stop from a full gallop. Then they simultaneously discharged their loaded guns from a distance with such marksmanship that not a single would fail in its aim. After that they suddenly retired to about a hundred paces, re-loaded their pieces and repeated the old process. All this was done with an alacrity and activity unparalled by other people of India. This caused a great annoyance to the enemy and made them helpless against it. The Sikhs, on their part, were no more troubled about bullets, shells and balls then, if they had been mosquitoes, flies or bees.

Another method was engaging the enemy at close quarters in a continued skirmish, advancing and retreating so rapidly and with such vigour that the enemy soon got puzzled. This process was continued until the man and the animal became equally exhausted. The front ranks then would retire to the rear and fresh troops would come forward to replace them in turn. The fatigued horses were let loose to graze for a while and the soldiers themselves would wash down their throat a little parched gram, and thus refreshed would renew their attacks.

An old tractic, so frequently resorted to by the Sikhs, was to discharge a sudden volley of bullets and arrows upon the enemy, engage them in fight for an hour or so, and then suddenly retire from the field. This gave the enemy an idea that the Sikhs had taken to flight. A detachment of the enemy pursued them. When the Sikhs found their pursures away from the immediate succour of their main body, they would, all of a sudden, come to a halt, return and attack them vehemently. Each Sikh fought hand to hand with his opponent, grappled his body to his, gripped and wrestled with him and threatened him with frowning looks, dreadful gestures, horrible distortions and hideous cries. They then throttled, tore and slaughtered him thus cutting the whole batch to pieces.

Sometimes combats between individuals were held. This was the most attractive form of fighting, because it allowed personal valour to come out glaringly. The Sikhs were light horsemen, each man carrying his food, forage, bedding, head and heel ropes for their animals, marching from 80 to 150 kms after a defeat, and then halting in complete readiness to fight on the following day.

At the time of Ahmad Shah's seventh invasions we come across two or three cases when the Sikhs preferred to have a pitched battle. We find them organised in a regular battle array to which we have already referred in these pages.

Raids

It was in their raids that the Sikhs were at their best. In the beginning of the period treated of in the previous pages we started with them as raiders and left them at the end as rulers, but still retaining an essential part of their old character. Their perfect self-confidence, the lightening-like rapidity of their movements and the manner in which they could extort money from the people made them a great terror, to which large tracts full of teeming population yielded so submissively that one or two Sikhs could easily over-awe a big village. This will be clear from an entry recorded by Forster when on his travels, dated the 28th February, 1783 at Kheynaspoor near Dehra Dun. It runs,—'I saw two Sicque horsemen, who had been sent from their country to receive the Siringaghur tribute, which is collected from the revenues of certain custom-houses. From the manner in which these men were treated, or rather treated themselves, I frequently wished for the power of migrating into the body of a Sicque for a few weeks—so well did these cavaliers fare. No sooner had they alighted, than beds were prepared for their repose, and their horses were supplied with green barley pulled out of the field. The *Kafilah* travellers wer contented to lodge on the ground, and expressed their thanks for permission to purchase what they required; such is the difference between those who were in, and those who were out of power.

Marching from 100 to 200 kms daily and continuing the exertion for many successive days, which might appear incredible to us, their incursions became formidable. As most of the Sikh soldiers had two or three horses each, they could quickly gather large booty. Franchline in his *Shah Aulum* (pp. 76-7) gives the following interesting details about the manner in which they conducted their predatory excursions. He writes, 'Inured from their infancy to the hradships of a military life the Seiks are addicted to predatory warfare in a manner peculiar to themselves alone. When determined to invade a neighbouring province, they assmeble at first in small numbers on the frontier, when having first demanded the *rakhi* or tribute, if it be complied with, they retire peaceably, but when this is denied, hostilities commence, and the Seiks in their progress, are accustomed to lay waste the country on all sides, carrying along with them as many of the inhabitants as they can take priosners and all the cattle. The prisoners are detained as slaves, unless redeemed by a pecuniary compensation. Griffin writes: "One thing, in their favour must be said, which raises them far above the Pindaris like men, and not like demons. There are few stories in Sikh History of outrage to women and torture to men such as stain the pages of South Indian History with cruelty and blood.

Horses

The Sikhs had achieved success rather to a wonderful degree in horsemanship. Without property, without home and without family, the Sikhs, in their days of persecution, had for all their worldly goods, their horses and their weapons, which were to them their dearest possessions, with whom they would most reluctantly part. Their horses were so expertly trained that they responded to their voice, touch of the hand and stroke of the heel. The men had cquired such practice in handling even a swimming horse that they could swim across a swollen and swift river with perfect easiness of mind. The love of a Sikh soldier for his horse was proverbial. They never hesitated in spending any amount of money in decorating and furnishing their horses, and, as a matter of fact, the quality of a horse and its equipment displayed the social and financial position of its owner. Its utility to them in the life of those days they clearly understood. "Though they make merry on the demise of any of their brethren," says Forster on p. 334 of Vol. I of his *Journey*, "they mourn for the death of a horse thus shewing their love of an animal so necessary to them in their professional capacity." Their horses were to the middle size, strong, active, patient, mild-tempered and noted for incredibel endurance. The Sikh horses were of the best breed in India 'owing to the use formerly made there of Arabian and Persian stallions, and something in the temperature of the air and water of the country.'

There were several good breeding grounds of horses. The horses of the sub-divisions of Fatahjhang, Pindi Gheb and Rawalpindi were much sought after; those of the Jehlam district, especially of the Dhan, were held in good estimation. The greater part of the Sikh cavalry was horsed from the Dhanni plains, north of the Salt Range. Some of them were fast, but nearly all were graceful remarkably enduring and able to go over the stoniest ground without shoes. The horses of Jhang and Multan bore a high reputation and the mares wer esteemed to be among the best in the Panjab. The horses bred along the Lahore border, in the Nakka country, were held in good repute. These were country-bred, large, strong and long-winded and were much fancied by the Sikhs. These were uncommonly fine mares or stallions. The Lakhi Jungle was also famous for a breed of excellent horses called the *Jungle Sazi*.

Horses were generally fed on gram, barley and a kind of grass called '*doop*' which is very nutritive, but *moth, bajra* and *tara-mira* were also in use. In the spring they were stuffed with green wheat and *gur*. The usual feed for a brood mare was 4 kg of grain a day besides grass. Colts were allowed to run loose in the young wheat, and were also given *jowar* and *moth*. Breaking in commenced when they were two years old. They were, at first, ridden bare back. An amble was the favourite pace, but an accomplished mare was taught to go through many exercises.

The prices of the horses ranged between two hundred and one thousand rupees George Thomas remarks that the breeders were averse to dispose of their brood mares, and if they were prevailed upon to do so, they would exaact double the price, though in general with regard to the foreigners, they could not be persuaded to part with a brood mare for any price.

Their food

The food of the Sikhs was of the simplest and coarsest kind, of littel variety and such as is used by the poorest people in India from necessity. Two or three meals a day were eaten, according to the season of the year and the amount of work to be done. Their best dish was the bread baked on pan and embers, taken in the morning with *lassi* (buttermilk) and in the evening with herbs and different sorts of pulses. They indulged in this luxary when at full leisure; but when in a hurry they washed down their throst hastily parched vetches and tares and a handful of gram. A large quantity of milk was consumed daily, and in its season a good deal of sugar-cane was munched. Salt, chillies, onions and other condiments if available were also used. *Dalya*, made from bruised wheat, *jawar, makai,* and *khichri* made for *bajra mixed with mung ki dal* were the favourite dishes. It was considered better to make the bread one part of gram with two of wheat, salt being mixed with it. This was called *'missi'* or '*besni*'. The thick '*roti*' made from wheat alone was called *'pani ki roti'*, the thin made after rolling out was called '*phulka*'. Pickle (*achar*) and some rough *chatni* completed their ideal dish.

On the occasion of a marriage or other ceremony superior food was consumed, and a great deal of sugar in some form or other (*gur, shakkar, khand*) was used. *Gur*, when it was to be bought, was eaten as a luxury in the cold weather; but when it was prepared at the '*kohlu*', it was turned to domestic use in the different stages of its making. The raw juice mixed with rice and milk was served up as a savoury dish by the good wife to her husband at his early morning meal. The '*karah prashad*', consisting of equal portions of flour, sugar and clarified butter with water a double portion of the whole, was the consecrated food and was eaten at all religions ceremonies, and at the *pahul* when all those initiated ate from one dish.

With the exception of beef, they had no objection to a diet of flesh, fowl, or fish. The animal must be killed after the *jhatka* fashion, *i.e.,* decapitation. *Jhatka* was not necessary when an animal was killed in sport. The necks of the birds were wrung, but those killed in sport were also accepted. Hunting of wild pigs was a favourite game. The Sikhs were, as they are up to the present day, remarkably fond of its flesh. They abhorred smoking tobacco, but intoxicated themselves with opium, *bhang* and spirits of their country manufacture.

Men, women and children ate the same food. The full meal for a man was one kilogram. The woman generally consumed as much as the man and no wonder, for a good Jat wife was by no means a lazy creature or devoid of muscle.

Dress

The Sikhs were simple and unostentatious in their dress. They generally wore undyed clothes made of home-spun cotton stuff. This consisted in the simplest from of three articles:—an ample turban of coarse cloth, of white or blue cotton, drawers (*kachha*) generally blue, and a kind of checkered plaid or blue cloth thrown loosely over the shoulders and coming down between the legs was confined round the waist by a belt of cotton. These with a pair of slippers made by the village cobbler, constituted the simple and inexpensive wardrobe of a Sikh for the greater part of the year. In winter he had a blanket of wool which usually cost Rs. 2 or a *duhar* or *chautahi*, a shet of very thick cotton stuff, double wove.

The chiefs were distinguished by wearing some heavy gold braceletes on their wrists, and sometimes a chain of the same metal bound round their arms; otherwise, no distinction appeared amongs them. On the occasion of a wedding a somewhat better dress was worn, and some colour was shown in the *pagri*, the white cloth being tied over one coloured yellow or some shade of red or green. Sometimes they affected these coloured *pagris* and the mixtures were often fanciful.

The Sikh women wore *pajamas*, called *suthan*, made of *susi*, coloured cotton stuff, and a *chadar* worn over the head and shoulders, either coloured in the case of young women, or uncoloured made of *garha* or *dhotar*, thick or thin cloth according to the season. This upper garment when coloured was of dyed cloth or of *phulkari*, *i.e.*, worked with silk flowers, or of *sitari*, another form of silk work; most women also wore a *kurta* or waistcoat. When going to another village they wore a *ghagra* or petticoat above the trousers, and a *choli* or bodice of coloured cloth.

The everyday clothes were always prepared from the village-made cloth, which though rough proved very strong and durable. The ordinary dyes were indigo for blue and safflower and red and yellow.

Amusements

As a general rule, the Sikhs were manly, robust and vigorous and were passionately devoted to sports. The boys generally played *Gullidanda*, and *Pitkaudi* or *Kabaddi*. The men used with great dexterity wooden dumbbells which were enormously heavy and long. They also lifted and threw heavy weights. Both these amusements contributed a great deal to the uprightness of their carriage and fine figures. The game of *saunchi*, too, was very popular.

The most universally popular sport was wrestling. At stated times in the year, large rural gatherings took place at some places to witness public matches. Prizes of horses, milch cows and scarfs were awarded to the best wrestlers.

Music, singing and dancing were all amusements much enjoyed by them, in particular at fairs. Dancing was generally performed by hired *nach* girls on the occasion of weddings or other festivities.

More intellectual anusement was sometimes found in listening to songs, sung by professional *mirasis* or *bhats*, a tribe of hereditary ballad singers, whose songs, ballads, and tales recited to the accompaniment of a fiddle or a tambourine, were in reality the favourite literature of the day. Occasionally a body of strolling acrobats visited a village and the people collected to see the exhibition. Snake charmers provided some recreation.

Women

The women were generally fine-looking, tall and graceful and their figures in youth were well-rounded and supple; but they were inferior in physique to the men probably from early marriage, frequency of pregnancy, poor diet and bad sanitary conditions. Their part was to guide the house. They ground corn, milked the cows and buffaloes, churned butter, cooked food, fetched water, span cotton for home consumption and attended to the sewing of family clothes, besides lending a hand to their husbands in the work of the field. The higher functions of the wife, however, were not unknown. She had a paramount influence in the household, by controlling the famlily purse and endeavouring in every way to prevent her husband from extravagance. Besides, she had the management of the family marriages; and if she was a clever woman her lord, if only for his own comfort, had to keep her in good humour.

In the holiday times the women's garments were gay with many colours and good deal of ostentation was displayed. A woman's social standing was greatly determined by her jewels in which the spare capital was invested, as the money could always be realized on occasion of need. Great expenses were incurred on marriages. Private marriages were condemned, and were but seldom contracted.

In the struggle of independence the Sikh women played no small part. They were splendid beings. They urged their husbands forward, even taking a part in the struggle themselves. Thus we could behold in them honour, heroism, faith, patriotism and liberty.

Fairs

The Sikhs were a lively and good-tempered people, fond of fairs, festivals and public assemblies. The principal fairs were the Diwali and Baisakhi, held at Amritsar in the months of November and April respectively. Two large fairs were. held at Tran Taran, in March and August. Religious fairs were also held at Goindwal, Khadur, Derah Baba Nanak, and other Sikh Shrines. A big fair of Hola Mohalla was celebrated with great enthusiasm at Anandpur.

GENEALOGY OF GURUS

8

Genealogy of Gurus

Appendix I

FIRST GURU

Baba Kalu — Mata Tripta
Guru Nanak — Mata Sulakhani
1469—1539

Sri Chand(S) | Lakshmi Dass(S)

SECOND GURU

Baba Pheru — Daya Kaur
Guru Angad — Mata Khivi
1504—1552

Amro(d) | Dattu(s) | Dasu(S)

THRID GURU

Baba Tej Bhan — Mata Bhakt Kaur
Guru Amardas — Mata Mansa Devi
1479—1574

Mohan(s) | Mohri(s) | Dani(d) | Bhani(d)

FOURTH GURU

Baba Haridas — Mata Daya Kaur
Guru Ramdas — Bibi Bhani
1534—1581

Prithi Chand (s) | Mahadeo (s) | Guru Arjan (s)

FIFTH GURU

Guru Arjan — Mata Ganga
1563—1606

SIXTH GURU

Guru Hargobind — Mata Gujri
1595—1644

Baba Gurdita(s) | Atal Rai(s) | Anil Rai(s)
Suraj Bhan(s) | sAmro(d)
Guru Tegh Bahadur(s)

SEVENTH GURU

Guru Har Rai — Mata Kishen Kaur
1630—1661
Ram Rai(s) Guru Har Krishen(s)

EIGHTH GURU

Guru Har Krishen
1656—1664

NINTH GURU

Guru Teg Bahadur — Mata Gujri
1621—1675

TENTH GURU

Mata Sundri — Guru Gobind Singh — Mata Jio
1666—1708

Ajit Singh | Jujhar Singh | Zorawar Singh | Fateh Singh

Guru Har Rai was the grandson of Guru Hargobind and first cousin of Guru Gobind Singh.

Gur Har Krishen was the grandson of Baba Gurditta (brother of Guru Teg Bahadur, thus in relation was also grandson of Guru Teg Bahadur).

Guru Teg Bahadur was Chacha (Uncle) of Guru Har Rai.

Guru Gobind Singh was first cousin of Guru Har Rai and Chacha (Uncle) of Guru Har Krishen.

HISTORICAL TABLE

THE SIKH GURUS
AND
THE PERIOD (YEARS) OF THEIR GURUSHIP

1. Guru Hargobind
2. Guru Gobind Singh
3. Guru Nanak
4. Guru Arjan
5. Guru Amardas
6. Guru Har Rai
7. Guru Angad
8. Guru Tegh Bahadur
9. Guru Ramdas
10. Guru Harkrishen

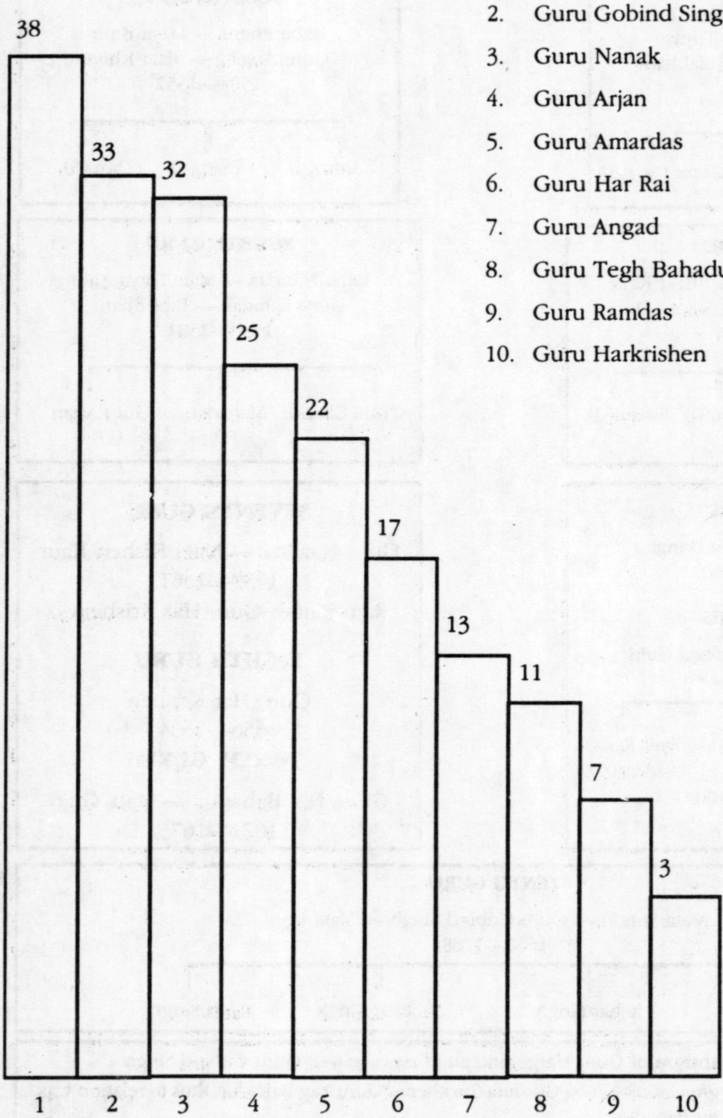

Total Years = 203

HISTORICAL TABLE V

The Sikh Gurus, their dates of birth, their dates of leaving this world, dates of transferring the Guruship and the number of days of stay in this world after the transfer of the Guruship.

Name of the Guru	**Date of Birth**	**Date of Departure From This World**	**Date of Fusing One Soul In Another Soul**	**Days of Stay in This World After Transferring The Guruship**
Guru Nanak	21 October 1469	22 September 1539	7 September 1539	15
Guru Angad	31 March 1504	26 March 1552	26 March 1552	3
Guru Amardas	5 May 1479	1 September 1574	30 August 1574	1
Guru Ramdas	24 October 1534	1 September 1581	1 September 1581	
Guru Arjan	15 April 1563	30 May 1606	25 May 1606	5
Guru Hargobind	19 June 1595	3 March 1644	3 March 1644	-
Guru Har Rai	16 January 1630	6 October 1661	6 October 1661	-
Guru Har Krishan	7 July 1656	30 March 1664	20 March 1664	10
Guru Tegh Bahadur	1 April 1621	11 November 1675	11 November 1675	-
Guru Gobind Singh	22 December 1666	18 October 1708	3 October 1708	15
Guru Granth Sahib	16 August 1604-1706			

HISTORICAL TABLE VI

THE SIKH GURUS

Name of the Guru	Age At Marriage	Number of Wives	Business Or Profession Before the Guruship	Faith Before Embracing Sikhism	Period of Service With The Previous Guru (Years)
Guru Nanak	18	1	Accountant / store-keeper with the Governor of Punjab (Government service)	Born in Hindu family	
Guru Angad	20	1	Trader-Shop (General store)	Worshipper of Durga	15
Guru Amardas	28	1	Farmer plus trader	Vashnavite	11
Guru Ramdas	19	1	Merchant	Became Sikh at a very young age	21
Guru Arjan	16	1		-	-
Guru Hargobind	12	3	-	-	-
Gur Har Rai	11	1	-	-	-
Guru Har Krishen	-	-	-	-	-
Guru Tegh Bahadur	11	1	-	-	-
Guru Gobind Singh	18	3	-	-	-

HISTORICAL TABLE VII
THE SIKH GURUS

Name of the Guru	Travels Within & Outsie India For The Missionary Work	Cities Founded	Total Shabads In Guru Granth Sahib	Number Of Ragas in Which The Shabads Are Compiled
Guru Nanak	From Tibet to Ceylon and From Assam to Mecca	Kartarpur	974 including Japji, Asa Di Var, Bara Mah	19
Guru Angad	-	Khadur	63 Sloaks	-
Guru Amardas	-	Goindwal	969 including Anand Sahib	17
Guru Ramdas	-	Amritsar	688 including Lavan	
Guru Arjan	Punjab	Taran-Taran	2,312 including Sukhmani Sahib	30
Guru Hargob-ind	Punjab, U.P., Kashmir	Kiratpur Hargobindpur	-	-
Guru Har Rai	Punjab	-	-	-
Guru Har Krishen	Delhi	-	-	-
Guru Tegh Bahadur	Punjab, U.P., Bengal, As-sam, Bihar	Anandpur	115	
Guru Gobind Singh	Punjab, U.P., Rajasthan, Andhra Pradesh, Maharashtra	Anandpur, Paonta-Sahib	Author of Dasam Granth One Sloak in Guru Granth Sahib	

HISTORICAL TABLE VIII

THE SIKH GURUS AND THEIR FAMILIES

Name of the Guru	Age At The Date Marriage	Age At The Birth of Children	Sons	Daughters
Guru Nanak	18	25 27	1. Shri Chand 2. Lakhmi Chand	None
Guru Angad	20	21 34	1. Dassu 2. Dattu	None
Guru Amardas	28	NA NA NA 60	1. Mohan 2. Mohri	1. Dani 2. Bhani
Guru Ramdas	19	24 26 29	1. Prithia 2. Mahadev 3. Arjan	None
Guru Arjan	16	32	1. Hargobind	None
Guru Hargobind	9, 18, 20	18 20 21 23 27 30.	1. Gurditta 2. Suraj Mal 3. Ani Rai 4. Atal Rai 5. Tegh Bahadur	1. Viro
Guru Har Rai	11	17 27	1. Ram Rai 2. Har Krishen	None
Guru Har Krishen	-	-	-	-
Guru Tegh Bahadur	11	45	1. Gobind Singh	None
Guru Gobind Singh	11, 18, 34	20 24 30 33	1. Ajit Singh 2. Jujhar Singh 3. Zorawar Singh 4. Fateh Singh	

HISTORICAL TABLE IX
THE SIKH GURUS AND THEIR CONTEMPORARY RULERS

Name of the Guru	Age	Name of The Indian Ruler	Age	Name of The King/ Queen of England	Age
Guru Nanak	70	Lodhi Dynasty- Sikandar Lodhi Mughal Dynasty Babur	47	House of Yorks Edward IV Edward V Richard III House of Tudors Henry VII Henry VIII	41 13 33 52 56
Guru Angad	48	Humayun	49	Edward VI	16
Guru Amardas	95	Akbar	62	Mary I Elizabeth I	42 70
Guru Ramdas	47	Akbar		Elizabeth I	
Guru Arjan	43	Jehangir	58	Elizabeth I House of Stuarts James I	59
Guru Hargob-ind	49	Jehangir Shah Jahan	54	Charles I	49
Guru Har Rai	31	Shah Jahan Aurangzeb	89	Charles II	55
Guru Har Krishen	8	Aurangzeb		Charles II	
Guru Tegh Bahadur	54	Aurangzed		Charles II	
Guru Gobind Singh	42	Aurangzeb		James II William III Mary II Anne	68 52 32 49

HISTORICAL TABLE X

WORLD PROPHETS AND THE AGE OF THEIR ENLIGHTENMENT

Name of the Prophet And His Faith	**Age At The Point of Enlightenment**	**Country of Brith**	**Date of Birth**
Abraham-Judaism	50 yrs	Canaan (Palestine west of Jordan)	2000 B.C.
Zoraster-Parsis	30 yrs	Persia (North East Iran)	618 B.C.
Lord Rama-Hinduism		Ayodhaya (U.P.) India	600 B.C.
Lord Krishan-Hinduism	5 yrs	Mathura (U.P.) India	500 B.C.
Gotam Buddha-Buddhism	36 yrs	Kapilavastu (Bihar)	560/500 B.C.
Mahavir-Jainsim	42 yrs	Bihar, India	599/500 B.C.
Jesus Christ-Christiantly	30 yrs	Bethlehem, Israel	4 B.C.
Hazrat Mohammed-Islam	40 yrs	Mecca, Saudi Arabia	570 A.C.
Guru Nanak	36 yrs 6 months 15 days	Talwandi, Punjab, Pakistan	1469 A.D.
Guru Gobind Singh	8 yers 11 months 19 days	Patna, Bihar, India	1666 A.D.

In May 1762, only three months after the great holocaust, the Sikhs gathered their forces again the defeated the Faujdar of Sirhind at Harnaulgarh, plundered and Jullunder Doab, re-captured the Doab between Ravi and Jhelum and blocked all the communication between Delhi and Lahore.

29.10

In October, the Sikhs gathered at Harimandir and celebrated the festival of Diwali. Abdali sent an envoy to have a peace treaty with the Sikhs. The Sikhs declined his offer.

29.11

Abdali marched towards Amritsar. A pitched battle was fought at the outskirts of Amritsar. The Sikhs inflicted a defeat at heavy losses on Abdali who fled to Lahore. This was the first battle victory of the Sikhs against Abdali himself.

29.12

The Sikhs avenged their holocaust and defeat at the hands of Abdali. Abdali appointed Kabuli Mal as the Governor of Lahore and left for Qandhar.

29.13

In the next two years, the Sikhs captured most of the important cities of Punjab and appointed their own nominees to look after the political and economic needs of the areas.

29.14

In October 1764 Abdali made his seventh invasion of India. He brought with him eighteen thousand Afghan soldiers, another twelve thousand Bluchs joined him near Eminabad. The Sikhs retreated to Lakhi jungle and waited for the right opportunity to attack Abdali.

29.15

In November 1764, the joint forces of Afghans and Baluchs invaded Amritsar. Sardar Gurbakhs Singh of the village Khem Karan, was guarding the Harmandir with only thirty other brave Sikhs. Abdali and his generals were amazed to see only thirty Sikhs facing an army of thirty thousand Baluchs and Afghans. All the Sikhs fell at the bullets and arrows of the Abdali's army.

29.16

Abdali blew up the Harmandir for the third time and filled the sarover with cow dung and the dead cows.

29.17

From Amritsar Abdali wnet towards Batala in pursuit of the Sikhs. Whichever way the army turned, the people were massacred. No one can count the number of things that fell into the hands of the crusaders.

29.18

In March 1765 Abdali returned back home. As soon as he crossed Sutlej the Sikhs fell upon him. The battle lasted for seven days. Abdali left the battle field and hastily headed for the frontier. This was the second defeat which the Sikhs and inflicted upon Abdali.

29.19

On 10th April 1765 the Sikhs celebrated Baisakhi at Harmandir sahib and rebuilt the shrine and cleaned the pool.

29.20

On 16th April 1765 Bhangi Sardar Gujar Singh and Lehna Singh forced their way into Lahore. Sardar Sobha Singh Kanhaya joined them the next day. On the plea of the inhabitants of the city no loot or plunder took place.

29.21

In October 1765 the Sikhs celebrated Diwali at Amritsar with great festivities without any obstruction or fear.

29.22

In the next twelve months various Sikh jathas had advanced up to Karnal in Haryana, Rewari and Chambel in Madhya Pradesh and Jaipur in Rajasthan. They came back to Punjab with heavy loot of money, gold and jewels.

EIGHTH AND NINTH INVASIONS OF AHMED SHAH ABDALI (1766-1772)

This period witnessed the Eighth and Ninth invasions by Abdali, the death of Abdali and the rise of the Sikhs as the future masters of Punjab.

30.1

In November 1766 Abdali invaded India for the eighth time. He crushed all resistance which came in his way. He went to Gujarat then to Sialkot and then turned to Lahore. The tree sardars evacuated Lahore and retreated to a place of safety.

30.2

Abdali entered Lahore on 22nd December 1766 and immediately summoned a conference of the elite of the city.

30.3

The elders of the city requested Abdali to appoint Sardar Lehna Singh as the Governor of Punjab, as he had administered the city without any bias of religion or creed. Abdali sent an envoy to the Sardar with gifts and in invitation. The Sardar refused to see Abdali.

30.4

Abdali did not know what to do with the people who could not be scared with death and who did not make friends with him.

30.5

In January 1767, General Jahan Khan, on the instructions of Abdali encircled Amritsar. This time all the Misls gathered in full strength and fell upon Jahan Khan. Five thousand Afghan soldiers were killed.

30.6

Abadli came to the rescue of Jahan Khan and the combined army of the two entered Amritsar in February 1767.

30.7

This time Abdali did not blow up or defile the Harimandir.

30.8

Abdali left Punjab for Kabul in March 1767. By the end of 1767 the Sikhs had re-taken the whole of Punjab.

30.9

In the North and North West, Gujjar Singh captured Rawalpindi. In the South and South East the Sikhs took over the Gangetic Doab. Thus they became the de-facto masters of Punjab in December 1767,

30.10

Abdali made his ninth and final attact on India. to re-conquer Punjab, in January 1769. The Sikh resistance did not allow him to go any further than Jhelum.

30.11

He returned to Qandhar as a defeated and broken man and died in October 1772.

RISE AND FALL OF SIKH MISLS (1772-1798)

This period lists the rise and fall of the Sikhs Misls and the foundation of the great Empire of Punjab, which later flourished under the strong reins of Maharaja

Ranjit Singh.

31.1

The period of the next 24 years of the Sikh history is both confusing and disconcerting.

31.2

This period witnessed the rise of the Sikh Misls, their in-fight and ultimate fall.

31.3

The misls were actually founded in 1748. On the Baisakhi day of 1748 the Dal Khalsa, under the command of Jassa Singh Ahluwalia, was organised into eleven misls. They were as follows:

Ahluwalia, Singhpuria, Sukerchakia, Nishanwalia, Bhangi, Kanhaya, Nakkai, Dallewalia, Shaheed, Karora Singhia, Ramgarhia, Though Phoolkia was the twelfth misl it was not a part of the Dal Khalsa.

31.4

After the last invasion by Ahmed Shah Abdali and his subsequent death, a novel sitation was created in Punjab.

31.5

Taimur, the son of Abdali, could wrest his control only on his father's conquests west of Indus along with Kashmir, Bahawalpur, Multan and Sindh.

31.6

The Mughal Emperor and shifted his seat to Allahabad from Delhi and was living there under the protection of the British.

31.7

Delhi was under the control of Najibuddaulah, a nominee of the Emperor.

31.8

The territory which lay between Indus and Jamuna was under the control of Sikh Misls.

31.9

Immediately after the death of Abdali, the Punjab was divided by the misls thus:

Ahluwalia—this misl took over the control of the area along river Sutlej i.e., Sultanpur and Kapurthala;

Ramgarhias—this misl levied tribute on Kangra, Nurpur, Chamba, Basohli and Mandi;

Sukerchakias—this misl took over the charge of Gujranwala and all area which lay around it;

Bhangis—this misl controlled the kingdom of Jammu;

Other misls—they earmarked their own territories and became their rulers or revenue collectors.

31.10

Apart from the Sikhs, Afghans and the Mughals there were four other forces trying to wrest power in and around Punjab they were, Jats, Rajputs, Rohillsa and Marathas.

31.11

In 1773-1774 the Sikhs advanced up to the outskirts of Delhi and plundered a number of villages. They killed Mullah Rahim Dad Khan the subedar of Panipat and took temporary control of the city.

31.12

In the spring of 1775 the leader of Bhangis and Karora Singhias defeated Zabita Khan, the Rohilla chief. He offered to the Sardars a large sum of money and also an assistance of quell the imperial resistance to enter Delhi.

31.13

In March 1776, the Sikhs with the help of Rohillas, defeated the Mughal forces near Muzaffarnagar and the whole of the Yamuna-Gangetic Doab was now under their protection.

31.14

In the summer of 1778, the Sikhs defeated the Mughal forces and entered the Capital. They stayed there for a few months and later crossed the Ganges into the territory of the Nawab Wazir. To weaken the Sikh strength, the Mughals resorted to diplomacy and made the Sikh Sardars suspicious of each other. The Sardars fell directly into their nasty plan and started plundering each other's domain.

31.15

In the autumn of 1779, Prince Farkhunda Bakht, with the help fo many Sikh Sardars besieged Patiala. With the appearance of Jassa Singh Ahluwalia on the scene, the Sardars, which indcluded Rai Singh of Buria, Baghel Singh of Jind and Bhanga Singh of Tannesar, deserted the Mughal Camp and joined the Sikh forces. The Mughal army was completely routed and lost many thousand soldiers and a large amount of equipment.

31.16

The years 1779-1785 gave to the Sikhs many opportunities to enter Delhi and unfurb the Sikh flag at the Red Fort, but no Sikh chief availed these God-given opportunities and openings. More than three times Sardar Baghel Singh entered the Mughal capital, Delhi, triumphantly. Each time, God had given him a chance to announce, from the historic Red Fort, the formation of the Sikh empire. But every time, the opportunity slipped from right under his nose. The same can be said of the other Sikh Sardars. This failure of the Sikhs to establish an empire could be attributed to their lack of knowledge in politics, statecraft and civic set-up. They were certainly great soldiers but were poor administrators. In March 1783, Baghel Singh, while in Delhi, ordered the construction of Gurdwaras at the sites of the execution and cremation of Guru Tegh Bahadur (Sis Ganj and Rakab Ganj) and the sites of the cremations of Guru Harkrishen, Mata Sahib Devan and Mata Sundri.

31.17

In April 1782, Najaf Khan the think-tank of the Mughal Emperor, died. In the next eight months and then in 1783 and in 1784, Baghel Singh, Jassa Singh Ahluwalis, Jassa Singh Ramgarhia and Karam Singh crossed Yamuna many a times and were given the change to become the rulers of Hindustan but they did not avail the opportunity. Instead of capturing Delhi they went over into the doab and crossed the Ganges at several points.

On March 11, 1783, Jassa Singh Ahluwalia entered the Red Fort and sat on the throne in Diwan-e-am. But a subsequent fight between the Sardars of Jassa Singh Ahluwalia's and Jassa Singh Ramgarhia's groups, made Jassa Singh Ahluwalia leave the Red Fort and reject the highest honour of becoming a Badshah (King) of the Sikhs. For the next nine months, from March to December Sardar Baghel Singh controlled the capital. The emperor and the royal courtiers hid themselves in their private apartments, which the Sikh Sardars did not plunder.

31.18

In the 1785 the Rohillas, the British and the Nawab Wazir of Oudh posted their joint forced along Yamuna to prevent Sikhs from crossing over.

31.19

In March 1785 and then in May 1785 the Sikhs signed two treaties with the Marathas. Under these treaties, the Sikhs agreed to proved the Marathas with a cavalry of five thousand men and in lieu of a jagir gave up the right to take 'raakhi' in certain specified territories. The treaties lasted only for a few weeks as neither the Sikhs nor the Marathas trusted each other.

31.20

In 1787 Sardar Baghel Singh with the Rohilla assistance defeated Mughal posts first at Meerut and then between Agra and Delhi.

31.21

From 1787-95, the struggle for the occupation of the Yamuna-Gangetic Doab went on. The Marathas, the Mughals and the British were the aspirants and the Sikh Sardars who could annexe the Doab were the least interested party.

31.22

The Sikh expansion under the Misl Sardars reached its furthest limit in 1795 when it was halted by British and Maratha alliance.

31.23

The Misl Sardars though failed in acquiring political gains in extending the boundary of Punjab beyond Yamuna, yet they gave to Punjab its lost glory and to the Punjabis their lost nationalism.

31.24

The set-up of the Misls was a leap of greatest significance in the Sikh history because it brought them together in a combat body for about forty years. It built in them a character of bravery and generosity.

31.25

The relationship of the Sikh Sardars with the Marathas, Rohillas, Mughals and British taught them basic knowledge of empire building.

31.26

The first Sikh-Maratha contact was in March-April 1758, when they came to conquer Punjab at the invitation of Adina Beg Khan, a Mughal faujdar, under the command of Raghunath Rao. Raghunath appointed Adina Beg Khan the Viceroy of Punjab for a annual tirbute of Rs. 7,500,000 and himself retired towards Maharashtra.

31.27

In 1759, Abdali defeated the Marathas and conquered Punjab. In 1760 Abdali fought a gruesome battle with Marathas at Panipat and completely annihilated the Maratha army. Sardar Ala Singh of Patiala, helped the Maratha army with rations when the wree dying of starvation.

31.28

During 1765-66 the Sikhs and the Marathas fought for and against each other in different battles.

31.29

In 1781, when the Emperor Shah Alam II appointed the Marathas to expel the Sikhs from Cis-Sutlej region, both came into a direct conflict with each other and became each other's enemy.

31.30

In 1785 Mahadji Sindhia, the Marathaa Raja of Gwalior, was appointed the Regent of the Mughal Empire with full powers by Emperor Shah Alam II. Mahadji Sindhia made friends with the Sikhs and entered into a number of treaties with them.

31.31

In 1795, Nana Rao, a Maratha general led an expedition against the Sikhs to expel them from the Doab. Nana Rao was compelled to retreat to Panipat.

31.32

The Maratha interference with the Sikhs came to an end with the British conquest of Delhi in 1803.

31.33

The misls rule of Punjab lasted for about 37 years. This period gave to the Sikh nation a few very daring army generals. If only the Sikhs could have produced statesman or politicians they would have ruled India after the fall of the Mughals.

31.34

Jassa Singh Ahluwalia was the head of Ahluwalia misl. He was born in 1718, in village Ahlu, 30 km southwest of Lahore, and died on 7 October 1783.

31.35

Baghel Singh Dhaliwal was the head of Karorisinia misl. He was an adopted son of Karora Singh who had founded the misl. Baghel Singh belonged to the village Chubhai, situated 21 km from Amritsar. Emperor Shah Alam II wanted to appoint the Sardar as the Regent of the Empire but he refused the offer. He had many other opportunities to unfurl the Sikh national flag on the Red Fort but he did not do it for reasons best known to him.

31.36

Baba Deep Singh was the founder of the Shahid misl. He was a Sandhu Jat of Pohuwind village in Jallandar district. He made four hand written copies of Guru Granth Sahib. He also fought heroically to liberate Harimandir from the Afghan occupation.

31.37

Raja Ala Singh was founder of Phoolkian mils and the Patiala state. He was born in 1691 at village Phul. He was baptised four times, as he had lapsed in his religious conduct so often. His first baptism came from Nawab Kapur Singh. He was the first in Phoolkian family to become a Sikh. He took baptism, a second time from Baba Deep Singh Shahid. Jassa Singh Ahluwalia baptised hin in 1761, this was Ala Singh's third baptism. He was baptised for the fourth time by Khushhal Singh in 1762.

31.38

Hari Singh Bhangl was the originator of the Bhangi misl. The word Bhangi is derived for hemp (bhang), a drug-plant. On account of addiction to this drug, this group came to be called Bhangi. Hari Singh was a Dhillon jat. He was a great soldier. He was at his best in fighting in the regions purely inhabitated by Muslims. There he entered like a roaring lion and subdued the enemy.

31.39

Jai Singh Sandhu founded Kanhiya misl. He was born in village Kanha Kacha, 21 km east of Lahore. Hari Singh Sandhu designed Nakai misl. He was born in 1706 in village Baharwal, near Lahore.

31.40

Khushhal Singh Jat was the architect of Ramgaria misl. One of the leaders of this mils. Jassa Singh, did the fortification of Ramgarh fort of Amritsar. Later he was known as Jassa Singh Ramgarhia. He was born in village Ichogil, 20 km from Lahore.

31.41

Budha Singh, a Sansi Jat, built Sukarchakia mils. Maharaja Ranjit Singh was a descendant of Sardar Budha Singh. Budha Singh was baptised by Guru Gobind Singh in 1692.

ARRIVAL OF THE BRITISH ON THE OUTSKIRTS OF PUNJAB (1453-1849)

This period discusses the conquest by the British in India and their advance towards Punjab.

32.1

The first European landed in India in 1453. He was a Portugese navigator named Vasco de Gama.

32.2

The British, East India Company received a charter from the Crown in 1600, to open trade with the East.

32.3

Captain William Hawkins of the company visited Jehangir in 1608 for business talks.

32.4

In 1612, the British were stopped by the Portuguese from landing at Sawally, a port near Surat. The British gave a crushing defeat to the Portuguese and put an end to their power.

32.5

In 113, the British built their first factory at Surat.

32.6

In 1639, the British founded the city of Madras.

32.7

In 1651, the British built a factory at Hugly.

32.8

In 1661, the King of England gave permission for the company to maintain an army to protect its interests in India.

32.9

In 1668, Charles II, the King of England, gave the city of Bombay to the company at a rental of Rs 10 per annum. The city was given to the King by the Portuguese as a part of dowry when he married Portuguese Princess Catherine of Braganza.

32.10

In 1690, the British founded the city of Calcutta.

32.11

In 1717, Farrukhsiyar, the Emperor of India gave a number of concessions to the British for their sea-borne trade. The concessions were a tribute for treatment which a company doctor gave to the emperor.

32.12

In 1745, the French captured the city of Madras; they had other parts of India in their possession as well. The important of these was Pondichery.

32.13

In 1757, with the victory at Plassey, the British East India Company became the chief foreign power in India. They started their official rule in India from the province of Bengal. The battle was fought on 23rd June 1757, and the British forced defeated Siraj-uldaula the Nawab of Bengal, at Plassey. The province of Bengal in those days comprised modern Bengal, Orissa and Bihar.

32.14

In 1761, the British captured Pondicherry and Madras and completely routed the French power from the Indian soil.

32.15

Robert Clive, the Governor of the company's possessions in India, was the founder of the British Empire in India.

32.16

Warren Hastings was the next Governor of Bengal. He remained in his post from 1772-1774 and was then promoted to become the first Governor-General of Bengal, which post he held upto 1785. He made no new conquests for the British. He defeated the Maratha and Haider Ali of Mysore to save the Bombay and Madras presidency for the British.

32.17

Lord Cornwallis was the second Governor-General. He was given more powers to rule the Indian states by the British Parliament. He remained in his post from 1786-1793.

32.18

In 1792 Cornwallis humbled Tipu Sultan of Mysore and extended the British supermacy in the South of India.

32.19

Lord Wellesley was the next Governor General of Bengal from 1798-1805.

32.20

In the period of Cornwallis, the Nizam of Hyderabad, Tipu Sultan of Mysore, the Marathas under the command of Daulat Rai Sindhia and the Nawab of Oudh had strengthened their positions and were conspiring to oust the British influence from their territories.

32.21

In 1799, the British defeated Tipu Sultan in the fourth Mysore war. The Sultan was killed and the territories under his control were shared between the British and their ally the Nizam of Hyderabad.

32.22

In the second Maratha war of 1803, the British annexed the territories of both West and North including, Cuttack, Aligarh, Agra and Delhi.

32.23

The territories of Tanjore, Surat and Carnatic were also annexed by the British after paying off pensions to their ageing rulers. The present state of Tamil Nadu and a large part of Andhra Pradesh were also taken over by the British in this period.

32.24

The third Maratha war was fought in 1804-1805 and the fourth and last Maratha war was fought in 1817-18. The Marathas were defeated and the whole area which is now named as Maharashtra and Madhya Pradesh as annexed by the British. The Maratha power came to a dead end.

32.25

The British fought the war of Nepal in 1814-16 and annexed a large part of the present Himachal Pradesh. The British later founded, in this area, the hill stations like Simla, Mussoorie, Nainital, Almora and Ranikhet.

32.26

In the first war of Burma in 1824-26, the British conquered the province of Assam and coastal provinces of Arakan and Tenasserim.

32.27

The British fought the first Afghan was in 1839-42, to check the advance of Russian towards India, and despite the heavy casualties and the initial defeat they entered Kabul and took over Qandhar and Gazni.

32.28

In 1843, the British annexed the province of Sind, defeating the emirs of Sind.

32.29

The state of Punjab was annexed in 1849, the lower Burma in 1852, the state of Oudh in 1856 and a large parts of present Uttar Pradesh in 1857.

32.30

In 1857, a military rebellion swept over a number of Indian states. It started in Meerut in 10th May 1857 and within a few days the whole of the Northern India and from the borders of West Bengal to Delhi and including central India joined in.

32.31

The mutineers entered Delhi and proclaimed, the last old and infirm Mughal King, Bahadur Shah II, the emperor of India. The British besieged the city of Delhi and other centres of rebellion activities and crushed the movement. Bahadur Shah was arrested and deported to Rangoon, where he dies in 1862.

32.32

The leaders of the mutiny were : Nana Sahib of Kanpur who after his defeat fled towards Nepal and nothing is known about his ultimate fate; Begum Hazrat Mahal of Lucknow, she also fled to Nepal after her defeat; Lakshmi Bai of Bundelkhand (Central India), she died fighting On 17 June 1858.

32.33

After the mutiny, the rule of the East India Company ended and India came directly under the control of the British Parliament and the Crown.

RISE OF THE SIKH EMPIRE DURING THE REIGN OF MAHARAJA RANJIT SINGH (1799-1839)

This period presents the time of the glory of Punjab and the formation of vast Sikh state by Sher-e-Punjab, Maharaja Ranjit Singh.

33.1

Ranjit Singh was born on 13 November 1780 at Gujranwla. His great-great grandfather, Buddha Singh, was baptised from Guru Gobind Singh and died heroically in 1716. His great grandfather, Naudh Singh died fighting against the Pathans in 1753. His grandfather, Charhat Singh, fought against Ahmed Shah Abdali and accidentally died with his own gun shot in 1774. His father, Mahan Singh, became the undisputed leader of Sukkarchak misl, fought a number of battles aginst the Afghan armies and died in 1792 when Ranjit Singh was only 12 years old.

33.2

Ranjit Singh was the only son of his parents. His mother, Mai Raj Kaur, was the daughter of the Kind of Jind. Ranjit Singh had no taste for books. His real love was horse riding, weaponary and military training.

33.3

In 1799, following the death of his mother Sardarni Raj Kaur and his closest adviser Lakhpat Rai, Ranjit Singh took the command of his Misl in his own hands. At that time he was 18 years old.

33.4

Ranjit Singh had five wives. His first wife was the daugher of the Sardar of Kanhaiya misl. Her name was Mehtab Kaur. This marriage took place in 1795. Mehtab Kaur bore him two sons, Sher Singh and Tara Singh; his second marriage was arranged in 1798 with Bibi Datar Kaur daugher of Rum Singh of Nakai, she gave him Prince Kharak Singh, who succeeded Ranjit Singh after his death. Ranjit Singh married a third time in 1800 with Maharani Jind Kaur, daughter of Manna Singh Aulak. Shie gave birth of Prince Dalip Singh, who was the last Sikh monarch, before the fall of the Sikh Empire. Ranjit Singh's fourth marriage took place in 1806 with a widow, Bibi Ratan Kaur, who bore him Prince Multana Singh.. His last marriage was solemnised in 1808 with Bibi Daya Kaur. She gave Ranjit Singh two sons, Prince Kashmira Singh and Prince Pashora Singh.

33.5

Ranjit Singh's five wives bore him seven sons. First wfie Mehtab Kaur died in 1813, second wife Datar Kaur died in 1818, third wife died Jind Kaur died, in England in 1891, the fourth Ratan Kaur died in 1811 and the fifth wife, Daya Kaur died in 1843. Ranjit Singh himself died in 1839 at the age of 59.

33.6

Shah Zaman, the grandson of Ahmad Shah Abdali, sat on the throne of Kabul in 1783. He attacked India four times. His first attck was in 1787, which was repulsed by the Khalsa forces. He attacked again in 1788 but was defeated by the Misl Sardars. His third attack was in 1796; this time he reached up to Lahore but the joint Khalsa army gave him a crushing defeat at the outskirts of Amritsar. His fourth and last attack came in 1798. When Shah Zaman reached Lahore, he was besieged by the misl Sardars. He shut himself up in the Lahore fort. Ranjit Singh reached the fort at the head of his forces and shouted aloud, "Oh grandson of Ahmed Shah, I the grandson of Charhat Singh, challenge you for a duel fight, come out from the fort if you consider yourself to be a man..."

33.7

The aftermath of the attempted attacks from Kabul made Ranjit Singh think that the Punjab needed a very solid and firm central government rather than a spiteful and coveteous misl system. He discussed his plan with his mother-in-law Sardarni Daya Kaur of Kanhaiya Misl, who agreed wholeheartedly with her son-in-law's enterprising and aspiring scenario.

33.8

Ranjit Singh conquered Lahore in 1799 and Amritsar in 1802. He defeated the Bhangi Sardars, the rulers of the two cities, and gave them large estates for their living.

33.9

On 13 April 1801 he was declared to be a Maharaja and was anointd as such, according to the Sikh traditions, by Baba Sahib Singh Bedi. New coins were minted in the name of Guru Nanak and Guru Gobind Singh and all the coins which were released on the first day were distributed amongst the poor.

33.10

Ranjit Singh annexed Kasur in 1801 and Multan in 1803. In next two years he brought the whole of the Central Punjab, from the Sutlej to the Jhelum under his control. He occupied Ludhiana in 1806. The Sikh Cis-Sutlej states as Nabha, Patiala and Jind appealed to the British for protection. The British and Ranjit Singh signed the Treaty of Amritsar, on 25 April 1809. By this treaty the river Sutlej was fixed as the boundary between the Sikh and British Empires.

33.11

Maharaja Ranjit Singh's advance southward of the Sutlej was stopped by the Treaty of Amritsar, now he turned his attention towards North, East and West.

33.12

He conquered the hill states of Kangra, Jammu, Jarsota, Rajouri, Bhimber, Noorpur, Jaswal and Chamba between 1807-1809...Kashmir was defeated in 1814 but officially annexed in 1819.

33.13

In Northwest Frontier, Attock was conquered in 1813, Peshawar in 1818, Dera-Gazikah, Hazara and Dara-Ismailkhan were annexed in 1821. An uprising in Peshawar was quelled by Maharaja Ranjit Singh in 1824, when he entered the town with great pomp and show. He was given a very warm welcome by the native population.

33.14

Ladhak in the Kashmir valley and Jamrod a border town of Afghanistan and India were conquered by the Maharaja in 1837.

33.15

The Maharaja was presented with the 'Kohinoor' by the Wafa Begum, the wife of Shah Sujan, the former ruler of Kabul, for saving her husband's life first from his brother Shah Mohammed and then from Fateh Khan the Wazir of Kashmir.

33.16

The Maharaja's two brilliant generals, Akali Phoola Singh and Hari Singh Nalwa died heroically defending the boundaries of India. Akali Phoola Singh, the Jathedar of Akal Takhat, died in 1818 in the battle of Naushera, and Hari Singh Nalwa, the commander-in-chief of the Khalsa died in 1838 defending the fort of Jamrod.

33.17

Maharaja Ranjit Singh died in Lahore, on June 27, 1839 after a severe attack of paralysis. He was 59 years old and had vary successfully ruled Punjab for about forty years. His empire extended from Sutlej to the outskirts of Afghanistan.

33.18

Maharaja Ranjit Singh was the Lion of Punjab. He was a very generous and kind ruler. He laid the foundation of the Sikh Empire and made Punjab the most powerful state in India. His cabinet included Sikh, Hindu and Muslim ministers. His famous Prime Minister was a Dogra-Brahmin, Raja Dhian Singh. His foreign minister was a Muslim, Faquir Aziz-ud-din. Diwan Bhawani Das and Raja Dina Nath were his famous Finance Ministers. Sardar Hari Singh Nalwa, a Sikh, Diwan Mohkam Chand, a Hindu and Illahi Khan, a Muslim were his war ministers.

33.19

For administration purposes, the Maharaja had divided his kingdom into four provinces, viz., Lahore, Multan, Kashmir and Peshawar. The head of the province was a called a Nazim. The provinces were subdivided into districts. Each district was under a Kardar. The villages were ruled by the Panchayats, which consisted of five elders of the village.

33.20

The judiciary consisted of lower village courts controlled by the Panchayats; the city courts were administered by the Kardars; the state courts were headed by the Nazims and the Adalat-e-ala at Lahore was chaired by the minister of Justice. The final court of appeal was Maharaja himself.

33.21

The chief source of the government revenue was a land levy with ranged from 1/3 to 1/2 of the total produce of the land. The other sources of income included custom and excise duties, nazrana, salt tax, jagir taxes and business taxes etc.

33.22

The Maharaja was above religious bigotry. He made Punjab a truly secular state. He was a national monarch. He was a practising Sikh and had regard for all other religions. He gave very valuable gifts to Hindu mandirs and Muslims mosques. He donated tons of gold to Harimandir to cover its domes with golden plates. Hence the name of Harimandir came to be known as Golden-temple.

FALL OF THE SIKH EMPIRE (27 JUNE 1839-29 MARCH 1849)

This period narrates the tragic drama of succession and the annexation of Punjab by the British.

34.1

Maharaja Ranjit Singh died on 27th June 1839 and the Punjab was annexed by the British on 23rd March 1849. In about ten years after the Maharaja's death the treacherous and unfaithful Dogras of Jammu with their well rehearsed plan double crossed the Sikh Sardars and sold the Sikh empire to the British.

34.2

The main villain of the first act of this bloody drama was Raja Dhian Singh, the Prime Minister, who murdered, in cold blood, four direct heirs of the throne and hundreds of their supporters. He poisoned Kharak Singh, eldest son of Maharaja Ranjit Singh; crushed to death, Naunihal Singh, son of Kharak Singh; killed Rani Chand Kaur, wife of Kharak Singh and murdered Sahib Kaur wife of Prince Naunihal Singh. He was murdered in 1843. The villains of the second act were two Dogra-Brahmins, Prime minister Lal Singh and Army-chief Tej Singh.

34.3

The turmoil began on the very eve of Maharaja Ranjit Singh's death. Raja Dhian Singh Dogra had started planning the modes of the killings during the illness of Maharaja Ranjit Singh.

34.4

Kharak Singh, succeeded to the throne after his father's death. Chet Singh Bajwa, a brother-in-law of the prince and his younger brother were murdered in front of Kharak Singh on 8th October 1839, in his palace. Other relatives of Chet Singh Bajwa arrested and put into prison and later brutally murdered.

34.5

Raja Dhian Singh made Naunihal Singh, the son of Kharak Singh, the defacto Maharaja and put Kharak Singh under house arrest. Kharak Singh was later poisoned to death. He died on 5th November 1840.

34.6

On the same evening, when Prince Naunihal Singh was coming back after cremating his father, an archway of the north gate of the Hazuribagh, was made to fall on him, at the signal of Raja Dhian Singh. Naunihal Singh was seriously injured and was rushed to the palace under the guard of Raja Dhian Singh. His request for a glass of water was dismissed by Dhian Singh. The palace gates were closed and not even Rani Chand Kaur, the mother of the Prince and Rani Sahib Kaur, wife of the Prince, were allowed in. The Prince was tortured to death in the palace and died the same evening though his death was officially declared on 8th November by Dhian Singh.

34.7

Rani Sahib Kaur, the wife of Naunihal Singh was pregnant at the time of death of her husband. On 27th November 1840, Rani Chand Kaur, the mother of Naunihal Singh was made regent till Sahib Kaur delivered her child. Sher Singh, a son of Maharaja Ranjit Singh and Rani Mehtab Kaur, put forward his claim for the succession.

34.8

On 9th June 1842, Rani Chand Kaur was brutally murdered by her maid servant, on the instigation of Raja Dhian Singh. She crushed Rani's skull with a grinding stone.

34.9

Sher Singh became the Maharaja on 9th June 1842. Sandhawalia Sardars were related to Rani Chand Kaur. After the death of the Rani, whom they had supported for her regency, their estates were confiscated and there were rumours of the Royal orders of their arrest and murder.

34.10

On 15 September, 1843, Ajit Singh Sandhawalia, killed Maharaja Sher Singh and his young son Prince Partap Singh in the garden of Maharaja's palace where he was camping to inspect a section of the army.

34.11

On the ssme day, Ajit Singh also killed Raja Dhian Singh, in the Lahore fort.

34.12

Hira Singh Dogra, the Dogra chief and a son of Dhian Singh, incited the army generals against the Sandhawalia Sardars. The army ambushed the Sandhawalia Sardar in the Lahore fort on 16th September 1843 and killed him along with his associates.

34.13

On 17th September 1843, Prince Dalip Singh, the youngest son of Maharaja Ranjit Singh nd Rani Jind Kaur was proclaimed Maharaja and Hira Singh Dogra as his Prime Minister. Dalip Singh, at this time was only five years old.

34.14

Princes Kashimra Singh and Peshaura Singh procliamed their right to the throne. The Khalsa army supported the right of Dalip Singh but recommended pensions and estates for the other two Princes.

35.15

Suchet Singh Dogra, an uncle of Hira Singh asked the Sikh army to dismiss the Prime Minister Hira Singh and his associate Pandit Jalla, a Brahmin priest for their misdeeds. The army chiefs rejected Suchet Singh petition and decided to remain loyal to the Prime Minister.

34.16

In 1844, Pandit Jalla accused Rani Jinda of having illict relations with Lal Singh Brahmin. The army chiefs called upon Hira Singh and Pandit Jalla to withdraw the accusation. Hira Singh turned down the Army's request and instead requested his uncle Gulab Singh Dogra, of Jammu, for help, to teach the army chiefs a lesson. In the fight which pursued both Hira Singh and Pandit Jalla were slain.

34.17

In 1845, Dalip Singh was engaged with the daughter of Chattar Singh of Attariwala. Prince Peshaura Singh captured the fort of Attock. Chhatar Singh Attariwala proceeded to Attock. Peshaura Singh submitted to him. The rebal forces later seized the Prince and murdered him.

34.18

On 21st September 1845, the army chiefs at Lahore killed Jawahar Singh, the brother of Rani Jinda for the conspiracy of murdering Prince Peshaura Singh. The army took over the overall control of Punjab and appointed one Diwan Dina Nath as its spokesman. It is surprising to note that, despite the planned killing of the successors of Maharaja Ranjit Singh by the Doogras and the ultimate Sikh resurgence, many of the chiefs of the army council were still Dogras-Brahmins.

34.19

Lal Singh and Tejj Singh, two Dogras-Brahmins, respectively, became the next Prime Minister and Commander-in-chief of the Sikh forces. Immediately after taking charge, they, along with Gulab Singh Dogra of Jammu, communicated with the British to sell them the Sikh military secrets for personal favours and money. They invited the British to annex Punjab and in return give them the top posts in the new set up.

34.20

In July 1844 Lord Hardinge was appointed the new Governor General of India. In September 1844, Broadfoot was appointed a military agent in Ludhiana. In December 1845 Lord Gough brought some elite military units from Meerut and Ambala to Ferozepur. General Littler was in command in Ferozepur cantonment. He had assembled a large number of boats to bridge the Sutlej to attack Punjab.

34.21

The first Anglo-Sikh war (1845-46) was thrust upon the Sikhs by the British. It consisted to five battles; battle of Mudhi (December 18, 1845), battle of Ferozepur (December 21, 1845) battle of Buddowal (January 21, 1846), battle of Aliwal (January 28, 1846) and battle of Sabrao (February 10, 1846). All the five battles brought havoc and destruction for the Sikh army for Tej Singh and Lal Singh had already communicated to the British the strength, layout, numbers and weak spots of the Sikh army. They deliberately directed the Sikh force to advance towards those targets, where they could easily fall into the enemy's ambush. They led many crack Sikh-army units directly into the death cell. It was not the British who defeated the Sikh army, it was the treachery of the Dogra minister and the Dogra chiefs. Thousands of Sikh soldiers were killed and drowned in Sutlej. The Sikh hero Sham Singh Attariwala died in this war. The battle of Ferozepur (December 21) which the Sikhs had won was turned into their defeat by the ugly and unpardonable designes of the Dogras.

34.22

The war was brought to a close by the Treaty of Lahore, 1846. The main provisions of the treaty were:

a. The Jullandar Doab and all the Sikh territories to the left of the Sutlej were tranferred to the British.

b. An Englishman, Sir Henry Lawrence, was stationed at Lahore as a British resident.

c. The numbers of the Sikh army and its guns were restricted and were to decided by the British.

d. An British army contingent was stationed at Lahore to maintain peace and order in the state.

e. Dalip Singh was recognised as the ruler of Punjab with a Council of Regeny. Lal Singh was re-affirmed as the Prime Minister (for his ugly and treacherous role).

f. A war indemnity of 15 million rupees was to be paid to the British.

34.23

As the Sikh treasury did not contain sufficient funds to pay off the war debt, the state of Kashmir was sold to Raja Gulab Singh, by the Birtish, for 10 million rupees. Thus Raja Gulab Singh who helped the British to defeat the Sikhs was rewarded by the British by making him the ruler of the most beautiful part of Ranjit Singh's Panjab.

34.24

In December 1846, Sir Henry Lawrence was given more powers to control the internal affairs of Punjab.

34.25

In 1848 Lord Dalhousie was made the Governor General of India. He had hardly been in India a few months when the second Anglo-Sikh was broke out.

34.26

Maharani Jinda was put under house arrest on 9 August 1847 and was deported to Benaras in 1848. In the province of Multan, Diwan Mulchand was replaced by General Kahan Singh, in December 1847. In the changeover two Englishmen, Vans Agnews and Lieutenant Anderson were murdered.

34.27

After the treaty of Lahore, 1846, the highest posts in the province were filled by the British and the salaries of the Punjabi employees were greatly reduced. These acts brought discontent and distrust in the army ranks and they called upon their leaders to liberate Punjab from the British. This led to a revolt and an uprising by the Sikhs at a number of strategic places in Punjab. This revolt later turned into the second Anglo-Sikh war.

34.28

The second war was fought at three fronts; battle of Ramnagar and Sudullapur (November 1848), battle of Chillianwala (January 13, 1849) and battle of Gujarat (February 21, 1849). The first two battles of Ramnagar and Sadullapur were faced by Sher Singh Attariwala in the North and Dewan Mulraj in the South. General Campbell and Lord Gough ambushed the Sikh rebellions forces and they had to retreat to Jhelum.

34.29

On 13 January, 1849 the third battle was fought near the village of Chillianwala. The Sikh army gave a crushing defeat to the British despite the fact that the British had a much larger and well equipped army. The British retreated across the Chaj to the banks of the Chenab.

34.30

The British collected all their power and support and fought the battle of Gujarat with the advancing Sikh forces. The Sikh soldiers fought heroically but the weight of numbers and superior armoury decided the day. The Sikh resistance was completely crushed on 11th March 1849 and by a proclamation dated 29th March 1849 the Sikh kingdom was liquidated and Punjab was annexed to the British India. Maharaja Dalip Singh stepped down from the illustrious throne to Maharaja Ranjit Singh never to sit on it again.

SPREAD OF THE CROWN RULE (1839-1900)

This era notes the period of Indian Mutiny, transfer of power from the East India Company to the Crown and the start of the time of economic reconstruction of India.

35.1

Before the conquest of Punjab the British had annexed most of the important states of India. The Marathas, the Moghuls and the Rajputs, all had been humiliated by the British before the fall of Punjab. The victory over Punjab made them the Supreme power of the whole of India.

35.2

Delhi was under their protection since 1803, when they defeated the armies of Sindhia, a Maratha King and captured Aligarh, Delhi and Agra. At Delhi the Mughal Emperor, Shah Alam, a blind old man of 83 was taken under protection.

35.3

After Punjab the British annexed Burma in 1852, Berar (Hyderabad) in 1853 and Satara, Jhansi, Nagpur and Oudh in 1856. Some of these states were annexed by lapse, some for misgovernment and others in lieu of a payment of a fine.

35.4

In 1857 an army mutiny took place in some of the Indian states. It lasted for more than a year and transformed the whole structure of the British rule in India.

35.5

The mutiny started from Meerut. On 24 April, 1857, eighty five soldiers in Meerut refused to use greased cartridges. A rumour had spread that the cartridges had been greased with the cow fat. On 10 May, the sepoys in Meerut had shot down their British officers and had burnt down their bungalows. The sepoys then marched towards Delhi. Nana Sahib in Kanpur, Begum Hazart Mahal in Lucknow and Lakshmi Bai in Jhansi joined the mutineers and killed British officers and burnt down their houses.

35.6

On reaching Delhi the Meerut sepoys declared the last Mughal, Bahadur Shah II, the Emperor of India. The mutiny came to an end in June 1858 and the rule of India was transferred to the Crown from the East India Company which had ruled India for about 100 years.

35.7

The mutiny was ill-organised and was ignited by a few selfish interests. For this reason, many Indian states did not participate in it. Notably, the Punjab did not enter in this mutiny, despite the fact that the Punjabis had been defeated by the British only eight years earlier and the wounds of their humiliation, at the hands of the British, were still fresh.

35.8

The mutiny, for sure, was not an uprising. It was also not a national movement. Only a few Princes took part in it. Those who claimed to be fighting for freedom were the people who, a decade earlier, had been the cause of the fall of Punjab and the humiliation of the Punjabis. The mutiny had no effective organisation. Every locality had its own leaders. There was no unity of purpose. The Muslims wanted to revive the Mughal empire, whereas the Hindus were anxious to set up the Maratha rule.

35.9

The restoration of the Mughal rule, by the influential mutineers, restrained the Sikhs from joining the rebellion, as the tales of the Mughal atrocities against their forefathers reacted sharply to Bahadur Shah's proclamation as the new emperor.

35.10

On 10/11 September 1857, Brigadier Hodson captured Bahadur Shah II, Begum Zeenat Mahal, their three sons and a grandson. The three Princes were stripped naked and were shot by Brigadier Hodson. The Sikhs took the corpses of the princes to Chandni Chowk and laid them out for display in front of Gurdwara Sis Ganj, where about 200 years before, Guru Tegh Bahadur had been executed by the order of the then Mughal Emperor Aurangzeb, an ancestor, of Bahadur Shah II.

35.11

An important outcome of the mutiny was that the service in the armed forces was thrown open to the Punjabis and specially to the Sikhs. An earlier regulation had already provided that the Sikh fraternity would on no account be interfered with, that the Sikhs should be permitted to wear their beard, and the hair of their head gathered up, as enjoined by their religion. Some races including as martial. Of the martial races the favourites of British officers were the Sikhs and the Gurkhas.

35.12

After 1857, the consolidation of the British rule in India was complete and the government drew up an economic plan to reconstruct India according to their own designs. The famines of Punjab (1861), Orissa (1865), South India (1876), Kashmir (1878) and Central India (1896) however, influenced their schemes and a comprehensive programme of constructing canals, roads, railway network and reclaming the desert was given the top priority.

35.13

The years 1837 onwards saw an exodus of Indian workers to contries in the Far East, USA, England and Canada. Indentured labour was recruited from Bihar and Uttar Pradesh to work on the sugar-farms of the British companies in Mauritias, Fiji, Trinidad, Jamaica and British Guiana. The Tamils was recruited to work as labourers in Malaya and Singapore. The Sikhs went out either as carpenters, masons or clerks in East Africa; as policemen in Malaya; as factory workers in Britain and as farmers in California and Vancour. The Gujeratis and Sindis set out their small business in these countries. Between 1837-1915, about 3.5 million Indians had settled abroad.

35.14

By the end of 1900, the glamour of the foreign rule had vanished and the rulers had become arrogant and unconcerned. The policy of discrimination by the British started dividing the community into religious groups. The positions of the junior army ranks were filled by the Sikhs and Punjabi Muslims and the seats of the junior civil servants went to the Bengali and Madrasi Hindus.

35.15

The city of Calcutta remained the Imperial captial up to 1912 when Delhi was made the new capital of India. The social and religious reformers like Ram Mohan Roy, Rabinder Nath Tagore, Surender Nath Bannerji and Swami Vivekanand showed their open concern about the British rule. The revolutionary slogan of Bal Gangadhar Tilak, "Swaraj is our birth right and we shall have it..." set the tune of struggle for independence. The punjabis in general and the Sikhs in particular plunged into this struggle in the early twentieth century.

35.16

Lord Canning was appointed the first Viceroy of India under the Crown. He remained in his post from 1858-1876. In 1861 the Indian Councils Act 1861 was passed by which a few nominated Indians were taken in the legislature. Lord

Canning was succeeded by Lord Elgin I in 1862, but after about a year and a half, he died at Dharamsala in November 1863.

35.17

Sir John Lawrence became the next Viceroy in 1864. He had been Cheif Commissioner of Punjab for some time and was known as the 'Saviour of Punjab'. He annexed Bhutan in 1865. Lord Mayo succeeded Sir John in 1869. He was stabbed to death by an Afghan convict, in 1872, at the harbour of Port Blair, when he was touring in the Andemans. Lord Northbrook took over as the new Viceroy in 1872. The Prince of Wales, afterwards King Edward VII, visited India in 1875. Lord Northbrook resigned in 1876 as he had differences with the Secretary of State. He was succeeded by Lord Lytton. On January 8, 1877, Lord Lytton laid down the foundation of Mohammedan Anglo-Oriental College at Aligarh. In 1920 this College was raised to the status of a University known as the Aligarh Muslim University. The British annexed Afghanistan in 1879.

35.18

Lord Ripon took over as the next Viceroy from Lort Lytton in 1880. The first Indian census was done in 1881. Punjab University was founded in 1882 in Lahore. In 1884, Lord Ripon resigned. He was the most beloved Vicerory of India. Lord Dufferin joined as the new Viceroy. During his period, the Indian National Congress was founded at Bombay on 28 December 1885. Lord Lansdowne succeeded Lord Dufferin in 1888. In 1892 the second Indian Council Act was passed, which introduced further changes in the composition, powers and functions of the Legislative Councils. The Act was a great disappointment. The Indian leaders where totally dissatisfied with it. Lord Elgin II took over form Lord Lansdowne in 1894 and served as the Viceroy until 1899. During his period the boundaries of Burma, China and Siam were fixed. The Punjab suffered a severe famine in 1896-97.

APPENDICES

1

Tulsi Das

I
EARLY LIFE

We know as little about the facts of the life of Tulsidas as about those of Shakespeare. Apart from legend and story, the documentary evidence relating to their lives is strikingly meagre. They were contemporaries - Shakespeare writing in "the spacious days" of the good Queen Elizabeth and Tulsidas in the equally spacious and constructive years of the reign of Akbar the Great. The official historians of the age take little notice of these great writers who were "not of an age but for all time." A modern historian of the age of Tulsidas, Vincent Smith, justly laments the omission. And yet there are hardly two other writers in all literature who in their own different ways have done more to unravel the mystery of the human situation or to move the hearts of millions of men and women over the centuries.

Tulsidas occupies a unique position among the world's great writers insofar as he was a poet who was no mere poet but a seeker engaged in a ceaseless endeavour to get into touch with Reality and a saint who was no mere saint but a humanist whose writings have made a tremendous impact on the life and culture of his people. His crowning achievement as one of the greatest exponents of the core of the Indian cultural and spiritual heritage is that he brought to his people a positive message of hope and fulfilment by going beyond the conflicting positions of the metaphysical speculators and asserting a living and vital faith in divine light and love and a divine personality which redeems and liberates.

The source material on which it is usual to build the story of the life and career of Tulsidas is not of a uniformly good quality. There is, on the one hand, a body of legend, laudatory verses and so-called lives coming from admirers, saints and disciples whose attitude is necessarily that of faithful fellow-travellers inspired by a glowing spirit of adulation and enthusiasm. To this category belong such books as the *Bhaktmal* of Nabhadas, a commentary on the *Bhaktmal* by Priyadas, *Mool Gosain Charit* by Baba Beni Madho Das, said to be a contemporary and disciple of the poet, and *Shiva-Singh-Saroj*, a collection of life-sketches of Hindi poets known to its author, Shiva Singh Sengar. On the other hand, there are the more familiar attempts of modern scholars to gather facts, sift evidence and reconstruct a life-story, insofar as it is at all possible to do so, out of a jungle of conflicting versions. At the head of works of this kind stands Sir George Grierson's 'Notes on Tulsidas' which appeared in 1893 in 'The Indian Antiquary.' Subsequent biographers of Tulsidas have quite evidently drawn heavily on the facts gathered and the conclusions arrived at by Sir George, but any creative attempt to project the image of the poet as it emerges from the pages of his own writings and in the light of his own cherished beliefs, experiences and inner conflicts has yet to be made.

Tulsidas himself does not mention the date of his own birth or the name of his birth-place and there is no entirely reliable or indisputably authentic evidence to enable us to fix firm dates and place-names. Writers relying mainly on the testimony of Baba Beni Madho Das mention *Samvat* 1554 (1497 A.D.) as his birth date, while H.H. Wilson's remark in one of his papers that Tulsidas "commenced his Hindi version of the *Ramayana* in the year of *Samvat* 1631 when he was thirty-one years of age" has persuaded many that he was born in *Samvat* 1600 (1543 A.D.) Various reference are given in support of both the dates but the reliability of both is open to question in view of what the poet himself has said about the circumstances of his life. In any case, it is not likely that he wrote his *Ram-Charit-Manas* at an impossibly late or early stage of his life.

There is, however, a fair consensus among scholars in favour of *Bhadrapad* 11, *'Mangalvar Samvat* 1589 (Tuesday, September 18, 1532 A.D.). It is a date which Sir George Grierson and a host of the best modern scholars consider most likely. Shiva Singh Sengar in his *Shiva-Singh-Saroj* states that Tulsidas was born "near about *Samvat* 1583" which is a date not far removed from *Samvat* 1589 (1532 A.D.). The date also happens to stand the test of astrological calculations perfectly.

The controversy over the exact birth-place of Tulsidas is not easily set at rest. Seven cities claimed the honour of being the birth-place of Homer and nearly as many are mentioned as the birth-place of Tulsidas.

All these places belong to Uttar Pradesh and out of the four most often mentioned three are situated within a fairly restricted area near Chitrakut. Sir George Grierson, who had good sources of information and the ability to subject them to dispassionate examination, was of the view that Tari on the banks of the Yamuna and only ten or twelve miles away from Rajapur had the best claim. One of the commentaries on the *Bhaktmal* has it that celebrated devotee of Sri Krishna, listed in an account of the deeds of two hundred Vaishnavas known as *Do Sau Vaishnavan ki Varta.* The claims about the house and the temple are based entirely on hearsay and doubts have been cast on the authenticity of *Do Sau Vaishnavan ki Varta* by competent critics. In any case, it is not possible that Tulsidas, who lost his mother soon after his own birth, had a real younger brother named Nand Das. The lynch-pin of the claim that Soron was the birth-place of Tulsidas is a line in the *Ram-Charit-Manas* where the poet says that he heard the story of Ram at Sukerkhet and the supposition that this Sukerkhet is another name for Soron. Firstly, saying that he heard the story of Ram at Sukerkhet is not the same thing as saying that he was born there. Secondly, and above all, there are substantial grounds to identify the Sukerkhet mentioned by the poet with the sukerkhet (or Varah Kshetra) situated on the confluence of the Saryu and the Ghagra, a few miles west of Ayodhya. Baba Beni Madho Das, a companion and disciple of the poet, who died in 1642 and wrote the well-known *Gosain Charit*, as well as Krishna Dutta Misra, author of *Gautam Chandrika*, a work written in 1624, only a year after the poet's death, state definitely that the place where the poet received his education at the feet of Narhari Das is situated at the confluence of the Ghagra and the Saryu. Earlier commentators on the *Manas* writing towards the end of the eighteenth century had no doubt in their mind that "Sukerkhet, that is, Varah Kshetra" stands "on the banks of the Saryu, west of Ayodhya." Tradition and ancient texts confirm that his Sukerkhet is a particularly sacred place visited by a large number of devotees. The Avadhi dialect in which the *Manas* is written and the cultural atmosphere it depicts are unmistakably reflected in the life and manners of the people of the region and it is fair to conclude that some of the earliest days of the poet's life were spent among them.

Tulsidas himself has stated that it was a good family in which he was born, but he vehemently protested that he did not care for caste labels. There are, nevertheless, good grounds for the belief that he was a Brahmin, probably of the Saryuparin variety, whose father was Atma Ram and whose mother was named Hulsi. But if exact dates and names are uncertain, the poet has described the circumstances of his birth and early life in no uncertain terms. There are references in many of his writings to the unlucky constellation of the stars under which he was born and the cruel manner in which he was separated from and left to his own devices by his parents. "My parents left me after I was brought forth into the world," he tells us. "Even the Creator did not send me out into the world with any luck; there were no rejoicings on my birth." The reason why the infant should have been separated from his home and family is not clear from the vague hints thrown out by the poet in his later writings. One tradition has it that he was an abnormal child whose mother died soon after he was born and the parents were frightened that he would bring no good luck to them. Sir George Grierson plausibly argued that since the boy was born under evil stars and a child born under such stars boded ill-luck to the parents, they abandoned him under the advice of astrologers and in keeping with the superstitious beliefs of the times. That his birth gave no joy to his parents and there were no rejoicings to celebrate the occasion is stated by the poet himself. Poverty as much as evil stars seem to have decreed that he should start life as an orphan without shelter or surety about his next meal.

Education

The misery of the early years of chill penury when Tulsidas went about with the begging-bowl from door to door remained a vivid memory with him throughout his life. In moving words he relates how the pangs of hunger took him to the doors of all kinds of men, how a few grains received in alms would be as welcome as the fulfilment of the four great ends of human life, how without food or raiment he ran from pillar to post, "begging by day and sleeping in some lonely mosque by night." "Luckless as I was," he tells us, "they avoided the very shadow of my body."

While there can be no doubt that his early years were marked by poverty and the need to fend for himself, we must not take these confessions in too literal a sense. It is necessary to read them in their context. Most of these confessions occur in his later works when he was looking back at his life in review from a certain high altitude, "all passion spent." When he says in the *Kavitavali* that his parents abandoned him and even the Creator wrote no luck on his forehead, he also says that Raghunath, the Lord and Master of his material welfare, did not fail him. When he talks again about his birth in a "house of beggars", the lines that immediately follow state in a spirit of devout thanks giving, that "the will of Tulsi's Lord Almighty negates all fate and forebodings and the Lord's name turns a straw into a thing mightier than the mountains." We may be sure, therefore, that his declarations about `the tattered clothes and earthen bowl' of his youth have much more to do with the central experience of his life, that the Lord redeems the unluckiest and most wretched of His creatures, rather than with any eagerness to dwell on the misery and privations of his early life.

It is only natural that in the circumstances in which young Tulsidas was placed he should have gravitated towards the company of the wandering sadhus who formed a very well-recognised section of society in those days. Indian society in the days of the Mughal emperors was made up of many worlds. There was, first, the world of the ruling chiefs and State officials given to grand living. There was the world of the common man, the peasants, traders and workers who made a bare living in normal times and were very hard hit indeed in the years of famine and scarcity. There was a third world of sadhus and learned men who had turned their backs against the world and set up seminaries of learning and philosophy. Apart from the mere escapists, there were many others who under the pressure of economic necessity or rigid social conventions willingly joined the company of these holy men and found both in safe heaven and mental calm. There were many opportunities in this company of overcoming the handicaps of birth and circumstances, acquiring knowledge and seeing life during travels on pilgrimage. Fate and circumstance seem to have put the feet of Tulsidas early on the road to this fraternity. As he puts it in the Vinaya Patrika, "taking pity on my miserable plight and saints said, `grieve not.'"

It appears that a holy man named Narhari Das or Narhariyanand took him under his protecting wings. There are hints of this meeting between master and disciple in a passage in the *Vinaya Patrika*. "Bound down by the strong shackles of Karma and the ego. I suffered greatly but the Lord of the suffering and the helpless, Sri Ram, freed me from this bondage of Karma when he saw how greatly

I suffered. The moment the Guru questioned me I replied, `I want to serve you. I have none whom I could call mine. I grasp your feet.' The Guru patted me on the back, held my arms and made me his own (disciple)." And the young boy was a very willing disciple indeed. All that he wanted, if he "was well treated", was his daily bread and a few clothes. There were those who would look down upon him but this did not perturb him. He had no ambition to have a place in the hierarchy of caste or to enter the life of a householder. To repeat the name of Ram was his only vocation. All accounts agree that he was a meditative type of pupil and not very wordly wise.

It is not difficult to see that the guru, Narhari Das, was well pleased with the new disciple who, at this stage, seems to have been known as and answered to the name Rambola. Who gave him this name we do not know. But it stuck to him for some time and fitted well with his practice of going about repeating the name of Ram. "I am'a servant of Ram. Ram has given me the name Rambola." This was good enough for him but throughout his life he was much better known as Tulsidas and it is likely that his guru gave him the new name.

It is stated that his Guru Narhari Das or Narhariyanand belonged to the school of Ramanand. But all that is certain is that he was a great devotee of Ram and deeply learned in the lore of Ram. He believed that the great discipline which led to spiritual well-being was the repetition of the name of Ram. It was a simple faith which the master inculcated in the mind of his pupil. "The Guru taught me that devotion to Ram is best and I like this (straight path) which is like the King's highway."

In the only direct reference which the poet makes to the lessons he learnt, he tells us that he heard the story of Ram at Sukerkhet. He was too young and immature, he tells us, to be able to imbibe the full import of the story but the good teacher repeated it over and over again. With characteristic modesty he goes on to add that it was only an inkling of the full meaning that he got at this stage. We may be sure, however, that he impression left on his mind was deep and abiding. He made up his mind that in good time he would write the story for the delight of his soul and the benefit of the common people in the language of the common man.

When the poet did begin to write his own version of the story of Ram, he did not fail to recall with gratitude "the lotus-feet" of his guru, "the very ocean of compassion, Hari himself in the shape of Nar (a human being), whose words are like the rays of the sun to dispel the deep darkness of illusion", and whose teachings laid bare "all the hidden and manifest jewels of the story of Ram in whatever mines they may be embedded." His guru, the place where he learnt his first lessons, the Saryu, Ayodhya and the life and culture of the people among whom he lived and moved in his early life left a permanent impression on his mental make-up and his writings.

Tulsidas spent several years at the feet of his master and developed a deep feeling for Ram both as a personal god and as a Presence immanent in the world. What texts he learnt and what trends of thought, besides a deep devotion to Ram, he pursued while at Sukerkhet he does not specify. But it is beyond doubt that he was singularly free from sectarian bias, keen to learn and full of the thirst for knowledge. One tradition supported by the author of the *Mool Gosain Charit*has it that Tulsidas remained with his guru, Narhari Das, only for a few years. The guru and his flock of disciples moved on to Kashi and thus an opportunity opened for him to pursue his studies at that ancient seat of learning. Shesh Sanatan, one of the most profound scholars of the day who had a passion for imparting knowledge to promising students, seems to have noticed the talent of the ardent, young pupil of Narhari Das. The moment it was apparent to Narhari Das that Tulsidas was eager to continue his studies under Shesh Sanatan, he decided to allow him to stay on at Kashi. There is a deep strain of the scholarship in the writings of Tulsidas and anyone familiar with the latter will agree that he used his time to the best advantage under the new guru. He tells us in the opening verses of the *Ram-Charit-Manas* how deeply indebted he was to the various *Vedas, Puranas, Upanishads* and the *Ramayanas* written by earlier poets for his source materials. It must have been a comprehensive and thorough-going education that he received, embracing various branches of learning including poetry, philosophy, religion and astrology. It is not unlikely that some of his respect for Advaita philosophy was developed under the influence of Shesh Sanatan. His scholarly training was also at the root of his impatience with those who belittled the *Vedas* and the *Shastras* without knowing what they were talking about. At the same time his learning was quite obviously vitalised by much independent thinking and experience of life.

Tulsi Das makes only oblique references in his works to his marriage and life as a householder. It is certain that the blows of misfortune, the treatment he had received at the hands of his people, the teachings of his guru and his own thoughtful study of the ancient texts had persuaded him that his surest refuge in life was Ram and the life divine.

In one of his later works, he recalls with nostalgia the days when he was well set as a wandered who made a living in the name of Ram and regrets his thoughtlessness 'in snapping the thread of his ties with the Lord and getting caught up in the ways of the world.' He had to take a decision about his future when his teacher Shesh Sanatan died and with his passing away Kashi lost its attraction for him for the time being. He had lived in the company of the sadhus but he himself was not one of them. According to tradition and the testimony of *Mool Gosain Charit,* the *upnayana* (sacred thread) ceremony of the Brahmin boy was performed duly and at the proper time. It is only natural that at the end of his studies the young man, who was now a scholar of some standing and endowed with "a handsome personality", should have thought of going back to his ancestral house and settling down as a householder. He must have had to build a house anew after the long years of absence but once he was set up in life again he must have been a very eligible match for the young girls of his community. There is a body of evidence in the writings of authors other than the poet which shows that his bride, traditionally known as Ratnavali, daughter of Dinbandhu Pathak, was an exceptionally intelligent, bright and beautiful young lady who shared her husband's religious interests and devotion to Ram. It was a happy married life. The young husband made a living by reciting the story of Ram, in which he was very well grounded, to enthusiastic audiences and, if a stray reference in the *Vinaya Patrika* is to be taken on its face value, his "middle age was spent in trade, agriculture and various expedients to make money."

Years of a happy married life sped by before the event which gave a decisive turn to his life took place. Both Baba Beni Maddho Das and Priyadas in his commentary on the *Bhaktmal* give an account of his renunciation of home and family life which is substantially similar. Tulsidas loved his wife so well that he would not allow her even to pay a visit to her parents. One day in his absence and without his permission his wife left for her father's house in the company of her brother who had come to see her. Unable to bear the separation, the young poet left the same night for his father-in-law's house even though he had to cross a river. The wife, taken aback by the ardour and impetuosity of her fond husband, might well have felt that he had crossed the limits and she told him in rebuke, "If you bore half the love that you have for my fleshly body towards Ram, you would surely be freed from the fears and sufferings of human life."

The words sank deep in the poet's heart and he took an irrevocable decision to renounce home and hearth.

It was a turning-point in the sense that he, took a definite decision as to what he was looking for. There could be no doubt that the foundations of faith in the love of Ram had been well and truly laid by his teachers and his own experience of life. Neither the success which attended his recitals of the story of Ram nor the conjugal bliss of his home life could keep him permanently bound down to the humdrum life of a householder. A stray spark was enough to rekindle the ashes of a deep-seated desire to go out and see Ram "face to face." It is significant that he is completely silent about the details of his married life beyond admitting in a stray line that he had learnt his lessons in true love from "advice given by his wife" or lamenting, as he does in the *Vinaya Patrika* "the indiscretions of his young age" when he fell victim "to the triple maladies of youth, woman and cupid."

The renunciation of Tulsidas was in his day and in the context of his own life as decisive as that of the other Indian saints and sages from Gautam Buddha to Vivekananda who left hearth and home, not to find a way of escape but to search for the truth and share their knowledge with their fellow-men. Tulsidas, in any case, had no respect for those who turned sannyasis because they had "lost a wife or the family income had dwindled." His mind was ripe for the great decision and it would appear that his marriage and family life were just an interlube in a pilgrim's progress towards spiritual self-realisation.

II
YEARS OF QUEST

The years in the life of Tulsidas that followed his renunciation of home and family were some of the most fruitful in developing his personality and outlook on life. It was during these years that he travelled up and down the country, gathering knowledge, studying men and affairs, meeting saints and sadhus and dwelling in meditation in a final bid to apprehend the Reality behind the apparent contradictions and disappointments of life. Unfortunately it is also a more or less dark period as far as dates and details are concerned. The places where he spent most of his time were Prayag, Ayodhya, Chitrakut and Kashi but he visited many other places far and near which find mention in his writings.

The place to which he naturally turned for solace, once he had made up his mind to renounce the life of a householder, was Ayodhya. There were many cultural and spiritual associations due to which the place was enshrined in his heart. It was Ram's own city and very much his own spiritual "home." It was near here that he had found refuge as a hapless and poverty-stricken child. But the idea uppermost in his mind at the moment seems to have been to travel to the great pilgrim centres of the country, such as Jagannath Puri, Rameshwaram, Dwaravati, Badrikashram and the heights of the Himalayas. Apart from tradition and the account of these travels in the *Mool Gosain Charit,* we have some very vivid descriptions of some of these places in his own writings. In a striking passage in the *Vinaya Patrika*, while praying to Nar-Narayan, he recalls the forests and mountain peaks of Badrikashram, the trials and hazards which the pilgrim has to face, the murderous attacks of armed robbers on the way and adds characteristically. "Lord, the journey of the spiritual seeker is not less difficult. Poor Tulsidas is equipped neither with the supporting staff of true renunciation, nor the traveller's money of a firm grounding in *dharma*."

His description in the *Ram-Charit-Manas* of Mansarovar in the Himalayas is equally alive with the warmth of feeling and it is not inconceivable that he had seen personally the blue mountain peaks and the jewelled stairs and transparent waters of the lake. The view certainly had enhanted his heart and was very much in his mind in choosing a title for his great epic.

There could be no doubt that Tulsidas was a ceaseless traveller in his youth and middle age and that with Ayodhya as his headquarters he visited many places, big and small, in northern India. References to these visits occur in his own works and in the works of contemporary writers. Places in Uttar Pradesh and Bihar which had anything to do with the story of Ram had naturally the strongest attraction for him. Thus in January during *Makar Sankranti* he would stay at Prayag. In February and March he would move on to Chitrakut. In April, the month in which his Lord

Ram was born, he would remain at Ayodhya. From there he would proceed to Kashi. After the rains he would go to Mithila because it would be the part of the year when his Lord Ram's wedding ceremony took place there.

There are many stories about happenings at various places and the good turn he did to an admiring host here, an erring priest there and devoted commoners everywhere.

It is only natural that during these travels he should have gathered a great deal of knowledge about men and affairs and with his keen, observant mind studied the manners and ways of the people he met. Describing the banyan tree in the hermitage of the sage Valmiki at Sitamarhi (between Prayag and Kashi), he says, "Even an ordinary banyan tree is dwelt in by god Siva but the spot is twice blessed because mother Sita lived in exile here and the sage Valmiki set up his hermitage. The people here are very soft-spoken, polite and obliging."

What Tulsidas was clearly looking for during these years was not a career as a holy man but the resolution of the intense spiritual questionings within him. He had turned his face against home but not against life, travel and literary activity. Some of his stray poems and minor works like *Ramagya Prashna* and possibly *Vairagya Sandipani* with its learnings towards the traditional disciplines were written at this stage of his life. Besides Ayodhya and Kashi, his chief haunts during these years were Prayag and Chitrakut.

Prayag was the place where two of the most ancient and authoritative exponents of the story of Ram had lived and taught. It is said that Tulsidas came to Prayag when the bathing fair of *Makar* was being held and all kinds of saints, ascetics and holy men were gathered together. The picture of Prayag which he draws in the *Manas* in the course of a long-drawn-out simile shows how Prayag and the society of saints were inseparable in his mind. But the physical charms of the place were not lost upon him. "A wave of delight sweeps over my heart," he tells us in the *Kavitavali*, "at the sight of the confluence of the white and dark waters of the Ganga and the Yamuna. It looks as if a horde of charming white young ones of the Celestial Cow were frisking about and grazing over a bed of green grass."

For Chitrakut he had feelings which were not only warm but also almost mystical. He believed that the best thing which anyone eager to cultivate the love of Ram could do was to stay at Chitrakut. "By the grace of Sita-Ram only a little effort would bring great good." He himself had made the experiment. "A course of bathing in the river, living on a fruit diet and the repetition of the name of Ram for six months," he tells us, brought him all sorts of merit and auspicious achievements. He was enchanted by the natural beauty of the place with its cloud-capped hills, shining rocks and transparent waters. In almost all his works he longs to be at Chitrakut, "the eternal huntress lying in wait to chase away the sins and sufferings of human life."

Legend and tradition are at one in giving an interesting story of the manner in which Tulsidas met Ram face to face at Chitrakut and it is a story so often repeated in all the accounts of the poet's life and so mysteriously referred to by him in his own writings that it might as well be repeated here in some detail.

It was a practice with Tulsidas to recite the story of Ram and the devotional fervour of these recitals attracted large gatherings. The god Hanuman, ever eager to hear the praises of Ram but anxious to conceal his own identity, used to attend these gatherings in the guise of a leper. He would be the first to arrive and the last to leave. Tulsidas came to get hold of the secret. At the end of his next recital, when all had left, he caught hold of the feet of the deity and told him how keenly he longed to see Ram "face to face." The deity could not refuse the prayer of so ardent a devotee and told the poet to wait and watch in Chitrakut. It happened one day that Tulsidas was sitting in Chitrakut lost in meditation. Just when two princes on horseback passed that way but the poet, whose eyes were fixed on the ground at the moment, missed the sight. The god Hanuman appeared the next moment and asked him, "Did you see the two princes on horseback? They were Ram and Lakshman." The poet was sorely disappointed.

The story goes on. The good god Hanuman reassured the disconsolate poet that he would have another view of Sri Ram the next morning. And the next morning when the poet was sitting by the river-bank in deep distress, Sri Ram appeared as a youth and asked him to put sandalwood paste on his forehead. This time Hanumanji was close by to give a timely hint and the poet had a full view of his Lord and Master. So charmed was he by the vision that he forgot all about putting sandal paste on Sri Ram's forehead and the god had to do it for himself.

We may or may not believe the story in its literal details, but the poet himself seems to have been powerfully moved by the happening. In poem in the *Gitavali* he definitely recalls it and laments how his eyes turned his own enemies, how he spoilt his own best interests by keeping his eyes fixed on the ground, how little he knew about the inscrutable ways of Providence, how everything happened in a trice, how "though waking, he was asleep."

The important point is that at this stage of his life, he was engaged in an intense heart-searching and examination of the problems of spiritual self-realisation and it was at Chitrakut that he got the answers.

In a revealing poem in the *Vinaya Patrika,* he reviews the incident and gives us an idea of how he himself viewed his relations with his Lord and Master. He tells himself, "Listen to this that I have to say and then do what you will. Look with your four eyes (the eyes that look at the outer world and the eyes turned inwards) and say, in all the three worlds and the three ages, is there anyone who is as keen about your welfare as the Lord? Housed in your physical body, you have forged all sorts of new relationships. Put to test, the fraud behind these relatives' hypocritical professions of love has been exposed. The dealings of the crowds of your friends were no better than transactions made with swindlers. And even clever gods must be seen as they really are. If they will do you one good turn, they will expect a millionfold return. And the acts of piety and religious merit too are fruitless—a mere weariness of the flesh unless inspired by the love of Ram. Without such love, it is like making sacrificial offerings over a heap of ashes or the rains pouring down on barren land. (The truth is) there is no master as full of compassion as Ram, none who is as ready to do good to all, at all times, in the beginning, in the middle and in the end, whose glory pervades the world and the *Vedas*. Wretch, how can you find rest or peace, if you forget the One who is the dearest, the very life of your life, the supreme benefactor, the One who purifies the lowliest and the most wicked? O Tulsi, remember evhat Ram, the gracious King of Kosala, has done for you and recall in your heart the episode at Chitrakut." The 'Chitrakut episode' acquires added significance when we read the poem just quoted along with some others in which he asks himself why, in spite of his purity and piety, his professed allegiance of Ram, his ceaseless travels across "countless forests and mountains", there is still a distance between him and his Master. The explanations and the directions given by the saints and philosophers do not satisfy him. Finally, he turns the searchlight inwards and discovers that the thief robbing him of his reward was within him and this thief he was able to detect only at Chitrakut.

It is apparent that a new consciousness about the will and purposes of the Divinity and the path that leads to the grace of God dawned upon him. These glimpses of Ram, "the all-pervading Reality which is the same in all the worlds", which he secured at Chitrakut, gave him a sense of self-confidence. He was now definitely nearing the end of a long quest and ready to record the faith he had acquired in the great epic, the *Ram-Charit-Manas,* which was immortalised him.

III
HIS TESTAMENT

It was on a Tuesday, the ninth day of *Chaitra* in the *Samvat* year 1631, that Tulsidas started writing the *Ram-Charit-Manas* in the city of Ayodhya on the banks of the sacred Saryu. The place and date are significant, Ayodhya being the birth-place and the day being the birthday of Sri Ram. Equally significant is the fact that it is the only date relating to his life which he has recorded with the greatest care and which is, therefore, beyond controversy. In terms of the Christian era, it was the last day of March in the year 1574, when by any reckoning he must have reached middle age and crossed a definite stage of his life. It is a pity he has not told us much about the men and ideas which influenced him between the years when he heard the story of Ram as a raw youth at Sukerkhet and he started writing his own version of it at Ayodhya. With his great thirst for knowledge, he must have been open to many influences, not the least of them the Advaita philosophy of Shankar taught by his scholarly teacher at Kashi. There are unmistakable traces of the impressions of Advaita philosophy left on his mind in the *Vairagya Sandipani* and in the *Manas*. Among the other disciples of Shesh Sanatan, there must have been some wedded to the Krishna cult. One tradition has it that Nand Das, the well-known poet and devotee of Krishna, was a fellow-student with whom he must have argued out points in the Krishna cult. He could not but have imbibed the best in the tenets of Saivism and there is ample evidence that he remained an ardent devotee of Siva till the end of his days. His own patron deity was Mahabir who, he tells up, "owned him from childhood", brought him up and saw him through all the vicissitudes of a chequered life. In fact, whenever a disciple or an admirer wanted to express his gratitude to the poet-saint, the one thing he would suggest was the setting up of an image and temple of Mahabir. The variety of the *Vedas, Puranas* and *Upanishads* and other source material that has gone into the making of his great epic has been candidly admitted by him in the opening verses of the *Manas*. What is significant and truly remarkable is the unity of the vision and faith which he developed in the midst of the variety of knowledge and experience he gained and the integrated view of life which he advocated in a world in which sectarian affiliations were the order of the day.

The core of his own faith seems to have been, first, that there is a Power and a Presence named Ram; second, that by nature it is full of love, grace and compassion; and last, that life's fulfilment consists in getting into touch with it through love, purity and selflessness.

The story of Ram, as he understood it, was ideally fitted for the enunciation and unfoldment of this view and the faith within him. Whether we also believe it or not that god Siva told him in a dream to write the story for the benefit of his soul and the good of mankind, there could be no mistake that the poet himself fervently believed that he was writing the *Ram-Charit-Manas* under divine inspiration.

Tulsidas sets forth his approach to the story of Ram in a long, illuminating preface to his great master-piece. The basic urge, he tells us, is "the satisfaction of my own soul" and as if to confirm this he repeats in the closing verses of his book that he had written it "to dispel the darkness of his own heart." This approach is plainly not that of a teacher or a propagandist but that of a seeker exploring the ways of Ram and eager to share the joy of exploration and discovery with the reader. He anticipates the criticism to which he will be subjected and the quarters which will criticise him. In utter humility he invokes the blessings of all—gods and men, previous writers on the subject, the doubters and the scoffers—and repudiates any ambition to show off as a scholar and poet. He knows he will be laughed at by the learned for writing not in Sanskrit but in the language of the common people and defends his choice because he is sure in his own mind that good poetry "like the Ganga, should do good to all."

The approach was so fundamentally different from that of the poets and the pandits of the day, so alive with the warmth and glow of a live experience that it must have raised many eyebrows in the ranks of the committed and professional exponents of theology. In the eyes of the metaphysical philosophers who tried to reduce the divinity to a mere abstraction devoid of personality, he was particularly suspect. And he took good care to dispose of the questions and the doubts which he knew would be raised.

There is the question, first, whether the Ram of his story is the same Brahma the *Vedas* describe and the yogis mediate on. "Yes," says he, "between the Finite and the Infinite, there is no difference. For the love of the devotee the Infinite, the Ineffable, the Formless, the Unborn becomes Finite even as water and snow are not separate."

He also meets any doubts about another article of his faith, the power and efficacy of the Name of Ram as an instrument of self-realisation. With the fervour of one who knows what he says he asserts, "The Finite and the Infinite are the two forms of Brahma the Indescribable, the Fathomless, the Beginningless, the Incomparable. To may mind, the name is greater than both because the Name brings both under its sway." "and please," he adds with transparent sincerity, "Do not treat this assertion of mine as a piece of bold fancy. I am saying something born of my own experience and love and faith. Knowledge both of the Infinite and the Finite is like fire. The Infinite is like the ire implicit in the wood. The Finite is like the explicit flame which all can see. That is why I have said that the Name is greater than even Brahma." For once he is at pains to argue the point. "The Name and He for whom the Name stands are one but they are related as master and servant." "The Name immediately calls up the form." "The Name is the witness of both the Finite and the Infinite." It is like "an accomplished interpreter" who explains the one to the other. And with deep devotional fervour, he extols the power of the Name. "The living Ram could bless only the people in the Dandaka forest but innumerable are the human hearts which his Name has purified and redeemed."

The poet had a method in prefacing the main story with these rather abstruse discussions as well as the philosophical dialogue between Siva and Parvati on the nature and identity of the Immanent Brahma and the Ram of his story. His normal manner is so entirely human and objective that he found it necessary to dispel misconceptions and specify the true levels of his own faith in the love of Ram.

Tulsidas's famed love of Ram (Ram Bhakti) is so unmistakably the dominant note of his epic that much of his meaning could be missed without a correct understanding of its true character. Tulsidas is not averse to a statement of the nine signs of *bhakti* given in the traditional texts. Ram himself enumerates them. "The first is the company of saints; the second, keen interest in the story of my deeds; the third, devoted service to the guru (teacher); the fourth, singing my praises without hypocrisy; the fifth, repetition of my name and firm faith in me as the *Vedas* enjoin; the sixth, self-control, moral purity and ceaseless practice of virtuous actions; the seventh, a sense of equality born of the consciousness that I am immanent in the world as also regard for saints even more than for me; the eighth, contentment with what is one's portion and refusal to see the shortcomings of others even in a dream; and the ninth, simple, guileless behaviour, heart-felt faith in me and a state of mind free from elation or depression."

This picture of the devotee who lives in God recurs in the *Manas* in the most significant contexts and the poet's greatest prayer elsewhere is that he may be granted the life of the true devotee whose mind is free from fear and anxiety, desire and egoism, unaffected by harsh words or high praise, whose heart is calm and at rest, full of goodwill for all and without malice towards anyone, who has attained the state in which the dualities of pleasure and pain are transcended.

It is apparent that his is a kind of *bhakti* which has much more to do with the development of the human personality than with set dogma or ritual. Essentially, it is a way of life which transforms and redeems. "Bhakti is free." It stands in its own right, "independently, without extraneous aids,' and `knowledge itself is subservient to it." It has its roots in love and simple faith and constant awareness of a presence as intimate and near and dear as "one's own father and mother." Far from being other-wordly or lacking in a sense of social responsibility, the love of Ram which Tulsidas advocates is to be practised and proved on the social level and in the context of human relationship. He accepts the world as it is, full of good and evil, joy, grief and suffering. The love of Ram transforms all. "Who knows who will go to hell and who to heaven? Life in the world here below is very good indeed for Tulsidas as a devotee of Ram."

In fact, it would appear that the entire story of Ram as the poet develops it in the pages of the *Ram-Charit-Manas* is designed to illustrate and emphasise the integrated life of those who are prepared to undertake and discharge responsibilities in the light of a great love and devotion.

Four persons, according to the poet, have really understood the nature and quality of true devotion—Siva, Hanuman, Lakshman and Bharat. All of them are as much active and indefatigable workers in the cause of Ram as repositories of the secrets of Ram-*bhakti.* The lesser characters are no less engaged in rendering the little bit of service they can. What matters is not the bit of service rendered but the spirit in which it is rendered. There is hope, therefore, as much for the boatman who ferries Ram across the Ganga and the monkeys and the vultures who labour in the good cause as for the sage and the saint. It is a very human level on which the story moves and that is why it wins the heart of the common man and touches his most intimate longings and aspirations.

Scholarly attempts have been made to identify the school of philosophical thought to which Tulsidas subscribed and it is remarkable that the advocates of all schools—the monists, the dualists, the believers in a qualified monism—are able to gather plausible points in favour of their own particular school. This only shows how at home the poet was in the tenets of each school while remaining faithful to his own integrated view of the life divine. He would rather say that "he alone can realise the self who has left behind the three illusions."

The ease with which Tulsidas is able to effect a synthesis between various philosophical positions and sectarian beliefs is one of the glories of the *Ram-Charit-Manas.* Throughout the great epic he is at pains to show the invalidity of the artificial divisions between the finite and the Infinite, the followers of the way of knowledge and the way of Love, the worshippers of Ram and of Siva. This synthesis is brought about not by refutation or special pleading but by showing in the lives and conduct of the characters he creates that the way of *bhakti* is but the way of works and the way of works is only the way of knowledge vitalised and fulfilled.

As a literary work, the *Ram-Charit-Manas* has most of the qualities of a great epic. The high seriousness, the wide canvas, the record of the accumulated wisdom, culture and experience of the race and the universal popularity which we associate with the great epics in world literature are all there. And the poet observes the formal rules laid down by literary tradition with a care which is apparent. In fact, in his own times he seems to have been looked upon by many of his most competent admirers as an incarnation of the sage Valmiki. But tradition and models do not prevent him from handling his material as he chooses. His main interest does not lie so much in narrating the story as in using it to portray the intimate transactions of love between Ram and those who open themselves up to His love. Naturally he is prone to stressing just those episodes and situations which are likely to throw into relief his own devotional attitude. The narrative might be held up, there might be some imbalance in the size of the cantos but he cannot resist the temptation of introducing plenty of dialogues, dissertations, invocations and prayers. This is almost certainly due to his rooted belief that the primary purpose of relating the story of Ram is to free, arouse and elevate the mind and that there is no story which cleanses, purifies and redeems as much as the story which is related in his epic.

The devotional element overshadows the story which makes Tulsidas *Ram-Charit-Manas* an epic with a difference. It is not surprising, therefore, that it is looked upon by many readers more as a religious scripture or a song celestial than as an epic cast in the traditional classical mould.

IV

AT KASHI

Although Tulsidas started writing the *Ram-Charit-Manas* in 1574 in Ayodhya, there are good grounds to believe that he was able to finish the work only in Kashi a few years later. Written in the wake of a great awakening at Chitrakut and in the congenial atmosphere of Ayodhya, the first three cantos are easily among the biggest and best in the whole book. The language and felicity of expression of these cantos, the culture which they reflect, the atmosphere in which the story moves and draws its sustenance have much to do with Ayodhya and the region known as Avadh. What persuaded Tulsidas to leave a place so much to his liking as Ayodhya, it is difficult to say. Various conjectures have been made. It is stated that his broadminded tolerance and freedom from sectarian prejudices led to differences with the *vairagis* of the place. Sectarianism of any kind certainly went against his grain. It is also possible that with all his deep-seated love for the city of Ram, he was not exactly happy with the state of affairs in the temples or the life of the so-called yogis and ascetics. In the *Dohawali* he regrets that only those people are worshipped as yogis an accomplished men who eat and dress in the most repulsive manner. "The temples and holy places," he says, "are dens of evil and corruption. The rulers rule by striking terror in the hearts of their subjects and the number of bullies and ruffians, ever ready to stir up trouble, runs into thousands." Tulsidas had no respect for the illiterate and intolerant men who donned the saffron robe only to make a living and we may be sure that they in turn distrusted him for his freedom from sectarian bigotry. In fact, he was very much in the camp of the learned men, the *acharyas* whose main engagement was the search for light and peace. It is not unlikely, therefore, that he should have decided to migrate to Kashi which was at that time the recognised centre of Hindu learning and religion. Even otherwise he must have been looking out for fresh fields and pastures new for the propagation of his message of faith and hope for mankind.

There is a distinct note of relief in the opening lines of the fourth canto of the *Manas*, where he says that Kashi is "the homeland of Siva and Parvati, a storehouse of knowledge and learning, a place which destroys sin and gives freedom from bondage" and that there is no reason why he should not spend his days there.

Tulsidas's reputation as a devotee who had seen Ram face to face at Chitrakut seems to have travelled and reached the people of Kashi before him. Naturally when the *Ram-Charit-Manas* was completed and came to the notice of people, it received instant and wide recognition on account of the author's love of Ram, his absorption in the theme, the freshness of his approach, his deep humanity and the music and the movement of his flowing verses. It also aroused controversy because a work of the deepest import and obvious merit was written not in Sanskrit, the sacred language, but in the language of the people, because it attempted a synthesis of conflicting schools of thought and belief and, above all, because of its emphasis on a simple and direct faith, free from complicated ritual and set observances.

Society in Kashi of the Mughal times was divided into many sections. There was the circle of learned scholars versed in Sanskrit lore; there were the members of the aristocracy; there were the leaders of various religious sects and their adherents who made a living as priests; and there were the poor, simple folk who were the victims of economic distress and social restraints. Genuine scholars like Madhusudan Saraswati recognised the merit of Tulsidas and paid handsome tributes to his skill as a poet and devotee. A few like the landed proprietor, Todarmal, and possibly the linguist and patron of letters, Abdur Rahim Khan-i-Khana, were drawn towards him as much by the beauty and the truth of his writings as by the purity and saintliness of his character. The people at large could not but have received his message of love, hope and faith with alacrity. But the custodians of religious sectarianism, specially the Saivas, definitely disliked him because they supposed wrongly that he was trying to spread the cult of ram at the expense of the cult of Siva. In any case, they could see clearly that if the spirit of broadminded tolerance which he sought to promote was allowed to grow, they might soon find their occupation gone. Interested parties hatched plots to harm and humiliate him. Time-honored tradition has it that thieves were hired to steal the manuscript of the *Ram-Charit-Manas.* The merits of the book were assailed and some of his more determined critics said that they would have nothing to do with the book unless god Siva himself put the seal of his approval on it. The traditional lives of Tulsidas are full of stories of miracles which saved him from the attentions of his opponents. The poet makes no direct reference to their misdeeds but there are many significant passages in his works which throw light on the nature of the opposition he had to face.

Tulsidas had a deep and sincere regard for god Siva. He had come to Kashi in the hope that god Siva would protect him and his interests as the guardian god of the city. He fervently believed that god Siva was both a god and a guru to him because he had derived the inspiration for the love of Ram from and through him. He had made Ram himself say, "He who opposes Shankar opposes me." But the sectarian bigots had no use for the sincerity and the nicety of the poet's position.

Tulsidas on his part could not have liked some of the ways of "the flock of ghost worshippers" who professed allegiance to god Siva. He disapproved of the methods of the controversialists who "hack the texts of the *Vedas*, the *Upanishads*, the *Puranas* and grammar like a block of wood" and "raise controversies to burn their own hearts and the hearts of others." He roundly condemend the unlettered sectarian sadhus who talked about "illusion and unreality" without really knowing anything about what they were talking about.

It is not difficult to see that this attitude of his was not in step with the times or the prevailing tendencies. Slowly but surely a regular storm of opposition gathered round him. And this opposition was not confined to wordy warfare. His opponents could go to any lengths in making him uncomfortable. In despair he tells Siva, the presiding deity of Kashi, "During the day I am jostled about by cheats and by night I am surrounded by thieves; unless you keep a kindly eye on me, my stay in this city would be made impossible."

One of the ways in which his opponents twitted him was to question his antecedents and in particular his caste, sect and upbringing. In the spirit of one almost at bay, the poet tells them in a number of passages that he had no caste and no sect and no desire to have one, that they were free to give him any names, that Ram was his only lord and master and "his enemies would meet the fate of the enemies of Ram."

There are indications that attempts were made to bring about his death. He makes no direct reference to actual acts beyond saying that, with Ram on his side, no one could kill him. He preferred to bear down opposition by patient suffering. Instead of blaming others, he would sooner search his own soul and seek an explanation of his situation in his own imperfections. There are numerous references to Kali, the Devil (representing the age of decay and evil) in his writings at Kashi. In the combat with the flesh and the Devil perhaps he had not been "sufficiently vigilant" or fully well-armed. It is a measure of his clear-sightedness that he saw in the midst of all the bigotry and ill-will round him that the answer to bigotry was not more bigotry and that what really moved his opponents to action was not religion but the lack of it. If, therefore, the voice of criticism died out in course of time and his opponents failed in their purposes; it was due as much to the purity of his motives and his ability to rise above the storm of passion and prejudice as to miracle and divine aid.

The favourite resorts of Tulsidas in Kashi were on the bank of the Ganga. He loved to be near the sacred river. "Drinking the water of the Bhagirathi and repeating the name of Ram is my daily routine," says he in the *Kavitavali*. A few spots in Kashi are specially associated with his life. He used to be the guest of his good friend Pandit Ganga Ram Joshi at Prahlad Ghat. In a chamber at Gopal Mandir he is said to have written parts of his great devotional work, the *Vinaya Patrika*. The god Hanuman was the poet's favourite deity and of the twelve temples of the god that he got built, one is situated at Sankat Mochan. At assi again there is a chamber where the poet is said to have spent some of the last days of his long life.

It is certain that Tulsidas acquired a high reputation both as a poet and as a man of God in his life-time. Not only poets and saints but also the people at large for whom he wrote in the language they understood flocked to him in steadily growing numbers. Two activities in which he seems to have been keenly interested were the construction of temples of Mahavir and the annual Ram Lila celebrations. At Assi Ghat he organised Ram Lila celebrations according to the story in the *Ramayana* and the place south of Assi, which used to be the Lanka of these celebrations, continues to be known by that name.

One of his best friends at Kashi, Pandit Ganga Ram Joshi, seems to have helped him in getting a number of temples of the god Hanuman built out of funds supplied by him. The story goes that the son of the Raja of Rajghat in Kashi lost his way while out hunting. The worried father summoned Pandit Ganga Ram Joshi to ask if the young price would return home. Pandit Ganga Ram Joshi promised to give an answer the following day and on return home talked to Tulsidas about the situation in which he was placed. Tulsidas, who had a lively interest in astrology, made calculations and predicted that the boy would be back home the following evening. The prediction proved true and the Raja rewarded the poet's friend by giving him a lakh of rupees which the grateful Pandit put at the feet of the poet. Tulsidas refused to touch the money but when his friend insisted, he agreed to accept twelve thousand rupees which he promptly spent on the construction of twelve temples of the god Hanuman, of which the one at Sankat Mochan continues to be one of the most popular in the city.

Another good friend was Todarmal, a landowner and devoted admirer, who enjoyed the poet's confidence. It is said that the poet put a manuscript copy of the *Ram-Charit-Manas* with him for safe custody and that it was at his instance that he was persuaded to stay on at Kashi when he had made up his mind to quit it. When Todarmal died, a *panchnama* (deed of arbitration) dated September 27, 1612 was drawn up under which Todarmal's landed property was partitioned among his successors. A few lines at the top of this deed are said to be in the poet's own handwriting. This deed remained with the members of the family of Todarmal for eleven generations and is now in the safe custody of the Raja of Kashi. Tulsidas seldom wrote anything about human personalities, but the moving lines he wrote on the death of Todarmal reflects the depth of his feeling for the friend he had lost. "The lamp of the life of a man truly large-hearted, ruler of four villages, has gone out in these evil days. Once had taken upon his shoulders the burden of the love of Ram, he refused to shake it off, although there were many who asked him to do so. Now that he has gone to the world of Ram, Tulsi is no longer worried; his only regret is that he will have to go through life without a pure-hearted friend." It is said that when Tulsidas had to leave Gopal Mandir on account of the opposition of the Gosains of Vallabh group, Todarmal asked him to come and stay in his own temple at Assi.

There are many stories which describe in graphic detail how the great poets and saints of the age—Surdas, Nand Das, Banarasi Das, Kashavdas, Hit Harivansh, Mirabai, Abdur Rahim Khan-i-Khana 'Rahim' and Raskhan—came in contact with Tulsidas or were moved by his poetry. In the absence of fixed dates and references in historical records, it is not possible to give credence to all of them. Nabha Das, the author of *Bhaktmal* and a contemporary of the poet, referred to him as an incarnation of Valmiki "born to redeem the depraved people of his day." There are good grounds to believe that there was a great deal of mutual admiration between Tulsidas and some of these poets. It is remarkable that these poets and admirers were drawn from quarters which normally would have very little to do with one another. Followers of the Krishna cult like Nabha Das and Nand Das who seem originally to have come to scoff remained to bless. Tulsidas was so evidently an admirer of the songs of Surdas that he emulated some of them and wrote a book of songs in praise of Sri Krishna, entitled *Gitavali*. Banarasi Das was a Jain poet of Jaunpur, but when he wrote a poem in praise of the *Ramayana,* Tulsidas promptly wrote one in praise of Parshwanath in the most devout strains. The Sanskrit scholar Madhusudan Saraswati belonged to the Saiva cult but this did not stand in the way of his acknowledging Tulsidas's devotion and poetical skill after due debate. Abdur Rahim Khan-i-Khana was a Muslim poet and administrator but the two poets had no hesitation in admiring each other. All this points as much to the esteem in which he was held as to the catholicity of his outlook.

He had friends and admirers in the ranks of the administrators also and two names, those of Rajas Man Singh and Jagat Singh, are particularly mentioned in this connection.

It is, however, difficult to substantiate or disbelieve entirely the story about his visit to the Mughal Emperor in Delhi. It is said that Emperor Jahangir on hearing about the miracles he had performed asked the poet to be his guest and to demonstrate his powers. The official historians of the day make no mention of this and the vague hints thrown out by the poet are not enough to give us a clear picture of what really took place. Priyadas in his commentary on the *Bhaktmal* says that when the poet met "the Badshah of Delhi" and the latter asked him to show miracles, Tulsidas replied, "These stories about miracles are false. One should put one's faith in Ram alone," which certainly is a reply in the poet's characteristic manner.

It is certain that during the later years of his life at Kashi, Tulsidas was a celebrity and some of the very important people of the day would come to see him. The poet himself does not seem to have been keen to establish contacts with the high and the mighty. Some at least of his visitors would have to go back disappointed because he was writing or lost in meditation. There are indications that he was a little uncomfortable when he found that he was being sought after by people in high places. "Time was," he tells us, "when I begged from door to door, and now the rulers of the land are at my feet." And he knew the reason why. Those were the days when "Tulsi was without Ram" and now Ram was by his side. That the Lord had "turned a handful of dust into one mightier than the mountains", that he was being hailed as one of "the great sages of the day" was the Lord's own miracle but Tulsidas seems to have remained unspoilt by this turn in his fortunes. "If a lean and poverty-stricken grass-cutter," he says, "should come by a mountain-load of gold, this would remove only the poverty of his house, not the poverty of his heart. Having passed through both the phases of poverty and prosperity and having found both doubly distressing, Tulsi has blackened the face of Poverty itself. He has ceased to be deluded by hope, having entered the service of Ram, the River of Compassion." He realised that mere material advancement was not good for a mans's spiritual health and was constantly reminding himself that the Lord was his only refuge.

There are many stories of the miracles which Tulsidas performed during this period of his life and these have been repeated so often and so consistently in the writings of poets and saints that it may be legitimately supposed that the simple and devout people among whom they were current did take them on their face value. It is easy to see that some of the veneration in which he was held did rest on his reputation as a miracle-worker who lived a charmed life. Quite a few of them, however, reveal his personality much more than his powers. He himself was so humble and gentle and utterly straightforward that it is difficult to associate any desire to indulge in magic or mystery with his dealings. It is more likely that the miracle that worked most powerfully on men's minds was his transparent sincerity, his calm unruffled mind, his wide tolerance and his compassion for the erring and the distressed.

During the years at Kashi he received a great deal of recognition and went out on many of his travels in Uttar Pradesh and Bihar, but his main interests were writing and meditation. It was during these years that he attained new heights of creative literary work and spiritual self-realisation.

V

POETICAL WORKS

The *Ram-Charit-Manas* which he finished within a few years of his coming over to Kashi is undoubtedly the work which brought the widest fame to Tulsidas and enjoyed the greatest popularity with his audiences. But he lived for nearly half a century after he had finished it and the majority of his works other than the *Manas* were written or collected after his reputation as the author of the immortal epic had been firmly established.

There are some very long lists of the works of Tulsidas but the consensus of opinion among scholars is that only twelve can be named as his own works with any degree of certainty. These twelve are the *Vairagya Sandipani*, the *Ramagya Prasna*, the *Ramlala Nahchhu*, the *Janaki Mangal*, the *Rama-Charit-Manas*, the *Parvati Mangal*, the *Krishna Gitavali*, the *Gitavali*, the *Vinaya Patrika*, the *Dohavali*, the *Barwai Ramayana* and the *Kavitavali*. Except in the case of a few, such as the *Ram-Charit-Manas*, the *Ramagya Prasna* and the *Parvati Mangal*, the poet gives us no indication as to when a particular work was written. This is perhaps natural as a majority of the undated works are collections of verses written from time to time. Of the manuscript copies of the *Ram-Charit-Manas* now available, the oldest written in 1604, some twenty years before the poet's death, is the one preserved at Ayodhya. Another old copy is preserved at Malihabad near Lucknow, the capital of modern Uttar Pradesh. And it is a measure of the intrinsic qualities of the *Manas* that of the making of commentaries and translations of the great epic both in Indian and foreign languages there is no end.

Ram and the story of Ram remained the principal theme and fountain-head of inspiration in all his major works but having written the great epic, the poet seems to have developed a pronounced tendency to express himself in song and lyric. The thin thread of the story of Ram by which the poems in a particular collections are sought to be held together often recedes in the background, and the poet's love of beauty, form, colour and music comes to the foreground.

The *Gitavali* relates the story of Ram in songs but there is no attempt either to develop the story or strike a balance among the various episodes. The charm of the songs consists in their naturalness, sincerity of emotion and musical quality. The poet deliberately chooses scenes and episodes which lend themselves to lyrical treatment. They have a charming pictorial quality and there is an intimate connection between the mood evoked and the musical *raga* in which they are cast. Tulsidas had evidently an interest in music and it is not unlikely, as tradition has it, that the poet wrote these songs for ardent young musicians who sang the glories of Ram before eager and devout audiences.

With all his preoccupation with matters of deep spiritual import, Tulsidas had a lively interest in the lives and fortunes of the men and women among whom he moved and in making them interested in the story of Ram. Three short but charming literary pieces, the *Ramlala Nahchhu,* the *Parvati Mangal* and the *Janaki Mangal* seem to have been specially written to please and interest the ladies.

The *Ramlala Nahchhu* is a book in twenty stanzas, describing the rites connected with the sacred thread and wedding ceremonies and recalls the auspicious occasion and joyous scenes in the King's palace at Ayodhya.

In the *Parvati Mangal* the poet describes the wedding of Siva and Parvati. He had described the episode earlier in the *Manas* but the *Parvati Mangal* as an independent literary work has a charm of its own. It is compact in form. The economy and simplicity of the style are striking, which is something of a triumph for an epic poet. For once we have the date 1586 when it was written long after he must have finished writing the *Manas.* It certainly should have provided an effective answer to the allegations of those who said he had glorified Ram at the expense of Siva.

There is a close resemblance between the *Parvati Mangal* and the *Janaki Mangal* both in style and theme. In the *Janaki Mangal,* the wedding of Ram and janaki is described in 216 stanzas, full of warm feeling and sensuous beauty.

All the three works are written in the language of the people, pure Avadhi, and in the metre mainly of the wedding songs, *Sohar,* to recall scenes which would delight the ladies. This shows not only how much the poet cared for the common people but also how keenly he felt that good poetry could be written to record common experiences for the common people in their own language.

It is significant that Tulsidas has written in praise of Sri Krishna with as full-throated ease as about Siva and in strains quite as sincere as those of Surdas. The language of *Sri Krishna Gitavali* is pure *Braj,* the language spoken in the region in western Uttar Pradesh which was the scene of Sri Krishna's exploits. The poems in this collection of songs, sixty-one in number, compare very favourable indeed with the best manner of the poems in the *Sursagar* of Surdas.

It would appear that Tulsidas made experiments in practically all the various literary forms that were extant and popular in his day and he touched nothing which he did not adorn. As a metrical form, the *Doha* had been used by a long line of Hindi poets and saints and Tulsidas himself had used it to great effect in his *Ram-Charit-Manas* to sum up or finalise ideas in a set of preceding lines. He must have seen how fit a vehicle it was for expressing crisp and quotable truth or observation in a concentrated form. Naturally there is a great variety of subject-matter in the *Dohavali* of Tulsidas, which is a collection of verses written at various times. From the maturity, insight and acuteness of observation in a very large number of them, however, it is natural to suppose that the collection was made at a comparatively advanced stage in the poet's literary career. Thirty-four *dohas* in a set known as 'Chatak-Chautisa' in this collection are remarkable for the presentation of the poet's own ideal and philosophy of love, love which seeks neither reward nor recompense, love which is utterly and entirely selfless, love which is an ever-fixed mark which neither storm not tempest can shake. There is also in the *Dohavali* a great deal of worldly wisdom based on close observation of trends in society, men and affairs.

Another metrical form which caught the fancy of the poet was the *Barwai,* which he used for writing yet another *Ramayana,* the *Barwai-Ramayana.* It is said that the original *Barwai-Ramayan* contained many more than the sixty-nine verses to be found in the editions now generally available. In any case, both the language, which is pure Avadhi, and the metre, which was rarely used, except by Tulsidas's contemporary, Abdur Rahim Khan-i-Khana, had a special appeal for the poet. It is a metre delicately designed to make for economy of phrase and concentration of ideas, highly responsible to the evocation of the finer shades of feeling and gracefully languid in movement.

The wide appeal of Tulsidas's language and style as a poet is due mainly to its simplicity, adequacy and directness. "What does it matter," he would say, "whether one writes in Sanskrit or the language of the people? What matters above all is true love." He believed strongly that it was not words but the sincerity of feeling behind them that shaped a poet's language and style. His own language and style went through a process of steady evolution from the pure Avadhi of his lesser works to the refined and fully developed, composite language of his major works such as the *Manas,* the *Kavitavali* and the *Vinaya Patrika*. It is a composite language in the sense that he uses with perfect ease and freedom and without any inhibition words drawn not only from Avadhi, Bhojpuri, Bundeli, Brajbhasha and Khariboli but also from Sanskrit, Arabic and Persian. The flexibility of his language is amazing. It would seem that it varies with the subject-matter in hand-a fully developed and refined Avadhi in the *Manas* and the *Barwai-Ramayan,* a perfected Brajbhasha for the *Krishna Gitavali,* the *Kavitavali* and the *Vinaya Patrika,* Sanskrit-laden lines for prayers and invocations and words drawn from Persian and Arabic, if the context demands it. Nothing seems to weigh with him as much as the basic need for naturalness, directness and effectiveness. If in the process it is necessary to take liberties with the rules laid down by the purists, he does not hesitate to do so in the larger interests of vitality, freshness and adequacy of expression. He is in this matter more the creator of a language and idiom of his own and an original craftsman than the follower of set rules and static tradition. He may be a little found of similes and metaphors but this is so not because he wants to show off but because he knows such devices will convince his readers.

The result is that he lives up to his promise that he would write poetry which may not please the purists and the pedants but which would win the hearts of the masses because it is full of the love of Ram.

The *Kavitavali* gives us rich material both about Tulsidas's own life and the life of the common man in the society of his time. Together with the *Hanuman Bahuk,* it contains 369 quatrains, mostly in Kavitta and Savaiya metres. In the earlier part of the work, the poet gives some unforgettable word pictures of situations in the story of Ram in quatrains of exquisite beauty, remarkable as much for the meaning as for the musical sound effects, the movement of the lines and the inherent lyricism. But by the time the concluding canto, the 'Uttar Kand,' is reached, the story of Ram comes to an end, the poet for once begins to talk about himself, his early life and struggles, his rise to fame, his allegiance to Ram and the rest of the work is the story not of Ram but of Tulsidas himself. Reviewing life from the vantage-ground of old age, he records with arresting frankness and sincerity the articles of his faith. He feels that man is not alone, that a life in tune with Ram has infinite possibilities, that life's greatest fulfilment is to live in God, above the dualities of poverty and affluence.

A keen social conscience is also in evidence in many of these quatrains. The poet is moved by the sight of "the Ravana of Poverty holding the world in his grip." He draws a graphic picture of people in dire distress asking one another, "Where shall we go? What shall we do?" because the farmers have no fields to cultivate, the beggars get no alms, the businessmen have no vocation, and servicemen seek jobs in vain. He observes that people in all ranks of society resort to questionable and immoral devices to keep body and soul together and arrives at the conclusion that "there are no fires more devastating than the fire of hunger." He is unhappy because people have given up the right path laid down by the Shastras and all sorts of new fangled beliefs hold the field. The misery, vice and poverty he saw all round him and the confusion created in men's minds by the so-called religious men seem to have persuaded him that there is no religion for man higher than the service of his fellow-men.

The *Vinaya Patrika* Ranks only with the *Ram-Charit-Manas* as one of the crowning glories of the works of Tulsidas. It is a collection of lyrical songs. In the epic, the poet had to express his love for Ram through the speech and action of others and the purposes of successful characterisation and dramatisation had to be met first. The general reader could see the deeper aspects of the poet's message of love only as through a glass darkly. In the *Vinaya Patrika,* which is in a real sense a sort of a spiritual biography, the poet is face to face with his Maker. He gives here, with fascinating candour and great intensity of feeling, a record of his endeavours to discover Reality and the true nature of the Way of Love. This has led to a widespread but mistaken belief that it is some sort of a philosophical treatise in verse. His intensely personal, intimate approach, sincerity of feeling and the lyrical quality of the songs, make it one of the finest collections of devotional verses in all literature.

The story goes that when Kali found that the life and works of Tulsidas were weaning people away from him and making inroads on his own domains, he threatened the poet with dire consequences. The good god Hanuman advised the poet to present a petition in the court of Ram. Both the title and the concluding verses of the collection lend colour to the story. But apart from the story, the feeling which inspires the poet, that he is laying bare his heart at the feet of his Master, helps both to organise the songs and to give them their unique devotional flavour. Each poem is a human record of the poet's struggle with the flesh and the devil, his attempts to solve the riddle of the universe, his eagerness to get into touch with the sources of light, peace and joy. And the conclusions he arrives at give us valuable hints both about him mature convictions and his inner personality. He finds that there is an all-pervading divinity "in the beginning, the middle and the end." To get into touch with it is the greatest opportunity of human life. Mere intellectual discussion is of little use here. It will not help a man to see light if he only sits enveloped in the darkness of a closed room by night and talks endlessly about a lamp and its light. If man could conquer anger, greed and ignorance, he could see light. But it is not so easy to conquer them Asceticism, austerities, elaborate rites and rituals are the ways suggested, but it is like making a rope of dust to bind down an elephant. Love, faith and surrender to the will of a Master who is full of compassion for the lowliest and the vilest are the only way.

The spontaneous feeling, the deep personal note, the unity and concentration of thought which we seek in the great lyric are all there in the songs of spiritual self-surrender collected in the *Vinaya Patrika*. There is no other work in which the authentic voice of the poet is to be heard more directly and distinctly.

Two calamities which overtook Kashi in his old age moved Tulsidas deeply. These were the famine and the great plague during the reign of the Mughal emperor, Jahangir. COntemporary records have it that the plague broke out in Agra about the year 1616 but from the manner the poet associates the epidemic with an astrologically evil period called 'Meen ki Sanichari,' it would appear that it visited Kashi even earlier. There is a note of deep misery over the plight of fellow-citizens in the powerfully objective picture of the havoc caused which the poet has drawn. He prays to his gods to spare Kashi for the City of Shankar had turned into a city of the dead and the dying.

Tulsidas himself suffered from some particularly painful disease about this time, which has led some writers to make the conjecture that he was caught by the plague and that his death too could be traced back to its after-effects. In the *Hanuman Bahuk* and elsewhere he does refer to his physical ailments and prays to his favourite deities to spare him. But there is nothing in these references which could help us to identify the disease or trace out the exact cause of his death. On the other hand, there are clear indications that at least once when he fell ill, he was saved through the good offices of his patron deity, Hanuman. Another ailment of his he describes as a pain in the arms which spread to other parts of the body. This ailment seems to have given him no end of trouble and in a number of quatrains in the *Hanuman Bahuk* he states how he prayed to all the gods in turn and in the end became silent, realising that he "must reap what he had sown." This turning of the searchlight inwards is so characteristic of the poet that it would be very farfetched to conclude that because his prayers were not answered, he lost all faith in divine intervention, or that he died of the plague.

It is true, nevertheless, that towards the end of his long life he was tired of his physical infirmities and wished that if the gods wanted him to continue to live, his "body should be free from ailments." He had lived a life full of years, honours and the bounties of the spirit. His only regret when "the ravages of old age had damaged the body completely" was that he had missed his opportunities, "failed to build a boat across the river of Ignorance, failed to sing the story of Ram as he had wished to, failed to emulate the example of devotees like Dhruva and Prahlad"; but it was very well with him as it was, because he had the assurance of the name of Ram in his heart.

It is apparent that he was mentally well prepared to face death with equanimity and that life came gradually and naturally to an end. "Having sung the praises of the name of Ram", he passed away in the year 1623 on the banks of his beloved Ganga on a day in July which was most probably a Saturday.

VI

HIS MESSAGE

A Halo surround the name of Tulsidas, the saint and author of the *Ramayana,* but this should not prevent us from looking at the very human, lovable and friendly man behind his writings. He had his full portion of life's rebuffs and handicaps. He was a pauper in childhood, his home life was wrecked when he was a youth; he was assailed on all sides when in middle life he decided to settle down in Kashi. It is a measure of the man's will to succeed that after every set-back the decided not to yield but to strive and pursue his quest with renewed vigour. "it is easy to talk about it but endless are the difficulties in the way with which only those who have pursued the path are familiar." But with all his high seriousness and fortitude he seems to have been a remarkable gentle and lovable man who would never make an enemy if he could help it. "A friend of the friendly, a lover of Ram, free from malice or rancour, detached, natural and simple in his dealings", he won the confidence of all who came in contact with him. Detached he certainly was in the sense that he could rise above public praise or citicism, but the impression that he was a recluse who did not encourage visitors and remained shut up in his study is very wide of the mark. He would not have been the welcome guest that the was in hall and hamlet during his long journeys to distant places, if he had shunned company. During the course of a journey to the eastern districts of Uttar Pradesh, he was hosted by Rajas and important men on the way but when he reached a village the inhabitants of which were known to be cruel and vicious, he refused to accept their hospitality. He preferred to stay outside the village with a milkman and was so pleased with his humble host that he granted him the boon that the members of his family would remain Ram's devotees, if they did not steal or make trouble for others. That a religious man like him should have been asked to witness a deed of arbitration drawn up to partition the estate of the landowner, Todarmal, shows both the confidence he enjoyed as an upright citizen and his readiness to do his duty to the memory of a dead friend.

The people who disliked him were the custodians of the vested interests of caste, creed and sect. They stopped at nothing in trying to bring about his discomfiture and hound him out of Kashi. But it is a measure of his tolerance that he bore no ill-will towards them and trusted that his God Ram would safeguard his interests. As he puts it, "Some say this Tulsi does a lot of evil, some say he is an impostor, some others that he is a sincere servant of Ram; the saintly take me for a great saint, the villains for a great villain. The waves of a million such true and false reports gather up round me. I ask no favours nor do I complain. I bear with all and do not let my heart be perturbed. The good and the evil which will befall Tulsi are in the hands of Ram. Varily, I am like the grass which thrives only in the soil of the love of Ram."

Tulsidas's tolerance stemmed directly from this mental outlook and was much more than a mere rule of conduct. "Knowing that this whole world was pervaded by Ram, he could not but salute everyone with folded hands."

Nevertheless, a great deal of firmness and courage of conviction went with his innate humility. His broad catholic attitude towards the religious beliefs of others is beyond question. He had respect for the followers of Siva, Sri Krishna, Lord Buddha and Mahavir. He sincerely attempted a synthesis of the various schools of Indian philosophy. But he adhered firmly to his own experiences in the quest for truth, truth as he saw it. All the storm raised by the Vaishnava Vairagis of Ayodhya or the persecution to which he was subjected by the Saivas of Kashi could not shake it.

There are many stories handed down by tradition about the man's goodness and the good turn he did to those in distress. Some of these, shorn of miracle and magic, throw interesting light on the man and his motives. There is the story of the Brahmin pilgrim who had committed a heinous crime in the eyes of the Shastras and come to kashi for expiation. The custodians of the Shastras treated him as an outcaste but the good poet not only owned him but also partook of food served by him in the name of Ram. There is another oft-repeated story that when he was told that Ram himself stood guard over his house by night, he gave away all his belongings to the needy and the poor. This gives us an idea not only of his selflessness but also of his colossal faith, as Rev. Edwin Greaves has pointed out, in God's "solicitude for his devotees."

He cared little for the accumulation of material wealth or public recognition. In fact, the good man believed that his physical ailments in his old age were somehow connected with his own shortcomings as a devotee.

In spite of all the stories are current about the miracles he is said too have performed, there is good reason to believe that he himself had little use for superstition and hypocrisy of any kind. He roundly condemned those who went to a shrine for a son or the restoration of their eye-sight or those who believed in ghosts and spirits or the pseudo-yogis who talked about the Invisible and the Unknowable.

One of the most striking aspects of Tulsidas's personality is his keen sense of objective beauty. He revels in the description of his blue-coloured deity, stressing a thousand details of the lotus eyes, the lotus feet, the pink palms and the yellow robes. The vignettes of Ram and Sita whether at the wedding altar, or in the forests during exile, or on their throne in Ayodhya are the warp and woof of his *Ramayanas* in various metres. Form, colour, beauty, sweetness and power are the qualities he sees in his Ram and the same qualities he extols in his writings. "I am willing to acknowledge anyone as my guru," he says, "who can expound knowledge without reference to ignorance; or describe light out of the context of darkness or set forth the formless without reference to form."

There are no records of his private life either at Ayodhya or at Kashi. But he had an intense personal feeling both for the Saryu and the Ganga. A bath in the river was part of the routine of his daily life and the milk and fruit diet which he prescribed as good for the seeker could also have been his own favourite diet.

The title 'Goswami' has stuck to his name so persistently that it has been suggested that for some time at least he was the head of a seat known as "the place of Gosain Tulsidas Ji" near Lolark-kund in Kashi. If this was so, he must have been rather uncomfortable in his situation because he expressly regrets that he had become a Gosain and forgotten the even tenor of his life. He was certainly averse to the institutionalisation of his experiences as a devotee and a seeker.

Two of his pet diversions were music and astrology, and it is not unlikely that he enjoyed a game of chess. With all his absorption in things of the spirit, he had a keen sense of humour. In his own gentle, subtle manner he would not spare the gods "who pose as altruists but are for ever scheming" or the lonely holy men who would have lots of feminine company as soon as Ram arrives in the forests and turns the rocks into moon-faced beauties!

There are hints in his own writings and in the writings of others that he had a fair complexion and a fine presence. A picture believed to be a copy of one made in his own life-time, and now in the possession of his friend Ganga Ram Joshi's successors at Prahlad Ghat, represents him as a rather lean and thin but self-possessed man of religion.

A great deal of wide-ranging scholarship went with his saintliness and it is impossible to miss his close familiarity with the principal schools of Indian philosophy on the one hand and the literary tradition embodied in the works of Sanskrit and Prakrit poets on the other. But he wore his learning lightly and, what is even more remarkable, he had a lively appreciation of the limitations of mere literary skill and intellectual sharpness. "The way of knowledge is like the sword's edge," he would say, "and the pitfalls are many and difficult to avoid." The man skilled only in the use of words can neither apprehend Reality nor rise above pain and suffering. Poetry, morality and scholarship are good in their spheres but all of them must be ministers of love. It is impossible to separate the love of God which he extols in his writings from the love of humanity. There is a deep strain of humanism in all his prayers to his God and in all his exhortations for the cultivation of the good life.

Four centuries have rolled by since Tulsidas wrote has *Ram-Charit-Manas* and if his message continues to have a hold on the minds and hearts of millions of his countrymen, it is because of its abiding value and inner vitality. It is a simple faith which he taught. "The love of Ram is born," he said, "in a simple heart and reflected in simple speech and action." Religious devotion for him was a way of life and it was no devotion, if it did not transform the life and it was no devotion, if it did not transform the life of the devotee and give him peace and the love of mankind. His main theme in his great epic is the victory of righteousness over the forces of darkness and evil. The weapons with which Ram fights and wins are "courage and fortitude, discrimination and self-control, a mind calm and unruffled and a heart full of love and compassion." This is so positive and so much the essence of the Indian view of life that its appeal to the Indian mind has been direct and irresistible.

Tulsidas felt that great poetry must be simple and as easily accessible a boon for all as the waters of the Ganga which makes for his immense popularity with the masses. The common man responds naturally to the manner in which he poses human issues in the context of human situations as he has to face similar issues in real life. The impact of such guileless but purposeful writing could not but be immediate and powerful.

No other poet in northern India has reflected more faithfully or more successfully the core of Indian thought and cultural tradition in his writings and none has left a more permanent impress on the evolution of the thought and cultural behaviour of the people over the centuries. This due to his deep concern for the human situation and complete freedom from sectarian affiliations. In an age in which most saints and thinkers of his stature would have thought of founding a sect or a school, he used all his gifts as a poet and a saint to arrive at a synthesis and harmonise viewpoints. In his own persuasive manner, he did much for the promotion of emotional integration among his people and in the long run he was much more successful than iconoclasts and crusaders.

The unit of the good society which he envisaged was the individual, and the ideal citizen of his Kingdom of God was a man who was free not only from ignorance and ill-will but also from disease and want. He recognised that there was no curse greater than poverty and no duty higher than doing good to others. He had much respect for an ordered life and the established norms based on sound judgment and the accumulated wisdom of the race, but the way of life which he himself preached recognised no distinctions of caste, sex or station in life. He had little patience with mentors who talked jargon and confused men's minds.

One of his crowning achievements was that he dispelled the mist of pessimism and abstract speculation which darkened and enveloped the lives of his people and gave them a healthy and positive creed, the keynotes of which were hope, joy, faith and fulfilment.

It is only natural that in our own time, Mahatma Gandhi, a great admirer of Tulsidas and a kindred soul, found much in the poet's writings to renovate the human soul and restore the people's faith in their national destiny.

VII
REPRESENTATIVE SELECTIONS

Renderings in English of some representative passages from the works of Tulsidas along with the original text in the Devanagari script are given below:

Ramlala Nahchhu

A short, early work, the *Ramlala Nahchhu* describes colourful, festive scenes associated presumably with the wedding of Ram.

गोद लिए कौसल्या बैठी रामहि वर हो ।
सोभित दूलह राम सीस पर आँचर हो ।।
बतिया सुघर मलिनियां सुन्दर गावहि हो ।
कनक रतन मनि मौर लिए मुसुकातहि हो ।।

"Queen Kaushalya sits with Ram in her lap, the ends of her sari spreading fascinatingly over the head of the bridegroom. The comely flower-girl standing close by holds up the golden wedding headgear, studded with precious stones, and sings and smiles charmingly all the while."

Vairagya Sandipani

In the *Vairagya Sandipani* the poet's main interest is in questions of moral discipline and philosophy.

रैनि को भूषन इंदु है, दिवस को भूषन भानु ।
दास को भूषन भक्ति है, भक्ति को भूषन ज्ञानु ।।
ग्यान को भूषन ध्यान है, ध्यान को भूषन त्याग ।
त्याग को भूषन शांतिपद, तुलसी ग्रमल ग्रदाग ।।

"The ornament of the night is the moon, that of the day the sum. The ornament of the devotee is devotion, that of devotion knowledge. The ornament of knowledge is meditation, that of meditation renunciation. The ornament of renunciation, says Tulsi, is pure, unalloyed peace."

Janaki Mangal

In the *Janaki Mangal* the poet describes the wedding of Ram and Janaki.

बर बिराज मण्डप मंह बिस्व बिमोहइ ।
ऋतु वसन्त बन मध्य मदन जनु सोहइ ।।
लागि झरोखन झांकहिं भूपति भामिनि ।
कहत बचन रद लसहिं दमक जनु दामिनि ।।

"The bridegroom seated under the wedding canopy enchants the world. He shines like the god of love in the midst of a forest in spring.

"The queens cling to the windows of the palace and look out (at Ram). As they speak their teeth shine like flashes of lightning."

Ram-Charit-Manas

Woven round the central story of the *Ram-Charit-Manas* there is a great deal of religion, mythology and philosophical exposition, which are used to formulate the poet's own devotion to Ram, who is both a personal deity and the Supreme Reality.

About the sources of his work, the poet says:

नाना पुराणनिगमागम सम्मतं यद्
रामायणे निगदितं क्वचिदन्यतोपि
स्वान्तः सुखाय तुलसी रघुनाथगाथा
भाषानिबन्धमति मंजुल मातनोति ।।

"Tulsidas puts forth this captivating story of Ram obtained from various *Vedas*, *Puranas*, *Shastras* and some other sources in the language of the people for the satisfaction of his own soul."

The greatness of the theme gives him much satisfaction:

जदपि कवित रस एकउ नाहीं, राम प्रताप प्रगट एहि माहीं।
सोइ भरोस मोरें मन आवा, केहि न सुसंग बड़प्पनु पावा।
धूमउ तजइ सहज करुआई, अगरु प्रसंग सुगन्ध बसाई।
प्रिय लागिहि अति सबहि मम भनिति राम जस संग।
दारु बिचारु कि करइ कोउ बंदिअ मलय प्रसंग॥

"Although my work may lack poetical qualities, the knowledge that it sets forth the glories of Ram reassures me, for who will not attain greatness by good associations? Even smoke, bitter by nature, ceases to be disagreeable as soon as it is joined by the sweet smell of incense. The Malaya sandalwood will continue to be worshipped because of its association with the Malaya mountain and the fact that it is only a piece of wood will not weigh will anyone."

He seeks the goodwill of all:

जड़ चेतन जग जीव जत सकल राममय जानि।
बंदऊं सब के पद कमल सदा जोरि जुग पानि।
देव दनुज नर नाग खग प्रेत पितर गन्धर्ब।
बंदऊं किन्नर रजिनिचर कृपा करहु अब सर्ब।
आकर चारि लाख चौरासी, जाति जीव जल थल नभ वासी।
सीयराममय सब जग जानी, करऊं प्रनाम जोरि जुग पानी॥

"Knowing that ram dwells in all things and beings, animate and inanimate, I bow at the lotus-feet of all, with folded hands. Be kind to me, all ye hosts of deities and demons, men, serpents, birds, ghosts ancestors, choristers of heaven, dark demons of the night. There are eighty-four lakh types of beings cast in four forms which inhabit water, earth and air. Knowing Sita-Ram to be immanent, dwelling everywhere and in all, I salute all with folded folded hands."

The descriptive passages in the *Manas* are some of the best. The following reveals the feelings of Sita when the princes Ram and Lakshman appear in King Janak's flower-garden:

चितवति चकित चहूं दिसि सीता, कंह गए नृप किसोर मनु चीता।
जंह बिलोक मृग सावक नैनी, जनु तहं बरिस कमल सित श्रेनी।
लता ओट तब सखिन्ह लखाए, स्यामल गौर किसोर सुहाए।
देखि रूप लोचन ललचाने, हरषे जनु निज निधि पहचाने।
थके नयन रघुपति छबि देखें, पलकन्हिहूं परिहरीं निमेषें।
अधिक सनेह देह भै भोरी, सरद ससिहि जनु चितव चकोरी।
लोचन मग रामहि उर आनी, दीन्हे पलक कपाट सयानी।

"Sita looks eagerly all round her, wondering which way the charming princes had gone. Whichever way her fawn-like eyes cast a glance, it would look as if a shower of rows of white lotus-flowers had fallen. The girl companions of Sita pointed to a spot behind the creepers where the two, dark and fair princes stood. Sita's eyes looked greedily at their fair forms. Joy filled her heart as though she had found her lost treasure. The sight of Ram's beauty made her eyes motionless and the eyelids ceased to drop down. So overpowered was she by an excess of love that she lost control over her body. It was like the *chakor* (the traditional moon-gazing bird) looking fixedly at the moon in winter. Through the gates of her eyes she took in Ram in her heart and smartly closed the doors by shutting her eyelids."

This is how those gathered at the court of King Janak see Ram before Siva's bow is broken:

जिन्ह कें रही भावना जैसी, प्रभु मूरति तिन्ह देखी तैसी।
देखहिं रूप महा रनधीरा, मनहुं बीर रस धरें सरीरा।
डरे कुटिल नृप प्रभुहिं निहारी, मनहुं भयानक मूरति भारी।
रहे असुर छल छोनिप बेषा, तिन्ह प्रभु प्रगट काल सम देखा।
पुरबासिन्ह देखे दोउ भाई, नर भूषन लोचन सुखदाई।
नारि बिलोकहिं हरषि हियं निजनिज रुचि अनुरूप।
जनु सोहत सिंगार धरि मूरति परम अनूप ।।
बिदुषन्ह प्रभु बिराटमय दीसा, बहु मुख कर पग लोचन सीसा।
जनक जाति अवलोकहिं कैसें, सजन सगे प्रिय लागहिं जैसें।
सहित बिदेह बिलोकहिं रानी, सिसु सम प्रीति न जात बखानी।
जोगिन्ह परम तत्वमय भासा, सांत सुद्ध सम सहज प्रकासा।
हरि भगतन्ह देखे दोउ भ्राता, इष्टदेव इव सब सुख दाता।

"Each saw the image of Ram according to his own mental attitude. To the warriors he was the very embodiment of valour. To crafty kings trembled to look at his mighty figure, the very image of Fear. The demons sitting in disguise felt as if Doom was staring at them. The citizens saw in the two brothers the jewels of humanity, and the delight of their eyes. To the hearts of the delighted ladies, they were rare personifications of Love and Beauty. The learned saw in the Lord the vast cosmic form with many mouths, heads, feet, eyes and hands. To King Janak's relatives, they were like their own near and dear kith and kin. In the heart of King Janak, they aroused love like that he had for his own children. To the yogis they were the Supreme Reality, motionless, pure, equal-minded, self-expressed. In the eyes of the devotees, they were their own deities who brought all manner or bliss."

Lakshman's simple faith and deep devotion are evidenced in the following lines, as he pleads with Ram to be allowed to accompany him to the forests:

दीन्हि मोहि सिख नीकि गोसाईं, लागि अगम अपनी कदराई।
नरबर धीर धरम धुर धारी, निगम नीति कहुं ते अधिकारी।
मैं सिसु प्रभु सनेंह प्रतिपाला, मंदरु मेरु कि लेहि मराला।
गुरु पितु मातु न जानउं काहू, कहउं सुभाउ नाथ पतिआहू।
जहं लगि जगत सनेह सगाई, प्रीति प्रतीति निगम निजु गाई।
मोरें सबइ एक तुम्ह स्वामी, दीनबन्धु उर अन्तरजामी।

धरम नीति उपदेसिग्र ताही, कीरति भूति सुगति प्रिय जाही ।
मन क्रम बचन चरन रत होई, कृपासिंधु परिहरिग्र कि सोई ।

"Lord, good is the advice you give me. But the coward that I am, it is beyond my reach. Only the exceptional men of fortitude, grounded in the scriptures and high morality deserve advice of such high import. I am only an infant brought up by your love. Can a young swan lift the burden of the Mandrachal and Sumeru mountains? Lord, I am telling you my sincere feelings. I have known no other teacher, father or mother. For me all relationships and bonds of affection, love and faith which bind men in the world and are extolled in the *Vedas* have come to be centred in you, dweller in our hearts. Let religion and morality be preached to those who care for reputation, power and a good end. But, Ocean of Compassion, could you give up one whose only concern is devotion to your feet in thought, speech and action?"

Moral philosophy is mixed up with a description of natural beauty when the rains set in and Ram misses Sita:

घन घमंड नभ गरजत घोरा, प्रिया हीन डरपत मन मोरा ।
दामिनि दमक रह न घन माहीं, खलकै प्रीति जथा थिर नाहीं ।
बरषहिं जलद भूमि निग्रराएं, जथा नवहिं बुध विद्या पाएं ।
बूंद ग्रघात सहहिं गिरि कैसें, खल के बचन संत सह जैसें ।
भूमि परत भा ढाबर पानी, जनु जीवहि माया लपटानी ।
सरिता जल जलनिधि महुं जाई, होइ ग्रचल जिमि जिव हरि पाई ।

"As the clouds gather up and burst in thunderclaps in the sky, my heart is shocked because my beloved Sita is not with me. There are flashes of lightning in the clouds, even as there is no constancy in the friendship of the wicked. The clouds come down on the plains to pour rains, even as the wise bend down with humility when they acquire knowledge. The mountains suffer the blows of the rain drops, just as the saintly suffer the blows of the rain drops, just as the saintly suffer the speech of the wicked. Water becomes dirty as soon as it touches the earth, even as the individual soul is spoilt when it is enveloped in illusion. The waters of the river are stilled on entering the sea, even as the self is at rest in union with God."

Ram gives this assurance to Vibhishan, from the enemy camp, once he seeks refuge with him:

जौ नर होइ चराचर द्रोही, ग्रावै समय सरन तकि मोही ।
तजि मद मोह कपट छल नाना, करऊं सद्य तेहि साधु समाना ।
जननी जनक बन्धु सुत दारा, तनु धनु भवन सुहृद परिवारा ।
सब कै ममता ताग बटोरी, मम पद मनहिं बांध बरि डोरी ।
समदरसी इच्छा कछु नाहीं, हरष सोक भय नहिं मन माहीं ।
ग्रस सज्जन मम उर वस कैसें, लोभी हृदयं बसइ धनु जैसे ।
तुम्ह सारिखे सन्त प्रिय मोरें, धरऊं देह नहिं ग्रान निहोरें ।

"A person may be enemy of all the world and its animate and inanimate beings but the moment he surrenders himself to me having given up pride, illusion, hypocrisy and deceit, I transform him into one like the, noblest of men. He who gathers together the threads of his affection for his mother, father, brother, wife, body, riches, home, friend and family and waves them into a string tied to me, he who is equal-minded, desireless, unmoved by joy, grief and fear-such a good man lives in my heart like riches and property in the hearts of the greedy. Saintly men are dearest to me. For them do I take this human form and for no other reason."

Vibhishan is worried that Ram is at a disadvantage against Ravan sitting well armed in his chariot on the battle-field. Ram recounts the weapons that bring true victory.

सुनहु सखा कह कृपानिधाना, जेहि जय होइ सो स्यंदन आना ।
सौरज धीरज तेहि रथ चाका, सत्य सीलदृढ़ ध्वजा पताका ।
बलविवेक दम परहित घोरे, छमा कृपा समता रजु जोरे ।
ईस भजनु सारथी सुजाना, विरति चर्म संतोष कृपाना ।
दान परसु बुधि सक्ति प्रचंडा, वर बिग्यान कठिन कोदण्डा ।
अमल अचल मन त्रोन समाना, सम जम नियम सिलीमुख नाना ।
कवच अभेद विप्र गुरु पूजा, एहि सम विजय उपाय न दूजा ।
सखा धर्ममय अस रथ जाकें, जीतन कहं न कतहुं रिपु ताकें ।

"Listen friend," says the merciful Lord, "the chariot which brings victory is different. The wheels of that chariot are bravery and fortitude. Its flags are truth and moral power. Its horses are force, judgment, self-control and service of fellow-men, tied to the chariot by the ropes of charity, compassion and equal-mindedness. Devotion is the skilled charioteer, selfessness, the shield, contentment, the sword, charity, the axe, intelligence, the mighty bolt, the elevated mind, the terrible bow. A heart, pure and unruffied, is the quiver, while the arrows are equality, disciplined life and self-control. The impenetrable armour is worship of the teacher and the Brahmin. There are no better weapons for securing victory. Friend, for one who sits in such a chariot, there are no more enemies to be conquered."

Dohavali

Dohavali is a collection of 573 couplets in some of which the poet makes acute observations on life and manners.

मनि मानिक महंगे किए, सहंगे तृन जल नाज ।
तुलसी एते जानिए राम गरीब नेवाज ।।
घर कीन्हें घर जात है घर छांड़े घर जाइ ।
तुलसी घर बन बीच हीं राम प्रेम पुर छाइ ।।
मुखिया मुखु सो चाहिए खान पान कहुं एक ।
पालइ पोषइ सकल अंग तुलसी सहित विवेक ।।

"It is enough to prove Ram's compassion that gold and jewels are scarce but straw, water and cereals (essential for supporting life) are easily available.

'If we build a house here (as a man of the world), we lose our (true spiritual) home; but if we renounce our hearth and home (social responsibilities), then again our home is ruined. To my mind, the best thing to do is to reside in the city of Ram which lies midway between the home and the forest.

"The chief should be like the mouth which is one for the purposes of eating and drinking but which nevertheless thoughtfully nourishes all the members of the body.

"What does it matter whether it (the language medium) is Sanskrit or the common dialect? True love is the one thing needful. If a rug serves better, what is the use of a shawl?"

Barwai Ramayana

In *Barwai Ramayana* the story of Ram is sung in the *Barwai* metre which with its soft musical qualities is specially suited for the delineation of the finer shades of feeling.

चंपक हरवा अंग मिलि अधिक सोहाइ
जानि परै सिय हियरे जब कुंभिलाइ ।
गरब करहु रघुनन्दन जनि मन मांह
देखहु आपनि मूरति सिय कै छांह ।
विरह आगि उर ऊपर जहं अधिकाइ
ए अंखिआं दोउ बैरिनि देहिं बुझाइ ।

"A garland of (white-yellow coloured) champak flowers looks well on the person of Sita. But it mixes so well with her complexion that it is possible to distinguish it only when the flowers have faded.

"Ram, do not be too proud of your appearance. Your (dark) figure is but a shadow of Sita's (resplendent) beauty.

"As soon as the fires of separation flame up in my heart, these two eyes prove my enemies for they (the tear-drops) extinguish it instantly."

Kavitavli

The *Kavitavali* is a collection of quatrains of exquisite pictorial and musical qualities dealing with the story of Ram and the story of the poet's own life and experiences.

These lines describe Sita as she leaves the city walls of Ayodhya on her way to the forest.

पुरतें निकसीं रघुवीरवधू, धरि धीर दए मग में पग द्वै ।
झलकीं भरि भाल कनीं जल की, पुट सूखि गए मधुराधर वै

फिर बूझति हैं चलनो अब केतिक पर्नकुटी करिहौ कित ह्वै ?
तिय की लखि आतुरता पिय की अंखियां अति चारु चलीं जल च्वै ।

"Exercising all her patience and her will-power, the bride of Raghuvir came out of the city and took two steps on the path (to the forest). Soon her forehead was covered with resplendent drops of perspiration. Her sweet lips went dry. And the next moment she was asking Ram, "How much more do we have to walk? Where are you going to set up your hut of leaves?" Tears droped from the eyes of the husband as he noticed his wife's impatience and eagerness."

As Ram and Sita are passing through the forests, the village women want to know from Sita how she is related to the young prince beside her:

सुनि सुन्दर बैन सुधारस साने सयानी हैं जानकी जानी भली
तिरछे करि नैन, दै सैन, तिन्हें समुझाइ कछू मुसुकाइ चली
तुलसी तेहि औसर सोहैं सबै अवलोकति लोचन लाहु अली
अनुराग-तड़ाग में भानु उदैं बिगसीं मनो मंजुल कंजकली ।

"When Sita heard the sweet nectar-like words of the village women, she at once saw through their clever question. She gave a side-glance and an understanding wink, smiled and went forward. Looking at Sri Ram with delight in their eyes, these village women themselves looked charming. It was as if lotus buds had blossomed forth in the lake love at the touch of sunrise."

Here is a lurid picture of Lanka on fire:

लगी लागी आगि भागि भागि चले जहां तहां
धीय को न माय, बाप पूत न सम्भारहीं
छूटे बार, बसन उघारे, धूम धुन्द अन्ध
कहें बारे बूढ़े 'बारि बारि' बार बारहीं
हय हिहिनात, भागे जात घहरात गज,
भारी भीर ठेलि पेलि रौंदि खौंदि डारहीं
नाम लै चिलात बिललात अकुलात अति
'तात तात' तौंसियत झौंसियत झारहीं ।

"People in fright run helter-skelter crying `Fire.' Mothers do not heed their daughters, nor fathers their sons. With dishevelled hair and clothes in disarray, the fumes of smoke choking their eyes, old men and young cry out for water. Horses neigh and break away, elephants trumpet and push at the huge crowds, crushing them down under their feet. Upset and terror-stricken, everyone calls at everyone else, `We are being baked as in an over by these scorching flames.'"

The poet looks back at his early life in some passages:

जाति के, सुजाति के, कुजाति के पेटागि बस
खाए टूक सब के, बिदित बात दुनीं सो
मानस वचन कायं किए पाप सतिभांय

राम को कहाइ दासु दगाबाज पुनी सो
रामनाम को प्रभाउ, पाउ, महिमा, प्रतापु,
तुलसी सो जग मनिग्रत महामुनी सो
ग्रति हीं ग्रभागो, ग्रनुरागत न रामपद

"Urged by the pangs of hunger, you had to beg at the doors of all kinds of high and low caste people. The world knows this. You won the reputation of being a man of Ram but you have not lived up to that reputation, having indulged in all kinds of evil in thought, speech and action. But behold the power, the influence, the greatness of the name of Ram; people now hail you, Tulsi, as the great sage (Valmiki). Even though you have witnessed a miracle so great as this, you have not, the luckless fool that you are, fixed yourself firmly in the love of Ram."

He is full of repentance:

भलि भारत भूमि, भले कुल जन्मु, समाजु सरीरु भलो लहि कै
करषा तजि कै परुषा बरषा, हिम, मारुत, घाम सदा सहि कै
जो भजै भगवानु सयान सोई, तुलसी हठ चातुक ज्यों गहि कै
नतु ग्रौर सबै विष बीज बए, हर हाटक कामदुहा नहि कै।

"You were born in this good country, Bharat, in good family, with (all the advantages of) a fine personality and good society. In such circumstances, he alone would be wise who would give up anger and harsh speech and, braving the rigours of heavy rains, cold winter, high winds and the hot sun engage himself in the love of God with the single-minded devotion of the *Chatak* bird because all else is like harnessing the heavenly cow, Kamdhenu, to a plough of gold to raise a harvest of poison."

He looks at the world and laments trends in life and society in his own times:

किसबी किसान कुल बनिक भिखारी भाट
चाकर चपल नट चोर चार चेटकी
पेट को पढ़त गुन गढ़त चढ़त गिरि
ग्रटत गहन गन ग्रहन ग्रहेटकी
ऊंचे नीचे करम धरम ग्रधरम करि
पेट ही को पचत बेचत बेटा बेटकी
तुलसी बुझाइ एक राम घनस्याम ही तें
ग्रागि बड़वागि तें बड़ी है ग्रागि पेट की।

"All today work only to make a livelihood-those who are taking education or resorting to various devices or ascending mountains or roaming about in dense forests in search of game. This applies to all sections of society the manual labourer, the farmer, the trader, the beggar, the minstrel, the servant, the nimble acrobat, the thief, the envoy and the magician. They will do anything, good or evil, moral or immoral, even sell a daughter or a son to fill their bellies. Tulsi says, `The pangs of hunger are more devastating than any other fires. Only the blue cloud that is Ram can extinguish this fire.'"

His sincerest note is heard when he sings about himself and Ram:

जागें जोगी जंगम जती जमाती ध्यान धरें
डरें उर भारी लोभ मोह कोह काम के
जागें राजा राजकाज सेवक समाज साज
सोचें मुनि समाचार बड़े बैरी बाम के
जागें बुध विद्या हित पण्डित चकित चित
जागें लोभी लालच धरनि, धन, धाम के
जागें भोगी भोग हीं वियोगी रोगी सोगबस
सोवै सुख तुलसी भरोसे एक रामके ।

"Yogis, roving holy men, sadhus and their parties are kept awake because they are keen to go into meditation or anxious to avoid lust, anger, illusion and greed. Kings are kept awake on account of state affairs. Their attendants and paraphernalia, the worries due to news about enemy activity. The learned keep awake in pursuit of learning; the greedy in pursuit of land, wealth and houses; the pleasure-seeker is kept awake in search of pleasure; the love-lorn and the diseased on account of the pangs of separation or ill-health. It is only Tulsi who sleeps well because of his abounding faith in Ram."

Vinaya Patrika

The *Vinaya Patrika* is a collection of devotional songs recording the poet's intimate spiritual longings and written in his most mature style. Renderings of a few songs are given below:

तू दयालु दीन हौं तू दानि हौं भिखारी
हौं प्रसिद्ध पातकी तू पाप पुंज हारी ।।
नाथ तू अनाथ को अनाथ कौन मोसों ?
मो समान आरत नहिं आरतिहर तोसों ।।
ब्रह्म तू हौं जीव तू ठाकुर हौं चेरो
तात मात सखा गुरु तू सब विधि हितु मेरो ।
तोहिं मोहिं नाते अनेक मानियै जो भावै
ज्यों त्यों तुलसी कृपालु चरन सरन पावै ।।

"Lord, you are full of compassion and I am indigent you are the alms-giver and I am the alms-man, I am a well-known sinner and you are the destroyer of sin. You are the lord and master of all who have none to protect them, and where is the orphan like me? There is none more miserable than I am and none who takes away men's miseries as you do. You are the Supreme Reality and I am the individual soul; you are the master, I am the servant. You are my father, mother, friend and guru, a well-wisher at all points. Many are the bonds of relationship between you and me. You may treat me as you choose. All that Tulsi asks for is that you will redeem him in the manner it is possible."

यह बिनतां रघुवीर गुसाईं
और आस बिस्वास भरोसो हरौ जीव जड़ताई ॥
चहौं न सुगति सुमति संपति कछु रिधि सिधि विपुल बड़ाई
हेतुरहित अनुराग रामपद बढ़ै अनुदित अधिकाई ॥
कुटिल करम लै जाइ मोहि जंह जंह अपनी बरिआई
तहं तहं जनि छिन छोह छांड़िए कमठअंड की नाईं ॥
या जग में जहं लगि या तनु की प्रीति प्रतीति सगाई
ते सब तुलसिदास प्रभु ही सों होहिं सिमिटि इक ठांई ॥

"This is my prayer, Raghuvir, my master. Take away all the hope, faith and trust I put in others and all the ignorance of the individual soul. I ask not for salvation or knowledge or wealth, spiritual accomplishments or surpassing greatness. All I want is that a disinterested love for your lotus-feet should grow and develop in me as the days pass by. Whatever the places to which I am driven by the force of ruthless *karma* (action entailing consequences), all I ask for is that you will not withdraw your affection for me even for a moment even as the tortoise does not part from its eggs. All love, all affection, all relationships, whatever binds this mortal frame to this world may be gathered up at a single point and directed only towards my lord and master. This is the prayer of Tulsidas."

असि कछु समुझि परत रघुराया
बिनु तब कृपा दयालु दास हित मोह न छूटै माया ॥
वाक्य ग्यान अत्यन्त निपुन भवपार न पावै कोई
निसि गृह मध्य दीप की बातन्ह तम निवृत नहिं होई ॥
जैसे कोई इक दीन दुखित अति असन हीन दुख पावै ।
चित्र कल्पतरु कामधेनु गृह लिखे न बिपति नसावै ॥
षटरस बहु प्रकार भोजन कोउ दिन अरु रैनि बखानै
बिनु बोले संतोषजनित सुख खाई सोइ पै जानै ॥
जब लगि नहिं निज हृदि प्रकास अरु बिषय आस मन माहीं
तुलसिदास तब लगि जगजोनि भ्रमत सपनेहुं सुख नाहीं ॥

"Raghuvir, Gracious Lord and Master of the devotee, it strikes me that unreality and illusion cannot be dispelled except by your grace. No one skilled only, in verbal knowledge can get over and cross this objective world. Darkness cannot be got over by a man who is shut up in a dark chamber by night and merely talks about light and a lamp. The privation of the poor wretch who starves for want of food and nourishment will not be removed by drawing a picture of *Kalpataru* (the wish-fulfilling tree) or the Kamdhenu (the celestial cow of plenty) on the walls. The satisfaction of good meal is known only to him who eats it, even if he should not say a word; but mere talk, day and night, about the six varieties of eatables will do him no good. Tulsidas says as long as there is no illumination of the heart (no direct apprehension of reality) and the objective world of desire continues to have its hold on the mind, there is no true happiness to be had even in a dream and the individual soul goes on roaming through endless earthly incarnations."

अब लौं नसानी अब न नसैहौं ।
राम कृपा भव निसा सिरानी जागे पुनि न डसैहौं ॥
पायो नाम चारु चिंतामनि उर करतें न खसैहौं
स्यामरूप सुचि रुचिर कसौटी चित कंचनहिं खसैहौं ॥
परबस जानि हंस्यो इन इन्द्रिन, •निजबस ह्वै न हंसैहौं
मन मधुकर पन कै तुलसी रघुपति पद कमल बसैहौं ॥

"My life has been wasted up to this time. I shall allow it to go to waste no longer. By the grace of Ram, the night that is this world has come to an end. Fully awake, I shall not go to sleep again. Having found the beautiful jewel of the name of Ram, I shall not allow it to slip out of the grip of my heart. I shall put the gold of my heart to the dark-coloured touchstone of the pure and engrossing form of the lord. As long as my faculties were controlled by others I was their laughing-stock; now that they are under my own control, I shall no more be an object of ridicule. I now that henceforth my heart like the bee shall for ever remain fixed to the lotus feet of Ram."

2

Namdev

I
HIS LIFE

On 29th April 1892, a biography of Namdev was published in Marathi entitled *Namdev Charitra,* written by Madhavarao Appaji Mulay. It had in the beginning appreciative opinions by greatmen like Justice Madhav Govind Ranade, Sir Ramakrishna Gopal Bhandarkar, Sri Gopalrao Hari Deshmukh (Lokahitavadi) and Lokamanya Bal Gangadhar Tilak. Tilak wrote as follows:

> "That great devotee of God who composed nearly a billion poems and pioneered the path of Devotion for the common people, and carried them to their destination successfully, should have been left neglected till now and no authentic biography of him should be available, is a matter of wonder. Namdev has in his *Abhangas* given the account of his forefathers and has also indicated important matters like the time of birth and death and the account of his contemporary saints. Nobody had attempted to collect all those *Abhangas* at one place, and so the biographies of the pioneers of this popular Path of Devotion were not reliably recorded. The present author has taken great pains in collecting all this information. one can determine the dates of his birth and death and also of his contemporaries like Dnyandev, Nivrittinath, Sopandev and so on."
>
> "The period of Namdev is very significant in the later history of India. At that time not only in Maharashtra but throughout India these saints laid the foundation of the Path of Devotion and showed the direction. Dnyandev, Kabir, Nanak and such saints of different provinces met and discussed many common matters, which are given in this book. As a devotee, poet and pioneer of the Path of Devotion, Namdev's life has a triple importance."

In Marathi Sri Ranganath Hari Bhalunkar has taken a resume of various controversies about the life of Namdev from 1892 to 1952. which are given below:

Sri Bharadvaj-Under this pseudonym Shivrambua Eknath Bharade wrote 16 articles in the paper 'Sudharak' (Reformer) from Poona. The first article was 'Were Dnyaneshwar and Namdev contemporaries?' and was published on 5.12.1898.

These sixteen articles were published during 1899. Sri Ajgaonkar, Huparikar, Baskar, Abhyankar, Keshavarao Damle and others tried to refute Bharadvaj's arguments in 'Kesari.' In the 'Mumbai Vaibhava' of Solapur, a 'Jidnyasu' ('Curious') also replied and so did K.N. Athalye, editor of 'Keralakokil.' Sri Shripatibua Bhingarkar wrote a long series of articles which was later published in book-form in 1900. Bharadvaj maintained that Dnyaneshwar the author of *Dnyaneshwari* and *Amritanubhava* was different from Dnyaneshwar the author of *Abhangas* or songs. He thought that the first Dnyaneshwar was probably of 1212 Saka and the latter was in the fourteenth century of Saka era. The author of Dnyaneshwari was a Saivite and belonged to the Nath sect and his father and preceptor or guru was Nivrittinath, while the composer of songs was a Vaishnava and his parents were Vitthalpant and Rukmini, and his guru Nivrittinath who was also his brother. The songster Dnyaneshwar had one more brother Sopanadeva and a sister Muktabai. The place of birth and 'Samadhi' of the first Dnyaneshwar was Apegaon; about the second nothing was definitely known, but he took 'Samadhi' at Alandi. The second Dnyaneshwar went on pilgrimage with Namdev.

Sri Bharadvaj did not accept the clear evidence of the birth of Namdev given in one poem clearly indicating: (1) Saka 1192 (2) Month of Kartik (3) Fortnight : Shukla (or the bright moon) (4) Date : Ekadeshi (5) Day : Sunday and (6) the name of the *Samvastsara* Prabhava. Bhingarkar saw the old manuscripts of Namdev in Pandharpur and said that it is not 'Prabhava' but 'Pramod' which is also current amongst the Varkaris. But Bharadvaj did not leave his obdurancy and maintained that 'Prabhava' was only 1309 Saka and so Namdev was of a later period and could have never seen Dnyaneshwar. But if 'Pramod' is accepted as the correct textual entry, then all the six points referred above are proved to be right.

Prof. Vasudev Balwant Patwardhan and Sri Ramkrishna Bhandarkar accepted Bharadvaj's version and placed Namdev in the fourteenth Saka century, while Pandit Panduranga Sharma, L.R. Pangarkar, S.V. Dandekar, Dr. R.D. Ranade, Dr. S.G. Tulpule decided that the date of birth of Namdev was Kartik Shuddha Ekadeshi of 1192 Saka. The year is thus A.D. 1270. This date is also corroborated by references in songs of contemporary saints like Gora the potter, Savanta the gardner, Narhari the goldsmith, Visoba Khechar, Chokhoba the sweeper, Banka, Sena the barber, Parisa Bhagawat and others. Similarly the dates of the 'Samadhis' of the brothers of Dnyandev are given by Namdev as Saka 1218 and 1219. So Bharadvaj's arguments do not stand any ground.

One of the testimonies in determining the age of any poet is his language. Bharadvaj argued that the language of namdev seems to be more modern than Dnyaneshwar's and so there must be a difference of at least a century between both. But in this matter, the fact that should be noted is that written language and language carried by oral tradition should be differentiated. As Namdev's Songs have references to *Yavana* and there are also *Yavani* (foreign) words, Bharadvaj argued that Namdev must have been after the establishment of Muslim power in Maharashtra. Muslims entered Maharashtra for the first time in A.D. 1318. So

Namdev may be belonging to the fourteenth century, this is what Bharadvaj reiterates. "In the *Dnyaneshwari* there is not a single foreign *(Yavani)* word." But as Namdev travelled with Dnyaneshwar in north India, he might have seen the broken temples and icons and so he referred to them in his works. As Namdev mentioned these, it does not mean that Muslim power must have established itself in the South at that time. Namdev was propagating his message for fifty-four years after Dnyaneshwars' *Samadhi* (end): The first Muslim attack on Paithan was in 1288 and the battle of Devagiri was fought in 1296. Namdev was continuing his work even after the establishment of Muslim power in Maharashtra. Hence Bharadvaj's arguments do not have any meaning.

The meeting of Namdev and Kabir also proves that Namdev was earlier. The dates of Kabir, as given by Bharadvaj are A.D. 1380 and 1420, which also stand to correction in the light of later researches. There are two legendary tales in Namdev's life that Panduranga (God) came in the form of a Malanga and a Pathan to test his dear devotee. Bharadvaj argued that how could it happen if Muslims had not entered Maharashtra. But Muslims did trade with South India and Konkan in early days, and individual traders had even settled down in those parts.

Nanak and Namdev met in the fourteenth century and so Namdev could not be earlier, is another argument put forth by Bharadvaj. Bhingarkar replied that there was a Nath-Panthi *sadhu* named Nanakswami and he had a debate with Gahininath of Nath-panthi about *Siddhi* and it is recorded in a work entitled *Gahini Pratap*.

Bharadvaj also maintains that Namdev and Changdev were not contemporaries. But Namdev's autobiographical *Abhangas* do mention that Namdev and his son were present when Changdev had taken 'Samadhi.'

The miracle of making the dead cow rise on her feet is mentioned in Nabhaji's *Bhaktamal* of 15th century A.D. and in the Granth Sahib where under Namdev-Vani the *pad* is mentioned "Sultanu Puchhai sunube Name." Bharadvaj says that this incident happened in A.D. 1367, when Bidar was established. V.K. Rajavade has published a *Bakhar* (historical record) about Mahim, in which in the sixth chapter it is mentioned that Devagiri was attacked by the Padshah in A.D. 1296 and Namdev was worshipping and giving religious discourses in Pandharpur.

The meeting of Bhanudas and Namdev is another point put forward by Bharadvaj in favour of fixing the date of Namdev one century later. What Bharadvaj assumes is that Bhanudas was the grandfather of Eknath. Bhingarkar says that there is no evidence for such assumption. Namdev had met a Bhanudas who had a brother named Suryadas. But the grandfather of Eknath had no such brother.

In 1913 Sir R.G. Bhandarkar wrote in his 'Vaishnavism, Saivism and Minor Religious systems':

"The date assigned to the birth of Namdev is as we have seen Saka 1192, that is A.D. 1270. This makes him a contemporary of Jnandev, the author of the *Jnandevi,* which was finished in A.D. 1290. But the Marathi of the latter work is decidedly archaic, while that of namdev's writings has a considerably more modern appearance. namdev's Hindi too looks more modern than that of the thirteenth century, when the poet Chanda flourished. It is difficult to say what is that due to. But it appears probable that the traditional date of Namdev's birth (Saka 1192) has been pushed backwards and that he is represented as a contemporary of Jnandev. We have seen in the former section, that Nabhaji in naming the successors of Vishnuswamin places Jnandev earlier and Namdev as later. If we are to judge from Namdev's Marathi and Hindi, his date must be put later by about a century.

"Some conception, however, of the time when Namdev flourished may be formed from the strong and definite sentiment as to the futility of idol-worship, which his guru is represented (in one of the hymns, viz., *Pashanacha dev bolechena kadhi)* to have expressed. Khechar, or Visoba Khechar as he is usually called, appears to have been an uncompromising opponent of idol-worship from the accounts given of him in the existing biographies. All previous writers including Ramanuja, as well as a great many that followed, excused idol-worship in some way or other. If then Khechar's attitude towards it was definitely hostile, he and his pupil Namdev must have flourished when the Mahomedan influence had for the first time become very powerful. The Mahomedans established themselves in the Deccan in the beginning of the fourteenth century of the Christian era, and their hatred of idol-worship must have taken about a hundred years to make its way into the understanding of religious Hindus."

"But a more direct evidence for the fact that Namdev flourished after the Mahomedans had established themselves in the Maratha country is afforded by his mention in a song (no. 364 Tukaram Tatya) of the destruction of idols by the `Turaks' i.e., Turks. The Mahomedans were often called Turaks in early times by the Hindus. Namdev, therefore, probably lived about or after the end of the fourteenth century."

"It will thus be seen that the date of Namdev's birth given with such details is quite wrong. unfortunately the historical spirit has by no means been the distinguishing feature of the intellectual life of early Indians, and we often confuse different persons together, and attribute to one what belongs to another. Some such confusion must have taken place in the present case."

Hari Narayan Apte gave Wilson Philological Lectures in 1922 and remarked:

"The divergence between language used in literary composition and that used in ordinary conversation, is always very great and will always continue to be great. In fact, it very often becomes a necessity. When a people grow into a nation and consequently the area, over which their language spreads, grows in extent, time works up differences and one and the same language is naturally divided into several dialects. Take the case of Marathi at the present time. How many dialects do you think it is divided into? Broadly speaking there are (1) Marathi in the Deccan (2) Marathi in Konkan (3) Marathi in Berar and Central India and (4) in Southern India. These are the four very broad divisions. But there are numerous sub-divisions under every one of these. In all Dr. Grierson has collected specimens of these dialects and sub dialects which belong undoubtedly to Marathi. Now when such process of divisions and sub-divisions takes place in the history of a language, and there arises a necessity for a language in which the educated people belonging to the several provinces can write and communicate their thoughts to one another, such a language automatically or by a natural process comes into existence. That is the reason why there has arisen a literary Marathi, a Marathi in which writers belonging to the several provinces write their compositions."

Bhalunkar argues that *Dnyaneshwari* was studied amongst a comparatively more literate and Sanskrit-knowing Brahmin class, whereas Namdev's hymns and songs were mostly carried by oral tradition from generation to generation. V.L. Bhave has pointed to old Marathi words in Namdev's autobiographical *Abhangas*. There may have been many interpolations and modifications in the copyists who wrote the *Abhangas* of Namdev.

The objection raised by Sir R.G. Bhandarkar was as follows:

"Similarly another youngman not fully acquainted with the critical method said that Namdev and Dnyandev were contemperaries but that the difference between their languages was due to mistakes of successive scribes. He thus believed that the scribes could reconstitute the grammar and lexicon of a language, forgetting to ask himself why the marvels effected by the scribes in the case of Namdev should not have been effected by them in the case of Dnyandev himself, whose language they had not altered."

It was replied by Sri Panduranga Sharma *(Chitramaya-jagat* in Vol. 13 No. 8) whose real name was Rao saheb Panduranga Dnyaneshwar Kulkarni- "Dnyaneshwar's philosophical writings are cryptic and in *Sutra*-from meant for the sophisticated. Such a compact poetic composition does not render itself to any corruptions. Namdev's Abhangas were sung by common people, they are outpourings of devoted illiterate persons, which later became more popular songs. For this reason, Namdev need not be punished by being relegated to a further century. The more any form of poetry is popular the more is the likelihood of its being modified and altered.

Dr. Nicol Macnicol also repeats what Bhandarkar said and maintains in the preface to his *Psalms of Maratha Saints* :

> "The language of Namdev's verses is much more modern than that of the Dnyaneshwari. So that though the tradition gives his date as from 1270 to 1350 the probabilities are that Sir R.G. Bhandarkar is right in placing him a century later."

But Prof. Vasudev Balwant Patwardhan delivering his Wilson Philological Lectures in Calcutta in 1917 replied to these arguments cogently and said that the language of the first poet of marathi Mukundaraja in his *Paramamrita* appears to be even more modern than that of Dnyaneshwari:

> "Reading this passage carefully we find that it reads almost like a modern passage. Excepting the forms in `u' of the nominative singular which, however, are not frequent in the passage and the forms *yaya* and *apleni* there are no traces here of old Marathi."

He further concludes:

> "...the fact remains that whatever the vocabulary, the grammar of the language of Nama's work *as it is presented* in the various Gathas is far too modern to admit of Nama's being a contemporary of Dnyaneshwar. If further research brings to light a copy of Nama's works which are nearer the Dnyandevi in archaism of grammar, idioms and vocabulary, I shall be glad to modify my statement. But till then I cannot help to conclude that an interval of more than a century divides the author of Dnyandevi and Namdeva.

Dr. J.M. Farquhar wrote an article on "The Historical position of Ramanand" in the Journal of Royal Asiatic Society of Great Britain and Ireland in April 1920 and proved Namdev as a contemporary of Ramanand in A.D. 1430. He argues that Ramanandi sect was popular from 1299 to 1410 and so the meeting of Namdev and Ramanand is doubtful. He quotes Bhandarkar and Macnicol's translations in support. Pandit baleshwar Prasad gave A. D. 1423 as the time of namdev in *Sant Bani Sangraha*. Bhalunkar replied that the term 'doubtful' is a mere guesswork. Baleshwar Prasad based his opinion on *Bhaktmal* of Nabhaji and *Mishra Bandhu Vinod*. Nabhaji's work is not very reliable as it is based on hearsay evidence of Sadhus. Sri Panduranga Sharma has replied to these arguments fully in the `Historical position of Namdeva' published in the Annals of the Bhandarkar Institute Vol. 8 (page 335-341) published in 1927.

The argument about the difference in the languages of Dnyaneshwar and Namdev does not stand scrutiny. bhalunkar quoting Rajwade gives details of the reasons of such linguistic variations due to differences in place, time, sex and caste of the speakers. Sri M.G. Bartakke wrote an article in *Lokshikshan* (May 1940) and found out so many archaic and obsolete Marathi words in the *Abhangas* of *Tirathwati* by Namdev. If this happens even after so many centuries, no doubt there existed much difference in Marathi spoken at various places and at various levels of society in the thirteenth century.

The statement that Dnyaneshwar and Namdev did not influence each other is refuted by Panduranga Sharma in 1925 in an article published in the Vol. 5 Nos. 1-2-3-4 of the quarterly of Bharat-Itihas-Sanshodhak Mandal.

In conclusion what is said in the Wilson Philological Lectures in 1916 by V.B. Patwardhan stands very much unrefuted:

"Here we have the Romance of a light that never was on sea or land, of a dream that never settled on the world of clay, of love that never stirred the passion of sex; a wonder that never was wrought by flesh and blood; of a mystery that never was revealed in caverns subterranean, of supernatural power that never found abode in giants and monsters. Here is the Romance of Piety; of faith, devotion, of the surrender of the human soul in the love, the light and the life of the ultimate Being. Here is the freedom of the freest of the free man. It is Romance of Bhakti spiritual love that we have here. That is the body and the soul of the great flood of poetry that starts with Namdeva.

"It is the heart's song to the heart. It is the outburst of the contents of the heart under excitement when the heart is touched or stirred, or thrilled or roused into passionate life.

"To come back too the main subject. Out of it and its exposition poetry sprang a new school of Lyric poetry that flowered in Namdeva. He, Namdeva, is the first...as far as the history of the Marathi Literature is known to us.. and perhaps the foremost poet of the new school. Dnyandev is certainly, potentially greater. but in actual accomplished work Namdeva is perhaps unsurpassed.

"We now come to the importance of Namdeva as Maker of Marathi Literature. Examine the Works of Namdeva and we find that the most poetic verses from him are those where he speaks from his heart and reveals either the dark spots present there or the struggle of the conflicting impulses; or again the ardent consuming desire he feels for communion with God or again the impatience and the distressing suspense verging on despair. These lyrics of a relentlessly tried soul are as passionate as they are intense and sincere. It would not be easy to parallel the following verses in romantic concept, in homeliness of diction, in truth of feeling, and in lyrical intensity.

(1) Tujhya charnache sutatan anusandhan
jail majha pran tatkshani (Avate, 338)
When I leave the quest of your feet; let my life be
forsaken suddenly.

(2) Tujhiya payi majhya mane dili budi-344
In your feet my mind is absorbed

(3) Ata honar te ho kan Pandhrinatha- 345
Now let anything happen O Pandhrinatha

(4) Jaywant aso Lakhshimicha Chuda- 306
Victory to the husband of Lakshmi

(5) Tu may mauli mhanoni aas keli-307
You are the Mother and so do I hope.

He is the founder and the best representative of a new genre of lyrical poetry and has so immensely influenced his successors.

The life of Namdev is surrounded by legends, like the lives of so many other saints. I am attempting a summary of these legends as given in the first Marathi-Printed biography by Sri Mulay.

There was a terrible jungle in the spot where present Pandharpur is situated. It was called Dindirvan A *deshasth* brahmin named Pundalik used to live his parents and serve there. His father was Janudev and mother Satyawati. At the age of five, his thread-ceremony took place, and for sixteen years he studied Vedas and scriptures. He was married and carried on the burden of the family. But he did not care for his parents. If he served his parents, his wife would castigate him. He illterated his old mother who used to do all the domestic work. He gave the best clothes and food to his own wife and treated the mother as a maid-servant. Tired of his maltreatment the parents decided to go on pilgrimage to Kashi. Pundalik permitted them to do so. The wife of Pundalik also insisted to accompany. On two horses rode Pundalik and his wife while the old parents walked behind, groomed the horses and lived on alms. One day they reached the *Ashram* of Kukkutaswami. There Pundalik saw some fairies in human form who came in the morning and cleaned the Ashram and disappeared. They later admonished him as a very sinful person as he maltreated his parents. The fairies were the four Holy Rivers. Kukkutaswami was the incarnation of Shravana in a sling. King Dashratha unknowingly hurt him. As his desire was unfulfilled he came back to this Earth. "When you have your parents, why do you go on pilgrimage. Better serve them." Pundalik made his parents ride the horses and made his wife walk behind. He served his parents for twelve years. Even Indra was afraid of him and tried his best to disturb his penance.

Once Narada came to Pundalik and told him the story of the importance of Dindirvan. The brick which was lying there was in fact Indra who was suffering under a curse, as he had deceived and raped Ahalya. As Moon was an abettor in this conspiracy he was also cursed to become a leper. Narada told Pundalik to offer this brick of Krishna when he came to this forest.

Sri Krishna remembered Rukmini and came in the form of a cowherd in her search. He saw her and stood almost struck by her presence. Putting both of his hands resting on his waist he watched her. Rukmini made great fun of this cowherd and even spoke harshly. Then Krishna showed to her his real form. And this re-incarnation of Vishnu was called Vitthal (*Veet* means a brick in Marathi,

Thala is the place) Pundalik did not care to see whether God has come and stood there near him, he was so much absorbed in the service of his parents. Later he begged pardon and called him Vitthal. God was pleased and gave him this boon that whosoever would utter Vitthal constantly, and take bath in the holy river Chandrabhaga, would be saved from the bother of the cycle of births.

Thus Pandharpur became a holy place and it was for Pundalik that Sri Vishnu came there. This form of Sri Vishnu, namely Vitthal, became the deity worshipped by Namdev.

Namdev's ancestory begins with Yadushet, who was a tailor by caste. The word 'Shimpi' in Marathi is used in *Bhaktmal* as Chheepa. The legend that he was born out of a mother-of-pearl or a shell is due to the verbal similarity between 'Shimp' and 'Shimpi.' He was the dweller of a village name Narasi Bamani near Karhad on the banks of Krishna. In the line of Yadushet, Namdev was the son of Damashet and Gunai or Gonabai. They had only one daughter Aubai and no son for a long time. He was born in the morning of Kartik Shukla Ekadashi in Saka 1192 (i.e. A.D. 1270). At the time of his birth, considering him to be the incarnation of Sanatkumar) Indra, Kuber, Varuna, Brahma, Shiva, Vishnu rained flowers on the earth and the firmament echoed with the sound of heavenly and vidine music.

At the age of two Namdev started repeating the name of Sri Vitthal. At the age of five when his teacher asked him to write on the slate 'Onama...' (Om Namah) he wrote 'Sri Vitthal' At the age of seven he took stones as gongs and repeated the same name of God and danced in ecstasy all day long. God himself came to accompany his in dance. God was repeating the name of Shiv as 'Har-Har'! while Namdev uttered 'Hari-Hari'! Namdev asked him about this difference between Shiva and Vishnu. God said both are the same.

Namdev was given some food (Naivedya) to be offered to the god Vitthal, in absence of Damashet. He went to the temple and insisted on Vitthal to take it, otherwise Mother would not eat. At his request God took the food. When his father returned, he did not believe in this story and so he was taken to the temple and shown this miracle. Sri Vitthal even drank the milk offered by young Namdeva, though it was hot. The legend further gives the dialogue of the mother of Namdev and God, who had burns in him mouth, but He gave some other excuses.

At the age of eight, Nama was married to Rajabai the daughter of Govindashet Sadavarte. On is the first Divali after the marriage namdev wanted God to come home and take holy bath early in the morning, so he went to the temple. God Vitthal agreed to do so if Namdev stood in his place. God also warned him not to stir and take the candy which the devotees offered. Namdev's parents took the God home and Namdev stood there in God's place as his shadow. When devotees started offering him candy and butter, he started eating. Some real devotees realized that the idol was Namdev and not God Vitthal.

In the biography by Mulay a detailed account is given of Gora the potter coming and trying to test the heads of various saints by patting them, as if they were unbaked pots. He reported to Dnyaneshwar that Namdev is raw and he is not fully baked as he has not found any Guru. So Namdev went out and found a Malang who had a bag, a tall cap, a begging bowl, a crooked stick and a horn and was accompanied by a dog (which was in fact the wish-cow) and in his right hand there was a smoking-pipe. Later this Malang converted Savata. Namdev refused to renounce his religion and so he tried to run away. But God was testing Namdev in this form of a Malang.

Then He took the form of a Pathan and ordered for Namdev's arrest for forced labour. Namdev asked Savata the gardner who was with him, to run away. Namdev ran upto the temple and was terribly upset later God revealed that in the form of Pathan He had tried to take him away. There are other stories of God coming with Rukmini in the form of a Muslim trader who told him "Go to the temple of Aundhya Naganatha where you will meet your guru visoba Khechar.' Namdev went to this place stopping at Aarne, where he met Savata, and then at Dhamangaon where he met Kurmadasa and later at Ter where he met Gora the potter.

Visoba Khechar tried to test Namdev by assuming the form of a leper. He kept his dirty foot over the Nagnath image and asked Namdev to remove it and to place where Shiva did not exist. Namdev tried to do so but to his great surprise such a place was not to be found. Whichever direction he turned Khechar's foot, the Shiva image sprang up. Namdev was convinced of the greatness of his guru Khechar after this miracle, Visoba asked Namdev to carry the old diseased guru on his back, out of the dark temple. Namdev was bathed in blood and mucid matter and was disgusted. Later on Visoba the guru, showed his real healthy handsome form, and proved that the way to God is a hard and strenuous way.

One month after this initiation at the hands of his spiritual preceptor, Namdev was asked to go and collect dues from a nearby village. While returning on the banks of the Man river in the village Manjari he baked his bread and kept it near the over and went to fetch water. A dog came there and picked up the bread and started running. Namdev thought that it is God Vitthal who is testing him and so he went running after the dog with a little utencil full of clarified butter, thinking that if the dog would eat the dry bread, it would suffer from a stomachache. Namdev had reached the stage when he considered every animate being as having a divine spark within it. God resumed his form and asked Namdev: "How did you recognize me?" Namdev said that he knew Him as his guru Khechar had taught him.

Namdev got a son who was named narayan. He had three more sons and a daughter. There was the devoted maidservant Janabai in his house who was the daughter of a Shudra Dama and his wife Kurund. She was the incarnation of the same woman who was Manthara in Treta (the age of Ramayan) and Kubja in Dvapar (the age of Krishna). Damashet maintained her as a member of his family.

On the bank of the river Chandrabhaga some devotees were saying that Valmiki had composed a billion shlokas. Namdev heard this and vowed that he would also compose verses in that large number. Out of these Abhangas many were composed by God himself and by many members of his family.

In the second part of this traditional biography, Mulay gives the story of his mother asking Namdev to do some business. So he went to Dada Savkar, a *Deshasth* Brahmin moneylender of pandharpur, to borrow from him some capital. Dada Savkar was a miser. Yet God gave him the good sense to lend Namdev two thousand 'hons' (gold coins) without any bondage or mortgage. Namdev thought that the best investment would be feeding the Brahmins. So a large party was arranged. Every one was invited to dine at Rakshasabhuvan. Namdev's party went on for five days. On the last day he fed everyone in the village. Dada Savkar was scared that instead of investing his capital, Namdev was squandering all the money. On the last day Dada Savkar was brought to the spot and namdev told him that the money spent was not by him but actually by Dada Savkar. He was made to say the *Sankalp* or the prayer-offering to God.

Dada was terribly annoyed and insisted on getting back all the money with interest. Namdev asked him to come to the river and go with him into deep waters upto his naval. dada was afraid but he was dragged and was made to dive. Here Dada Savkar saw a great miracle, *darbar* of the Mughal king. There was so much gold and such jewels, pearls, rubies and diamonds that he was flabbergasted. Dada was taken to this court and made to feel himself as one of them. He stole one of the golden bars But when he came up on the level of water, everything disappeared. He was so much scared that he left all the articles given by the king to cook for himself Then he was asked "Did you receive all the money you had lent to Namdev?" Dada said, "Well, my life was saved and that is enough."

On one of the Kartik Shukla *ekadashis* God tested Namdev in the form of an old famished Brahmin who came in the form of a beggar and asked Namdev for alms. Namdev said that the could not give him food on *ekadashi*, which was a day for fasting. Hearing this, the Brahmin swooned in the courtyard and gave up his life. Namdev was so much shocked that he offered his own life, as he thought that the death of the Brahmin was due to his not giving him food. Namdev ordered for two pyres being arranged on the bank of Chandrabhaga including one for himself. The Brahmin came to life and showed his real form as God Vitthal.

Raka was a Gujarati potter in Pandharpur, who was a devotee of Vitthal and lived with his wife Banka and daughter Vanka. One day by mistake three kittens were put into fire, as they were sheltered by the mother cat in one of the earthen pots kept ready for baking. When the fire was set, the cat came and wept and moved around that fire. Banka and Raka were so much aggrieved that they begged of Panduranga, and after the third day when the pots were taken out of fire, to their surprise the kitten came out alive and unscathed. He was so much influenced by God that he left his business of a potter and decided to live as a mendicant. One day his daughter Vanka was taking her bath in the river Chandrabhaga where Namdev's daughter Limbabai was washing her clothes. The dirty water of the washings polluted Vanka. Limbabai was angry when Vanka admonished her. Limba said "O you potter's daughter, why should you have such ideas of untouchability?" Vanka said "Well your father worships a God with a form. My father worships a formless God and so I think I am polluted by you." Limba went and told the story to Namdev, who went and asked God about it. God and Rukmini took Namdev to the forest where Raka was roaming with his wife Banka collecting faggots. God tested him asking Rukimini to put her golden bracelet below drywood. Raka thought that is better to hide it with dust, lest his wife got tempted. The wife who was following, saw the golden bracelet shining, and put some more dust to hide it fully, lest the daughter, who was following, got tempted. The daughter saw it and was very sorry for such parents who still thought about the difference between gold and dust. Namdev saw this other worldiness and non-attachment of Raka, Banka and Vanka and was convinced of their saintlihood.

Another story of Gora, the potter of Terdhoki is given by Muley. He was the one who had called Namdev rather raw or helf-baked after patting the heads of all of the saints. One day while Gora was pounding the clay for preparing his pots, he was so ecstatically absorbed in the name of Vitthal that he did not see that his young infant came crawling and got mixed up with the earth and was dead. The mother had gone out to fetch water. When the mother returned and saw the dead child pounded up in the clay she raved with anger and pain. As her words disturbed Gora's devoted singing, he rushed to be at her with the potter's wheel. But she took the name of Vitthal, and on his name warned him not to touch her.

Later he married the younger sister of Gora's wife The father-in-law requested him to treat the younger sister in the same manner as he treated the elder one. Gora had no interest in household. But one day when he saw that one night his hands lay on his wife's body he repented, and in that frenzy that he could not keep his vow of continence, he cut both of his hands with a sickle and sat praying. God came there in the form of a guest-potter and asked him not to worry. God and his wife Rukmini, with Garud as the donkey, did all the potter's selling business. The pots of terdhoki with the signs of conch, discus, lotus were found in the market at Pandharpur. Everybody was surprised at the skill of the potter who was handless. One day when Namdev was singing and giving his congregational sermon (Kirtan), he suddenly asked Goroba along with other devotees to raise the hands and praise God. Goroba had no hands and so he was ashamed. Namdev asked him to clap his hands in whatever manner he liked. Suddenly the miracle happened. As flowers come to trees in the spring season, Goroba got his palms and hands. The elder wife of Gora requested Namdev to get her son back. Namdev asked her to call him. And lo, and behold, the child came crawling. Everybody was surprised at Namdev's divine power.

One day Gonai had cold and she was coughing. Namdev was asked to bring the bark of a particular bramble-like medicinal tree from the forest. Namdev went with his axe and while he tried to cut the bark, to his great surprise he saw red juice flowing out of the trunk. He was so much pained that he hit his own foot, and started peeling out his own skin of the same size as the bark. God came and rescued him when he bled profusely and feel unconscious. God touched the tree and Namdev's foot and the bark was restored, so was the skin brought back to the foot and the wounds were healed. Gonai's coughing was also cured.

At Bedar there was a Brahmin who had taken a vow that he would bring Namdev from Pandharpur and listen to his devotional music. At first Namdev refused to leave pandharpur, but at God's request he agreed to go there. He was accompanied with so many devotees that the king of Bedar though that an army is coming to invade him. He ordered his chief minister Kashipant to arrest Namdev. With the help of twenty-five guards he got him arrested. The Sultan killed a cow and asked Namdev to make her alive, or otherwise the Sultan would convert all the people with Namdev heard the voice from Heaven and put the head of the dead cow near her carcass. She was rejuvenated. As the devotees of God were troubled by the king, black, yellow and red snakes were suddenly seen all over the town and king's people were bitten by them and they died So Kashipant, the minister came to Namdev and requested him to save the Kings' men. Namdev was sympathetic and the forgave the minister and the king.

At paithan while Namdev was singing and travelling, his companion Kurmadas, who had no hands and fee, expressed his desire to go to Pandharpur. God came in the form of a Brahmin and took him along with Dnyandev and Namdev. In the way they stopped at Arenbhende where Savata the gardener was worshipping God. God told Savata that those two people, Dnyaneshwar and Namdev were the thieves who were after him and so he wanted some place to hide. Savata took his gardener's knife, opened his own stomach and asked God to hide there. He wrapped a blanket around his stomach. Now Dnyandev and Namdev began to search for their companion. They saw Savata in ecstacy as God was literally near his heart. Namdev was very much afraid that he had lost the company of God. God came out of Savata's belly and thus made Namdev realize that the pride of any devotee as the only and the greatest was false. At Laul Kurmadas t ɔk *samadhi,* after meeting the two saints and God. At that spot every year on Ashadhi and Kartiki *ekadashi* big holy fairs are held.

The story of the miracle of the touchstone is still more interesting. Parisa Bhagvat was given by God a stone which worked like a miraculous thing because it turned every metal which came in its contact into gold. Parisa Bhagvat's wife Kamalaja was a friend of Rajai the wife of Namdev Rajai told her friend that Namdev was not doing any business and did not earn, so she had to suffer from grinding poverty. Kamalaja secretely loaned this miracle-stone and Rajai got all her iron and brass utensils turned into gold and sold them. When Namdev came home and saw such a change in the household with all new things and so much of good food and clothing, he was surprised. Rajai innocently told the story of the stone. Namdev asked her to show him the stone. Namdev asked her to show him the stone. While Rajai went inside the house to cook the dinner, Namdev took this stone to Chandrabhaga river and threw it into water. Parisa Bhagvat learnt of this and was very angry. He asked Namdev to bring his stone back. Namdev dived in the water and brought many sand-stones and asked Parisa to pick his *Paris* (the touchstone) out of them. To his great surprise all those stones carried the same quality. Bhagvat was convinced of his power and asked Namdev to bless him. He said "O Namdev, saints like you are the real touchstones. Whomsoever you touch will be turned into gold. You are a living philosopher's stone."

Then the stories about Janabai being helped by God Vitthal, how God returned Namdev to his mother and how he came in the form of Keshavshet and gave to Namdev's wife and mother ample gold coins, are also wel-known.

Stories about the travels of Dnyaneshwar and Namdev are repeated. Sri Nivrittinath, the elder brother of Dnyaneshwar, also accompanied them. They met the saints Savata, Kurmadas, Bhagavat, King Jagatpal and his guru Kukundraj and Gora on the way, He reached Kapildhara where a Brahmin Kamalakar and his wife Shuddhamati requested them to honour their house and invited them to dine. At first they refused but at their five-year old son Gopal's insistence Namdev agreed. When Namdev and his friends went to dine, God tested Kamalakar assuming a snake's form and biting his son Gopal who went to fetch fuel. After this there was further testing when the saints insisted on Kamalakar and his wife's eating with them, even when they knew that Gopal was dead. Namdev made the dead rise. Thus Gopal and his parents were reunited.

The pilgrims went further from Dharateerth to Aundhya Nagnath where they met Haripal, the hunter. He was a highwayman, yet he was a devotee of Vithoba. He left Jagpal Sheth and his wife unhurt as they told him that they were going on pilgrimage to Pandharpur. This Sheth and his wife were God and Rukmini in disguise, who tested this devotee, and gave him a gold armlet to be used for feeding the guest-saints.

At Nagnath, Mamdev was insulted by the Brahmin priest and driven out of the temple. Namdev started singing and the miracle of the door of the temple turning to his side is described. Such a miracle is also described in Kabir's life.

Then they went to Pratishthan (Paithan) where they met Bhanudas. Here the bad Brahmins troubled him by saying "Namdev and friends are of lower castes, and so they had no right to be saints. They are all fake." Upon this another miracle happened and the God of gods Indra descended down with hundreds of singing devotees with nine lakh ochre flags. The critics and deriders were put to shame. Those who came to scoff remained to pray.

They went to Devgiri and stayed at Sajjan Kasai (the butcher). Then they went to Ellora, Ghrishneshwar, Kacheswar, Shukreshwar, Panchvati, Tryambakeshwar, Dwarka, Dakorji and Junagarh. At Junagarh they met Narasi Mehta. There are many *abhangas* composed during this journey. They contain metaphysical discussions as well as moral discourses. In this work the further places of pilgrimages mentioned are Allahabad, Bharadvaj Ashram, Ayodhya (where they met saint Pipaji), Chitrakut (where they met Tulsidas) and then reached Benaras. Here they met Kabir. Obviously in this account there is lot of historical inaccuracy and anachronism.

Kabir's wife went to a trademan to borrow the necessary provisions. The grocer was lascivious. He promised to give her the necessary things on the condition that she satisfied his lust. She agreed and told the story to her husband Kabir. She promised to go to the grocer after having fed the guest-saints. in the meanwhile, it started raining heavily. In the mud and slush Kabir himself carried her on his shoulders to that grocer. The grocer was shamed. The grocer came to see and bow down before Kabir, Namdev, Nivrittinath and Dnyaneshwar; and he also got his salvation.

It is said that Dattatreya, Matsyendra and Gorakh all the three great gurus met Nivritti, Namdev and Dnyaneshwar. Thus Namdev stayed for a week in Benaras. They went to Marwar and while crossing Rajasthan Namdev was very thirsty. Dnyaneshwar went to bring deepest water from a well for him. This miracle happened at Koledji, that God himself made the well overfill with water.

They returned to Tera Where they met Gora again. Then they went to Bijapur where Sena the barber and Dadu the weaver met them They went to Ghataprabha, Malaprabha, Rishyamuk Parvat, Kishkinda Nagari, Tungabhadra and Kumarteerth, the place of Kartikswami. Here Nanankswami was also travelling alone. Namdev enquired the cause for this. Nanak replied that he needed no disciples, the five elements were there. Nanakswami gave food to these saints. Namdev miraculously brought the idol of Kartikswami to dine with them. Nanak was surprised to see this. Then Namdev and others departed to Vyankatesh, Mallikarjun, Kirti Ramraja and Rameshwar. Here they met Maruti (Hanuman). They went to Tamraprani, Karvir, Virat nagari (Nepal) and reached back Alandi and Dehu. At Dehu they blessed Vishwambhar the first person in the line which bore Tukaram. They all returned to Pandharpur via Bhimashankar.

Parentage

Leaving aside the miracle-believers who think that Namdev was not born of human parents of was an incarnation of Sanat Kumar, Mahipati maintains Damashet and Gonai found this child swimming in a shell in the river Chandrabhaga. So Priyadas thinks that he was the son of a widow from a devotee Vamdev. Garsa De Tassy thinks that he was one of the children who was picked up. Janabai mentions that Gonai got him as a result of a vow. All sources agree that Damashet and Gonai were the father and mother of Namdev, who had one sister Aubai. Namdev had four sons and one daughter.

The stories about Namdev's childhood are the same in all sources. But the incident of his being a dacoit and murderer has been refuted by Pataskar, as it is not mentioned in any contemporary verses about him, nor in any later verse-biographies or poetic references to him. In all the *Gathas* of Namdev only one *pad* published in a *gatha* after 1894 mentions this incident. But even Muley who wrote his biography three years earlier, had not known of this *pad*. If Namdev's heart was changed and later he settled in Pandharpur, how could his deep devotion to Vitthal from his early childhood be explained. Ajgaonkar says that Namdev killed 84 cavalry men of the king; but how could such a heroic person remain unknown in history.

Guru

about his preceptor there are three opinions; Sant Dnyaneshwar, Visoba Khechar and Sopandev. But Visoba Khechar seems to be the most correct answer, if one takes all the biographies into account. Janabai's reference to Sopandev, the younger brother of Dnyandev is merely figurative.

Travels

About his travels described in his *Tisthavali* all biograhers are unanimous. He went with Dnyaneshwar to several places in southern, western and northern India. His travel to Punjab was done in the last phase of his life.

Date of Death

About the *samadhi* of Namdev Parikha (or sa?) Bhagvat gives Ashadh Shukla Ekadashi as the day. In Ghuman it is considered to be second of Magh. On this day there is a big fair held in Ghuman. Bohardas was supposed to be the successor of Namdev. Legends about this disappearance from his sleeping room and going to his mother in Pandharpur are not quite reliable. But very little evidence is there about both these dates.

Works

There is no authentic edition of his works published as yet. The Maharashtra State Government had undertaken such a project five years ago but has not yet produced any authentic edition. One thing is certain that 2,500 *padas* in Marathi commonly attributed to Namdev may not be all composed by him. Some are by Vishnudas nama, who may be another person. In Hindi nearly 234 poems are found, but of which two are also found to be in the name of Gorakhnath, and two under Kabir. The 61 *padas* in Guru Granth Sahib in Panjabi may be all by Namdev. because of such variety and possibility of innumerable interpolations, Namdev's language has also many ranges; Marathi, old Rajasthani, Brij, Panjabi, Khari Boli have all entered in his poems In one poem Kannada, Gujarati and Urdu are also used.

II
PHILOSOPHY

To understand Namdev's philosophical approach, it is necessary to know his times, his traditions and the very roots of the *Bhakti* movement. In the Atharva-Veda the Vratyas are described as those who do not believe in the Yajna rituals, but depended on individual penance. As they believed in Vratas (Vows) they were called Vratyas.

In Kathopanishad the Absolute or Brahman was described with many negative attributes like unapproachable, non-formal, unfron, unending, eternal, sublime, beyond words and so on. The Nath Panth called it Niranjan. The Shvetashetar-Upanishad uses the word Nirguna for the first time:

Karmadhyakashah Sarvabhutodhivasi Sakshi Cheta Kevalo Nirgunashcha

(He presides over all actions, He resides in all beings, He is the witness, He is the consciousness, He is the Absolute and is quality-less)

The Brihadaranyaka Upanishad equates the soul with God, the Atman with Parmatman. Geeta further elucidates this Absolute as indestructible, omnipresent, un-distributed and beyond all sensual apperception.

Buddhism regarded all difference between men and men as artificial and untenable. Defying all scriptural authority and caste or Varna, differences attached to birth, Buddha regarded Nirvana as the only permanent value. All else was transitory and ephemeral. The Nirguna Saints, Yogis and Tantriks too propogated this equality amongst all men. Only the importance of Guru is accepted by the followers of the path of Yoga.

Early Hinduism was polytheistic and believed in the theory of incarnation. Later it evolved into some kind of formless godheads, worship and meditation, through Vedanta. It was confronted with monotheistic Islam and later with Sufism. The Nirguna saints followed a middle course and tried to create a synthesis between Vedanta and Sufism. They formulated a new kind of Sadhana or penance which was a combination of the three-fold ways of knowledge, devotion and action.

The Vedic system of worship consisted of hymns, panegyrics, Stotras, animal sacrifice. It slowly culminated into an eleborate ritualism of sacrifice. But later even this system was transformed into pure devotion and purity of action. The inner heretic and rebellious practices led into reformation, Jain, Buddhist and materialistic Charvaka sects were such deviations and revisionist courses. Some of them questioned the very sanctity and sensibility of the old orthodox practices.

The various sects prevalent before Namdev could be summarized as follows:

1. Smarta Sampradaya of Shankaracharya

2. Sahajayana of Siddha Sarahapa
3. Jain Munis after Mahavir
4. Natha-Sampradaya of Gorakhnath
5. Various sects of Bhakti:
   a. Alvars of the South and Saivite saints
   b. Vaishnava Acharyas and Saints
   c. Kashmir Saivism
   d. Varkari Panth
   e. Mahanubhava Panth
   f. Sahajiyas of Bengal
   g. Lingayats of Karnatak
   h. Sufis and Muslim saints

Let us briefly take a resume of the achievements and limitations of these sects. Shankaracharya (788-820 A.D.) was born in Malabar at Kaladi. His father was Shivaguru and mother was Subhadra. He was a Namboodri Brahmin. He had a remarkable command over Sanskrit, 279 books are attributed to be composed by him. He was a keen debater and a sharp logician, He travelled widely throughout India.

"Brahma Satyam Jaganmithya Brahmojiven no param" (Brahma is the only truth, the World is illusion. Brahma and the soul are not different, the one includes the other) is the substance of his teaching. His greatest weakness is the problem of Maya. He is not able to explain the purpose of the origin of this Creation; he takes recourse in the Brahma-Sutras to various analogies. Shankaracharya's philosophy became too abstruse and dry for the commoner and he himself had to write more musical hymns like Saundarya-Lahari. He was also criticized as a crypto-Buddhist, as his Brahman was very much similar to the Buddhist ultimate principle of Void or Shunya.

Shankaracharya's Smarta sect worshipped the five gods with equal devotion: Shiva, Vishnu, Shakti, Ganesh and Surya. He also believed in the Vedas and other scriptures which were called *Shrutis* of "Those which were heard." Though God in several forms was worshipped, yet there was an undercurrent of one all-pervading godliness which was non-dualistic. Namdev was influenced by this philosophy of unqualified monism. Actually Namdev carried the massage of Vedanta to the common masses and so Dr. R.D. Ranade called the age of these saints as the Age of Democratic Mysticism.

Post-Buddhist sects in India are so many that it is almost a confusing picture. yet Mahapandit Rahul Sankrityayana has given a very fine and detailed picture of the religious conditions in India in the introduction to his *Dohakosh* published by Bihar Rashtrabhasa Parished. buddhism branched off into two main currents-The Hinayana and the Mahayana. Later Mantrayana and Vajrayana were also added to it. It was a curious mixture of the Buddhist phenomenalism and asceticism with

Tantric secretive anti-social practices. Mahayana is strongly influenced by Hindu Bhakti cults as revealed in ı nanti Bhikshuk's work in Hindi published from Vishvabharati, Shantiniketan. Mahayana tried to codify Buddhas's message.

Vajrayana is associated with the eighty-four Siddhas. They turned Buddha's Shunya and Karuna into Prajna and Upaya; they also borrowed the Chinese and Tibetan principles of Yub and Yang (man and women principle) and imagined the state of their meeting as Yuganaddha. Budhichitta was turned into Vajrasatya. Out of this a queer mixture of hedonism and stoicism ensued. It was called the doctrine or the Greatest pleasure Mahasukha-Ved. The five *makars* became essential and to go beyond their sensuousness through abandon and liberated behaviour, was one of their targets. Dr. Rameshchandra Mazumdar has quoted in his History of Bengal in part I, the Charyapadas which denote how this Vajrayana turned into Sahajayana. One of the essentials was decasting oneself and free mixing with women of lower castes like Dombi, Natini, Rajakini (washerwomen) or Chandal was permitted. In Sarahpad's poems such a Dombini figures, which becomes later the symbol of Maya in Kabir and Tukaram's writings.

Sarahpad's criticism of the upper castes, particularly of the hypocricy and the gap between their precept and practice is repeated in several *padas* of saints like Namdev or Tukaram. Sarahpad says, "Brahmins do not know the real secret, they repeat Vedas like parrots mechanically. They take the clay, water and grass and chant *mantras* without knowing their meanings. This kind of fire-worship and fire-sacrifice is a sure way of spoiling one's eyesight with smoke. They wear ochre robes but in practice they are not ascetics at all. The Shaivites besmear their bodies with ashes, but they have not really conquered their senses. Many wear long unkempt hair and burn lamps in the day or carry bells with them; some mendicants grow their nails or wear dirty rags, some wander naked and take off their hair by plucking them out and do all kinds of peculiar and unnatural practices. All of them thought that they would reach the ultimate state of Shunya in an easy or spontaneous (`Sahaj') way. All severe body-bending and physical masochism was not necessary. By the meeting of Kamal (Lotus) and Kulish (The thunderbolt or the diamond in some cases), the two symbols of the female and male principles, on e can reach the Vision and enjoy the blessed beatitude in a natural way. The term `Su-rati' (which meant smriti or memory as well as sexual union) attained a special meaning and it was pitted against the caste-exclusive Shruti (Vedas or testimony). Siddhas named wed Sarahpa; the sufflx `Pa' was the short from of `Pad' or feet. From the eighth to the twelfth century the later Buddhists like Vajrayanis attempted some kind of synthesis in Shaivism, Buddhism and also the then current Bhakti cults. The Nath panthi Jogis and Gorakhnath's Hath-yogis were influenced by these practices. In Namdev the great importance attached too the guru is due to such influences. Dr. Hazariprasad Dwivedi's *Nath-sampradaya* in Hindi proves this point; so does R.H. Dhere's Marathi work on the same subject.

Later Jainism also insisted on purity of action and means. Devasen (circa 932) who composed *Bhava sangraha* and *Darshan-Sar* preached equality of castes Ram Singh of the eleventh century attacked the malpractices of the so called higher casters in his *Pahud Doha*. In this work, in the *doha* 206, he says:

Mantrun, Tantun, Shaiyanu, dharanu
 Nami uchhasah kijjai karanee
Emai Paramssukkha muni subbai,
 Eti Galgal kamun ruchchai

(Chanting of Mantras, Tantra, all the teachings of meditation (dhyana, oharana and breath-control - why for, to what purpose? Muni (Ramsingh thinks that all these practices are simply ridiculous to him to attain ultimate bliss this botheration is unnecessary).

Muni Ramsingh and Joindu (Yogindra) have attacked and exposed idolatry and proved the futility of image-worship. Instead they insisted on introversion. These sects were atheistic and they laid more stress on subjective purity. In Namdev and other democratic saints of him time like Gora, Savata and others one finds many echoes of the sayings of these Munis and Bhikkhus. They all criticized the rot that had set in orthodox hide-bound Brahmanical Hinduism.

Nath Panth propagated by Guru Gorakhnath was another such revolt. The late Dr. Rangeya Raghav (T. Narasimhachar) in his Ph. D. Thesis in Hindi on *Gorakhnath* has written in details about the life and philosophy of this almost legendary figure. When did this sect start is not exactly known, the roots of all such sects are hidden in historical antiquity. But it is believed that Adinath was the first Nath Guru. Adinath is also the name of a Jain monk. It was also called as *Avadhut* sect and *Siddh Kaul Mat*. The followers were also popularly known as *Kanphate* or Jogis with the split ear-lobes. The word Nath has been analysed as one who is establishing (—Tha) the Brahman in the form of Nada (Na). They all believed in reaching the Highest stage where some kind of music or divine sound was heard.

The practices of the Shakti-worshippers current at that time were mixed in these tenets of Nath sects. Thus Adinath is considered to be Shiva, and this sect has a close resemblance to Kashmir Trik philosophy. Matsyendranath and Jalandharnath were the two disciples of Gorakhnath. There are twelve different sect which branched from Gorakhnath, Kabir, Jaisi, Surdas and later saints. All devotional poets have described these Jogis vividly. They were wandering minstrels and mendicants, who carried begging-bowls and horns and accosted each other by the term 'Allakh' (A-laksha=un-attainable, invisible). They carried with them a musical instrument called *'Kingri'*. Matsyendranath, Machhindra, Minanath, Minapad are the names of some important yogis of the Nath panth. He was in the line of Gurus of Dnyandev or Dnyaneshwar. Namdev imbibed the principles of Nath panth through his great respect for and the company of Dnyaneshwar. While Matsyendra was connected with Shaivite Kapaliks,

Jalandharnath (on whose name the place Jullunder was founded) was connected with Buddhist kapaliks. Namdev in his travels to Punjab was definitely acquainted with these kinds of mendicants also.

In the history of religious sects and schools in medieval Hinduism, the most interesting sociological phenomenon is that the very exclusiveness, corrupt practices and hypocricy they sought to attack in orthodox and bigoted sects slowly and gradually corroded these liberal and rebellious new schools. Thus in India the attempt at any change or break-through very quickly defeats its own purpose. The Rebels turn into worse kinds of Establishment dan this process of fossilization of any fresh attempt at free-thinking is repeated time and again. Any attack on the conservative frame-work is easily recognized as another sectarian off-shoot and the roots of the *banyan* tree became more and more strengthened. Buddha was thus made into one of the *avataras* or incarnations of Vishnu and admitted in the Hindu Pantheon. So were the tenets of Nath sect absorbed in the mainstream of Bhakti.

Nath panth did not believe in Vedas as the sole authority, but preached some kind of inner intuition, as the ultimate testimony. They did not believe in the elaborate sacrificial rites, but took 'Om' as the ultimate principle. Book-knowledge was abhorred and personal realization or subjective experience was insisted upon. This brought in the inevitability of direct communion through Guru. Instead of the scriptures the word got an upper hand. In the matter of ultimate salvation or emancipation, the Nath sect has much similarity with the ultimate Nairatma of the Buddhist Mahayanis. They did not think that the process of identity with the Ultimate or Absolute ends with the knowledge of non-duality, but they tried to go beyond where the real Bliss lies. The concept of Hindu heaven is here substituted by the Mahasukhavati of Buddhists.

The Naths elaborated a kind of Yoga practice in which the Serpent-Power or *kundalini* was to be awakened. For this they gave an interesting description of the six different seats of power or lotuses in the body. By breath-control one conquered these seats and reached the highest where the undisturbed or limitless (Anahat or Anhad) Nad or the 'Supreme Sound' is heared. As the penitant *sadhak* advances in his yogic practices he goes beyond this Nad or sound and reaches the state of beatitude or *samadhi.* Such a person becomes a siddha: In Gorakhnath's *Hathayoga Pradipika* and in Dnyaneshwar's *Anubhavamruta* there are references to this yogic system. But Namdev was unlettered in the sense that he was not exposed to any systematic Sanskrit learning. He absorbed all these terms through hearsay and listening to many practising wandering yogis. Namdev's specific contribution was to bring about a synthesis in the way of knowledge and the way of Devotion. He thus democratized the devotional approach which was previously considered limited to upper castes and so exclusive. According to Dr. B.N. Mundi, "Gorakhnath's original banyan tree branched into various forms in various provinces and states: in Nepal, Assam, bengal, and Panjab. In Maharashtra the branches took roots and one finds Varkari, Mahanu-bhava, Datt, Anand, Chaitanya and Samartha as the different names of these offshoots." (page 71)

Was there any teed-back from the South during this period in the movement of devotional saints in Maharashtra? Shaivite and Vaishnava sects flourished in Tamilnad in the first millenium of the Christan era. From the second century onwards, the twelve Alvars preached their spiritual message. Rev. G.U. Pope has given a feel of the original sublimity and music in his verse translation of the *Divya Prabandham* texts. The South, in general, did not have many doubting Thomases, Jainism and Buddhism had not uprooted the beliefs of the orthodox Hindus in idol-worshipping; though Shaivism had the seeds of the worship of the formless godhead and Shankaracharya distilled his Vedanta as metaphysics of Pure Reason. Yet the common people had not questioned the masters. The overwhelming influence and on-slaught of Islam had not reached the South fill the twelfth century.

Raghunathacharya or Nath Muni (850-920) is said to have collected five thousand Prabandham *Padas* of Alvars; out of which 1300 are composed by Nammalvar. But before the Alvars and later also simultaneously 63 Maha-Saivites propagated their tenets through very fine metaphysical and mystic poetry. The Shaiva saints were from various castes: some were farmers and even. Shudras, all of them were not necessarily Brahmins. Nandan was an untouchable. The Shavites had ousted the Buddhist and Jain influences and even the traces which remained were very feeble. In Karnatak the Jain and the Virshaiva saints could easily establish themselves. While Basaveshvara, the founder of Virshaivism, preached a philosophy of defying the framework of caste, Dasas also absorbed the same process of democratization.

Vaishnav Acharyas who revived the worship of Rama and Krishna were as follows:

1. Yamunacharya	(960-1040)
2. Ramanujacharya	(1026-1136)
3. Madhvacharya	(1197-1275)
4. Nimbarkacharya	(1113-1151)
5. Vallabhacharya	(1298-1429)

It was Ramanujacharya who is relevant to the kind of Bhakti Namdev propagated. It was the way of Absolute Faith in the grace of God. Technically it involved *Prapatti* or complete surrender. Ramanuja gave the right of this total submission to the fourth and the lowest castes and sub-castes also. Now salvation was no more the monopoly of the upper few or the twice-born only.

Coming to Maharashtra, the Varkari sect was the most influential sect as far as namdev was concerned. The term Varkari is a marathi one which means one who goes on pilgrimage, or does a 'Vari.' Pandharinath or Vitthal is the main deity For having His glimpse (darshan) the devotees go every Kartik and Ashadh, in groups. This was an attempt to go back to the original forms of worship. This was rooted in the Narayaniya sect propounded by Narada and Shandilya in the *Bhakti-Sutras.* Scholars go to the extent of interpreting Heraclites as mentioned in Megasthenes as 'Hari-Krishna' of the Shaursenas. As these devotional schools laid all their faith in Vishnu, so they were called Vaishnavas and they called their ultimate object of worship 'Bhagavan' or 'Bhagvat' and so they were termed Bhagavatas. In A.D. 140 Heliodorus pillar raised by the Greek viceroy at Taxila, the 'Devadeva Vasudeva' has mentioned the Gupta kings in the eighth century as calling themselves Parama Bhagavat. On the Coromondal coast in the stone-edicts of the Pallavas Bhaghavat religion was popular in the third and fourth centuries of the Christian era. The valabhis of Gujarat in the sixth century were Bhagavatas. Banabhatta in his Harsha-charita mentions Pancharatra and Bhagavat as the two important sects.

The Bhagavat way of absolute devotion to one Good was the direct influence of Shrimad-Bhagavata, the holy book of the Vaishnavas. The Varkari panth combined in it the catholicity of the Nath Panth, its reliance on the Guru and the desire to serve the common people, and giving an equal treatment to all persons irrespective of caste and creed, as also found in the Lingayats of Karnatak. It is very difficult to trace its exact origin in Maharashtra as little historical evidence is available.

The famous popular *pada* is *'Sant Krupa Jhali'* "By the grace of saints, the building was completed. Dnyandev laid the foundation for this temple. Name, has servant enlarged it. Janardan Eknath gave it the pillars of Bhagavat. Tukaram became the pinnacle. Sing with patience all together. Bahini says the flags are fluttering. "It is no use elaborating this song.

All the Varkaris have in common one object of worship: Vitthal, whose temple is in Pandharpur. Pundalik is the main devotee who built this temple. About the crown (which is like a Shiva-Lingam) on the head of the main image there is lot of discussion. So is about the word 'Pandhari' itself, which is the Marathi word for white, derived from the Sanskrit 'pandur,' and is attributed to be the colour of Shiva. Vishnu is proverbially blue. Some historians attribute the popularity of this deity too some kind of Shaiva and Vaishnava unity. A deity like Hari-hara was already worshipped in Karnatak and in Andhra. At Tirupati Lord Venkats had a similar crown

The Varkari sect was influenced by Vasugupta's Shiva-sutras. Dnyaneshwar was influenced by Kashmir Shaivism, According to Dr. R.D. Ranade, the Varkaris fast on Monday as a token of reverence to Shiva. The Varkaris do not believe in caste differences. This was the sect which brought about the synthesis between the Nirgun and Sagun forms of devotions. Though Varkaris are considered Vaishnava they are very close to Pancharatra. The worship of Vitthal as one Absolute God and the realization of the Supreme as a matter of individual experience brings them closer to Vedanta. The Varkaris insist on pilgrimage (to Pandharpur), singing of hymns in a congregational manner and an austere life. These practices seem to be very similar to many non-Hindu sects too.

Amongst the Varkaris, on the one hand there are Yogis like Nivritti and Dnyaneshwar, and on the other Bhaktas like Namdev and Gora. The Varkaris further branched into several sub-sects like Chaitanya, Swarup, Anand and Prakash. The names themselves indicate the stress on one or the other aspects or mystic realization. The followers of this pathway to God are found in Vidarbha, Gujarat, Karnatak, Andhra and Bengal.

The other important devotional sect in Maharashtra, on which recent researches have thrown much light, was Mahanubhav. It is also called Jayakrishni Panth (in Punjab), Mahatma Panth and Achyut Panth. It was anti-Vedic and partly pro-Islam too. Sri Chakradhar originally from Gujarat was its propagator. But the first founder is supposed to be Gundoba, Gundam Raul or Govind Prabhu of Siddhupur in Vidarbha. Chakradhar was originally Harpaldeva, the son of Vishaldeva the Samvedi, Nagar Brahmin minister of malladeva-rai of broach in Gujarat, He fought many battles, enjoyed two or three marriages and later got disgusted of all pomp and regal splendour and went to Vidarbha. This Chakradhar founded this sect and had 500 disciples including women. His date is given to be Saka 1073 to 1185. He worshipped Krishna and Dattatreya. Chakradhar gave even the Shudras the right to *Sanyasa*; which was a matter borrowed from Buddhism. Nagadevacharya (Saka 1158-1224) continued his work. Later Bhaskar Kavi, Keshavaraj Suri, Damodar Bhatt, Gopal Vyas, Mahibhatt, Mahadai a and others organized and enlarged this sect.

The philosophy of the Mahanubhavas was rather simple. They believed in four elements: Jeev (Being), Devata (Gods as objects of worship), Prapanch (World as illusion) and Parameshwar (the Absolute). The world is transitory, the absolute is eternal. The soul of the beings is bound, the Absolute is free. They seem to be dualists. Gods are many, so are the beings which have miniature or symbolic bodies (Linga-deha). It is the Absolute who gives the knowledge and thus one is emancipated from the bondage of the illusory world. They also insist on non-violence, renouncing family life, good conduct. The respect for the guru is an additional matter. Without him the realization is not achieved. Every thing connected with the Guru is to be venerated. in this matter they seem to be next to Buddhists. The grace of the Guru was the most important catalytic and so personal communion was also emphasized. It was called *prasad-sevna*. They put on black robes; and did not believe in untochability. They served Marathi language and literature in a remarkable manner. Out of their Great Seven Books, four are concerned with Krishna's life.

In Karnatak an important sage in the Lingayat Panth was Allam Prabhu who was a Nath Siddha. He is also considered as one of the disciples of matsyendranath. Even in Basavesvara's *Vachanas* and in Akka Mahadevi's hymns, there are echoes of Guru Gorakhnath's *Hathayoga pradipika.* It is the opinion of one of the scholars. (see Sri Dhere: Guru Gorakhnath p. 201). Allam Prabhu later had difference of opinion with Gorakh, and in 1265 A.D. Revana Siddha who came with Navanathas became a disciple of Vir-Shaivism. Mamdev's conversion from the worship of God with from, into the principle of a formless God, seems to be a result of these various philosophies current in India.

Amongst such philosophies Sufism was also a very strong influence. Sufism arose as a protest against orthodox Islam. But Setu Madhavrao Pagdi maintains in his Marathi work 'Sufi Sampradaya' that it is not correct. They insisted on *Marifat* or direct communion and the value of a preceptor. In 1061 A.D. Hazrat Dataganj, who came to Lahore from Ghazni in the form of a captive, wrote *Kashful Mehjub.* He was intiated into Sufism in Baghdad. He brought this philosophy into India, furthered by Fakhruddin of Phenuphonda in South (died 1147 A.D.) and Syed Mohamad Bandanivaj Gesudaraj (1217-1320 A.D.) who wrote *Merajul Ashaqui,* an early book of Hindui language. The four sects of Indian Sufis were Chistiya, Subhandiya, Qadariya and Nakshabandi. All of them had one thing in common: Love for God and belief in His omnipresence and omniscience.

The Pratyabhijna of Kashmir Shaivism has much is common with Sufi's direct experience. Some Scholars maintain that Varkaris in Maharashtra were influenced by these philosophies, though their sources were very different. It is interesting to note that the Sahajiya Vaishnav in Bengal also maintained the same ecstasy of love as an essential for God-Realization. The Buddhish Sahajiyas talk of 'Prajna' and 'Upaya' and Bauls sing of 'Sahaj.' Jaideva's *Gita Govind* and Vidyapati's *Padas* have described the amours of Krishna and Radha and Krishna and Gopis in the same spirit of God meeting the soul. All of them were different from the abstract Vedanta dialectics.

In the Guru Granth Saheb Jaidev, Sadhna, Veni and Trilochan are also mentioned as contemporaries of Namdev. Jaidev in the sacred book *(Gaudi 16)* is referred to as 'Jaidev Nama Vipra Sudama' Kali Jge Nama Jaidev.' Whether this Jaidev is the same as the composer of *Gita Govinda,* born in Orissa (or Bengal?), son of Bhojdev and Radhadevi, is a matter of dispute amongst scholars. In the Granth-Sahib the two *padas* in Raga Gurjari and Maru seem to be influenced by Patanjala Yoga-Sadhana.

Sant Sadhna may be Sajjan Kasai according to Marathi biographers of saints, as some of the events in their lives are common. His one *pada* is in Rag Bilawal (No. 58, Guru Granth Saheb). In *Sant Gatha* there are six *padas* of this saint. There is the same sincere feeling of pouring out his heart before God in this poet. It seems that the poet was in great distress when he sang this hymn

Sant Veni's three *padas* are given in Guru Granth Sahib in Siri Rag, Rag Ramkali and Rag Prabhati, Guru Arjandev had made Veni as his Guru is another reference in Rag Basant Malhar. These *padas* refer to Yoga sect.

Sant Trilochan was an elder contemporary of Guru Nanak. His birth year was probably 1266 A.D. From the *padas* in Guru Granth Sahib it seems Namdev and Trilochan had a dialogue. Trilochan said:

Name Maya mohiya-kahe Trilochan meet
Kahe chheepahun chhaile-Ram no labahun cheet

(Nama is engrossed in Maya, says Trilochan his friend. Why spread over this printing (or fabrics), without keeping Ram in the heart.)

Namdev has replied to this in these words:

Nama kahe Trilochana-munhte Ram sambali
hath haun kari kam sanu-chitta Niranjan nali

(Name says-O Trilochan the mouth utters Ram, The hands and feet do their work, keeping the heart in Niranjan, the Abstract Absolute)

Saint Ravidas has referred to Namdev, Kabir, Trilochan, Sadhna, Sena together as persons who have 'swum through this ocean' and gone beyond, Priyadas Mahipati and Purandar have given some stories about them. Trilochan Das was a trader by caste. His four *padas* in Guru Granth Sahib have some reference to Maharashtra. These *padas* criticize fake sadhus, expose the meaninglessness of the illusory world and extol importance of God's name. He refers to 'Vithoba' also.

In the Kashmir poetess Lalla Dyed or Lalleshwari whose utterings are collected by Dr. Grierson and Barnet in "Lall Vakhyani" and by Prof. J.L. Kaul also in his articles and the booklet on `Lol lyrics,' there are echoes of the same intense love for the Abstract and the formless God as seen in latter Namdev and Kabir. It is difficult to establish any link, but the influence of Sufism seems to be working all over North India, including Kashmir, in the medieval age.

Poetesses in all Indian languages have played a very important role is underlining this ecstasy of God-realization. Andal and Avvaiyar in Tamil, Akka Mahadevi in Kannada, Lall Dyed and Haba Khatun in Kashmiri, Mirabai and Sahajobai in Rajasthani and Brij Bhasha, Molla in Telugu and Muktabai and Janabai in Marathi are good examples. janabai has composed some *abhangas* about Namdev's life.

In the Psalms of Maratha Saints there is an account of Janabai as follows:-"One of the members of Namdev's household has also a place among the Maratha poet-saints. This is a Sudra woman, named Janabai, who, according to the story, became a domestic slave of the poet because of her admiration of his devotion. She spent her whole life in his service and Vithoba's. The god is declared in the legend to have been constantly in her company, grinding corn for her, drawing water, helping her to wash the clothes. It is not always clear, however, whether the *abhangas* do not really describe, not a personal relationship of communion, but a recognition of the divine immanence in all things, When she says that-"in the inner shrine of contemplation Pandurang comes to meet us and clasps up to his breast," it is difficult to believe that she is not describing an experience of spiritual fellowship. But when she says, referring to the household occupations:

Grinding, pounding this our game,
Burn we up all sin and shame

there is here more than a suspicion of Advaita doctrine. She is reaching beyond the Maya, the "sport", of life and its duties, to an identity with Brahman beyond the distinction of good and evil. This is fully unveiled in another *abhanga,* which after expressing a feeling that has all the appearance of being parallel to that daily comradeship with Christ which Christian saints have ever sought, betrays itself in its conclusion as no more than a metaphysical affirmation of identity with the All.

The utterance of the name of God; Smaranam (Sumarni), is the first step in nine-fold Bhakti. Namdev, as his name itself suggests, insisted on this aspect of Bhakti.

Dr. R.D. Ranade writes in his Mysticism in maharashtra about Namdev's insistence on the name of God.

"Among all the Saints of Maharashtra, we find a perpetual insistence on the significance and efficacy of the Name of God; and of all these saints, we may say, Namdeva's insistence upon the Name is the strongest. "If I were to leave meditation on Thy feet even for a while," says Namdeva, "my lifebreath will vanish instantly. If there were a cessation to the utterance of the name of God in my mouth, my tongue will split a thousand-fold. If my eyes were not to see Thy beautiful form, they would come out forcibly from their sockets" (Abg 49). Through mystical experience, through devotion, through deceit, through the torments of Samsara, let the name of God always dance upon the tongue (Abg 51). There is neither time nor season for the meditation of God. There is neither a high caste nor low in His meditation. He who is the Ocean of love and pity shall come to the succour of all (Abg 54). The great Siva was tormented by the poison called Halahala, and yet his body became cool when he meditated on God. In the eighteen Puranas, says Namdeva, the only remedy narrated is the utterance of the Name of God (Abg 55). The Pandavas, even though they were enveloped in a house of fire, were saved because they meditated on the name of God. The cow-herds could not be burnt by fire, because they held God in their hearts. Hanuman could not be burnt by fire, because he meditated on the name of Rama. Fire had no power over Prahlada, because he constantly uttered the name of God. Sita was not burnt by fire, because she set her heart upon Raghunatha. The home of Bibhishana was saved in the holocaust at Lanka, says Namdeva, because he meditated on the name of God (Abg 59). The covering of untruth, which envelops a man's words, shall never depart except through a meditation on God (Abg 61). The Name of God is the Form of God, and the Form of God is the Name of God, There is no other remedy except the Name of God, says Namdeva, and anybody who says there is another is fool (Abg 64). God may remain concealed; but He cannot conceal His name. When we have once uttered His name. He cannot escape from us (Abg 66). Let the body live or depart, fix your mind upon God. I shall never leave Thy feet, says Namdeva, shall keep Thy Name in my mouth, and set my heart aflame with Thy love. I only implore Thee, says Namdeva, that Thou shouldst fulfil my resolve (Abg 67). To be in Samsara is even a pleasure, when the mind is once set upon God (Abg 68). Poor Brahmins do not know the secrets of realisation. God can be attained by meditation on His name only. I implore the young and the old, says Namdeva, to cling fast to the Name of God. In all your religious ceremonies, you should think only of God, and nothing else (Abg 72). They paint the pictures of the Sun or the moon, but they cannot paint the picture of light. They can put on apparel of a Sanyasin, but they cannot imitate his dispassion. They may perform a Kirtana, says Namdeva, but they will miss the nature of God-love (Abg 75). With a Vina in my hand and with the name of God in my mouth, I shall stand up in the temple of God. i shall renounce all food and water, and shall think of nothing but God. I shall forget my mother, or father, or wife, or children. I shall lose all bodily consciousness, and merge it in the Name of God, says Namdeva (Abg 77.) If, in such a condition, Death comes to devour me I shall sing and dance in joy. My only wish is, says Namdeva, that I should serve Thee from life to life (Abg 80)."

Macnicol has translated fourteen Abhangas of Namdev, out of which we quote two to give an idea of the philosophical depth of his poetry:

391 *(Tatva pusavaya gelo vedajnasi)*

From Vedic students first the truth I sought,
And found them full of "Thou Shalt, Thou shalt not"
Never shall they possess tranquillity,
For mighty in them is the power of "me."

From Scripture scholars sought I once again
The form divine, but found them rent in twain
Not one agrees with what the others say,
But pride and error lead them all astray.

Next in Purana I sought that form so fair
But still, alas, no place of rest was there.
The preachers preach of Brahma but set their mind
On lust, and so true peace they never find.

Ask of the Haridas the way devout;
You will find in him no faith at all but doubt

He tells in words the Name's high excellence,
While all the time engrossed with things of sense

Weary with seeking, here at last am I,
Low at they feet, O Pandurang I lie
My worldly life is full of tears, but thou
('Tis Nama cries), O save me now.

(2) *The Reign of Peace*

583 *(Avagha samsara sukhach karin)*

Now all my days, with joy I'll fill
  Full to the brim
With all my heart to Vitthal cling
  And only him,
He will sweep utterly away
  All dole and care;
And all in sunder shall I rend
  Illusion's snare.

O altogether dear is he
  And he alone,
For all my burden he will take
  to be his own

Lo, all the sorrow of the world
  Will straightway cease,
And all unending now shall be
  The reign of peace

For all the bondage he will break
  Of worldly care
And all in sunder will he rend
  Illusion's snare

From all my foolish fancies now
  Let me be free
In Vitthal, Vitthal only is
  Tranquillity.

Dyaneshwar called the poetic power of Namdev as 'sweeter than nectar' and 'deeper than ocean.' Molseworth called him the first poet of marathi literature. Prof. Patwardhan described Namdev as 'the first and foremost of the new school of lyric poetry in Marathi.' Dr. Tulpule finds in him 'afflorescence of imagery, use of many ancient words.' Prof. N.R. Phatak calls him a real rebel.' Dr. Vinaymohan Sharma has described him the 'first propagator of Nirguna Bhakti and the guide and preceptor of saints like Kabir.'

Namdev's poetic and philosophic legacy can be summarized in the words of Dr. Govind Trigunayat and others as the synthesis of action and non-action, egalitarianism, non-attributiveness of the Absolute, unending deep feeling of live, belief in omnipresence of God, non-dualism as opposed to polytheism, insistence on devotion and chanting of name, master-and-slave relationship between God and the devotee, mystic intuition, social reform, the non-ritualistic manner of worship and the usage of people's language.

Acharya Ramchandra Shukla discusses the change in Namdev's philosophical attitude and the shift in the manner of worship from Saguna to Nirguna. In his famous 'History of Hindi literature,' Shukla says in these words: "Namdeva had not applied himself to Saguna Bhakti on account of any imitiation from a *Guru*. He had done so on his own, by a spontaneous and innate urge. Dnyandev was always explaining him that no knowledge is possible without a Guru. Saints talk about Nirguna Brahma and show the way to God-realization through the teachings of a Guru. Dnyandev went on insisting on the knowledge or pure Nirguna form. Without a Guru everything was futile. So he went to Visoba Khechar of Nagnath. He has said:

My mind is the needle, my body is the thread
Name the tailor at the feet of Khechar bowed his head

and also:

My life was made fruitful by my Guru
All my misery was over, he gave happiness
Knowledge and charity my Guru taught me
Life is void without Rama's name

he has also said-

Whom shall I worship?
I do not see anyone different (that Him)
If one keeps his faith in one stone
On another stone one treads
If that stone is God, we are also God
Namdev says let me worship only Hari.

Ramchandra Shukla quotes his 'Nirgunibani' and gives two instances:

—Had there been no mother, no father, no action, no body

Neither we would be there, nor you, no one would know
who came from where
There would have been no moon, no sun, no water
would be mixed with air
No scriptures, no Vedas, where would have Karma
come from?

—Pande, your Gayatri (Cow) was eating the field of a Muslim
With a lame foot, she came limping
Pande, your Mahadev came riding a white bullock
Pande, we also saw your Ramchand coming
He fought with Ravan in vain, lost his own wife
Hindu is blind, the Turk is one-eyed
the Knower is wiser than both.

Such admonition of both Hindus and Muslims and their orthodoxies is also seen in Kabir.

The worshipper of idols insisted on a direct devotion to a personal God and indicated that an Abstract Absolute is also symoblically possible. But the worshipper of the formless only insisted on Knowledge.

In Namdev, his poems about Saguna worship are in Brijbhasha or in traditional language, but the later poems coloured with Nirguna feeling are in Sadhukkari or Nathpanthi's Khari Boli.

Neither do I know living, nor my doing
I am bound with fine bindings
Neither have I knowledge, nor meditation
Hari is filling everything
I am orphan without virtues
I am separated from You
Namdev says let me go to the resort of Hari
Otherwise people would scoff

Namdevache Abhanga

From Ajgaonkar's Book

No.1 *(Vitevari ubha)*

Standing on the brick the saviour of the poor
He extends both his arms to meet all
He does not see the good or bad qualities

He meets them again and again O Kashiraja
Such a kind soul asks for everyone
He enquires about the great and small
He gives an equal darshan to all
He is standing equipoised
Nama says he likes the saints
He is standing to embrace them

No. 6 *(Sampada sohela)*

The wealth and festivities do not please me
I am fond of only Pandhari
I love only to go to Pandhari
When is the Ashadhi Ekadashi
When will the Ekadashis of Ashadhi and Kartik would fall
He is asking every person going that way
Nama says he is so much absorbed with the idea
That Chakrapani is waiting for him

No. 17 *(Tujhiya satvene)*

Vedas speak with your power
The sun moves because of You
You are such omnipotent master of universe
Knowing this secret I came to you
The clouds rain, sit on mountains
The wind asks of your power
Nama says nothing moves at all
You are O God Panduranga the basis and support

No. 156 *(na Padhave ved)*

Do not study Vedas, no need to know the scriptures
Only remember the tenets of Nama
No knowledge of Brahma, no renouncement
Simple path of Bhakti with the saints
With all the rituals how many in this kali
have really crossed this sycle of births
Nama says the secret is told to me by saints
There is no other peace and resort than this

Hindustani Padas

No. 2142 *(Heen deen meri jati)*

I am low and poor by caste O Pandhari rai
Why did you make Nama a tailor
He made Nama with the gongs, he came to the temple
The Brahmin priest drove him out
Nama said 'Allakh' behind the temple
The temple began to turn round wherever Nama Turned
Cows are of many colours, milk is of one colour
How are you Brahmin and how are we Shudras
My mind is the needle, my body is the thread
Nama the tailor bows at the feet of Khecharji

No. 2145 *(Ham to bhule Thakur)*

We are lost in the Master
Why do you have false frenzy
The rivulet became ocean
Why do you weep O well
The lemon became sandal in the company of sandal
Why should asaphoetida weep
By Guru's grace Nama became a Sadhu
Seeing this these hypocrites started weeping

No. 2224 *(May na hota)*

Had there been no mother, no father
Had there been no action, no body
We would not have been there, nor you
Who would have come from where
There is nobody else except Ram
Just as the birds dwell on the tree
Had there been no moon, no sun
Water and wind would have been one
There would have been no scriptures, no Vedas
Where did this rebirth come from?
Khechar Buchar Tulsi-garland
I received them as blessings of the Guru
Nama says Pranava is highly shining and fiery
Only Sadguru can show it

III
HYMNS OF NAMDEV
INCLUDED IN THE *GURU GRANTH SAHIB*

Gauri

(1)

O God, Thou didst cause stones to float;

Why should not man float over by repeating Thy name?

Thou didst save the courtesan, the shapless hunchback, the hunstman, and Ajamal.

Even the murderer who shot Krishan in the foot was saved-

I am a sacrifice to those who utter God's name-

Bidur, the son of a handmaiden, Sudama, and Ugarsen, who obtained regal state;

Men without devotion, without penance, without family and without god works, were saved by Nama's Lord.

Asa

(2)

There is one God of various manifestations contained in and filling everything; withersoever I look There is He.

Maya's variegated picture hath so bewitched the world, that few know God.

Everything is God, everything is God, there is nothing but God.

One string holdeth hundreds and thousands of beads; God is the warp and woof.

Waves and foam and bubbles cannot be distinct from water.

This illusion, the world, is the play of the Supreme God; on reflection thou find it different from Him.

Fleeting phantoms, illusions of dreams man deemeth real advantages.

My guru instilled into me right ideas, and when I awoke to reason my mind accepted them.

Saith Namdev, behold the creation of God, and reflect on it in thy mind;

In every heart and in all things uninterruptedly there is only the one God.

(3)

If I bring a pitcher and fill it with water to bathe the idol,

Forty-two lakhs of animal species are in the water; God is contained in them;

why should I bathe Him?

Wherever I go there God is contained;

God supremely happy ever sporteth.

If I bring flowers and weave a garland to worship the idol,

The been hath first smelled the flowers; God is contained in the bee, why should I weave Him a garland?

If I bring milk and cook it with khir to feed the idol,

The calf hath first defiled the milk by tasting it;

God is contained in the calf; why should I feed Him?

In this world is God; in the next world is God; there is no part of the world without Him.

Thou are, O God, in every place; Nama representeth, Thou fillest the whole earth.

(4)

My heart is a yard measure, my tongue a shears.

With it I measure and cut of Death's noose.

What care I for caste? What care I for lineage?

I repeat the name of God day and night:

I dye what ought to be dyed, and I sew what ought to be sewed.

I cannot live for a ghari without God's name:

I perform worship and sing God's praises;

During the eight watches of the day I meditate on my Lord.

My needle is of gold, my thread of silver-

Nama's soul is attached to God.

(5)

The serpent casteth its slough, but not its poison:

Since thy heart is not pure,

Why perform mock meditation and repetition of God's name?

Thou art as the crane watching for fish in the water.

The man who eateth the food of lions,

Is called the god of thieves.

Nama's Lord hath settled the quarrel;

Drink God's elixir, O double-faced one.

(6)

If thou see the Supreme God, thou shalt have no other desire;

If thou think of the worship of God, thou shalt keep thy mind free from care.

O my soul, how shalt thou cross over the world's ocean filled with the water of evil passions?

O my soul, thou hast been led astray on seeing the deceitful world.

A calico-printer's house gave me birth, yet I became saturated with the guru's instruction,

Through the favour of holy men Nama hath met God.

Gujari

(7)

If Thou give me an empire, what glory shall it be to me?

If Thou cause me to beg, how shall it degrade me?

Worship God, O my soul, and thou shalt obtain the dignity of salvation,

And no more transmigration shall await thee.

O God, Thou didst create all men and lead them astray in error:

He to whom Thou givest understanding knoweth Thee.

When I meet the true guru, my doubts shall depart.

Whom shall I then worship? none other would be seen
but Thee. One stone is adored.

Another is trodden under foot:

If one is a god, the other is also a god-

Saith Namdev, I worship the true God.

(8)

He who hath no trace of impuriry, who is beyond impurity, and who is perfumed as with sandal hath taken His seat in my heart.

No one saw Him coming; who knoweth Him, O sister?

Who can describe, who can understand the All-pervading and Unknowable?

As the trace of a bird is not perceived in the sky,

As the path of a fish is not seen in the water,

As a vessel is not filled with the mirage-water of the sky,

Such is God, Nama's Lord, in whom these three qualities are blended; His coming or going is not seen

Sorath

(9)

When I sing of God, then I behold Him;
Then I, His slave, obtain contentment.
Accept divine instruction, O man; the true guru shall cause thee to meet God.
Where the heavenly light shineth,
There playeth spontaneous music.
'God's light is all-pervading'-
By the guru's favour I know that.
In the chamber of the heart are jewels
Which glitter there like lightning
God is near, no distant,
And His Spirit completely filleth mine.
Where the inextinguishable sun of God's word shineth,
There earthly lamps grow pale;
Through the guru's favour I have known this.
God's slave Nama hath been easily absorbed in Him.

(10)

A near neighbour asked Nama, 'By whom didst thou have this hut rebuilt?
'If thou show me the carpenter, I will pay him twice the wages thou didst.'
'O my sister, my Carpenter cannot be given thee;
Lo! my Carpenter pervadeth all things;
My Carpenter is the SUpport of the soul.

If any one want such a hut to be built, the Carpenter will require love for His wages.

When man breaketh with his family and all his friends, then the Carpenter of His own accord cometh to him.

I cannot describe such a Carpenter; He is contained in everything and in every place.

As when a dumb man tasteth the great flavour of nectar, if thou ask him, he cannot describe it.

Hear the praises of the Carpenter, my sister-He restrained the the ocean and fixed Dhru as the polar star.

Nama's Lord recovered Sita, and bestowed Lanka on Babhikhan.'

(11)

Without covering it with leather the drum of the brain playeth;

Without waiting for the month of Sawan the thunder roareth,

And it raineth without clouds.

If any one consider the real state of things,

I have met my dear Lord.

By meeting Him my body hath become perfect;

Having touched the philosopher's stone I have become gold.

In word and thought I have strung the gems of God's name.

I feel real love for God, my doubts are dispelled:

On questioning the guru my mind is satisfied.

As the pitcher is filled with water,

I know that the world is filled with the one God.

When the disciple's mind accepted the guru,

The slave Nama recognized God.

Dhanasari

(12)

Men dig deep foundations and build palaces thereon.

Was any one longer lived than Markand who put grass on his head and thus whiled away his days?

Only God the Creator is dear to me;

On man, why art thou proud? this unsubstantial body shall be destroyed.

The Kauravs, Duryodhan and his brothers used to say, 'Everything is ours.'

Their umbrellas extended over a space of twelve jojans, yet the vultures devoured their bodies.

Lanka was all gold; was any one greater than Rawan?

What availed him the elephants tethered at his gate? In a moment they became the property of others.

The Yadavs practised deception on Durbasa, and obtained the fruit thereof.

God showed mercy to His slave; Namdev singeth His praises.

(13)

I have restrained the ten organs of sense; the very name of the five evil passions I have erased.

Having extracted the poison from the seventy-two tanks of the heart, I have filled them with ambrosia;

I shall not allow the poison to return again.

The ambrosial word I utter from my heart; my spirit I instruct not to attach itself to worldly things.

I have destroyed worldly love with an axe of adamant:

I touch the guru's feet and implore him.

Turning away from the world, I have become a servant of the saints and I fear them.

I shall be saved from this world the moment I cease to be entangled by Maya.

Maya is the name of the Power which placeth man in the womb; abandoning it I shall obtain a sight of God.

The man who worshippeth in this way shall be freed from all fear.

Saith Namdev, O man, who wander abroad? obtain God in the way I have told thee.

(14)

As water is dear to the traveller in Marwar, and the creeper to the camel;

As the huntsman's bell at night is dear to the hind; so is God to my soul-

Thy name is beautiful, Thy form is beautiful, very beautiful The colour, O my God-

As rain is dear to the earth, as the odour of flowers is dear to the bumble-bee;

As the mango is dear to the kokil, so is God to my soul.

As the sun is dear to the sheldarke, as the lake of Mansarowar is dear to the swan;

As the husband is dear to the wife, so is God to my soul.

As milk is dear to the child, as a torrent of rain to the mouth of the chatrik;

As water is dear to the fish, so is God to my soul.

All penitents. sidhs, and munis seek God, but few have seen Him.

As Thy name is dear to all creation, so is Vitthal to Nama's heart.

(15)

Before the world a lotus was formed;

From it proceeded Brahma, and from Brahma all men.

Know that everything else was produced from Maya, who leadeth the world a dance.

First a voice proceeded from God;

Afterwards Maya proceeded from God

Through that voice the parts of this Maya and of that God blended and the world was produced.

In this garden of God men dance like water in the pots of a well;
Women and men dance.
There is no god but God-
Argue not on this point.
If thou have doubts,
God saith, Consider in thy heart that this world and I are one.'
The world is like water-pots, sometimes above, sometimes below.
Wandering about I have come to Thy gate.
God-Who art Thou?
Nama-I am Nama, Sire-
O Lord, save me from the world which bringeth death.

(16)

O Lord, the purification of sinners is Thy daily work;
Hail to those saints who have meditated on my God.
On my forehead is the dust of God's feet,
Which is far from even demigods, worldly men, munis, and saints.
Compassionate to the poor, O God, destroyer of pride,
Nama hath found the asylum of Thy feet, and is a sacrifice unto Thee.

Todi

(17)

Some say God is near, others that He is far away.
To say He is near or far is, as it were, to say that a fish could climb a date-tree.
Why, SIr, talkest thou nonsense?
They who have found God have concealed the fact.
Men who are pandits shout the Veds,
But the ignorant Namdev only knoweth God.
Who that uttereth God's name retaineth the stain of sin?
Sinners have become pure by uttering His name.
In the company of God His slave Namdev hath acquired ocular evidence.

He hath ceased to fast on the eleventh day, and why should he go on pilgrimages?

Saith Namdev, my acts and thoughts have become good.

Who hath not gone to heaven by uttering the name of God under the guru's instruction?

(19)

There is a play on three sets of word.
There is a pot in a potter's house, an elephant in king's house,
A widow in a Brahmin's house-sing randi, sandi, handi O!
Asafoetida in a biniya's house, horns on a buffalo's forehead,
A lingam in a temple of Shiv-sing line, sing, hing O!
Oil in an oilman's house, creepers in a forest,
Plantains in a gardener's house-sing ket, bel, tel O!
Gobind in the company of saints, Krishan in Gokal,
And God in Nama-sing Ram, Siyam, Gobind O!

Tilang

(20)

Of me who am blind Thy name, O King, is the prop.
I am poor, I am miserable, Thy name is my support.
Bounteous and merciful Allah, Thou art generous;
I believe that Thou art present before me;
Thou art a river of bounty, Thou art the Giver, Thou art exceeding wealthy;
Thou alone givest and takest, there is none other;
Thou art wise, Thou art far-sighted; what conception can I form of Thee?
O Nama's Lord, Thou art the Pardoner, O God.

(21)

Halloo! my Friend, halloo my friend, how art Thou?
I am a sacrifice unto Thee, I am a sacrifice unto Thee.
God is Thy forced labour, exalted Thy name;
Whence hast Thou come? where hast Thou been? and whither art Thou going?
This is the city of Dwaraka; tell the truth.
Handsome is Thy turban, sweet Thy discourse;
But Why should there be a Mughal in the city of Dwaraka?
Among several thousands of people Thou art the only Mughal seen;
Thou art the very picture of the king of sable hue;
Thou art the Lord of the horse, the Lord of the elephant, and the Ruler of men.
Thou art Nama's Lord, the King of all, and the Giver of salvation.

Bila

(22)

The guru hath made my life profitable-
I have forgotten sorrow and obtained joy within me.
The guru hath granted me the eye-salve of divine knowledge.
O my soul, without God's name man's life is vain.
Namdev knoweth God by keeping Him in mind;
My soul is absorbed in Him who giveth life to the world.

Gaund

(23)

Where I to perform the horse-sacrifice,
Give my weight in gold as alms,
Bathe at Pryag,
It would not be equal, O Nama, to singing God's praises.
O listless man, worship they God.
Were I to offer rice-balls at Gaya,
Dwell at Banaras,
Recite the four Veds,
Fulfil all religious offices,
Restrain my senses under the guru's instruction,
Perform the six duties of Brahmans,
Read the conversations between and his consort-
All these different occupations would be useless; O my soul, lay them aside,
And remember, remember God's name.
Worship Him, Nama, and thou shalt swim across the world's ocean.

(24)

As the deer followeth huntsman's bell,
And giveth to its own life rather than cease its attention,
In the same way I gaze on God.
I do not leave Him to turn my mind in another direction.
As the kingfisher gazeth on the fish,
As the goldsmith meditateth stealing gold while fashioning it,
As the lustful man gazeth on the wife of another,

As the gambler meditateth cheating while playing kauris,
So Nama ever meditateth on God's feet-
Wherever I gaze there is God.

(25)

Float me over, O God, float me over!

I am unskilful and know not how to swim; O God, my Father, give me Thine arm.

He to whom to true guru hath taught knowledge, is changed in a moment from a man into a demigod.

I have obtained the medicine by which, though begotten by man, I have conquered heaven.

Place me even for a short time where Thou hast placed Dhru and Narad.

By the support of Thy name many have been saved: this is Nama's private opinion.

(26)

I am ardently longing for the Friend-
Without her calf a cow is lonely,
Without water a fish writheth,
So without God's name doth poor Nama.
As the calf, when let loose,
Sucketh his dam's teats and swalloweth her milk,
So Namdev hath obtained God-
When man meeteth the guru he showeth the Unseen-
As the wicked man loveth another man's wife,
So Nama loveth God.
As man's body burneth in the bright sunshine,
So doth poor Nama without the name of God.

(27)

By repeating the name of God all doubts are dispelled-
Repeating the name of God is the highest religious exercise-
By repeating the name of God caste and lineage are effaced.
That God is the staff of the blind man.
I bow before God! I bow before God!
By repeating God's name Death tortureth not.

God took the life of Harnakhas,

And made for Ajamal a dwelling in heaven.

The courtesan who taught her parrot to repeat God's name was saved-

That God is the apple of mine eye-

By repeating the name of God, Putana full of deceit,

The destroyer of children, was saved;

By remebering the name of God the daughter of Drupad was saved;

Gautam's wife though turned into a stone, was saved.

God destroyed Kesi and Kans,

And conferred the gift of life on Kalinag.

Nama representeth, by repeating the name of such a God fear and trouble depart.

(28)

They who worship Bhairav shall become sprites;

They who worship Sitala shall ride on donkeys and scatter dust-

For myself I take the name of the one God;

I would give all other gods in exchange for it.

They who repeat the name of Shiv and worship him,

Shall ride on an ox and play the drum;

They who worship the great mother Durga,

Shall be born as women instead of men.

Thou callest thyself, O Durga, the primal Bhawani,

When it came to my turn to be saved, where didst thou hide thyself?

Under the instruction of the guru, O my friend, cling to God's name-

Nama representeth, thus saith the Gita.

(29)

To-Day I Nama saw God, I now admonish the fool-

O pandit, thy gayatri used to graze on the boor's field,

He took a stick and broke her leg; since then she hath walked lame.

O pandit I have seen thy great god Shiv going along on a white bullock.

In his consort Parbati's house a banquet for him was prepared, he killed her son.

O pandit, thy Ram Chandar-I have seen him too going along;

Having lost his wife he fought with Rawan.

The Hindus are blind, the Musalmans purblind;

The man who knoweth God is wiser than either.

The Hindus worship their temple, the Musalmans their mosque.

Nama worshippeth Him who hath neither temple nor mosque.

Ramkali

(30)

A boy taketh paper, cutteth it into a kite, and flyeth it in the sky.

While conversing with his companions, he keepeth his attention on the string.

I have pierced my soul with God's name,

As the goldsmith's attention is engrossed in his work.

The queen's female servant taketh her pitcher, filleth it with water,

Coverseth laughingly and pleasantly, yet keepeth her attention on the pitcher.

It the cows of a city with ten gates be yet loose to graze,

And they go grazing for even five miles, they will remember their young, and return each by her own gate.

Saith Namdev, hear, O Trilochan, when a child is laid in its cradle,

Its mother, whether engaged at hame or abroad, keepeth her thoughts on her child.

(31)

The endless songs and poetry of the Veds, Purans, and Shashtars I will not sing;

I will play unbeaten music in the imperishable region of God;

Ceasing to love the world I will sing of God.

Imbued with Him who is beyond expression and indestructible, I shall go to the abode of the Inscrutable One.

I will cease to hold my breath in the right or left nostril or between them both.

I deem the left and right nostril the same; I shall be blended with the light of God.

I will not go to see places of pilgrimages nor enter their water; I will not annoy men or lower animals.

The guru showed me the sixty-eight places of pilgrimage in my heart where I will bathe.

I will not nave myself glorified and congratulated by my select friends.

Nama saith, my heart is dyed with God, and I shall be absorbed in Him.

(32)

When there was no mother, no father, no karma, and nobody;

when we were not and you were not, who was there and whence did he come?

O God, no one hath any relation:

Man's dwelling in this world is like the perching of a bird on a tree.

When there was no moon, no sun, when there was only water and air blended together,

When there were no Shastars and no Veds, whence did Karma come?

I have by the favour of the guru obtained God, for whom the Jogis suspend their breath, and fix their attention on the bridges of their noses, and the Bairagis wear necklaces of sweet basil.

Nama representeth, God is the primal Essence; when there is a true guru he showeth Him.

(33)

If one perform penance with body reversed at Banaras, and die at a place of pilgrimage; if one burn one's body with fire, or strive to make it survive for a kalpa;

If one perform the horse sacrifice or offer secret presents of gold, all that would not be equal to the name of God.

O hypocritical man, renounce deception practise it not;

Ever and ever take God's name.

Wert thou to go to the Ganges and the Godavari every twelfth year, bathe at Kedarnath,

And make offerings of thousands of cows at the Gomti;

Wert thou to perform millions of pilgrimages, freeze thy body in the Himalayas, all would not be equal to the name of God;

Wert thou to offer horses, elephants, women with their couches, lands, and make such gifts continually to Brahamans;

Wert thou to purify thy body and offer its weight in gold, all would not be equal to the name of God.

Look for the pure dignity of Nirvan, and be not afterwards angry with thyself, of attribute blame to the god of death.

Nama representeth, drink the real nectareous elixiriof my kind Raṃ Chandar, the son of Jasarath Rai.

Mali Gaura

(34)

Happy, happy that flute which Krishan played!

A very sweet unbeaten sound issueth from it.

Happy, happy that blanket which Krishan wore!

Happy, happy that ram and his fleece it was made from.

Hail, hail to thee, mother Devaki,

In whose house god, the lord of Lakshmi, was born!

Blest, blest the forest glades of Bindraban,

Where Nama's god Natayan sported,

Played his flute, herded his cows,

And was happy.

(35)

God, my father, hail to thee, dark complexioned Vitthal with the long hair!

Holding in thy hand the discus, thou didst come from heaven and save the life of the great elephant;

Thou didst save Draupadi when her clothes were being torn off her in Duhasasan's court;

Thou didst save Ahalya the wife of Gautam;

How many hast Thou purified and saved:

Thus the lowly Namdev without caste hath entered Thy sanctuary.

(36)

In every heart God speaketh, God speaketh;

Doth anyone speak independently of Him?

There is the same earth in the elephant and the ant;

vessels of many kinds are made from earth.

In mobile and immobile things, in worms and moths, and in every heart God is contained.

Think of the one God who is endless; abandon all other hope.

Nama representeth; I have become free from desires;and in this state who is Lord and who is slave?

(37)

When i entered the`asylum of God the Bridegroom, I obtained the four stages of salvation and the four supernatural powers.

I have been saved, I have become famous through the four ages, and I have put the umbrella of praise and fame over my head.

Who hath not been saved by repeating the name of the Sovereign God?

They who listen to the guru's instruction and associate with holy men are called saints.

On beholding the effulgence of the guru, who is conspicuous with his shell, discus, necklace, and sacrificial mark, Death becometh afraid.

Man then becometh fearless, and by the power of God thundereth forth that he hath escaped the pain on transmigration.

God gave kind Ambarik the gift of salvation, and aggrandized Babhikhan with sovereignty;

The Lord gave the nine treasures to Sudama, and made Dhru immovable in the north pole, where he is fixed to the present day;

Go having assumed the body of Narsinh the man-lion, killed Harnakhas for the sake of his saint Prahlad.

Nama saith, Vishnu is in the power of the saints, and is till now standing at the door of Bali.

Bhairo

(38)

O my tongue, if thou utter not God's name,

I will break thee into a hundred pieces.

O tongue, dye thyself with God's name;

meditating on God's name dye thyself with a good dye;

false, O My tongue, are all other occupations.

The dignity of Nirvan is only obtained through the name of God.

Wert thou to worship countless millions of other gods.

If would not be equal to repeating God's name alone

namdev representeth, this O my tongue, and say 'O God, Thy forms are endless.'

(39)

God dwelleth near him

Who coveteth not another's wealth or another's wife.

I will not look at him

Who repeateth not God's name.

sAs beast is that man

Whose heart is estranged from God.

Namdev representeth, a man without a nose

Doth not look well even with the other thirty-two marks of beauty.

(40)

Nama having milked his brown cow took

A cup of milk and a jug of water for the idol.
'Drink milk and my mind will be at ease;
Otherwise my father will be angry.'
A golden cup filled with milk
Nama took and placed before the idol-
The saints alone abide in my heart-
On seeing Nama the god smiled;
On giving milk to the idol the worshipper Nama went home,
And God appeared unto him.

(41)

I am a mad woman and God is my spouse;
It is for Him i decorate myself elaborately.
Abuse me well, abuse me well, abuse me well, o people;
My body and soul are for my beloved God.
I hold no idle discussion with any one;
I sip with my tongue the elixir of God.
Now I know in my heart that such an arrangement hath been made,
By which I shall meet God with banners and music.
Whether any one give me praise or blame,
Nama hath met God.

(42)

Sometimes man is not satisfied even with milk, molasses, and clarified butter;
Sometimes he beggeth morsels from house to house;
Sometimes he picketh up pulse-sweepings.
Remain as God hath placed thee, O brother-
The greatness of God cannot be described-
Sometimes man rideth on prancing steeds;
Sometimes he hath not shoes for his feet;
Sometimes he putteth himself to sleep on a couch with a clean coverlet;
Sometimes he cannot get straw to sleep upon-
Saith Namdev, the Name alone saveth;
He who hath found a spiritual guide shall be delivered.

(43)

I went, o Lord, with laughter and gladness to Thy temple,

But while Nama was worshipping, the Brahmans forced him away.
A lowly caste is mine, O King of the Yadav, why was I born a calico-printer?
I took up my blanket, went back,
And sat behind the temple.
As Nama repeated the praises of God
The temple turned towards His saint.

(44)

As food is dear to the hungry,
As the thirsty need water,
As the fool is attached to his family;
So God is dear to Nama.
Nama's love is devoted to God,
And he hath easily severed himself from the world.
As a woman is smitten with a strange man,
As a greedy man loveth wealth,
As woman is dear to the lutful.
Such is Nama's love for God.
That is real love by which God attacheth man to Him,
And by which through the guru's favour duality departeth.
Love for him who filleth my heart shall never be sundered;
Nama hath applied his heart to the true Name.
As the love between a child and its mother,
So is my soul imbued with God.
Namdev representeth I love God;
he dwelleth in my heart.

(45)

As a fool leaveth the wife of his home,
Hath intercourse with a strange woman, and is ruined.
As the parrot is pleased on seeing the simmal,
But at last dieth clinging to it,
So the home of the sinner shall be in hell-fire;
He shall continue to burn and never have respite.
He never goeth to see where God is worshipped,
He leaveth the right path and goeth the wrong one,

He forgetteth God and suffereth transmigration,
He rejecteth ambrosia and eateth a load of poison.
When a dancing girl arriveth on the dancing floor,
She putteth on rich dresses, adorneth herself,
Danceth to measure,and modulateth her voice,
While death's noose is on her neck.
He on whose forehead such destiny hath been written,
Quickly entereth the protection of the guru.
Saith Namdev, this is my decision-
O saints, thus shall you obtain salvation.

(46)

Sanda and Marka went and complained to Harnakhas-

'Thy son Prahlad will not study and we are tired of teaching him;

He singeth God's praises, beateth time with his hands, and corrupteth all the other pupils;

He repeateth the name of God;

In his heart he remembereth God.'

The queen represented to her son-'The king hath reduced the whole earth to subjection:

My son Prahlad, thou doest no bidding: he hath some design on thee.

A council of his enemies met and passed a resolution, 'We will lengthen his life.'

They terrified him by throwing him from a height, by putting him into water and fire, but God changed for him the properties of matter.

Harnakhas enraged drew his sword, and threatened him with death, saying, 'Show me who will save thee.'

Prahlad replied, 'God who weareth yellow clothes, the Lord of the three worlds, is in the pillar.'

Upon this God tore Harnakhas with his nails, and rendered demigods and men happy.

Saith Namdev, I meditate on that God who bestoweth salvation.

(47)

The emperor said, 'Ho, you Nama,
Let me see the deeds of your God.'
The emperor had Nama arrested-
'Let me see your God Vitthal;

Restore to life this slaughtered cow,
Otherwise I will strike off thy head on the spot.'
'Your majesty, how can that be?
No man can reanimate what is slaughtered.
All I could do would be of no avail;
What God doeth taketh place.'
The emperor fell into a passion,
And set a huge elephant at Nama.
Nama's mother began to cry-
'Why dost thou not abandon the God of the Hindus and worship the God of the Musalmans?'
Namdev: 'I am not thy son, nor art thou my mother;
Even though I perish, I will sing God's praises.'
The elephant struck him with his trunk,
But this Hindu trampleth on mine honour.'
The Hindus said, 'O king, hear our prayer
Take Nama's weight in gold.'
'If I take a bribe I shall go to hell;
Shall I amass wealth by abandoning my faith?'
While Nama's feet were being chained
He sang the praises of God and beat time with his hands.
The Ganges and the Jamma may flow backwards,
But Nama will repeat God's name.
When seven gharis were heard to strike,
The Lord of the three worlds had not yet arrived.
God afterwards came mounted on His gurur,
Which beat the air with its wings.
He took compassion on his saint,
And came mounted on His gurur,
'Say but the word and I will turn the earth on its side;
Say but the word and I will upturn it altogether.
Say but the word and I will restore the dead cow to life,
So that every one may behold and be convinced.'
Nama said, 'Spancel the cow.'
They put the calf to her and milked her.
When the pitcher was filled with the milk the cow gave.

Nama took and placed it before the emperor,
And the time of trouble came on him.
He implored Namdev through the Qazis and the Mullas-
'Pardon me, O Hindu, I am thy cow.'
Nama said, 'Hear, O monarch,
Hath this credential been exhibited by me?
The object of this miracle is
That thou, O emperor, shouldst walk in the paths of truth and humility-
Namdev, God is contained in everything.'
The Hindus went in procession to Nama
And said, 'if the cow had not been restored to life,
People would have lost faith in thee.'
The fame of Namdev remained in the world;
He took saints with him to salvation.
All trouble and sorrow befell the revilers-
Between Nama and God there is no difference.

(48)

When one ḥath a Guru, he meeteth God;
When one hath a guru, he is saved;
When one hath a guru, he goeth to heaven;
When one hath a guru, while he liveth he is dead-
True, true, true, true is the guru;
False, false, false is all other service than his-
When one hath a guru, he inculcateth the Name;
When one hath a guru, he runneṭh not in the ten directions;
When one hath a guru, he is far removed from the five evil passions;
When one hath a guru, he dieth not of grief;
When one hath a guru, he obtaineth the ambrosial word;
When one hath a guru, heareth the story of the ineffable;
When one hath a guru, his body becometh immortal;
When one hath a guru, he uttereth the Name;
When one hath a guru, he seeth the three worlds;
When one hath a guru, he knoweth how to reach the exalted position;
When one hath a guru, his head toucheth heaven;

When one hath a guru, he is ever congratulated;
When one hath a guru, he is ever estranged from the world;
When one hath a guru, he abandoneth slander;
When one hath a guru, he deemeth evil and good the same;
When one hath a guru, good destiny is written on his forehead;
When one hath a guru, evil passions seduce not his body;
When one hath a guru, the temple turneth towards him;
When one hath a guru, his hut is rebuilt for him;
When one hath a guru, his bed cometh forth from the river;
When one hath a guru, he batheth in the sixty-eight places of pilgrimage;
When one hath a guru, the quoit of Vishnu is impressed on his body;
When one hath a guru, he performeth the twelve adorations;
When one hath a guru, all poisons become wholesome;
When one hath a guru, doubts are dispelled;
When one hath a guru, he escapeth from Death;
When one hath a guru he crosseth over the terrible ocean.
When one hath a guru, he suffereth not transmigration;
When one hath a guru, he obtaineth the advantages of the eighteen Purans;
When one hath a guru, he obtaineth the eighteen loads of vegetables.
When one hath a guru, there is no resting place-
Namdev hath entered the guru's protection.

(49)

Come God, the Qalandar
Wearing the dress of an Abdali.
The firmament is the hat on Thy head, the seven nether regions Thy slippers;
All animals with skins are Thy temples, thus art Thou decked out, O God!
The fifty-six millions of clouds are Thy robes and the sixteen thousand queens of Krishan Thy waistbands;
The eighteen loads of vegetables are Thy clubs, the whole world is Thy salver;
Nama's body is Thy mosque, his heart Thy priest who tranquilly prayeth.
O Thou with and without form, Thou who are wedded to lady Lakshmi,
While I was worshipping Thou hadst my cymbals taken from me; to whom shall I complain?
Nama's Lord is the Searcher of all hearts, and wandereth in every land.

Basant

(50)

If a servant run away when his master is in trouble,

The servant shall not be long-lived, he shall bring shame on his father and mother's family,

I will not abandon Thy service, O Lord, even though men scoff at me,

Thy lotus feet dwell in my heart,

As man accepteth death to secure wealth,

So the saints relinquish not God's name.

Pilgrimages to the Ganges, Gaya, and Godavari are worldly acts;

If God be pleased, Nama shall be His worshipper.

(51)

The waves of covetousness sound like a cataract, my body is drowning therein, O God.

Float me over the ocean of the world, O God, float me over, Father Vitthal.

In this gale I cannot steer my boat, I cannot reach Thine opposite shore, O God.

Be compassionate and cause me to meet a true guru, take me across, O God.

Nama saith, I do not even know how to swim; give me Thine arm, give me Thine arm, O God.

(52)

As an ant draggeth along a bit of cow dung,

So this cart fashioned from dust and seed

At first moveth slowly;

But afterwards the world driveth it with a rod.

By darling soul goeth to the wash-tank.

The washerman dyed with love washeth it with the water of God's name;

My heart is fascinated with God's feet.

Saith Nama, Thou O God, who art everywhere diffused,

Have compassion on Thy worshipper!

O man, why hast thou gone into a forest of evil passions?

Thou hast partaken of the thieves' plant and gone astray.

A fish abideth in water,

And taketh no notice of the deadly net;

It swalloweth the bait to gratify its palate,

So man is bound by the love of gold and woman.

When the bees hoard up a great store of honey,

Man taketh the honey and throweth dirt on the bees.

The cow storeth up milk for her calf,

But the milkman tieth the calf up by the neck and milketh the cow.

For wealth man maketh great endeavours;

That wealth he taketh and burieth in the ground.

He amasseth a great deal, but the fool understandeth not.

That his riches shall remain on the earth and his body become dust.

He burneth with great lust, wrath, and avarice;

He never joineth the company of holy men.

Saith Namdev, seek God's protection;

Become fearless and worship God.

(54)

Why layest Thou not a wager with me, O God, that there is nothing but Thee?

The servant is known from his master, and the master from his servant; this is my game with Thee.

Thou art God and Thine own temple, Thou worshippest Thyself.

From water proceed waves, from waves water, though both have different names in conversation.

Thou art the Singer, Thou art the Dancer, Thou art the Trumpet-player-

Saith Namdev, Thou art my Lord, Thy servant is imperfect; Thou art perfect.

(55)

The man who worshippeth none Me is in Mine own image;

The sight of him even for a moment removeth man's three fevers, and his touch extricateth man from the pit of family life.

A saint can release one bound by Mr, but I cannot release one bound by a saint.

If a saint seize and bind Mr at any time, I can say naught to him.

I am bound by men's merits; I am the life of all things, but my slave is My life.

O Namdev, My love shall shine over him whose heart hath such faith.

Malar

(56)

Serve God who is unknowable and stainless.

Give me, O God, the gift of service for which saints beg.

God's palace hath pavilions on every side; in heaven is His gorgeous dwelling and mansion;

He filleth equally the seven regions of the world.

In His palaċe dwelleth the ever youthful Lakshmi;

The moon and sun are His lamps, the wretched mountebank Death, who levieth a tax on all, His Judge-

Such a Monarch is God.

In His mansion Brahma with four faces who created the whole world is the fashioning potter;

In His mansion enthusiast Shiv, the world's teachers, preacheth pure divine knowledge;

A His gate are the mace-bearers Evil and Good, and the accountants Chitr and Gupt;

Dharmraj the destroyer is His porter-

Such a Monarch is God.

In His mansion are the hearalds, the heavenly dancers, the rikhis, and the poor minstrels who melodiously sing;

All the Shastars are His actors, His theatre is stupendous, Kings sweetly sing His praises,

The winds are His waving chauris,

His handmaiden is Maya who hath vanquished the world,

His fire-place is the blind pit of hell fire,

Such a monarch is the Lord of the three worlds.

In His mansion the tortoise is a bed; Vasuki with its thousand hoods the cords to bind it.

His flower-girl is the eighteen loads of vegetables, His water-carrier the ninety-six millions of clouds;

The Ganges is the perspiration of His feet,

The seven seas His water-stands,

All living things His water vessels-

Such a Monarch is the Lord of the three worlds-

At His mansion wait Arjan, Dhru, Prahlad, Ambarik,

Narad, Nejai, the Sidhs, the Budhas, the heralds, and the heavenly dancers who extol Him and play before Him.

In God's mansion are so many living beings

Within all of whom He is diffused.

Namdev representeth, seek God's protection,

Whose standard all his saints bear.

(57)

Forget me not, forget me not,

Forget me not, O God!

Those misled Brahmans of the temple were all furious with me;

Calling me a Sudar they me and turned me out: what shall I do, Father Vitthal?

If Thou give me salvation when I am dead, nobody will be aware of it; save me now.

If these pandits call me low, then, O God, Thine honour will be in the background.

Thou who art called the compassionate and merciful altogether unrivalled is Thine arm-

God turned round the front of the temple towards Nama, and its back towards the pandits.

Kanra

(58)

God the Searcher of hearts,

Like a body reflected in a mirror,

Dwelleth in every heart; nothing produceth an effect or impression on Him.

He is free from all entanglements and devoid of caste.

When one looketh at one's own face in the water, the water can produce no impression on it,

So nothing can produce an impression on Vitthal, Nama's Lord.

Prabhati

(59)

Only the heart knoweth its own state; either keep thy secret to thyself, or tell it to a man of understanding.

Since I repeat the name of God, the Searcher of hearts, why should I be afraid?

God, the Lord of the earth, hath penetrated me.

My God is diffused in every place.

Shops are only phantoms, shopkeepers are only phantoms, cities are only phantoms.

The different grades of men who inhabit the earth are phantoms, and the world wandereth in error.

When the heart is imbued with the guru's instruction, duality is easily effaced.

All things are subject to the Commander's order; He is fearless and regardeth all alike.

He who knoweth and worshippeth the Supereme Being, uttereth words of divine knowledge.

Nama saith, I have obtained the Life of the world in my heart; He is invisible and wonderful.

(60)

God was in the beginning before the ages and in every age: His end is not known.

God is contained in everything uninterruptedly; thus is His form described.

The unbeaten strain resoundeth for him who repeateth God's name-

Happy is my God-

The sandal-tree by its perfume is pleasant to the other trees of the forest;

Through God who was before all things all who perfumeth like sandal, common wood becometh sandal.

Thou, O God art as the philosopher's stone; I am as the iron; in Thine association I have become gold.

Thou art compassionate, Thou art the jewel and the ruby

Nama hath been absorbed in the True One.

(61)

The inscrutable Being invented a play-

God is concealed in every heart,

No one knoweth the nature of the soul's light

What we overselves have done Thou knowest.

As an earthen vessel is produced from clay,

So Vitthal created the world.

The soul's entanglements depend on its acts;

It is itself responsible for what it hath done,

Namdev representeth, the soul obtaineth the result of its thoughts;

The soul which always remaineth fixed on the Inscrutable One, becometh immortal.

IV

BABA ATTAL—THE CHILD OF MIRACLES

The ways of God are beyond the rationality and comprehension of man. He often works wonders which are called miracles, inexplicable by any material causation and human argumentation. He bestows miracular powers in peculiar ways and by His grace Baba Attal was Attal Rai who was the son of Guru Har Gobind, the sixth Guru or spiritual Enlightener of the Sikhs. The term "Baba" means an old or elderly and respectable man, which is applied to both types of persons; really advanced in physical age and the young children for their extra=ordinary or prodigous spirituality or divinity. It was for this spiritual power of Attal Rai that he was called "Baba Attal", who was born on the 22nd of December, 1619. A.D. at Amritsar in Punjab, India. The word Attal means inevitable as whatever was uttered by Baba Attal was inevitable to happen. The name of Baba Attal's mother was Nanaki who was a lady of deep devotion of God, poius and generous.

The parents loved their all children but they were especially fond of Baba Attal. The Guru-father knew the spiritual powers of Attal Rai. So he used to seat him in his lap and say to him, "My dear son, God has bestowed on you many spiritual powers, but you should not display them or dissipate them for trivial things and purposes. You must be particularly cautious in using them against the will of the Lord as Guru Nanak has taught us in the very first pauri or stanza of Jap, Ji, "Hukam Razai chalna nanak likhiya naal." (We must obey the will of the Lord, the destiny which He inscribed for us in the very beginning). The young Attal Rai fondly listened to his father's remonstrations, smiled back and often said, "My respected father, these spiritual powers are gifts received from you and they are so much inexhaustible that in whatever way or to whatever extent they are used they will not be diminished." Saying this, he used to jump out of his lap and go to play with his play-mates.

Attal Rai was very fond of playing, "Khido-Khoondi", a game played with a khoondi (A crooked stick) and a "khido" (A ball made of wrapped up yarn and bits of cloth). As a matter of fact the modern game of hockey has originated from Khido-Khoondi. At that time Amritsar was a small but spacious town and not like the present city of Amritsar, very suffocatingly and densely populated. Attal Rai used to get up early in the morning, take his bath, squat cross-legged in "sukhasan", or easy posture, take his breakfast, go to his father sitting at Akal Takhat, pay his homage to the Guru Granth Sahib, congregations and then play khido-khoondi with his friends. His special place of playing was around the present tank called Kaulsarnamed after Bibi Kaulan, the daughter of Rustam Khan, a Muslim qazi of Lahore, who became so much deeply devoted to Guru Har Gobind and his teachings that she fled Lahor along with the Guru and used to live near this tank. She used to love Attal Rai with the true love like a mother. Attal Rai had a regular practice of taking cooked food from his home and distributing it among the poor and hungry people waiting for him around Kaulsar. Hence in his very childhood he became famous for his generosity for the indigent and needy people. One thing was certain that he always distributed cooked food, ready and fit to be eaten and never distributed raw food, to be cooked by the recipients after receiving it. So the poor people used to gather near the tank and used to sing in love for Baba Attal, "Baba Attal, Pakian pakaiyan ghal" (O Baba Attal, send us the cooked food ready to be eaten").

At that time there lived at Amritsar a Soni Khatri named Gurmukh who had a son named Mohan. Mohan was of the age of Attal Rai and was his bosom friend. Attal Rai had a special charm in playing khido-khoondi with Mohan, who was also a kid of very exquisite beauty, buoyant health and good habits. The little children used to pass most of the day in playing. One day the children kept on playing till dusk when Attal Rai had scored against Mohan and he was to play the role of picker and baller against the hits of Khoondi administered by Attal Rai but feeling it too late and dusky, all the boys wended their ways home with a decision that Mohan would repay his game, throwing and picking the ball next morning.

At night Mohan got up from his bed and went out for answering the call of nature. It was a very dark night. As he walked out of the room, he was bitten by a cobra. He shreiked violently and fell down unconscious. His parents got up and lifted him from the ground. They were shocked and cried loudly but within a few minutes, Mohan died of the cobra bite. Next morning the day dawned but still there prevailed night and darkness of sorrow and gloom for the partents of Mohan. They placed the dead body of Mohan on the ground and spread a white sheet of cloth over it.

Attal Rai got up as usual, took his bath, said his prayers, ate his breakfast, went to see the holy sight of congregation and his father. Then he repaired to the house of Mohan as the last evening's decision of game was lurking in his mind. But alas! on entering the house of Mohan, he saw the heart-rending scene of crying and lamentation of Mohan's parents and other relatives, around his dead body. Attal Rai became very sad to learn the death of his dear friend but lovingly said to the mother of the deceased, "Dear mother, don't weep. Mohan is only pretending to be in a sound sleep so that he may avoid to do his subordinate role of playing khido-khoondi with me, which he promised last evening. I will wake him up. How can he run away from his promise?" Saying this, he pulled up the neck of the dead Mohan by the crook of his stick and exhorted him, "Mohan get up and say "Wahiguru". Let us go and play, it is already too late". Lo, the powers of the Lord are indescribable. Mohan got up smilingly saying "Wahiguru" (Wonderful God).

All the people who were present there were surprised by the performance of the spiritual power of Attal Rai and the news spread like wild fire. A Sikh ran to Guru Har Gobind and happily related to him all that had happened, but to the surprise of the informant and other congregations, Guru's mood became rather grave over the news.

Just after that Attal Rai approached his father jumping and bumping in joy to have his seat in his lap and then receive a lot of love from him. Anyhow, the child detained himself to do it seeing the angry looks of his father and quietly sat amongst the congregation, close to the Guru. Guru Har Gobind admonished Attal Rai saying, "Oh dear son, you have done an unpardonable act of the display of your spiritual power by reviving your dead friend, Mohan. I always warned you not to interfere in the will of God. A resignation to the sweet will of the Lord is the real test and criterion of a true spiritualist and the display of miracles is prohibited in the domain of spiritualism. Truly, you have revived your friend Mohan, but this circle of deaths shall never end. Tomorrow some other people will come to you to give life to their dead and to whom you will do this favour and to whom you will refuse your gift? You will be partial, if you favour some people and refuse others, but to a man of God, all are equal and alike without any discrimination of caste, creed, colour, country, community and class. Dear son, I am not happy with you as by displaying your miracles, certainly you have done a wrong thing."

This admonition by the father shocked the child Attal Rai. He quietly and seriously withdrew from the presence of his father and went away with his cast-down face. He did not play any game on that day. Surely he remained absorbed in deep thoughts and contemplation, determining not to live any longer on this earth and leave the mortal frame of his body. He went to the tank of Kaulsar. Bibi Kaulan had left Amritsar to live at Kartarpur near Jullundur. He took bath in the tank, squatted at the parapet close to the bank of the tank supporting his chin on his stick. Then he absorbed himself in prayer, meditation and contemplation and thus he fell into a trance in which the divine bird of his soul took flight to heaven, for ever leaving the material cage of his body. He left this world as a repentence for the offence of displaying miracles. It happened at Amritsar on the 16th of September, 1628 A.D. when he was passing through the ninth year of his age.

Guru Har Govind presently learnt the passing away of his son, Attal Rai but he did not become sad at all and said to the members of his family and other followers who were present there, "It is good. I am glad that Attal Rai has realised himself as a true spiritualist. All shall die. None of us will live for ever. We must gladly bow to the will of the Lord. The name and fame of Attal Rai shall live for ever and the people will remember him with love, devotion and respect."

Since that time onwards, Attal Rai was addressed as Baba Attal. His body was cremated exactly at the spot where his soul bid farewell to his body and a shrine was made there in his honour and memory in 1628 A.D. The present nine storeyed shrine was constructed in 1784 A.D. and is known as Gurdwara Baba Attal. All the people who go to visit the Golden Temple, Amritsar, seldom miss to pay homage to this holy shrine and spontaneously the words escape the lips of the devotees, "Baba Attal, pakiyan pakaiyan ghal" (Oh Baba Attal send us the cooked food just ready to be eaten).

All the persons who are sincerely on the spiritual path cannot help being deeply touched by the historic story of Baba Attal. I observed and experienced it with the most recondite sentiments when my friend and meditation student, Marty Refner Wolfe originally from Indianapolis, Indiana, a mid-west State of U.S.A. but living at San Francisco, visited this shrine on the 11th of November, 1980 and hearing the story, meditating on it, kept shedding her tears of "vairag" or devotion within, while seeing the drawings on the walls of the shrine and on the top of the shrine from where she saw the view of whole of the city of Amritsar and miles away around it. Even to-day, the poor and hungry people throng to this place and the devoted followers carry cooked food there and distribute it among them, while the recipients and the onlookers devotedly sing or say, "Baba Attal, Pakiyan paainyan ghal."

V
RAV DAS

Rav Das is the author of many hymns in the Granth Sahib. He was certainly a disciple of Ramanand and a contemporary of Kabir, but otherwise there is nothing known regarding his precise date, parentage, or place of birth. When Rav Das arrived at years of discretion he began to wait on saints. He used to present them with everything he could procure from his father's house. His father was displeased at this and gave him a separate place of residence. Though his father's wealth and means were considerable, yet he gave nothing whatever to his son. The latter, who by this time had entered the married state, supported himself and his wife by making shoes, and lived very happily. Whenever he saw a holy man he supplied him gratuitously with covering for his feet. He afterwards built a hut, set up in it and idol which he had made from a hide, and applied himself to its worship. When he was reproached for making an idol out of a hide, he defended himself by descanting on the various advantages of hides. Drums used in worship were made from hides. The cow held sacred by Hindus had a hide. God is contained in animals which have hides, &c., &c.

Rav Das was ever immersed in his devotions, a circumstance which led to the abandonment of his trade and the deterioration of his circumstances. He soon presented all the external marks of poverty and hard life, yet his heart was glad and happy in the contemplation of God. It was during this period of distress that a holy man desired to render him assistance. Rav Das gave him bread to eat and lavished every attention on him. His visitor in return presented him with a philosopher's stone, explained its qualities, and told him to keep it carefully. Rav Das replied that he did not require it, as his property and wealth consisted in the name of God. When the visitor saw that Rav Das absolutely coveted nothing, he implored him to accept the philosopher's stone. Rav Das told him he might leave it in the thatch of his house, by which he meant that the article was not worth acceptance. The visitor obeyed Rav Das and departed. On that occasion Rav Das composed the following hymn :—

God's name is the great wealth of God's saints;
Day by day it increaseth and in no way decreaseth.

Nothing can steal it either by day or night; its possessor sleepeth secure in his home.

O God, what need of a stone hath he who possesseth this wealth?

After the lapse of thirteen months the visitor returned and found Rav Das in the same circumstances as before. He asked him what had become of the philosopher's stone. Rav Das replied, 'It must be where thou didst put it; I have been afraid to touch it.' Upon this the visitor took it from the thatch and departed, fully satisfied that Rav Das desired no earthly wealth.

One day the saint found five gold coins in a basket employed to hold accessories of worship. The result was that he began to fear even devotion to God, lest it might bring him wealth. Then God said to him in a vision, 'Although thou absolutely desirest nothing, yet accept the wealth I give thee now.' Rav Das promised to do so. A pious admirer gave him money with which he built a sara, or resthouse, wherein he entertained holy men. He then built a temple and so decorated it with a canopy, fringes, cords of gold lace, wall lamps, chandeliers, &c., that visitors on seeing its beauty became enchanted. After that Rav Das built a two-storied house for himself on the site of the hut he had hitherto used as a temple, and there he continued to worship with perfect love.

Rav Das experienced the ordinary fate of men suddenly enriched. The Brahmans, through envy and jealousy, complained to the king of Banaras that there was no authority in the Shastars for a shoemaker to make an image of God, yet Rav Das had without any fear or compunction set up such an image and was worshipping it and offering it homage. He ought therefore to be made to suffer for his presumption. The king summoned Rav Das, but was so much impressed with the dignity and reasonableness of his defence that he found no difficulty in immediately declaring him guiltless of any offence against religion.

Jhali, the Queen of Chitaur, hearing of Rav Das's fame, visited him and became a disciple of his. At this her attendant Brahmans waxed highly indignant. They said that the queen had lost her reason, and they went and complained of her to the Rana, her husband, who had accompanied her to Banaras. He sent for Rav Das, and heard the charges of the assembled Brahmans against him. They represented the supreme importance of caste, and the impropriety of allowing a shoemaker to usurp a higher spiritual or social position than that in which he had been born. Rav Das replied, 'What is dear to God is devotion; He payeth no heed to caste.' Upon this the Brahmans proposed to refer the matter to the arbitrament of prayer. They read the Veds for three full hours and repeated many spells, but did not succeed in inducing God to persuade the Rana of Rav Das's guilt. When it came to Rav Das's turn, he said, 'O Great King, be true to thy name of Pardoner of sinners.' He then sang a couple of stanzas. The first line of the first stanza is :—

O come without delay or call me into Thee.

The first lines of the second stanza are :—

O God of gods, I Thy protection crave;
Have mercy on me, knowing me Thy slave.

The Rana was easily convinced of Rav Das's innocence and expressed himself accordingly. Upon this it is said all present became believers in Rav Das's sanctity.

After that Queen Jhali left Banaras, and returned to her kingdom, where she decided on holding a thanks-giving festival. With great modesty and humility she invited Rav Das to be pleased to attend it. He accepted her invitation and went to Chitaur. His visit afforded her intense pleasure. She distributed a large sum of money in alms on the occasion, and invited the principal Brahmans of her state to meet the holy man. The Brahmans knew that the queen's guru had been a shoemaker, and it would be better for them to take raw provisions of their own and cook them than partake of food proffered by the queen. They accordingly had food cooked for themselves, but, when they sat down to eat it, it is said, they saw Rav Das seated between every two of them. They then believed in his divine mission and fell at his feet. It is stated that he gained many disciples on that occasion. Rav Das composed the following after the entertainment :—

Clever men,[1] I am notoriously a tanner by caste,

But in my heart I meditate on God.

If wine be made even with Ganges water, you holy men will not drink it;

But if wine which is impure, or other liquid be put into Ganges water, the later will not be altered.[2]

The palmyra palm-tree, sirs, is admittedly impure,[3] as its leaves[4] are also deemed;

But if God's words he written thereon, men will worship it and bow before it.

My trade is dressing and cutting leather and daily removing dead cattle round about Banaras.

Yet prominent Brahmans now prostrate themselves before me, since I, the slave Rav Das, have sought the shelter of Thy name, *O God*.

Rav Das is said to have been such a perfect saint of God that his conversation and poetry were like suns to dispel the darkness of doubt and infidelity. He performed the meritorious acts prescribed in the Veds and the Shastars. Orientals believe that if milk mixed with water be placed before a swan, it can by its peculiar bill separate both, and drink only the milk. In the same way Rav Das selected virtue from vice, made choice of good acts and avoided things forbidden.

The following compositions of Rav Das are found in the Granth Sahib.

Hymns of Rav Das

God being light and the soul also light, there is no difference between them except that the soul is encumbered with a body.

Sri Rag

Between Thee and me, between me and Thee what difference can there be?
The same as between gold and the bracelet, between water and its ripples.
If I did not commit sin, O Eternal One,
How shouldst Thou have gained the name of Purifier of sinners?
Thou who art the Lord, art the Searcher of hearts :
The servant is known from his master, and the master from his servant.
Grant me the wisdom to worship Thee with my body.
Rav Das, some rare person who destroyeth his evil passions,[1] may explain this.
Though Rav Das's birth is low, he is a candidate for God's favour.

Gauri

I

My associations are low—I think of it day and night—
My birth is mean, mine acts are crooked.
O God, Lord of the earth, Giver of life to men,
Forget me not, I am Thy slave;
Remove my troubles, make Thy servant full of love for *Thee*.
I will not forsake Thy feet even though my body perish to-morrow.
Saith Rav Das, I seek Thy protection, *O God*.
Quickly come to Thy servant, delay not.

II

There is a city named Beghampur,[1]
Where pain and sorrow find no place;
There is no fear to tribute or of tax;
There is nor care, nor sin, nor dread nor death,
Now have I found an excellent abode
Where ceaseless happiness doth reign, my friends.
There firm and for aye is sovereignty of God,
No second or third is there adored2, He ruleth alone;
Inhabited and ever famous is that city;
Its people are full dowered with wealth.
Theirs it is to wander as they please;
None restraineth them known in the palace,
Saith Rav Das, emancipated tanner,

My friends become my fellow citizens there.3

It is said that a Labana offered an ox to Rav Das. On refusing the present, the saint wrote the following :—

III

The road to *God* is very difficult and sleep, and I have *already* one useless ox.

My one prayer to God is, 'Preserve my capital, O God.'

Is there any merchant of God *who will join me?* My goods are laden and about to start.

I am a merchant of God, and deal in divine knowledge.

The wealth I have loaded is God's name; the world hath loaded poison.

Ye recording angels, who know this world and the next, write whatever nonsense you please *about me, I care not*;

The club of death will not touch me since I have cast away all entanglements.

This world is like the *fleeting* colour of safflower,

But the colour of my God is the *permanent* dye of madder, saith the tanner Rav Das.

Rav Das prays for divine favour.

IV

As a pit full of frogs[1] which know nothing of different countries,

So my mind infatuated with evil passions taketh no thought of this world or the next.

O Lord of all the world, grant me a sight of Thee for a moment;

My mind is not clear, O God, and so I cannot understand Thy condition.

Take pity on me that my doubts may be dispelled, and teach me right understanding.

Even supreme Jogis cannot explain Thine attributes which are beyond expression.

The tanner Rav Das prayeth for Thy love and service.

The following was Rav Das's reply to a holy man who asked the questions contained in the hymn.

V

In the Sat age was truth, in the Treta sacrifice, and in the Dwapar the performance of worship.

In the three ages these three observances were established, but in the Kal age the Name is the only support.

How shall I be saved?

No one explaineth to me.

How my transmigration may cease.

There are many forms of religion described, but everyone appeareth to adopt his own.

What are those acts by which I may be saved, and by the performance of which I may obtain all things?

If what are merits and what demerits be decided by listening to the Veds and Purans,[1] doubt *shall result;*

Doubt shall *thus* ever dwell in the heart; who shall dispel pride?

Man washeth his body with water, but in his heart there is evil of every description.

How shall purity result? My purity is such as the elephant practiseth.

As by the sun's light night departeth, as all the world knoweth;

As copper when touched by the philosopher's stone at once becometh gold;

So if the supreme philosopher's stone, the guru, be found by destiny,

The perturbed mind shall meet God *who* is in the heart, and the doors of adamant shall be opened.[2]

The doubts, the entanglements, and the sins of him who maketh the way of devotion firm in his heart shall be cut away;

He shall restrain his mind, obtain happiness, and meditate on Him alone who possesseth *all* qualities and yet posesseth none.

Many efforts have I made to ward off the noose of doubt, but, however much I tried, I did not succeed.

Love and devotion have not sprung up in me, therefore Rav Das is sad.

Man is a prey to all the five senses and their attendant passions, and not to one predominating and overmastering sense alone like the lower animals. Hence the following hymn :—

Asa

I

The deer, the fish, the bumble-bee, the moth, and the elephant perish each for one sense;

So what hope is there for him who *like man* hath five implacable enemies?

O God, man loveth ignorance;

His lamp of discrimination hath grown dim.

The thoughtless are born again as creeping things which distinguish not between good and evil;

They have now obtained human birth so difficult to obtain, *and yet* in it they associate with the base.

Men and lower animals, wherever they are, are born subject to their previous acts,

And the noose of Death which hangeth over them can by no means be warded off.

Rav Das, renounce worldly love, dispel doubt, and make the guru's divine knowledge thy religious fervour.

O Thou, who dispellest Thy worshipper's fear, grant me supreme bliss at last.

Rav Das prays for the saints' virtues and devotion

II

The company of the saints, who are Thine image, is my life.

Through the divine knowledge of the guru I recognize the saints as gods of gods.

Grant me the company of the saints, a taste for the saints' converse,

The saints' love, O God of gods,

The saints' good works, and the saints' way, that I may become attached to what they are attached.[1]

I pray for one thing more, the miraculous gem of devotion.[2]

Show me not the wicked and the sinner—

Between the saints and the Infinite there is no difference;

Rav Das saith, he who knoweth this is wise.

Rav Das is exalted by holy association.

III

Thou art sandal, I am the poor palma christi[3] plant, I dwell near Thee :

From a humble shrub I have become a lofty *tree* : Thine excellent perfume abideth *in me*.

O God, I have sought the protection of Thy true congregation.

I am without virtues, Thou art beneficent,

Thou art white[1] and yellow twisted silk; we are the poor worms[2] *who toil and make it*.

O God, may I continue to associate with the saints as the bee with the honey!

My caste is low, my lineage low, and low is my birth;

I have not served my sovereign God, saith the tanner Rav Das.

For God's love Rav Das would sacrifice himself.

IV

What would it matter were my body to be *cut* in pieces?
Thy slave, O *God, only* feareth that Thy love may depart :
Thy lotus feet are the home of my heart![3]
By drinking the nectar of His *name,* I have found God who is my wealth.
Prosperity, adversity, worldly love, and wealth screen God from man;
In them Thy servant is not absorbed.
Thy slave is bound by the rope of Thy love;
Saith Rav Das, what advantage is it to escape therefrom?

God's name saves saints and sinners.

V

God, God, God, God, God, God, God;[4]
By remembering God, saints and sinners[5] are saved.
Through the name of God, Kabir became renowned, and the accounts of his sins of many births were torn up.
Namdev as in duty bound[1] gave milk to god to drink;
Wherefore he had not the pain of being born again in the world.
The slave Rav Das is dyed with God's love,
And so, through the favour of the guru, he shall not go to hell.
They who think not of God shall be condemned.

VI

How *man,* a puppet of clay, danceth!
He looketh and looketh, heareth, speaketh, runneth about.
When he acquireth anything he is proud,
But when his wealth is gone he beginneth to weep.
In thought, word, and deed he is fascinated by pleasures,
So when he perisheth he is contained somewhere else.[2]
Saith Rav Das, the world is a play my, brethren;
I have established loving relations with the True Actor.[3]

The object of the following hymn is to show that nothing offered to God by idolaters, even according to their own ideas, is pure, and that the true offering to God is the sincere heart.

Gujari

The calf hath defiled the milk in the cow's under *by tasting it;*

The bumble-bee bath spoiled the flowers, and the fish the water—
My mother, where shall I find anything to offer in God's worship?
I cannot find other flowers superior to these.
Serpents twine round the sandal-tree;
Poison and ambrosia dwell together;
Incense, lamps, and consecrated bread are polluted.
How shall thy slave perform Thy worship?
Let me dedicate and offer my body and soul as my worship.
Thus, by the guru's favour, shall I find the Pure One.
I cannot perform Thine adoration and worship *according to Hindu rites;*
Saith Rav Das, in what condition am I?[2]

Rav Das concludes that everything is God.

Sorath

I

When there was egoism in me, Thou wert not with me; now that Thou art with me, there is no egoism.

Huge waves are raised by the wind in the ocean, but they are only water in water.[3]

O God, what shall I say? Through illusion things are not as they are supposed to be.

A king sleepeth on his throne; in a dream he becometh a beggar;

He suffereth pain at losing his empire, *though* it is intact : such hath been my condition.

Like the story of the rope and the serpent, I have now had the secret[4] explained to me.

On *seeing* several[5] bracelets I erroneously supposed *that they were distinct from the gold;* but what I then said I now say no longer.

In all things the one Lord assumeth various shapes; God sporteth in all hearts.

Saith Rav Das, God is nearer to us than our hands and feet; it is what taketh place by His will that taketh place.

Rav Das so loves God that he feels he has a claim on His mercy.

II

When Thou didst bind us with a noose of illusion, we bound Thee with a bond of love;

Try to release Thyself; we have been released by adoring Thee.

O God, Thou knowest how we feel towards Thee;

Now what wilt Thou do wish us, such *being our love for Thee?*

Man catcheth a fish, sliceth it, cutteth it up, and cooketh it in various ways;

He biteth and eateth it, still it forgetteth not the water.[1]

The Supreme Ruler is no man's heritage; He belongeth to him who loveth Him.

Though the screen of illusion be spread over the whole world, yet it troubleth not the saint.

Saith Rav Das, my devotion to the one God hath increased; to whom shall I tell this now?

Shall I still suffer misery for the removal of which I worship Thee?

Rav Das on introspection finds himself wanting.

III

I obtained this birth difficult to attainment as the reward of merit, but it passeth away in vain *on account of my* want of discrimination.

Say of what account would a palace and a throne like King Indar's be without devotion to God?

I have not thought of the pleasure in the Supreme God's *name,* a pleasure in which all other pleasures are forgotten.

What we ought to have known we know not; we have become mad, and not considered what we ought to have considered, and so our days have passed away.

Our passions are strong, and our discrimination weak; our understanding cannot either into God's designs.

We say one thing, and do another; worldly love hindereth us from understanding.

Saith Rav Das, I, Thy slave, am sad at heart;

Avert Thine anger from me and have mercy on my soul.

We should fix our attention on God who can adequately reward us.

IV

God is an ocean of pleasure; in His power are the miraculous tree, and gem, and cow.

The four advantages, the eighteen miraculous powers, and the nine treasures are in the palm of His hand.

Why repeat not, 'God, God, God,' with thy tongue,

And abandon all other device of words?

The epic poems, the Purans, the Veds of Brahma, are *all composed* out of thirty-four letters.[1]

Bias having reflected expressed his conviction that there was nothing equal to the name of God.

Very fortunate are they who tranquilly contemplate and fix their attention upon God; they shall afterwards be freed from their troubles.

Saith Rav Das, the fear of death and birth fleeth from him who hath put the light of *divine knowledge* into his heart.

The saint's relation to God.

V

If Thou art a hill, then I am Thy peacock;[2]
If Thou art the moon, then I am Thy chakor;
O God, if Thou break not with me, I will not break with Thee:
If I break with Three, whom shall I join?
If Thou art a lamp, then I am Thy wick;
If Thou art a place of pilgrimage, then I am Thy pilgrim.
I have joined true love with Thee;
Joining Thee I have broken with all others.
Wherever I go there is Thy service;
There is no other Lord like Thee, O God.
By worshipping Thee Death's noose is cut away.
Rav Das singeth to obtain Thy service.

Man is too proud of his body though its origin and its end are contemptible.

VI

The body is a wall of water supported by a pillar of air; blood[1] and semen are its mortar.

The poor soul dwelleth in a skeleton of bones, flesh, and veins;
O mortal, what is mine and what is thine ?
As a bird percheth on a tree, *so doth the soul on the body.*
Thou layest foundations and buildest thyself a house;
Three and a half cubits shall be thy measure *at last.*
Thou curlest thy hair, and wearest thy turban on the side of thy head;
But thy body shall become a heap of dust.
Even though thou possess lofty palaces and beautiful women,
Without the name of God thy game is lost.
My caste is low, my lineage low, and base is my birth:
I have sought Thy shelter, O God, saith the tanner Rav Das.

The following was addressed to some one who reproached Rav Das for not following his trade :-

VII

I a cobbler know not how to mend shoes,

Yet people want me to mend their shoes.

I have no awl to stitch with;

I have no knife to patch with.

People have been thoroughly ruined by mending shoes[1]—

I have attained my object without mending shoes.

Rav Das repeateth God's name;

I have now no concern with Death.

Rav Das's devotion and hope in God.

Dhanasari

I

There is none so poor as I, none so compassionate as Thou; *for this* what further test is now necessary?

My my heart obey Thy words! fill Thy servant therewith.

I am a sacrifice to Thee, O God;

Why art Thou silent?

for many births have I been separated from Thee, O God: This birth is on Thine *own* account.[2]

Saith Rav Das, putting my hopes in Thee I live; it is long since I have seen Thee.

Rav Das's love for God.

II

I remember Thee, O God, in my heart; I behold thee with mine eyes; I fill mine ears with Thy hymns[3] and praises;

I make my mind the honey-bee, I put Thy lotus feet into my heart, and with my tongue I utter Thine ambrosial name.

May my love for god not decrease!

I have bought it dear in exchange for my soul.

Without the companionship of the saints no love is produced, and without love no service is performed for Thee.

Rav Das offereth one prayer to God—preserve mine honour, O my sovereign Lord.

God's name is for Rav Das equal to all the Hindu oblations.

III

Thy name, O god, is mine Arati and mine ablutions;

Without the name of God all display is vain.

They name is my prayer-mat, Thy name my saffron-grater, Thy name the saffron which I sprinkle *for Thee*;

Thy name is the water, Thy name the sandal, the repetition of Thy name the grating thereof,[1] taking it I offer it unto Thee;

Thy name is the lamp, Thy name the wick, Thy name the oil I pour therein;

Thy name is the light which I have applied to it, and which hath enlightened the whole world;

Thy name is the string, Thy name the necklace of flowers; all the eighteen loads of *vegetables* are too impure[2] *to offer Thee*.

Why should I offer Thee the work of Thy hands? Thy name is the chauri which I wave over Thee.

The whole world is engrossed in the eighteen *Purans*, the sixty-eight *places of pilgrimage*, and the four sources of life.

Saith Rav Das, Thy name is the Arati; the true Name is the food I offer unto Thee, O God.[3]

God alone can save man from his evil passions.

Jaitsari

O Lord, I know nothing;

I have sold my soul to mammon.

Thou art styled the great Lord of the world, and we the sensualists of the Kal age.

The five evil passions which have corrupted my heart,

Have at every moment thrown a barrier between Thee and me.

Whithersoever I look, there is a stock of Trouble.

I am not yet satisfied, although the Veds bear witness *to God*.

As for his sin, on the body of Indar, the paramour of *Ahalya* Gautam's wife, a thousand vaginae formed;

As the head of *Brahma* adhered to *the hand of Shiv* the lord of Uma[1] *for his sin*,

So these wicked enemies, *the deadly sins*, have bound and beaten me *also a sinner*.

I am very shameless, and have not yet grown weary of their company.

Saith Rav Das, whither *shall I go?* What shall I do?

Except God's protection whose shall I seek?

The saint and the sinner under the allegories of a good and a bad wife contrasted.

Suhi

I

The good wife knoweth her spouse's worth;

She renounceth pride and enjoyeth conjugal happiness;

She giveth her husband her body and soul, and maketh no distinction *between him and herself;*

She seeth no one else, heareth no one else, and speaketh to no one else.

How should she, into whose heart no sorrow hath entered,

Know of the woes of others?

The bad wife[2] who hath not served her spouse continually

Is unhappy, and loseth both worlds—

The way by the bridge of Sirat[3] is difficult—

She shall have no companion, and must go alone.

In grief and in pain, O god, I have come to Thy door;

I am very thirsty, and I have received no answer *from Thee.*

Saith Rav Das, I have come to Thy protection; effect my salvation as Thou thinkest best.

As everything here changes, man should make provision for the hereafter.

II

The days which come, pass away again;

We must march on, nothing remaineth stable.

Our companions are going, we too must go;

The journey is long; Death standeth over us.

Why sleepest thou? Awake *for God's service,* O silly one;

Thou thoughtest life a real thing in this world, *when thou oughtest to have thought of God.*

He who gave thee life conveyeth thee sustenance,

And in every heart openeth a shop.[1]

Worship God, lay aside egoism;

In thy heart remember God's name betimes.

Thy life hath come to an end, yet thou hast not prepared thy way;

It is evening, and darkness is on every side.

Saith Rav Das, O fool and madman,

Didst thou not reflect that the world is a transitory abode?

Man can only rely on God, not on property or relations.

III

Man buildeth lofty mansions with halls and kitchens,
But after *Death* he cannot remain in them for a ghari.
This body is like a wainscoting of grass;
When the grass is burnt, it is blended with the dust.
Even thy relations, thy family, and thy companions
Set up a cry, 'Take him out quickly!'
The wife of thy house who embraced thee *in life*,
Crieth out, 'Ghost ! ghost !' and runneth away from thee.
Saith Rav Das, *Death* hath plundered the whole world,
But I have escaped by repeating *the name* of the one God.

VI
OTHER REFORMERS

JAIDEV

Jaidev, the well-known author of Gita-Govinda was a native of Kinduviloa or Kandoli in Burdwan, and the most distinguished poet in the court of Lakshman Sen. The beauty and tender love of his wife appears to have inspired him with the gripping and lyric drama and mystical allegory of Gita Govinda. There are only two hymns by Jaidev in the *Adi Guru Granth*. The language of these hymns is a mixture of Prakrit and apbhransh. Lassen and Pischal believe that even the original Gita-Govinda was in Prakrit and Apabhransh, and it was given Sanskrit form much later.

parmad purkh manopaman sat adi bhavratan

Primal Being, sublimely beautiful,
Primal Truth, all pervading,
Supremely wonderful, transcending nature :
Why then not contemplate Him, the Redeemer.
Devote thy mind only to the Holy Name
Which is ambrosia and the essence of life.
For those who remember the Lord
There is no fear of birth, of old age, and of death.

If thou desirest to defeat the angel of death
And all his ministers,
Praise and bless Thy Lord,
And do virtuous deeds.
The bliss of the Lord is unchanging
Now, and in the past, and in the future.

Man, if thou seekest to do virtuous deeds
Renounce thy greed, renounce thy coveting
Of thy neighbour's wife, all sins, all sinful desires,
And make the Lord thy refuge!

In heart and in words and in deeds
Devote thyself solely to thy Beloved Lord.
Without such devotion, what profit is there
In yoga, temple rituals, alms, and austerities?

O man, repeat the Sweet Name of the Beloved
Who is the bestower of all power upon men!
Jaidev openly seeketh his refuge in Thee :
Who art now, hast been, and Who pervadest all!

Gujri, 526

BENI

Beni was in all probability a contemporary of Namdev. A scholar and a poet with no livelihood, he told his wife that he was employed by the Raja for the interpretation of scriptures but every day he went to the forest for quiet meditation. But as he brought no money home, she became impatient. It is said that by strange circumstances Beni was given an honourable post and led a happy, saintly life.

tan candan mastak pati

The body thou smearest with sandal paste,
And on the forehead thou stickest basil leaves,
But in thy heart thou hidest a murderer's knife.
Thou lookest on folk like a thug, deceptively;
Like a crane watching for fish, thou watchest thy neighbours.
Yet such a profound devotee thou seemest to be
Thy very breath seemeth suspended in meditation!

Thou bowest for a long time before the beautiful idol;
But thou hast an evil eye, and thy nights
Are given over to quarrelling.

Thou bathest thy body every day,
Keeping two dhotis, performing every ritual;
Thy speech is sweet as milk,
Thy heart like a drawn dagger;
It is thy way to cheat thy neighbours of their cash!

Worshipping stones,

And making circles of flour to honour Ganesh,
Thou keepest vigil at night
To take thy share in the *ras lila* service,
Thy feet dance, but thy heart planneth wickedness :
Sinful is such a dance, O sinful man!

On the deer skin thou sittest,
With a rosary of sacred basil,
Scrupulously clean are thy hands,
On thy forehead are religious marks,
But falsehood is in thy heart :
O wicked man, not in this way
Wilt thou earn the greetings
Of the Lord Krishna.

He who has not known the Supreme God
He is blind, and all his observances are vain,
Saith Beni, enlightened by the Guru, meditate on God!
Without the True Guru none find the way.

Rag Prabhati, page 1351

DHANNA

Dhanna was a farmer born at Dhuan in the State of Tonk near Deoli. Thus little peasant boy had a very innocent soul. Seeing a Brahmin leading a very comfortable living by merely worshipping the idol he also sought the grace of God by worshipping the stone. For six days and nights he sat in meditation, and the God he sought in the stone revealed Himself within him. For further guidance in spiritual life he became the disciple of Ramanand. There are four hymns by Dhanna in the *Adi Guru Granth*, mostly against idol worship.

bharamat phirat bahu janam bilane

In error and illusion I have passed many lives;
My body, my mind, my worldly possessions are transient.
Held and defiled with the sins of greed and lust
I have forgotten God, the diamond.
To the crazed mind the fruits of sin are sweet :
It hath forgotten discrimination.
My passions, turning away from virtue, grow stronger :
Again I am weaving the cycles of birth and death.

I did not know the way of Him who dwelleth in the heart;
I burned with sin and fell into Death's noose.

I gathered the fruits of sin, and filled my heart with them.
There was no room left in it for the Supreme God.

Then the Guru caused the supreme treasure
Of knowledge of God to enter into my heart.
I centred my mind on the Lord in deep absorption,
It entered into my heart that He is One.
Embracing His love and service, I knew comfort :
I was satisfied, I was seated, I was set free.

He whose heart is filled with that Divine Light
Which also filleth creation,
He recognizeth the One
Who transcendeth all illusions.
Dhanna hath obtained God as his treasure :
And in the company of the Lord's saints
He hath become at one with the Lord.

Rag Asa, Page 487

TRILOCHAN (1267-1335)

Trilochan was a friend and contemporary of Namdev and both of them lived in close association with each other. Trilochan was initiated into religious life by Gyuan Dev but was introduced to mystic life and experiences by Namdev. He had a quarrelsome wife and although he tried to give her all worldly comforts and the attention she demanded, he refused to pray for a son for her. There are four hymns of Trilochan in the *Adi Guru Granth.*

antar mal nirmal nahi kina

Thou who hast not cleansed the dirt from thy heart,
Why wearest thou the outer garb of a hermit?
And thou who in the unfolding lotus of thy heart
Hast not enclosed thy Lord,
Why hast thou adopted complete renunciation?

And thou, learned Brahmin, Jai Chand,
Thou hast gone astray in error and illusion;
For all thy learning, thou knowest not
God as the Primal Joy :

Thou, yogi, eating in every house
Hast fattened only thy body;
For gain thou wearest thy patched coat.

For gain thy beggar's ear-rings.
Thou hast rubbed thyself with the ashes
Of the dead from the cremation ground,
But since thou hast no Guru
Thou hast not found the One Reality!

All of ye, why these holy mutterings?
Why practice all these outwards penances?
Ye might as well all churn water!
Remember the Lord in His Peace
Who hath made the millions of worlds!
Why, O holy beggar, carrying thy water-pot

Trudgest thou to the sixty-eight holy places?
Trilochan says : Listen, O foolish mortals!
What does it avail to thrash husks instead of corn?

Rag Gujri, page 525

HYMNS OF THE CONTEMPORARY SAINTS'

MARDANA (1460-1530)

Mardana was a Muslim, a professional rebeck player of the village Talwandi, who played and sang folk songs only to beg his food from door to door. Guru Nanak asked him to give up begging and string his music to his divine song to which Mardana readily agreed. With his blunt manners and wit like that of Shakespeare's Touchstone, Mardana accompanied Guru Nanak on his long Missionary journeys, particularly his visit to the Muslim World of the Middle East. Mardana died at Kartarpur about nine years before Guru Nanak passed away. Besides the succeeding Sikh Gurus, Mardana is the only Sikh disciple who was permitted to use Guru Nanak's name in his hymns. Guru Angad addressed himself as Nanak the Second, while Mardana addresses himself as Mardana Nanak I. This abiding bond between Mardana and the Guru is expressed in all the three hymns of Mardana we have in the *Adi Guru Granth*.

kayan lahan ap mad

In the vat of the body
Egoism is the wine,
Desire and low cravings
Are its companions.
The cup of ambition is
Abrim with falsehood.
And the god of death
Is the cup bearer;

By drinking this wine O Nanak,
One gathers multiple sins.

Make knowledge your yeast,
The praise of God the bread you eat
And the fear of God your meat.
This, O Nanak, is the true spiritual food.
Make divine Name your sustenance.

Var, *Bihagra;* page 553

SATTA AND BALWAND

Satta and Balwand were Muslim Bards who were also probably father and son. Being adept in Classical Music they were employed by Guru Angad to sing divine hymns. When young Guru Arjan became the Guru, they once demanded an exorbitant sum of money for the marriage of their daughter out of the public funds, which the Guru refused. They 'went on strike', thinking that the popularity of the Guru depended upon them. The Guru henceforth asked his disciples to learn music and never depend on the professional bards. Satta and Balwand soon repented. They have given a joint composition of eight hymns which tells us a good deal about Guru Angad and the reasons why Guru Nanak selected him as his successor in preference to his sons, and also explaining the unity of spirit in all the Gurus.

lehne di pheraiai nanak dohi khatyai

Because of the devoted service of Lehna
Nanak proclaimed him as his successor.
The same divine light of Nanak shines in Him.
His ways of life are the same,
Only the body he has changed.

An umbrella of spiritual sovereignty,
Is held over his head,
As he occupies the throne of Guruship.
With unstinted devotion he served Guru Nanak,
And followed the arduous path
Leading to union with God.

Food was given free
From the Guru's inexhaustible store.
Out of the infinite gifts of the Lord,
He himself partakes much
And bestows freely on others.

The praises of God are sung,
And His grace like light descends from heaven;
A glimpse of you, O True King,
Is enough to wash the sins of thousands of births.
Truly has Guru Nanak made Angad his successor
How can we desist from proclaiming this truth;
Guru Nanak's sons did not obey him
They turned their backs to the True Guru.
Insincere were their hearts,
Defiant were their attitudes,
Loads of sins they carried on their heads.
Guru Nanak appointed him as the Guru,
Through him, Nanak himself reigns as the Guru;
He who has imparted the Guruship,
Has brought about all this;[1]
Lo, who has won and who has lost?

Ramkali Var Satta Balwand, page 966

RAVIDAS

Ravidas was a cobbler by profession and a disciple of Ramanand. He resembled in every respect St. Boehme, the cobbler mystic of the West. Members of the highest caste became his disciples, prominent among whom was Princess Jhali of Chitore. There are forty-one hymns by Ravidas in the Adi Granth, written in the vernacular Hindi of Uttar Pradesh.

tohi mohi, mohi tohi antar kaisa

Between Thee and me, between me and Thee,
How can there be likeness or difference?
Likeness or difference as between gold
And a bracelet made of it, as between water
And the waves that move on its surface!
Were I not a sinner, O Eternal Lord,
How couldst Thou have the title of Redeemer of Sinners?
Thou, O Lord, art the Searcher or hearts.
Through God, the Master, we know the saints, His Servants :
Through the servants of God, we know God.
Grant me O Lord that my body may be Thy shrine.
Few, O Ravidas, see God in everything.

Siri Rag, page 93

begampura sehar ko nau

There is a place called City-of-no-Sorrows.
There is no grieving, no man suffers there.
There are no tax-gatherers. No one levies tribute.
There is no worrying, or sin, or fear, or death.
My friends, I have found myself a wonderful hometown
Where everything is good, everyone is happy!
There the sovereignty of the Lord is permanent
There all are equal, none second or third.
It is a populous and famous city.
The citizens are wealthy, and they move
As freely through the city as they please :
No high official of the palace impedes them.
My friends, says Ravidas, the emancipated cobbler,
Become my fellow citizens in this realm!

Gauri, page 345

kahan bheo jau tan bheo chin chin

What would it matter that they rent my body?
Thy slave feareth only, Lord that Thy Love may depart!
Thy feet are the lotus, and my soul flitteth
Like the honey-bees sucking their nectar,
I have found my treasure!
Gains, losses, worldly desires and wealth
Shut us from God; Thy slave hath not become lost in them!
Thy slave is bound to Thee by the rope of Thy Love!
O Ravidas, how can it benefit thee
To seek to break free from His rope?

Rag Asa, page 486

jab ham hote tab tum nahi, ab tuhi mai nahi

When I think of myself
Thou art not there
Now it is Thou alone
And my ego is swept away.
As billows rise and fall
When a storm sweeps across the water,
As waves rise and relapse into the ocean
I will mingle with Thee.
How can I say what Thou art

When that which I believed is not worthy of belief.
It is as a King asleep on the royal couch
Dreams he is a beggar and grieves,
Or as a rope mistaken for Serpent causeh pain,
Such are the delusions and fears;
Why should I grieve,
Why be panic-stricken?
As a man who seeth several bracelets
Forgets they are made of a single substance, gold,
So I have been in error but am no more,
Behind all the various manifestations there is one God;
In the motions of every heart it is God that throbs.
Ravidas, He is nearer to us than our hands and feet!
As the Lord willeth, so all things come to pass!

Rag Sorath, page 657

nagar jana meri jat bikhyat camaran

O people of the city everyone knows
I am a cobbler by trade and tanner by caste,
One of the low caste, and yet within my heart
I meditate upon God. If wine, which you think impure, is made
Of the holy water of the Ganges, you holy men
Will not drink it, but if that wine,
Or any other liquid you think impure,
Is poured in the Ganges, the river remains holy.
They make toddy from palms so the palm's leaves are impure
Yet if Holy Scriptures are written on paper made from palm-leaves
Men worship that paper, and bow before it.
Of low caste, by trade I am a cutter of leather :
In Benaras I carried dead cattle to the outskirts.
Yet noble Brahmins now bow low before me;
Since the slave, Ravidas, takes his shelter in Thy Name.

Rag Malar, 1293

RAMANAND (1340-1430)

Ramanand was born at Melukote near Madras and was the disciple of Raghvananda, the third in the spiritual descent from Ramanuja. Though he strictly practised most Ramanuja's ethical principles he was more inclined towards his Bhakti-Cult than towards his Vedanta theology. He came to North India quite early in life and settled at Benaras. He tried to reconcile the personal mysticism of Islam with the Vaishnav theology of the Hindus, as a result of which the most prominent Hindu, Muslim and Pariah Saints of his time were the disciples. There is only one hymn by Ramanand in the *Guru Granth*.

kat jaiai re ghar lago rang

Whither need I go to seek holiness?
I am happy here within myself at home.
My heart is no longer a pilgrim :
It has become tied down to itself.

Restlessly one day I did want to go :
I prepared sandal-wood paste,
Distilled aloe wood, and many perfumes :
I set out towards a temple of worship :
Then my Guru showed me God in my own heart.

Whatever holy place I seek as pilgrim
All I find is worship of water or stones,
But Thou, Lord, equally pervadest all things!
I have studied all the Vedas and the Puranas :
There or elsewhere thou mayest seek God
If God is not her in thy heart!

O gracious Guru, I am beholden unto thee
Who hast cut away my doubts and my vacillations!
Ramanand's Lord is the all-pervasive God :
The Guru's word removeth countless delusions.

Rag Basant, page 1195

VI. PARMANAND

Parmanand was Brahmin Vaishnavite disciple of Ramanand who lived at Barei near Sholepur. Though he is the author of innumerable poems, only one of his poems has been preserved in the *Adi Guru Granth*.

tain nar kya puran sun kina

Mortal man, what has been thy profit
From hearing the Puranas?
Thou hast not acquired a single-minded
Spirit of devotion to thy Lord!
Thou hast not given alms to the wretched.
Thou hast not put away thy lust.
Thou hast not put away thine anger.
Greed of gain has not left thee :

Thy lips are not clean of slander.
Thy outward shows of worship
Have all been utterly in vain.

Still thou robbest men on the roads
And breakest into men's houses to steal,
That thus, O criminal, thou mayest fill thy belly.
Fool, thou hast done such folly
As after death will earn thee an evil name!
From cruel violence thou hast not freed thy mind :
Thou hast not cherished mercy for living creatures.
Parmanand saith : In the company of the blest
Thou hast not joined in their holy speech!

Rag Sarang, page 1253